THE MUSLIM QUESTION IN EUROPE

Peter O'Brien

THE MUSLIM QUESTION
IN EUROPE

Political Controversies and Public Philosophies

TEMPLE UNIVERSITY PRESS
Philadelphia • *Rome* • *Tokyo*

TEMPLE UNIVERSITY PRESS
Philadelphia, Pennsylvania 19122
www.temple.edu/tempress

Published 2016

Library of Congress Cataloging-in-Publication Data

Names: O'Brien, Peter, 1960– author.
Title: The Muslim question in Europe : political controversies and public philosophies /
Peter O'Brien.
Description: Philadelphia, Pennsylvania : Temple University Press, 2016. | Includes
bibliographical references and index.
Identifiers: LCCN 2015040078| ISBN 9781439912768 (cloth : alk. paper) | ISBN
9781439912775 (paper : alk. paper) | ISBN 9781439912782 (e-book)
Subjects: LCSH: Muslims—Europe—Politics and government. | Islam and
politics—Europe.
Classification: LCC D1056.2.M87 O27 2016 | DDC 305.6/97094—dc23 LC record available
at http://lccn.loc.gov/2015040078

♾ The paper used in this publication meets the requirements of the American National
Standard for Information Sciences—Permanence of Paper for Printed Library Materials,
ANSI Z39.48-1992

Printed in the United States of America

9 8 7 6 5 4 3

For

Andre, Grady, Hannah, Galen, Kaela, Jake, and Gabriel

Contents

Acknowledgments

have accumulated many debts in the gestation of this study. Arleen Harrison superintends an able and amiable cadre of student research assistants without whose reliable and competent support this book would not have been possible. Special thanks go to Ana Esparza and Alyssa Alfaro, who compiled the reference lists. Trinity University thrice awarded me summer research stipends as well as academic leaves in 2011 and 2015. In 2011, the German Academic Exchange Service (DAAD) gave me a Research Visit Grant. Gökçe Yurdakul graciously hosted the visit at the Institute for Social Sciences at the Humboldt University in Berlin. Dagmar Vinz also deserves thanks for arranging the "Politics of Diversity" seminar that I offered in 2011 as part of the Gender and Diversity Masters Program at the Free University of Berlin. The students gave me valuable feedback for what amounted to an initial presentation of the general argument of the book. For inviting me to give guest lectures about the book's themes at their universities, I am indebted to Sieglinde Rosenberger (University of Vienna), Nermin Abadan-Unat (Boğaziçi University), Gökçe Yurdakul (Humboldt University of Berlin), Karin Goihl and Schirin Amir-Moazami (Free University of Berlin), and Sheila Pantlind (Aquinas College). Special thanks go to Gary Freeman, Gökçe Yurdakul, Schirin Amir-Moazami, Sieglinde Rosenberger, Tina Olteanu, Matt Barrusso, Stanley Fish, Jocelyne Cesari, and Bonnie Honig for providing critical readings of all or some of the manuscript. The serendipitous ways in which my scholarship intersects with that of Garth and Elizabeth Key Fowden make our annual visits (whether in Limni, Berlin, or

Cambridge) highly stimulating. Jane Key continuously provided a delicate balance of critical feedback and reassuring encouragement, not to mention mastering "the awful German language" (Mark Twain) while accompanying me during frequent protracted stays in Berlin. Those stays would never have been as delightful as they were for us without the indispensable assistance and dear friendship of Doris Thürmann and Frank Gottsmann and Barbara and Gottfried Gügold. Finally, I dedicate the book to the younger generation of our loving extended and blended family. May these fine young adults devise and implement more constructive and congenial ways to live with diversity than my generation has!

1

Introduction: Clashes *within* Civilization

> The most striking feature of contemporary moral utterance is
> that so much of it is used to express disagreements, and the most
> striking feature of the debates in which these disagreements are
> expressed is their interminable character. . . . There seems to be no
> rational way of securing moral agreement in our culture.
> —**Alasdair MacIntyre**, *After Virtue*

In our times political controversy seems to follow Muslims wherever they go. This is no less true of Europe, where an estimated twenty million Muslims now reside mostly as a result of large-scale postwar immigration. Non-Muslim Europeans acrimoniously debate how best to handle these "new" Europeans of Muslim heritage. For their part, the Muslim Europeans, comprising approximately 4 percent of the European Union's (EU's) population, hardly speak with one voice. Indeed, a central conclusion of this book is that European Muslims disagree vehemently but generally along the same ideological contours of discord that generate controversy among non-Muslim Europeans. To wit, there exists no great, let alone unbridgeable, gulf in outlook or lifestyle forever separating "Islamic" from "Western" civilization. We should be wary of the "clash of civilizations" thesis originated by Samuel Huntington (1996), popularized by the Western media, and applied on European soil as a microcosm of the global clash by an array of best-selling authors (Sarrazin 2010; Fallaci 2006; Ye'or 2005).

I urge instead that we start from the premise of *clashes within Western civilization*. I have in mind profound philosophical-turned-political fissures that have emerged in the modern era. These rifts may have been briefly smoothed over (or suppressed) during the generation immediately following World War II (WWII), during the so-called "end of ideology" (Bell 1960), which coincided with the original wave of postwar immigration to Western Europe (Messina 2007: 188–89). Mass immigration of Muslims to Europe presented a particularly salient (but hardly the lone) occasion for these strains to resurface and intensify beginning in the 1960s in Britain and on the Continent in the 1970s and 1980s. Heightened salience involved what Miller (2000) observed as the shift of immigration issues from low to high politics from little noticed or discussed to highly salient, appearing regularly in headlines, political speeches, international summits, and so on. One common way of reading this switch from low to high politics is to contend that the newcomers caused the problems that merited the heightened attention. This is the reading I want to counter. The controversies swirling about immigration—"this cauldron of political and policy debates" (Hollifield 1997: 40)—are better understood as deep-seated *intra-European* tensions rather than as clashes between a preexisting, presumably largely unified Western Europe and a recently settling (invading) non-European "Other" ("Islam").

Before I outline (and label) the outlooks generating the tensions, let us take a moment to look concretely at some of the political controversies surrounding European Muslims. This will allow the wider contours that I want to stress to come into visible relief, including why these intense controversies are not likely to be resolved any time soon. Consider the headscarf flashpoint (O'Brien 2009). Those who support banning the veil (as the French government has done in public schools since 2004) contend that the sartorial religious practice not only exemplifies but also proselytizes for the oppression of women. Others endorse the ban less out of an interest in women's rights than because they see it as the most visible symbol of the dilution of their culture by immigration. Given higher fertility rates among Muslims, so goes the argument, immigration will purportedly culminate in making the majority (culture) a "minority in its own land." Others see the right to cover as a litmus test for the sincerity of the much-touted freedom and tolerance of Western democracies. Many feel that Western European publics and governments fail the test miserably. Some critics don the veil as a sign of resistance to and condemnation of a long history (since the Crusades) of the domination of "Orientals" by Europeans.

Consider additionally the issue of secularism. In contrast to the United States, with its legal separation of church and state, most European governments have long-standing formal or informal relationships with Christian and Jewish denominations. These arrangements in one way or another channel state resources to promote recognized religious communities' undertakings. For example, most European governments help fund private confessional schools and/or subsidize the provision of religious, denomination-specific education in the public schools. It is only natural that European Muslims would seek to gain similar state aid for Islam, and they have done just that in virtually every European land where they comprise a critical mass (Laurence 2012). Typically, Muslims have demanded that they alone should determine the form and content of publicly subsidized Islamic instruction. After all, must one be a devout, even erudite Muslim to know what is most important about Islam to impart to pupils?

Many critics of Islam (including convinced secularists of Muslim descent) severely doubt Islam's democratic credentials and even go so far as to maintain that Islam and liberal democracy are fundamentally incompatible. While some want officials to spurn any relationship with Islam altogether, others call on the state to monitor and regulate public Islamic education in order to ensure that its form and content do not transgress liberal democratic tenets (for instance, gender equality). Most European states have, in fact, opened up dialogues with Muslims aimed at gestating so-called "Euro-Islam," an interpretation of the noble creed that is compatible with and conducive to liberal democratic mores and customs purportedly prized in Europe. Several Muslim organizations have taken umbrage at this paternalistic supervision, assailing it as thinly veiled cultural imperialism of the most insidious variety. Indignantly they have established their own privately funded and operated Islamic schools. Indeed, a few of these schools (and the organizations that oversee them) have been exposed as breeding grounds for vehemently and at times violently anti-Western thoughts, deeds, and actors.

Terrorism, needless to say, has become a salient issue, especially since the attacks of September 11 (9/11), as well as the Madrid, London, and Boston bombings and Paris attacks of 2015. Some scholars discern the "securitization" of immigration policy, by which they mean the tendency of officials, but also media, to view immigration primarily through the lens of its supposed threat to domestic security (Chebel d'Appollonia 2015; Kaya 2012; Givens, Freeman, and Leal 2008). Yet nothing approaching consensus regarding the best way to guarantee security seems discernible. Some have interpreted the terrorist attacks as a wake-up call that Western governments have put their publics at undue risk by maintaining a policy of relatively open and easy immigration and by granting extensive civil, political, and social rights to the newcomers. On this view, the state should deprioritize the rights and privileges of immigrants (by whom is putatively meant Muslims, often including naturalized Muslims) whenever they create even the suspicion of a threat to the security of "natives." Arrest and deport first! Ask questions and prove guilt later! One need only illustrate this stance as such to bring immediately to mind the counter-argument: human rights are sacrosanct and too important to permit their suspension or transgression for any individuals in the name of homeland security. A free society cannot be a 100-percent-secure society. Moreover, a demonstrable commitment to liberty and equality represents, in the end, the most effective weapon against the terrorists and their would-be sympathizers, a position opponents consider to be the utmost (and perilous) expression of bleeding-heart naiveté. Add to these arguments the viewpoint that the fixation on Muslims as potential terrorists by the Western media (and unofficially by security officials whose profiling targets Muslims) represents not only an apocryphal distortion, not only an ire-raising affront to peace-loving Muslims, but, because it is both, the single most effective recruiting tool for the very terrorists whom European governments wish to thwart. Why the preoccupation with immigration? After all, most of the London Tube bombers and Paris shooters were British subjects and French citizens born in Britain and France, respectively. Europe has been spawning homegrown terrorism since at least the anarchists of the nineteenth century. Investigate the reasons why rather than scapegoat Islam.

In this sampling of the controversies, we can detect three normative poles around which the vying stances cluster. Each pole represents something akin to a moral center of gravity that yields a moral compass one can use to chart an ethical way through any specific issue arising from immigration. The first pole underscores equality and liberty for all. Whenever and wherever one detects the claim of (especially innate or unearned) superiority and inferiority (for example, Muslim lives and limbs are dispensable); whenever and wherever one detects the forcing of an innocent, adult human being to act against his or her will (for instance, compulsion to don the veil), one's moral compass should point to potential immorality, a deep intuition that "this can't be right." The second pole concentrates moral awareness around the we-group, that wider collectivity beyond the obvious circles of immediate friends and family with whom one identifies or feels a sense of we-ness even when one does not personally know the members (for example, nation, ethnicity, religion). This second moral compass points to immorality whenever the well-being and continued flourishing of that we-ness, however understood, seems imperiled. The moral inclination is to defend the we-group, most often against an allegedly threatening they-group (thus, Muslims take "our" jobs or insult "our" customs). The third pole is actually an amoral pole. Its pointer signals trouble whenever it detects a claim to possess the moral high ground. Its center of gravity is a fully politicized sensibility that behind any claim to moral superiority lurks an ulterior, self-serving, political motive (say, the persistent domination of Muslims in the name of "emancipating" or "enlightening" them).

Each pole just limned represents something like the pithiest expression of a major normative outlook, or what I will call "public philosophy." I dub these "liberalism" (pole 1), "nationalism" (pole 2), and "postmodernism" (pole 3). This book contends that these three broadly understood philosophical traditions (schools of thought) represent the most influential normative forces in the politics of immigration in Europe today. Other isms, such as Protestantism, Catholicism, communism, fascism, and (explicit) racism, have drifted to the margins; others clearly more centrally visible, such as democratic socialism, feminism, multiculturalism, (implicit) racism, and

Islamism, can be (and are in this book) interpreted as variants (subcategories) of the broader three public philosophies.

Liberalism, Nationalism, and Postmodernism

I strongly wish to avoid misunderstanding in regard to labels. I devote a few paragraphs at this juncture to explaining (in broad and loose terms) my understanding of the labels "liberalism," "nationalism," and "postmodernism." My hope is that even if readers might prefer slightly different labels, we would all nonetheless (roughly speaking, of course) be considering the same three seismic developments in Western thought and society that I describe below. Labels inevitably involve generalization. I concur with Peter Gay (2002: 5), who sagely observes that "while it may be hard to live with generalizations, it is inconceivable to live without them."

Liberalism originated as a product and project of the Enlightenment. It emerged among brave, forward-looking men and women of the seventeenth and eighteenth centuries who sought to liberate humankind from the twin forces of darkness: ignorance and tyranny. Pioneering minds, such as John Locke, Baron de Montesquieu, Jean-Jacques Rousseau, Immanuel Kant, and Adam Smith, employed their prodigious reasoning powers to discern and articulate universal moral principles that the thinkers believed not only were comprehensible to all persons but also demonstrated the rectitude of man's yearning to be free. Liberalism insists on the inherent equality of all persons regardless of where and when they exist. From this fundamental equality derives the self-evident, inviolable right of each person to think, worship, work, and live as he or she wishes so long as he or she does not impede another's right to do the same. Furthermore, each individual must have an equal and voluntary say in determining the laws that govern him or her. Democracy, on this view, also represents the surest way to foster impartial government—that is, a government of laws based on rational, universal principles rather than of individuals moved by whimsical desire. Initially enunciated in philosophical treatises, these ideas eventually became anchored (never perfectly) in law first in countries such as Great Britain, the Netherlands, the United States of America, and France and eventually in the rest of Europe and beyond in what we today generally recognize as liberal democratic governments. Liberal laws established rights of property and person against arbitrary seizure, led to the abolition of serfdom and slavery, and gradually whittled away at forms of legal discrimination. Over time liberal democratic laws extended the franchise to more and more persons. Liberal laws established not only the free market but also, in time, the regulation of that market with an eye to redistributing its rewards more equitably throughout society. Liberalism, as I conceive it, deserves the lion's share of normative credit for inspiring and legitimizing the long and hard-fought process in (Western) Europe of securing for all citizens fundamental civil, political, and social rights (culminating in the postwar liberal democratic comprehensive welfare state) that T. H. Marshall so famously traced in *Citizenship and Social Class* (1950). The mention of social rights—"from the right to a modicum of economic welfare and security to the right to share to the full in the social heritage and to live the life of a civilised being according to the standards prevailing in the society" (Marshall 1950: 8)—should unmistakably signal that, in my conception of liberalism, (democratic) socialism represents a corollary of the broader moral theory and social movement demanding the equality and freedom of all. I gloss over the sniping from the left charging conventional liberalism with possessive individualism as well as the scare tactics from the right equating social democracy with creeping communist totalitarianism. The two generally agree on the same lofty goal of emancipating individuals; they differ only on the means to achieve it—an honest, consequential, but ultimately intramural debate.

Wherever humans feel humiliated, dehumanized, or forced to act against their will, they can turn to liberal values for moral support. They have done so and they continue to do so. Liberalism remains vital in our times thanks to the boost it has received from compelling intellectuals such as John Rawls and Jürgen Habermas and from courageous activists such as Martin Luther King, Jr., Nelson Mandela, Lech Walesa, Václav Havel, Aung San Suu Kyi, and Malala Yousafzai. It has been—in fits and starts no doubt—transforming our world from one oriented around corporate identities and entrenched stratifications to one centered on the individual unleashed to smash (in time) hierarchies of all sorts in favor of human rights and democratic governance.

Nationalism emerged in protest against liberal universalism. Coined by Johann Herder in 1774, "nationalism" first became common in political parlance in the middle of the nineteenth century. But well before that, sharp minds and tongues, such as Herder, Edmund Burke, Johann Fichte, Joseph de Maistre, and Guiseppe Mazzini, who abhorred the French Revolution and the Napoleonic expansionism that sought to impose its political order outside France, rejected the Enlightenment's pivotal notion of a single, universal human nature. They maintained instead that people were fundamentally different and that these inerasable differences stemmed from being members of different nations. Each nation was said to possess a particular character—Herder called it a "soul" (*Volksgeist*)—that organically takes shape by virtue of the fact that members of a given nation share a common history, language, and homeland, and common customs, mores, and tastes. Moreover, they share as well a common expectation and hope that their nation will survive and thrive into the future so that their progeny will be able to inherit, honor, and contribute to their culture and its collective achievements. They form a "community of destiny." Nationalism teaches that because each nation is particular, an idiosyncratic organic whole, it alone can know wherein consists the nation's well-being. It deductively follows that each nation (or people) must govern its own affairs, must have its own state. The nation-state, understood as the best possible congruence between nation and state, represents the moral and political ideal of nationalism. Despite a comparatively brief discrediting by its association with fascism, nationalism has been revived as a normative public philosophy in the work of prominent postwar scholars such as David Miller, Dominique Schnapper, Alain de Benoist, Marco Tarchi, Samuel Huntington, and Ernst-Wolfgang Bökenförde. A moral offspring of nationalism's particularism that stresses relative political autonomy for any bona fide cultural community has also found expression through communitarian philosophers such as Charles Taylor, Michael Walzer, and Hans-Georg Gadamer.

Peoples' endeavors to create and keep their own states have massively altered the modern world in successive waves of independence movements and nation-state formations. The first flowed forth over the course of the nineteenth century and transformed Europe (and the Americas) from a continent of absolutist empires and smaller kingdoms into one of nation-states. A second wave washed across Africa and Asia as new nations-states (often fledgling and cobbled-together) sought independence from European colonial empires. A third wave drowned the Soviet Bloc starting in 1989 and formed the independent nation-states of Central Europe and Central Asia.

The first wave culminated in World War I, the fragmentation of the Habsburg and Ottoman Empires into nation-states, and the founding of the League of Nations in 1919, when 44 states signed the League's covenant. Today the League's successor, the United Nations, consists of 193 member states. Because 97 percent of people live in their birth country (Hampshire 2013: 4), practically everyone on the planet has a national political identity (represented by the individual passport). All one need do to discover the importance of passports (all of which, save Vatican City, are at this point national) is to set out on international travel. It is hard to imagine a normative political vision that has had a greater concrete impact on the modern era than nationalism.

Postmodernism too entails a critique of Enlightenment liberalism. But its critique reaches far beyond liberalism to a rejection of any and all claims to absolute certainty, including the sense of wholeness and purpose that the members of a nation can purportedly enjoy when securely ensconced in a national polity. An instructive metaphor here is anti-foundationalism. Postmodernism represents an experiment to approach life precariously (even precipitously) without a metaphysical foundation that anchors us in some self-serving illusion that our existence fits neatly into a greater order or serves some ultimate end. It was Friedrich Nietzsche, with his philosophical "hammer," who shattered the foundation of Western thought: that monist presupposition widely held in the West since Plato that cosmos rather than chaos ultimately reigns, that we inhabit a *uni*verse whose inherent order we can comprehend. Nietzsche averred that what we take for absolute truth is but a lie that we have conveniently forgotten is a lie. Alleged truths are nothing more than linguistic metaphors rather than facts that correspond to an objective reality that confirms their validity. Our existence is ultimately one of infinite metaphors or contingent perspectives with no final arbiter to determine which of them is objectively true. Furthermore, what drives each perspective is a cloaked, deeply rooted will to power, a largely unconscious psychological urge to dominate others by forcing them to conform to our preferred interpretation of how the world ought to be.

Nietzsche's perspectivism has been profoundly explored and augmented in, for example, Ludwig Wittgenstein's theory of "language games," Maurice Merleau-Ponty's notion of "prereflective consciousness," or Martin Heidegger's idea of "Enframing." Each theorizes perspectives that stand in for—quite literally re-present—rather than actually coincide with any objective reality. These postmodern musings have reached perhaps their richest expression in Jacques Derrida's idea of *différance*, a ceaseless string of referrals between signified and signifier that can be deconstructed to show the absence of any fixed starting point. Sigmund Freud, of course, pioneered our exploration of the unconscious and how its sublimated urges affect our conscious lives. His work has been broadened and deepened by the likes of Erich Fromm, Herbert Marcuse, Jacques Lacan, Luce Irigaray, and Julia Kristeva. A number of major thinkers have enriched our understanding of the intersection of power and knowledge. Max Weber, for one, discerned in the modern rational outlook a totalizing force that would culminate in the disenchantment of the world—that is, in the total domination by bureaucratic rationality and administration, despite the fact that this bureaucratic outlook was just one of a wide range of world-organizing perspectives, none better than the other in some irrefutably demonstrable way. Max Horkheimer and Theodor Adorno (and other members of the Frankfurt School) developed the argument that the Enlightenment spawned a dialectic of not just increasing knowledge of the world but also increasing domination of those things known, including human beings with the advent of the human sciences. This strand of thinking has arguably attained its most trenchant exploration in Michel Foucault's hugely influential reconceptualization of power as a "power-knowledge nexus" in which the normalizing power of knowledge replaces older forms of brute physical force in the governing of human beings and societies.

Because postmodernism is the youngest of the three public philosophies, its concrete impact on our lives is perhaps not yet as readily recognizable as liberalism's generation of a world of individuals or nationalism's production of an international field of allying and vying nation-states. The sway of postmodernism manifests itself wherever we find challenges to accepted canons. These come forth in the academy with the criticism, say, of "dead white man's history." We encounter it too in the arts with the blurring of High Art and pop culture in the work of an Andy Warhol or the collapsing of the distinction between artist and viewer by Joseph Beuys. Works inspired by such postmodern pioneers now overflow modern art museums and galleries across Europe. The postmodern spirit permeates, however, well beyond purely "intellectual" venues. Think, for instance, of the growing interest in non-Western medicine that has spawned a multibillion-dollar industry peddling alternative healing techniques on practically every corner and computer. We experience a postmodern world also wherever we witness the proliferation, fragmentation, and combination of identities, especially identities conventionally not associated with one another. Thus, we increasingly find hyphenated persons who insist that they are Turkish Dutchmen or French Muslims, or Pakistani-Anglican-homosexual-vegan Britons for that matter. On the rise are hybrid families forged through the growing number of mixed marriages whose offspring go by names such as Muhammad Smith or Dominique Khaldun. Europe's large cities especially brim with such hybrid persons who conspicuously defy stereotypes and undermine conventional expectations regarding identity. Their stories are dramatized in multiple books, like Zadie Smith's *White Teeth* (2000, TV serial in 2002), or popular films, including Olivier Nakache's and Éric Toledano's *Intouchables* (2011), Fatih Akin's *Soul Kitchen* (2009), Buket Alakus's *Einmal Hans mit scharfer Sosse* (2013), Phillippe de Chauveron's *Qu'est-ce qu'on a fait au Bon Dieu* (2014), which reach into every home. They are the nation's soccer stars, such as France's Zinedine Zidane or Germany's Mesut Özil. Finally, the postmodern sensibility turns up in increasingly widespread political cynicism. The expanding distrust of political institutions and personalities coupled with the mounting alienation from politics documented by numerous pollsters in Europe reflect a withering expectation that politics is or can be about serving the common good (Dalton 2006; Inglehart and Welzel 2005). For ever-larger numbers of Europeans, the self-serving, ruthlessly calculating politician willing to do and say anything to gain or maintain power represents the norm rather than the exception. To the extent that European publics have come to expect bias, distortion, manipulation, and corruption in politics rather than being astounded and appalled, they are crossing over, whether knowingly or not, to the postmodern viewpoint expressed in Nietzsche's notion of the will to power. Similarly, when viewers and readers take biased, partisan reporting and analysis of politics to be normal and consider the expectation and aspiration for objectivity passé and Pollyanna-ish, they have essentially adopted Nietzsche's (1968: 267) perspectivism, whereby there are "no facts, only interpretations."

Kulturkampf

My simplified sketch of the course of modern political thought is the story of unfulfilled hopes and unintended consequences. We have not arrived at the intended destination of modernity's founders. The ultimate hope inaugurating and driving the modern era (since René Descartes) has lain in the anticipated discovery of secular certainty to replace the (perceived) onto-theological certainty of the past that was deemed immature and indefensible by modern minds (Toulmin 1990). In terms of morality, the aim was to deduce moral laws to correspond to the physical laws of nature discovered by the likes of Isaac Newton and other natural scientists.

But such ethical certainty and consensus have proven elusive. The heated controversies surrounding just such an issue as the Muslim question remind us daily of the conspicuous "battle over discourse" (Hampshire 2013: 32) that prevails in the West. The controversies would appear to be irreconcilable and mounting. "It is hard to find a democratic or democratizing society these days that is not the site of some significant controversy over whether and how its public institutions should better recognize the identities of cultural and disadvantaged minorities" (Gutmann 1994: 3). Europe lacks a political ideology possessing enough moral authority to unite all. On the contrary, Europe appears well on its way toward a value pluralism teetering on relativism, as well as to a nasty politics of bitter discord in which each party relentlessly if not ruthlessly seeks to impose its specific agenda on its detractors. Such is the portrait of our political universe painted by Alasdair MacIntyre (1984) in *After Virtue*. The lack of commonly held standards is the regrettable culmination of Western modernity across the entire spectrum of cultural life according to Jacques Barzun's (2001) *From Dawn to Decadence: 500 Years of Western Cultural Life*.

I generally see eye to eye with these deservedly esteemed scholars but prefer a more positive interpretation. My reading builds off the work of Isaiah Berlin. Whereas MacIntyre and Barzun mainly animadverted on the emergence of profound value pluralism, Berlin discerned in it the prospect for profound philosophical maturation. Maturation to greater philosophical (and presumably political) sophistication could transpire if value pluralism were to result in the abandonment of monism. In *The Crooked Timber of Humanity*, Berlin argued that monism represented the underlying presupposition of Western thought from Plato to his own time. Monism, he claimed, reposed on three presuppositions:

> The first position is this: to all genuine questions there can only be one correct answer, all the other answers being incorrect. . . . The second assumption is that a method exists for the discovery of these correct answers. . . . The third assumption, and perhaps the most important in this context, is that all the correct answers must, at the very least, be compatible with one another. (Berlin 1991: 23–24)

The Oxford don broke the spell that monism held over him via his investigation of Romantic nationalism. In his probing exploration into the thought of its seminal thinkers, in particular Giovanni Vico and Herder, Berlin determined it impossible to conclude that the ideology resulted from faulty reasoning. Rather, it started from different axioms from, and therefore reasoned through to incompatible conclusions with, his own preferred liberalism. But the axioms were unassailably reasonable and the reasoning compellingly sound. Hence, a rational way to dismiss nationalism as error eluded the committed liberal. Berlin was left no responsible option but to conclude that rationality was plural, that there could be more than one right answer to a given query and that there could be multiple upstanding visions of the good life that nonetheless contradicted one another. "Some among the Great Goods cannot live together. That is a conceptual truth" (Berlin 1991: 13).

I augment Berlin's analysis by adding postmodernism as a third public philosophy with its own internally convincing reasoning. I read these three public philosophies as the currently predominant players in an enduring *Kulturkampf,* or struggle for ideological hegemony in modern European politics. Ongoing arguably since the outbreak of the Reformation in 1517, the *Kulturkampf* has seen some public philosophies come and go, gain and then lose their competitive edge against rivals (for instance, Marxism). Liberalism, nationalism, and postmodernism stand today in competition but unable to defeat one another decisively. Each provides compelling reasons for believing its tenets. Each has been articulated by great seminal savants and is defended by persuasive contemporary apologists. Each has accumulated scores of theses and mountains of corroborating evidence to validate its conclusions. Each stands stoutly armed with arguments to fend off attacks and criticisms from rivals.

The metaphor of *Kulturkampf,* though useful, has its shortcomings. The image draws desired attention to the unavoidable ideological clashes of the three outlooks that I want to underscore. This emphasis on *intermural* disagreement automatically entails accentuating the *intramural* commonalities binding each of the three. That said, none of the three represents a monolith. Within each school there exist vying theories and theorists, different points of emphasis, and varieties of strategies. I will treat these finer distinctions within liberalism, nationalism, and postmodernism in Chapter 2. However, my underlying theme stresses that the differences within each school of thought resemble family quarrels—that is, differing outlooks that, in the end, concur when it comes to the most important values that should govern the public sphere. Liberalism stakes its lot with individual autonomy, nationalism with communal homogeneity, and postmodernism with insuperable heterogeneity and discord.

Messiness

Such attention to nuance within the three camps still leaves us with an all too orderly impression of the influence of these normative outlooks on politics. In treating the basic theoretical principles of each public philosophy, Chapter 2 might leave the impression that the concrete political world is filled with easily identifiable liberals, nationalists, and postmodernists. Real politics, of course, is fuzzier. Political actors do not march forth onto the political battlefield like footballers sporting jerseys clearly demarcated with an "L," "N," or "P" so that the analyst can clearly spot them. In this book philosophically consistent political actors represent the exception rather than the norm. Legislation itself—in democracies typically the result of complicated manipulations, compromises, negotiations, and concessions—is all the more inconsistent and contradictory.

Gary Freeman describes immigration policy as "an extremely messy reality," with "ramshackle, multifaceted, loosely connected sets of regulatory rules, institutions and practices" (2004: 946). Virginie Guiraudon (2003) has applied James March and Johan Olsen's (1989) "garbage can" theory of organized chaos to immigration policy making. James Hampshire (2013: 2) maintains that "the intractable nature of immigration policy is not a failure of governance but rather a reflection of contradictory imperatives of the liberal state." We wind up, then, with "a mixed bag not fully assimilationist, pluralist, or multicultural" (Freeman 2004: 960). Freeman sagely cautions social scientists against excessive optimism with regard to coherently fitting this policy mess into neat explanatory typologies.

In these pages I explore the hypothesis that the policy messiness that Freeman and others uncover stems, in part at least, from normative messiness. Normative messiness differs from mere discord between distinct normative camps. Messiness arises through imprecise and incomplete application of normative theories that obfuscates their critical differences. In the repartee of daily politicking, we rarely if ever encounter the public philosophies trotted out in full form—that is, as the intricate, comprehensive theories that I sketch in Chapter 2. Rather, we more often come across mere fragments of these larger normative outlooks that have become unmoored, so to speak, from their theoretical home. Few political actors have the time, inclination, or capability to trace a deployed fragment back to its mother theory, let alone explain the grand theory in its entirety. Few political activists are what Martin Carstensen (2011: 148) calls "paradigm man"; most work rather like the improvising "bricoleur" pragmatically and strategically using philosophical fragments like tools in a toolkit (see also Mehta 2011: 38–39). Hampshire (2013: 25) observes that politicians tend to want to "fudge" the immigration issue by sending "different messages to different audiences."

The resulting ideological "bricolage" generates normative muddle that in turn fosters policy messiness. When political actors employ normative fragments as "performative utterances" (Hampshire 2013: 152) or "schemas" (Bowen et al. 2014b: 14) in specific contexts separated from their mother theories, they make themselves less aware of, or at least less intolerant of, philosophical inconsistency and contradiction. Below the reader will encounter repeated examples of quite glaring philosophical inconsistency in the normative arguments of political personalities, parties, and organizations. Such contradictions irk theorists, but they do not appear to trouble political agents much. Make no mistake. Slogans like "France for the French" and "No human being is illegal" do philosophically contradict one another, but the contradiction goes less noticed in politics or, if discerned, is not given much import. Tolerated and perhaps deliberate inconsistencies find their way into immigration policy and contribute to its becoming "an awesome accumulation of contradictions" (Schierup, Hansen, and Castles 2006: 77) and "a messy state of affairs" (Boswell 2009: 251). As Margaret Levi (2013: 187) observes, "Bad policies are often good politics."

Mutual Fragilization

Another normative dimension in understanding policy messiness is "mutual fragilization." I borrow the concept from Charles Taylor's *A Secular Age*. There Taylor (2007: 303–4) interprets mutual fragilization as "certainly one of the main features of the world of 2000, in contrast to that of 1500." The Canadian philosopher has in mind a heightened awareness, in our times, of views opposing our own. Increasingly, however, these are construed not as the palpably false, immoral humbug of deranged or debased adversaries, but rather as the plausibly correct and prudent convictions of sensible fellow humans who happen to disagree with us.

We live in a condition where we cannot help but be aware that there are a number of different construals, views which intelligent, reasonably undeluded people, of good will, can and do disagree on. We cannot help looking over our shoulder from time to time, looking sideways, living our faith also in condition and uncertainty. (Taylor 2007: 11)

Richard Rorty (1989: 73) discerns something similar with the proliferation of "ironists"—that is, persons so atuned to inescapable contingency that they cannot take their own convictions fully seriously. Zygmunt Bauman (1993: 11) speaks of "endemic inconclusivity."

We might think of political antagonisms accompanied by diffidence and ambivalence as softer or gentler differences of opinion. To be sure, seemingly confident, uncompromising voices sound forth, like an Ayaan Hirsi Ali (2006) fully convinced that Islam tramples women's rights plain and simple. There can be little doubt that one consequence of the ongoing *Kulturkampf* is a hardening of positions among some adversaries. Jagged clashes between opposing parties would seem to close off the kind of empathy toward others' viewpoints that can open the door to the unifying "fusion of horizons" so nobly yearned for by Hans-Georg Gadamer (2007). I applaud the German hermeneutist's compelling urgings. But in the pages that follow, I am more interested, following Taylor, in exploring the emergence of a phenomenon that falls short of consensus. I have in mind a spreading disposition characterized by heightened awareness of discord that breeds increased expectation and acceptance of difference, diffidence, and ambivalence. Perhaps years of accumulated collective experience with an ongoing *Kulturkampf* have

> opened a space in which people can wander between and around all these options without having to land clearly and definitively in any one. In the wars between belief and unbelief [in this book public philosophies], this can be seen as a kind of no-man's-land; except that it has got wide enough to take on the character rather of a neutral zone, where one can escape the war altogether. Indeed, this is part of the reason why the war is constantly running out of steam in modern civilization, in spite of the efforts of zealous minorities. (Taylor 2007: 351)

Martin Schain, like Freeman, underscores the messiness of immigration policies. In his transatlantic comparative study, he finds a "contradiction of policies in different arenas" that governments regularly and quite knowingly, if tacitly, tolerate (Schain 2008: 276, 283). Such glaring inconsistencies, he avers, "reflect the complexities of the democratic political process" (Schain

2008: 275; see also Hampshire 2013; Bertossi and Duyvendak 2012). Normative fragmentation and fragilization, as I aim to show, is an important but underexplored example of these complexities. Normative fragmentation and fragilization need not persist. Some person or party might very well reconfigure fragments in a new way that would seem so compelling to most involved that they would embrace it and establish an overarching consensus. Rogers Brubaker (2001: 531) discerns something like this in the "return of assimilation." Christian Joppke (2009: 120) contends that "diversity" has become the "master rhetoric in all Western states." Jonathan Laurence (2012: xix) observes "a new political consensus" to integrate Muslims into existing institutional arrangements in numerous European lands. I do contend that European states and publics find themselves in a single, international (even global) discourse regarding immigration, but it remains a constantly fluctuating discourse shaped by abiding discord, principally among liberalism, nationalism, and postmodernism.

Methodology

My analysis employs a mainly constructivist methodology. Constructivism reposes on the premise that ideas matter. They form the expectations that we bring to the world and thereby shape the way we experience it (Béland and Cox 2011). Ideas are not, then, separate from or secondary to an independent social reality; they are constitutive of it (Berger and Luckmann 1967). Specifically, I work with the notion of public philosophy (Mehta 2011; Favell 1998; Lowi 1969). Of a kind with what other constructivists label "worldviews" (Weber 1949), "frames" (Bleich 2003), "political discourses" (Connolly 1993), "repertoires of evaluation" (Bowen 2010: 6), "policy paradigms" (Hall 1993), or simply "political ideologies" (Freeden 1996), a public philosophy is a loosely integrated, internally varied vision of how the public sphere ought to appear and function. A public philosophy determines for a political actor under its sway what stands out as significant as opposed to insignificant in the political arena. It shapes what comes forth as a problem in need of being addressed and prescribes what passes for a desirable solution. It is that set of expectations, ultimately normative, that inclines a political actor toward one position but away from another, to be perturbed by large-scale immigration rather than pleased, to view the newcomers as a threat rather than a benefit to one's life and land.

Most importantly, a public philosophy is an organic entity, a living tradition of related ideas that constantly morphs (Berman 2011; Freeden 1996). A public philosophy has a birth, an unfurling life, and presumably someday a death (a passing into political oblivion like, say, royalism, fascism, or Stalinist socialism). Needless to say, the latter fate has yet to befall liberalism, nationalism, or postmodernism. A public philosophy forms around a core set of tenets, fundamental and interconnected presuppositions, theories, and principles, typically enunciated by seminal thinkers acknowledged as such inside and outside the tradition. However, because a public philosophy is a protean tradition, offshoots and variations of the core ideas inevitably spring forth. These are typically developed by subsequent thinkers working self-consciously with the tenets of the masters in an effort to explore, expand, and improve them. There is a mutually dependent relationship between seminal and subsequent thinkers. Though the latter would have nothing to inspire them without the pioneering intervention of the former, the pioneers' ideas would, without their expositors' efforts, fade into oblivion—that is, turn into largely ignored ideational relics seriously considered by none but a few specialists in the history of ideas. A public philosophy, then, resembles an extended family rooted in a common (philosophical) ancestry but expanding to include many related yet still distinct individual members (dead and alive).

I offer family portraits, as it were, of liberalism, nationalism, and postmodernism. Perhaps it is better to think of them as caricatures—sophisticated caricatures, I hope, but caricatures nonetheless. I do not pretend to offer anything like a comprehensive history of liberalism, nationalism, or postmodernism of the kind one would expect to find in a volume such as *Nationalism: Its Meaning and History* (Kohn 1955). Again, such an effort exceeds the scope of this study and remains only tangentially related to its purpose: making sense of normative influences on contemporary immigration policy. My approach is informed more by what Michel Foucault (1979a: 30–31) calls the "history of the present." I assemble the caricatures with an eye to how each public philosophy is understood (and deployed) *today* in the politics of immigration. Aspects that do not figure much or at all in current debates (for instance, the kind of unabashed Aryanism/Anti-Semitism that played such a critical role in the nationalist thinking of the first half of the twentieth century) will receive only passing mention in the caricatures. The same holds for dimensions of the three isms that do not pertain much to politics proper (for instance, the Romantic art associated with nationalism or the mark of postmodernism on contemporary literary criticism or architecture). The sources on which I draw to create the caricatures are the primary works of the thinkers treated as well as prominent secondary interpretations of those works.

I treat the public philosophies as *political* ideologies. I thus structure the caricatures in a way that facilitates analyzing them as performative discourses that *do political work* by legitimizing and advancing some concrete agendas as opposed to others (Schain 2012: 370–71; Schmidt 2010: 15–20). This interest in examining public philosophies not merely as theories but as real forces in the day-to-day politics of immigration—the ultimate aim of the book—has a number of important consequences for the organization of the study.

In the first place, Chapter 2 is a service chapter, preparing the ground for the main analysis that takes place through four case studies carried out in subsequent chapters. These examine the following policy areas and the debates surrounding them: (1) citizenship (especially naturalization policy), (2) the so-called "headscarf controversy" (*l'affaire du foulard*), which has mushroomed beyond France to all corners of Europe, (3) secularism (mosque-state relations), and (4) domestic security (especially as it pertains to immigrants and refugees). The rationale for the choice of these four is explained further below. I can say at this juncture that each of the four studies focuses on persons of Muslim heritage residing (or seeking to reside) in Europe. Whether fairly or unfairly, they are the group around which the most controversy exists (Dancygier 2010: 286). As Anne Norton (2013: 2) observes, "The figure of the Muslim has become the axis where questions of political philosophy and political theology, politics and ethics meet."

Second, I intend the caricatures to operate in a way analogous to Max Weber's ideal type. They exist nowhere in real politics in the form in which they are represented in Chapter 2. However, formulating the public philosophies as pure theory (ideal types) generates heuristic devices that enable us to identify liberal, nationalist, and postmodern arguments or rationales when they are being deployed in politics. I must warn, however, that there is a limit to how much neat ordering the serious student of politics can do. Politics, especially democratic politics, tends to be messy. It is the nature, and perhaps even the beauty, of the beast (Blyth 2011). As intimated, many if not most political actors' stances do not square neatly with the theories of liberalism, nationalism, or postmodernism. Most people's beliefs are indeterminate, inconsistent, and mutable (Carstensen 2011; Geuss 2008: 2–6). Typically we encounter but fragments of the theories, and often fragments from two or more theories employed by a single actor or articulated in a single policy. It might irk some readers with a proclivity for consistency when I associate, say, Nicolas Sarkozy with a liberal position on one page and a nationalist one on another page. Inconsistent or not, the truth is that the former French president, like scores of other political actors, espouses normatively inconsistent or slippery positions.

Michael Freeden (1996: 37–41) maintains that just such inconsistency prompts many political theorists to shy away from the study of politics proper. Theorists scoff at the dumbing down and pandering by politicians. As a result, the conventional approach to the study of political philosophy has been to limit inquiry to the works of other political philosophers— essentially what I do in Chapter 2. I concur with Freeden that this convention regrettably relinquishes analysis at arguably the most important point—namely, where political ideas become forces in real politics as opposed to mere ideas in thinkers' minds. Pure theorizing about normative issues that pertain to immigration is far more advanced than the empirical investigation of how normative ideas affect politics (Schain 2012: 370; Bloemraad, Korteweg, and Yurdakul 2008: 155; Koopmans et al. 2005: 150). Empiricists tend to steer clear of normative factors because they resist exact measurement and quantification. The impact of normative ideas on politics winds up in a no-man's land neglected by both theorists and empiricists alike. "For too long," complains Seyla Benhabib (2004: 143), "normative political theory and the political sociology of the modern state have gone their separate ways" (see also Bader 2007: 22). Several studies have pointed to the influence of normative factors on immigration policy, although accompanied by the claim that their impact demands deeper exploration (Sainsbury 2012: 277; Triandafyllidou 2010b: 2; Gest 2010: 65; Messina 2007: 76; Koopmans et al. 2005: 182–209; Sniderman, Hagendoorn, and Prior 2004; Lamont 2000: 9).

This study aspires to be a constructive piece in building the bridge across the normative-empirical divide. Doing so entails tracing what Freeden (1996: 37) calls the "morphology" of political ideologies from their inception in seminal minds to their development and further exposition by subsequent theorists to their application in politics by political actors. All three aspects of "how ideas go from individual thought to collective action" (Schmidt 2010: 15) are necessary to come to grips with how normative ideas weigh upon politics. This is a formidable challenge that prevents me from pursuing other intriguing and important avenues of inquiry. For one, I pay little attention to how agents *acquire* normative ideas. My accentuation of normative fragments would seem to suggest an instrumentalist approach that reads actors as rational agents who choose normative fragments with an eye to advancing perceived interests. But I do not exclude from possibility structuralist accounts whereby social structures, for instance, class, ethnicity, religion, gender, or geography, lead actors to adopt certain views rather than others. Institutionalist approaches, which hold that a major institution can in effect transfer a prevailing ideology to those who come into contact with it, are plausible as are other theories of socialization, such as the impact of family (see Bleich 2003: 188). The point to underline here is that I do not take a position in this study. I examine how ideas are deployed rather than acquired by political actors.

Needless to say, normative theories, fragmented or whole, are hardly the only forces at work in politics. Indeed, policy analysts have identified a range of nonnormative factors that color immigration policy. These include demographics (Koopmans, Michalowski, and Waibel 2012), health of the economy (Anderson 1996), political opportunity structures (Koopmans et al. 2005), international crises (Tichenor 2002), interstate politics (Betts 2011), media salience (Givens and Luedtke 2005), type of party in power (Goodman 2014), strength of radical right parties (Koopmans, Michalowski, and Waibel 2012), policy venues (Guiraudon 1998), level of government (Schmidtke and Zaslove 2014; Dancygier 2010; Money 1999), courts (Kawar 2015; Joppke and Torpey 2013), institutional and legal heritage (Goodman 2014; Brubaker 1992), history of colonialism (Howard 2009), political access (Dancygier 2010; Freeman 1995; Kriese et al. 1995), asymmetry of available resources (Smith 1999; Mann 1987; Castells 1975), ethnic origin (Rex 1996), type of political actor, such as (opportunistic, ideological) elected officials versus (pragmatic, problem-solving) administrators (Howard 2009; Ellermann 2009; Schain 2008), cross-national learning (Goodman 2014: 219; Astor 2014: 1728–29; Laurence 2012: 19), institutional habitus, such as school as opposed to hospital as opposed to military (Bowen et al. 2014a), and administrative rationality or "governmentality" (Cohen 2009: 116–25). I will allude to such factors as they seem relevant to a particular normative stance under examination. I want to make clear, however, that I undertake in these pages no systematic weighing of the various factors to determine precisely where normative influences fit into the overall equation. That obviously important effort exceeds the scope of this book (see Hampshire 2013: 51–54; Schain 2008; Tichenor 2002). My study deliberately spotlights but one dimension of the politics of immigration. I do not purport, then, to provide a full explanation of how a given policy becomes law or why a given political actor espouses the view(s) he or she does. I aim rather to show that fragmentation and fragilization in the normative sphere contribute to the "dizzying" complexity (Hampshire 2013: 132) and "the bewildering diversity" of immigration policies (Bader 2007: 26).

Plan of the Book

As discussed, Chapter 2 treats liberalism, nationalism, and postmodernism as vying public philosophies locked in a protracted *Kulturkampf*. In addition to outlining tenets and reviewing seminal and contemporary thinkers of each public philosophy, I also stress variants within each philosophy as well as how they relate to issues of immigration. For example, I highlight two long unfurling strands of liberal theorizing that differ on how best to achieve the shared goal of individual autonomy for all. The first, which I dub "liberal voluntarism," stresses negative liberty or freedom from undue state intervention in the lives of its citizens, who are presumed to be able to achieve self-improvement on their own. Much warier of the formidable enemies of freedom, what I call "liberal perfectionism" emphasizes positive liberty and calls on the state to mold citizens into reliable practitioners and defenders of freedom. The first seeks a liberal society, the second a society of liberals. The first seeks freedom from the state, the second freedom through the state. These strands evince themselves in the work of contemporary normative theorists who deal with issues of diversity caused by immigration. Liberal multiculturalism morally bars the state from favoring any particular ethnic, religious, or other cultural group (including that of the majority), while liberal assimilationism exhorts the state to resocialize newcomers to the purportedly predominant liberal values of the receiving country through such measures as mandatory civics courses. However, we should take care neither to exaggerate the differences nor to understand these categorizations as firm and exact. Voluntarism and perfectionism represent two poles between which liberal thinkers and stances swing.

Their philosophical kinship comes clearly to the fore when liberalism is contrasted with nationalism and its stress on cultural particularism and communal solidarity. Again I underscore two diverging tendencies that, however, share the overriding normative goal of collective political autonomy for the culturally homogenous nation. "Egalitarian nationalism" embraces this goal for every nation and envisages independent nations living in peace with one another precisely because their national self-determination is honored. By contrast, what I term "antagonistic nationalism" sees "our" nation in a zero-sum game of competition with other nations and stresses national solidarity in response to real or imagined threats to national independence. Succinctly, egalitarian nationalism strives for the flourishing of *all* nations, antagonistic nationalism for the flourishing of *our* nation. As far as immigration is concerned, the first tendency has morphed into communitarianism, emphasizing the right of transnational immigrant minority communities to enjoy collective cultural autonomy and security analogous to that of the majority culture. The second manifests itself in xenohostile nativism that deems immigration and immigrants divisive, even irredentist forces that subvert national unity and well-being.

Postmodern perspectives too tend to range along a continuum between two poles. "Hobbesian postmodernism" perceives no alternative to a harsh struggle or turf war among persons and groups espousing incompatible values. However, in the postmodern reading the battle has no overpowering state to keep the peace, as famously theorized by Thomas Hobbes in *Leviathan*. A second, let us say gentler, inclination that I term "hospitable postmodernism" urges us to embrace unsettling alterity and hybridity and explore in our unexpected encounters still unimagined solutions to cultural conflict. The first variety turns up in normative reflection on immigration in the claim that the best we can hope for is, in the end, an always tenuous modus vivendi among conflicting cultural groups. The second finds expression in the interest in and celebration of "everyday multiculturalism" (Wise and Velayutham 2009)—that is, the pragmatic, context-specific, and always provisionary ways in which common folks confronted with cultural conflict manage to negotiate and accommodate their differences.

Chapter 3 examines the issue of citizenship. Requirements for naturalization as well as legal residence establish the most immediately relevant conditions under which immigrants live. By setting the bar of legality, they also directly and dramatically affect the untold numbers of "illegal" immigrants in destination countries in addition to aspiring immigrants in sending countries. In an "age of migration" (Castles and Miller 2009) framed by a stratified global economy of the affluent North and impoverished South, implementing the requirements of legal immigration becomes one of the most important and daunting tasks facing governments (Cornelius et al. 2002). At a deeper level beyond mere border control, stipulating naturalization requirements represents for a demos what Joppke (2009) calls a "mirror of identity." Defining what it takes to become a citizen—to become "one of us"—forces a citizenry to contemplate who "we" are. What should and what does constitute the integral traits of our political identity? To this fundamental political question, we will see, there exist myriad conflicting answers that, however, generally fall within the normative contours formed by liberalism, nationalism, and postmodernism. The varying normative stances find their way into complex citizenship policies across Europe and cast doubt on the putative comparative claim that there exist distinctive national understandings of citizenship, such as French republican, German ethnonationalist, and British or Dutch multicultural (Goodman 2014; Howard 2009; Koopmans et al. 2005; Brubaker 1992).

Chapter 4 investigates the veiling controversy. The extraordinary salience of this debate over a mere article of clothing stands as compelling testimony to the power of normative ideas to shape politics. Keep in mind that veiling is practiced by a minority of members of a minority religious sect in Europe. The policy of banning or permitting covering cannot, then, except in the wildest of imaginations, have serious material (or nonnormative) consequences (and thus motivations) in the same way that, say, an open immigration policy can affect rates of unemployment or the de facto minimum wage. And yet the headscarf controversy has often come to stand as a metaphor for the broader immigration debate as a whole, an extremely complicated and intricate subject matter that gets simplified down to whether one approves or disapproves of covering hair. On the face of it, the policy itself would appear straightforward: permit or proscribe veils. This is largely true, though the exact conditions under which veiling is permitted or proscribed vary widely. Normative fragmentation shows up markedly in the arguments for and against banning. Put differently, liberal, nationalist, and postmodern fragments turn up coexisting and allying with one another, so to speak, on the side of banning the veil despite the fact that the broader theories from which they stem are philosophically incompatible. The same turns out to be true with the case against banning. The veiling controversy, then, offers a telling example of normative fragmentation and fragilization that make it possible for positions fundamentally at odds to combine in the messy business of politicking.

Chapter 5 addresses secularism. Once considered a fait accompli that unequivocally positioned Europe in the vanguard of history and progress, secularism today is being revisited by Europeans, Muslim and non-Muslim alike (Habermas 2006; Casanova 1994). Muslim fundamentalists and Islamists, estimated at four or five million strong in Europe, tend to resist secularization, often highly conspicuously and controversially. They contend that European-style secularism unjustly requires the pious to relegate their religious beliefs and practices to the private sphere, degrading them to a level of superficiality on par with a pastime. Muslim resistance has led some Christians to reevaluate the deal that they struck with the secular state and to press for a larger, even leading place for Christian heritage and belief in the public sphere. Liberal voices contend that the modern state can and must maintain its neutrality while incorporating a modernized "Euro-Islam" into the European secular order. Postmodernists see in the reopening of the secularism question a perfect example of why it is immature folly to consider any normative order so self-evidently superior that it can remain immune to politicization. Secularism is anything but cut-and-dried in Europe, and rapidly changing policies toward Islam, Christianity, and other creeds are moving in many different directions.

Chapter 6 analyzes the issue of domestic security. Security concerns have, since 9/11, fully infiltrated the politics of immigration. Indeed, they bleed into every dimension of immigration, including the three case studies of Chapters 3, 4, and 5. Thus, is she hiding a bomb beneath that burqa? Are they harboring a terrorist cell in that mosque? Should we be more suspicious of our Muslim citizens and residents than the rest? Such questions evoke the specter of a dark European past. Is Europe in the process of recreating a category of second-class citizens analogous to the Jews of yesteryear? Are Europeans resurrecting on their own soil the kind of apartheid regimes they once imposed in their colonies? In arguing that such a grim process is well under way if not completed, postmodern and postcolonial voices have given some of the stigmatized Muslims reason to think that they must take their defense into their own hands. Even rumor and innuendo of such rebellious undertakings have stirred nationalist calls to unshackle the state and fully enable it to protect the nation by whatever means necessary. What has changed regarding security is that what were once considered extraordinary means, such as torturing and terrorizing, the mere mention of which raised automatic moral indignation, have been de-tabooed and are now being discussed as arguably appropriate responses to perceived insecurity.

Chapter 7 concludes the book by suggesting ways in which its approach contributes to the broader corpus of literature studying immigration. The case study chapters demonstrate Taylor's mutual fragilization, a matured normative milieu characterized by widespread diffidence and ambivalence toward competing public philosophies. Keenly aware that fragilized voters can be persuaded by a broad, almost kaleidoscopic mélange of normative stances, political actors in different contexts opportunistically invoke well-sounding fragments of philosophically incompatible normative world-views with little or no concern for consistency. Viewing them as improvising bricoleurs who deploy fragments of the three public philosophies like tools in a tool kit enables us to better expose and comprehend policy messiness. The approach of normative bricolage provides a more nuanced way of understanding the impact of moral arguments on the politics of immigration than the conventional Left-Right dichotomy employed in many studies (Sainsbury 2012; Howard 2009; Lahav 2004). By interpreting the normative discourse as a *Kulturkampf* that has ensued for centuries across the whole of Europe (and beyond), this book furthermore aims to offer a refreshing and revealing alternative to the conventional nation-state comparisons that stress path dependency and distinct national styles (Goodman 2014; Koopmans et al. 2005; Fetzer and Soper 2005; Favell 1998; Joppke 1996; Brubaker 1992).

2

Kulturkampf

Enlightenment is man's emergence from his self-incurred immaturity. Immaturity is the inability to use one's own understanding without the guidance of another. . . . The motto of Enlightenment is therefore: Sapere aude! Have courage to use your own understanding.
—**IMMANUEL KANT**, *Political Writings*

Next to love of parents for their children, the strongest instinct both national and moral which exists in man is love of his country.
—**EDMUND BURKE**, *The Works of the Right Honourable Edmund Burke*

Perhaps nobody yet has been truthful enough about what "truthfulness" is.
—**FRIEDRICH NIETZSCHE**, *Beyond Good and Evil*

I employ the German notion of *Kulturkampf* (literally, "culture struggle") to connote an ideological battle among liberalism, nationalism, and postmodernism. As intimated in the preceding chapter, I contend that none of the three public philosophies has been able decisively to discredit or defeat its rivals philosophically or politically. Each public philosophy has distilled such compelling arguments for its integral tenets that it has proven able to defend itself against philosophical or political marginalization. The enduring normative stalemate produces fertile ground for the emergence of mutual fragilization. Although each public philosophy doubtless has its share of staunchly committed proponents, a great number of political activists and citizens develop normative ambivalence. The latter results from a combination of budding diffidence regarding moral stances with which one closely identifies and creeping sympathy toward positions with which one does not closely identify. Mutual fragilization intensifies with fragmentation—that is, when normative slogans become detached from the systematic mother philosophy and deployed as performative utterances designed to sway political actors. Empirical demonstration of both mutual fragilization and fragmentation will have to await the case study chapters.

The current chapter aims to familiarize readers with liberalism, nationalism, and postmodernism as public philosophies. I want to create enough familiarity that readers can easily identify liberal, nationalist, or postmodern fragments as such when they come forth in the discourse on the Muslim question treated in subsequent chapters. I also aim to prepare readers for mutual fragilization. This I do by deliberately presenting generous interpretations of liberalism, nationalism, and postmodernism. I portray each public philosophy in its own terms and best light. I lay special stress on the reasoning buttressing arguments that figure prominently in the politics of immigration in Europe. Rather than side with a particular public philosophy, I wish to impress upon readers the plurality of persuasive normative outlooks that deal with European Muslims.

Liberalism

The intellectual origins of liberalism lie in the European Enlightenment of the seventeenth and eighteenth centuries. Pioneering thinkers of that era, such as Locke, Rousseau, Kant, and many others, argued that liberty, equality, reason, and progress represent righteous ends befitting all human beings. Regardless of liberalism's complex evolution over time, the philosophy's central aspiration remains to this day a society of free and equal human beings exercising their individual and collective reason to improve their lives.

For the *philosophes* of the Enlightenment the most redoubtable obstacles standing in the way of this lofty ideal were ignorance and tyranny taught and imposed by the unholy alliance of altar and crown. The (for the most part Roman Catholic) church was accused of preaching not only error and superstition but also, worse, blind obedience to authority. For instance, Baruch Spinoza, whose *Tractacus Theologico-Politicus* [1670] represented one of the earliest and most scathing critiques, charged: "Philosophy has no end in view save truth; faith . . . looks for nothing but obedience and piety" (1951: 189). Of the many human tragedies and follies that resulted from rampant credulity none came in for more scorn than the religious wars all too frequently endorsed by priests and waged by princes. In *Le Bon sens* (*Common Sense*), published in 1772, Baron d'Holbach lamented:

> In all parts of our globe, intoxicated fanatics have been seen cutting each other's throats, lighting funeral piles, committing, without scruple and even as a duty, the greatest crimes and shedding torrents of blood. . . . For what? . . . On behalf of a being, who exists only in their imagination, and who has made himself known only by the ravages, disputes, and follies, he has caused upon the earth. (Quoted in Bronner 2004: 165)

David Hume derided the Crusades as "the most signal and most durable monument of human folly that has yet appeared in any age or nation" (quoted in Tyerman 2006: xiv). With his characteristic wit, Voltaire (1969: 295) caustically quipped in 1769: "The Church must surely be divine, since seventeen centuries of roguery and imbecility were not capable of destroying it." The church was also said to be implicated in political tyranny by way of its support for the notion of the divine-right king whose absolute mundane authority was purportedly authorized by God. Locke (1980: 48), for example, in *Two Treatises of Government* [1689], excoriated the doctrine as nothing more than a continuation of the state of war of every man against every man wherein, however, the monarch has an overwhelming advantage. Across the English Channel, the Dutch republican Eric Walten (1689: 6) condemned monarchy as a euphemism for "slavery."

For the *lumières*, French and non-French alike, the cure for this sorry state of affairs was a strong dose of reason—that is, enlightenment. This did not necessarily have to mean an antipathy for religion per se. The preference rather was, to quote Kant's famous title from 1793, *Religion within the Bounds of Mere Reason*. Whether atheist, deist, or otherwise, Enlightenment thinkers generally shared the belief that reason rather than scripture, human rather than divine authority, ought to be the final arbiter (on earth) of what was true or false (Spragens 1981: 53). Moral philosophers enviously sought to emulate natural philosophers like Newton, whose great discoveries of the physical laws of nature were widely disseminated, for example, in the popular *Encyclopedia* of Denis Diderot and Jean Le Rond d'Alembert (Israel 2006: 201–3). The moral philosophers postulated the existence of a rationally ordered metaphysical universe whose eternally valid moral laws, like natural physical laws, were comprehensible through reason. In 1770, d'Holbach maintained that "morals is the science of the relations that subsist between the minds, the wills, and the actions of men, in the same manner that geometry is the science of the relations that are found between bodies" (Holbach 1970: 98). Kant (1996: xi) declared reason supreme in all matters:

> Our age is the genuine age of criticism, to which everything must submit. Religion through its holiness and legislation through its majesty seek to exempt themselves from it. But in this way they incite a just suspicion against themselves, and cannot lay claim to that unfeigned respect that reason grants only to that which has been able to withstand its free and public examination.

The great appeal of reason lay in its presumed universal accessibility. All humans were postulated to have the capacity to think rationally, one reason debate should be free and public. In his *Discourse on Methods* [1637], Descartes (1971: 7) maintained that "the power of judging well and of distinguishing truth from falsehood, which is what we properly mean by good sense or reason, is naturally equal in all men." Similarly, Kant (1949: 228) declared reason to be "clear, irrepressible, and distinctly audible even to the most ordinary man." Humanity's universal capacity to reason meant that the moral laws could not only be discovered but also verified and internalized by all human beings. A universal and knowable morality for all of humankind made possible the realization of Friedrich Schiller's noble vision of "all men becoming brothers" that Ludwig van Beethoven unforgettably put to music in the final movement of the Ninth Symphony.

The universality of human reason confirmed the moral validity of equality and liberty for all. For centuries elites of various stripes had sought to legitimize their superior power by proclaiming their superior wisdom. But if all humans possess the equal ability to reason and reason is the final arbiter of right and wrong, it followed that all persons must be naturally and fundamentally equal. "Being furnished with like faculties," wrote Locke in the *Second Treatise*, "there cannot be supposed any . . . *subordination* among us." Furthermore, if all individuals can think rationally, they should be free to lead their lives as they see fit rather than being made to follow the imposed direction of self-appointed superiors—"a liberty to follow my own will in all things where the rule prescribes not; and not to be subject to the inconstant, uncertain, unknown, arbitrary will of another man." By "rule" Locke meant "no other legislative power, but that established, by consent, in the common-wealth" (Locke 1980: 17). Being subject to the laws of a government formed by the rational consent of the governed (or social contract) was not seen as a violation of individual liberty. The rational consent of the governed meant that democratic law amounted to self-legislated morality rather than heteronomy. Of course, if all persons were equal, then one's rightful liberty had to end where it impinged on another's. Thus Kant (1949: 128), in *The Idea for a Universal History with Cosmopolitan Intent* [1784], wrote that each citizen should be allowed to seek "his welfare in any way he chooses, as long as (his way) can coexist with the freedom of the others." In *Ancient and Modern Liberty* [1819], Benjamin Constant nicely expressed the centrality of individual autonomy for liberalism:

> Liberty is everyman's right to be subject to the law alone, the right of not being arrested, tried, put to death or in any way molested, by the caprice of one or more individuals. It is every one's right to express his own opinion, to attend to his own art, to come and go, to associate with others. It is, lastly, every one's right to influence the

administration of the state either by nominating all or some of its officers, or by his advice, demands and petitions, which the authorities are in a greater or less degree obliged to take into account. (Quoted in Ruggerio 1927: 167–68)

Rational, free, and equal persons could be expected to improve their lot both individually and collectively. The Enlightenment bequeathed to posterity an extraordinary enthusiasm for progress. "The course of human affairs as a whole," wrote Kant (1991: 234), "does not begin with good and then proceed to evil, but develops gradually from the worse to the better, and each individual is for his own part called upon by nature to contribute towards this progress to the best of his ability." Though the obstacles were doubtless great, Enlightenment thinkers believed that one day all persons could be liberated and educated to take control over their lives and steer them toward betterment. No one deserved to be deemed so destitute, benighted, or subjugated that the liberating rays of enlightenment could not shine upon him. "The perfectibility of the person," declared Marquis de Condorcet (1804: 371), "is indefinite."

Liberal Voluntarism and Perfectionism

Liberalism not only champions but also depends on liberty, equality, rationality, and progress for its legitimization. Because it claims to be a self-legislated morality, liberalism requires persons who are granted liberty and equality to act rationally and progressively. Essentially, it needs persons neither to prevent nor to endanger their own freedom or that of anyone else. If they do either, they cast doubt on the very universality of human reason on which liberalism morally rests.

There has long been a debate within liberalism regarding how much government intervention, if any, is needed to achieve liberal ends. Isaiah Berlin (2002) famously analyzed the debate as one between negative and positive freedom. The former emphasizes freedom *from* government intervention into one's private affairs and the latter the freedom *to* develop with government assistance into a better person capable of genuine self-mastery. Others label the two outlooks "classical" and "modern" liberalism (Ryan 2012: 24). I prefer the labels "liberal voluntarism" and "liberal perfectionism" but I have in mind a distinction similar to Berlin's. Liberal voluntarism wants persons to have free choice, while liberal perfectionism wants them to make the right choice. It deserves underscoring that the two represent poles between which liberal philosophers and philosophies gravitate rather than enclosed camps with firm delineations of members and nonmembers. There prevails an unavoidable "slipperiness" between them (Ryan 2012: 22).

Liberal voluntarism worries more about governments that make mistakes than individuals who do so. Individuals should be free to err because error can represent an important dimension of the beneficial learning process leading into maturity. By contrast, when the state errs, its errors ramify widely. With this in mind, John Stuart Mill (1975: 15), in *On Liberty* [1859], laid out the harm principle, whereby "the only purpose for which power can be rightfully exercised over any member of a civilized community, against his will, is to prevent harm to others. His own good, either physical or moral, is not a sufficient warrant." The English utilitarian provocatively articulated his opprobrium for social engineering, indeed for any kind of pressure to conform, when he wrote: "If mankind minus one, were of one opinion, and only one person were of the contrary opinion, mankind would be no more justified in silencing that one person, than he, if he had the power, would be justified in silencing mankind" (Mill 1975: 23). A few years earlier, Alexis de Tocqueville (1952: 62–63), in *L'Ancien Régime et la Révolution* [1856], had averred that "each man, being presumed to have received from nature the enlightenment necessary to conduct himself, has from birth an equal and inviolable right to live independently of others in all that concerns him alone, and to forge his own destiny as he wishes." Compelling citizens to do the right thing amounted to nothing more than the illusion of progress, a cure that was worse than the disease: "A State which dwarfs its men, in order that they may be more docile instruments in its hands even for beneficial purposes, will find that with small men no great thing can really be accomplished" (Mill 1975: 141). Kant (1998: 107) too had denounced a government that would police or legislate morality: "Woe to the legislator who would want to bring about through coercion a polity directed to ethical ends! For he would thereby not only achieve the very opposite of ethical ends, but also undermine his political ends and render them insecure."

In the twentieth century, the critical distinction between the right and the good emerged within liberal discourse. As experience with (relatively) freer societies accumulated, it became obvious that free persons would not, as many Enlightenment thinkers had hoped, converge on a unified vision of the good life. As mentioned, Berlin argued that there were equally rational and compelling reasons for embracing liberalism as there were for espousing nationalism, even though the two philosophies were incompatible and incommensurable. "The necessity of choosing between absolute claims is then an inescapable characteristic of the human condition" (Berlin 1969: 169). Similarly, Rawls (2001: 3) developed the notion of "reasonable pluralism":

I believe a democratic society is not and cannot be a community, where by a community I mean a body of persons united in affirming the same comprehensive, or partially comprehensive, doctrine. The fact of reasonable pluralism which characterizes a society with free institutions makes this impossible. This is the fact of profound and irreconcilable differences in citizens' reasonable comprehensive religious and philosophical conceptions of the world, and in their views of the moral and aesthetic values to be sought in human life.

From the perspective of liberal voluntarism, the fact of reasonable pluralism should not alarm the state. The liberal state should focus its attention on guaranteeing rights rather than supporting a particular vision of the good life. It should concern itself with "procedural consensus" rather than substantive ethics (Habermas 1998: 226). It should stipulate and regulate the (fair) rules but not the results of the political game. It should act as umpire rather than coach. Government should ensure coercion-free public discourse in which all have an equal say in the making of laws that pertain to them (Habermas 1984; 1987a). Another metaphor is that of the "night watchman" (Nozick 1974: 26–27). The state should guard against the violation of its citizens' rights but refrain from instructing citizens what to do with their rights. The emphasis on rights rather than the good should include above all guaranteeing individual liberty and equality before the law and maintaining the rule of law. In this vein, Brian Barry (1996: 538) asserts that "the basic idea of liberalism is to create a set of rights under which people are treated equal in certain respects, and then leave them to deploy these rights (alone or in association with others) in pursuit of their own ends."

By contrast, liberal perfectionism fears bad choice. Many Enlightenment thinkers harbored doubts about the liberation of the masses. Kant (1838: 264) observed that the "*Volk* consists of idiots"; Hume (1754: 250) regretted that the "bulk of mankind" are "governed by authority, not reason." No one more famously voiced the concern than Rousseau (1967: 7), who in the opening line to the first chapter of *Du contrat social* [1762], penned the unforgettable observation: "Man is born free, and everywhere he is in chains." The chains were centuries of subjection to repression, ignorance, and poverty that the Geneva native had detailed in the *Discourse on the Origin and Basis of Inequality among Men* [1754]. Rousseau (1967: 22) further maintained that it, therefore, is often necessary that men should be "forced to be free." This represented no contradiction for the Genevan polymath, as he explained in his beloved novel *Émile* [1762], so long as the mandated instruction led to self-mastery in the end. As for politics, Rousseau (1967: 41) contended that "the people always desire what is good, but do not always discern it." Rousseau (1967: 42, 43, 45) theorized the need for a "great leg-islator" who "by his genius" would possess a prophet-like combination of wisdom, prudence, and charisma that would enable him to "compel with-out violence and persuade without convincing." His noble and indispens-able task was to guide individual citizens to transcend their petty, parochial interests, come together as a body politic and generate the "general will" (*volenté générale*) in the public interest. Additionally, the legislator was to establish and preach a "civil religion" (*religion civile*) whose basic tenets were to inspire harmony and loyalty to the state (Rousseau 1967: 145–47).

> He who dares undertake to give institutions to a nation ought to feel himself capable . . . of altering man's constitution in order to strengthen it; of substituting a social and moral existence for the independent and physical existence which we have all received from nature. (Rousseau 1967: 43)

Although the French (Rousseau to be sure but also Henri de St. Simon and Auguste Comte) are often loathed or lauded for social engineering, oth-ers too discerned the need for a guiding hand of the state. Kant (1991: 134), for one, wrote:

> If a certain use to which freedom is put is itself a hindrance to free-dom in accordance with universal laws (i.e. if it is contrary to right), any coercion which is used against it will be a hindrance to a hin-drance of freedom, and will thus be consonant with freedom in ac-cordance with universal laws—that is, it will be right.

Similarly, Mill (1975: 16), who worked for the East India Company, believed that "despotism is a legitimate mode of government in dealing with barbar-ians, provided the end be their improvement, and the means justified by actually effecting that end."

Arguably the most consequential thrust for positive liberty has come, since the mid-nineteenth century roughly, with the insistence on and struggle for *social* in addition to civil and political rights for all (Marshall 1950). Whether called "New Liberalism" in Britain or "Social Democracy" on the Continent, the principal aim of this progressive movement turned out to be to provide working-class individuals the same basic opportuni-ties that upper- and middle-class persons presumably can give themselves independently (Habermas 1962). The tradition reproached laissez-faire capitalism for generating and tolerating miserable living conditions for the masses that not only impoverished them but also effectively blocked them from developing self-respect and self-mastery (Ryan 2012: 33–34).

In his wartime report *Social Insurance and Allied Service* [1942], William Beveridge argued that a comprehensive social welfare state was necessary to free Britons from the "Five Great Evils of Want, Disease, Idleness, Ignorance and Squalor" (quoted in Hemerijck 2013: 122). In fact, welfare states that provided social security "from cradle to grave" were eventually realized across northwestern Europe in the generation following World War II (Hemerijck 2013: 121–25).

Other theories of positive liberty look beyond social rights to fostering civic-mindedness. Republicanism, for example, has long insisted that only through civic engagement with fellow citizens can individuals realize their full potential. Even when free, a life lived exclusively in the private sphere remains parochial and impoverished—that is, less than it should be (Viroli 1997; Pocock 1975; Arendt 1958: 22–78). Quentin Skinner (1990: 304) argues that "if we wish to enjoy as much freedom as we can hope to attain within political society, there is good reason for us to act in the first instance as virtuous citizens, placing the common good above the pursuit of any individual or factional ends." What Cécile Laborde (2002: 611) dubs "civic patriotism" requires

> of citizens . . . that they be willing to engage in the [public] conversation, that they see it as their own, and that they learn the skills which allow them to participate in it. So, while requiring that all citizens be socialized into the same political culture, it does not take this culture as a fixed legacy but as a "lived" experience.

Republicanism contends that citizens ultimately learn civic virtue only by doing citizenship—that is, by actively engaging in self-government. They therefore need to be encouraged and in some cases enabled by the state to participate in public life and dialogue. Such support, according to Laborde (2008: 24), necessitates "not only the just distribution of goods and resources but also the expansion of basic powers, virtues, and capabilities, including those of personal autonomy, civic skills, and self-respect." Persons who lack these qualities should not be left alone by the state, as liberal voluntarism posits, but rather helped to help themselves.

Deliberative democracy represents a turn in democratic theory from mere choice to informed choice. It represents an attempt to go beyond guaranteeing mere access to decision-making to guaranteeing the quality of decision-making (Keenan 2003; Richardson 2002; Fung and Wright 2001; Drysek 2000; Benhabib 1996; Buchstein 1995; Barber 1984). According to deliberative democracy, good decisions only emerge through and at the conclusion of rational collective deliberation. All impediments to rational discussion need to be eliminated. These include not only external obstacles, such as coercion, intimidation, and deception, but also internal obstructions, such as adherence to superstition or the inability to reflect critically. Habermas (1998: 44) stipulates the necessary conditions for the domination-free communication at the core of deliberative democracy as

> (i) that nobody who could make a relevant contribution may be excluded; (ii) that all participants are granted an equal opportunity to make contributions; (iii) that all participants must mean what they say; and (iv) their communication must be freed from external and internal coercion so that 'yes' or 'no' stances that participants adopt on criticizable validity claims are motivated solely by the rational force of the better reasons.

Deliberative democracy is functioning as it should when citizens can provide a reasonable account of the arguments for and against a specific policy that was adopted, including an appreciation of, not necessarily however agreement with, why one line of reasoning prevailed over the others.

The liberal democratic state should enable all its citizens to deliberate rationally, offering assistance to those not able to do so independently.

> Because most citizens live most of their lives in civil society outside of conventional politics, deliberative theories seek to structure civil society so as to better equip citizens to deliberate in politics. . . . As democratic theorists have long recognized, democracy cannot thrive without a well-educated citizenry. An important part of democratic education is learning how to deliberate well enough to be able to hold representatives accountable. Without a civil society that provides rehearsal space for political deliberation, citizens are less likely to be politically effective. (Gutmann and Thompson 2004: 35)

It follows that the liberal state should foster those organizations that encourage rational deliberation and not shrink from proscribing those that discourage or threaten it (Gutmann and Thompson 2004: 61). Critics who object to government overreach must keep in mind that democracies, because they are governed by the people and not by some enlightened despot or cadre, have an existential interest in well-educated citizens. Tolerating widespread civic apathy invites poor governance at best and political suicide at worst. After all, "we cannot simply assume that people are good liberal democrats." In some circumstances, "liberalism with a spine" is called for (Macedo 2000: 5).

Cosmopolitanism and Liberal Multiculturalism

Both liberal voluntarism and liberal perfectionism have profound implications for the politics of immigration. To address the former first, it prescribes a *thin* conception of citizenship that translates into advocacy for cosmopolitanism and liberal multiculturalism. According to cosmopolitanism, citizenship should not require any *thick* or profound attachment to or identification with a larger group. In order to guarantee individual autonomy, the rights of democratic citizenship should never be contingent on one's creed, race, gender, ethnicity, or, most importantly for immigration, one's nationality. Citizenship should be de-territorialized and de-ethnicized and attached to personhood rather than peoplehood (Delanty 2009: 131). Residence itself (in some accounts legal or even long-term) should suffice to make immigrants eligible for rights fully equal to those of native citizens (Ellermann 2014; Carens 2013; Tonkiss 2013; Abizadeh 2012; Beck and Grande 2007; Benhabib 2004; Habermas 2003; Rubio-Marin 2000). Rainer Bauböck (2007: 2423), for example, endorses "stakeholder citizenship" for all "individuals whose circumstances of life link their future well-being to the flourishing of a particular polity."

Cosmopolitanism implies a commitment to liberal multiculturalism. If the liberal state welcomes all, then it should not concern itself with telling citizens which language(s) to speak, god(s) to worship, lifestyle(s) to lead, group(s) to embrace. Their affiliations are their own private affair. Indeed, liberal multiculturalism reconceptualizes robust affiliation with a particular culture from a vice that threatens to undermine liberal universalism to a virtue that enhances personal autonomy. Vigorous affiliation with a chosen tradition can enrich and strengthen one's personal beliefs. Moreover, just such a sense of secure belonging and connectedness can fortify an individual to resist the fearsome pressures of conformity in mass consumer society (Bielefeldt 2007; Kymlicka 1995).

> Liberal multiculturalism [as] a normative principle that affirms . . . a political attitude of fostering and encouraging the prosperity, cultural and material, of cultural groups within a society, and respecting their identity, is justified by considerations of freedom and human dignity. . . . The preservation of their culture is justified only in terms of its contribution to the well-being of people. (Raz 1994a: 189, 186)

If cultural identity and pride are integral to personal autonomy, as is for example private property, then the liberal state should protect them as well. In Will Kymlicka's (1995: 113) words, the state "should aim at insuring that all national groups have the opportunity to maintain themselves as a distinct culture." The state should adopt a neutral position that refrains from privileging any particular cultural expression or group over others. In Joseph Raz's (1994a: 174) "liberal multiculturalism," the state "consists . . . of diverse communities and belongs to none of them." Exclusivist notions—"Italy is for the Italians," "French is the language of France," "Britain is a Christian country"—should enjoy no normative sway in truly cosmopolitan and multicultural societies that treat all human beings with equal respect and dignity.

> The neutrality of the law vis-à-vis internal ethical differentiations stems from the fact that in complex societies the citizenry as a whole can no longer be held together by a substantive consensus on values but only by a consensus on the procedures for the legitimate enactment of laws and the legitimate exercise of power. . . . Hence the ethical integration of groups and subcultures with their own collective identities must be uncoupled from the abstract political integration that includes all citizens equally. (Habermas 1998: 225)

Liberal Assimilationism

As far as immigration is concerned, liberal perfectionism translates into preference for liberal assimilationism. The latter urges the state to encourage, demand, and even test the assimilation of immigrants to liberal values, usually generally understood as the moral principles anchored in the receiving country's (liberal democratic) constitution. Habermas (1998: 229), for instance, claims that "constitutional patriotism" must be mandatory:

> A democratic constitutional state . . . can require of immigrants only the political socialization described in (1) ["Assent to the principles of the constitution"] (and practically speaking can expect to see it only in the second generation). This enables it to preserve the identity of the political community, which nothing, including immigration, is permitted to encroach upon, since that identity is founded on the constitutional principles anchored in the political culture and not on the basic ethical orientations of the cultural form of life predominant in that country.

By requiring identification with the liberal values of the constitution, liberal assimilationism prescribes a *thicker* form of citizenship that entails in some important respects becoming liberal-minded. Although Habermas (1998: 227) has said that "loyalty [to the constitution] . . . cannot be legally enforced," if one wants to require it, then disloyalty must either be penalized or corrected through mandatory instruction. It is not surprising that Habermas (2008a: 27) in his reflections on "post-secular society" writes:

The constitutional state confronts its citizens with the demanding expectations of an ethics of citizenship that reaches beyond mere obedience to the law. Religious citizens and communities must not only superficially adjust to the constitutional order. They are expected to appropriate the secular legitimisation of constitutional principles under the very premises of their own faith.

This reflects a political identity so thick as to affect the way persons worship. Laborde (2002: 609) too advocates a thick requirement for immigrants that "includes familiarity with collective institutions, political rituals and rhetoric, types of discourses, and accumulated habits and expectations stemming from previous conversations." Her "critical republicanism" mandates "autonomy-promoting education" for those unable or unwilling to embrace individual autonomy for all persons: "Vulnerable individuals—in particular female members of minority groups—must be equipped to resist the multiple forms of domination they are potentially subjected to: public and private, secular and religious, ethnocentric and patriarchal" (Laborde 2008: 168–69; see also Scheffer 2011: 309–10).

Like liberal voluntarism and liberal perfectionism, liberal multiculturalism and assimilationism represent normative poles between which liberal theories tend to gravitate. I thus deliberately quoted Habermas under both rubrics to underscore just this point. Other theorists too demonstrate "slipperiness" between thin and thick notions of liberal citizenship. Although Raz (1994a: 174) endorses "liberal multiculturalism," for example, he also notes the necessity of a common political culture:

> Members of all cultural groups . . . will have to acquire a common political language and conventions of conduct to be able to participate effectively in the competition for resources and the protection of group as well as individual interests in a shared political arena. (Raz 1994b: 77)

Because it champions liberty but does so with absolute moral certitude, liberalism will always harbor a built-in tension between voluntarism and perfectionism, what Spragens (1981) calls the "irony of liberal reason" (see also Gray 1996: 21–22).

Nationalism

The origins of nationalism are contested. Some consider it a purely modern phenomenon, accompanying, for example, industrialization (Gellner 1983) or the expansion of the print medium (Anderson 1991). Others stress older roots. The book of Genesis, of course, associates the creation of different nations of peoples speaking different languages with God's destruction of the Tower of Babel. Patriotism has its etymological roots in the Latin word *patria*. Originating in Roman times and surviving throughout the Middle Ages, *patria* connoted loyalty to one's community, but community understood in a much more parochial sense than the modern nation. There existed too the notion of *natio* closely associated with *lingua*. Students at medieval universities were, for instance, enrolled according to their *natio*, typically determined by their mother tongue. Caricatures of whole peoples—the "niggardly English," "stern Germans," "passionate Italians," "lazy Irish," and so forth—have been bantered to and fro in Europe for ages. In a more systematic, scholarly manner, John Armstrong (1982) uncovered "nations before nationalism," something like identifiable ethnic tribes bearing common, persistent characteristics that distinguished them from other tribes and who in modern times would gain or seek a nation-state. Anthony Smith (1986) calls roughly similar groupings *ethnies*, each of which was conscious of itself as a people with a history and without which modern European leaders could not have built nation-states as we know them today. There were also states and territories, such as France, England, the Netherlands, and arguably Sweden, assembled and governed by absolutist monarchs that appeared identifiably national—that is, French, English, Dutch, Swedish—in contrast to multiethnic empires such as the Habsburg and Ottoman dynasties, well before the nation actually governed in the modern democratic sense of a sovereign people in control of a state came into being (Marx 2003).

Particularism

That modern democratic nation-state was first proclaimed (in Europe) by the *Declaration of the Rights of Man and the Citizen* in 1789. Article III reads: "The nation is essentially the source of all sovereignty." This is why Rousseau, the celebrated philosopher of the Revolution, is sometimes called the intellectual father of modern nationalism (Smith 1991: 88), though in truth he championed republicanism modeled on the ancient *polis*. It was actually Johann Gottfried Herder who coined the term "nationalism." The Lutheran pastor of Bückeburg and one-time student of Kant insisted that the Revolution was distinctively *French*. Against its proponents, especially Napoleon I, who conquered far and wide across Europe in the name of defending and spreading the purportedly universal values of the Revolution, Herder retorted that the Revolution was particularistic. He argued that the principles of the *Declaration* could not have the same meaning for Germans (or any non-Frenchmen for that matter) because they were written in the French, not the German, language; that the Revolution could never inspire the Germans in the same way because it was launched and lived by Frenchmen and not by Germans; that the republic founded by Frenchmen in 1789 could never feel like the right model for Germans because they did not found it. Every phenomenon, Herder averred, is inescapably a product of the ultimately unique context—language, culture, time, place—in which it comes to life and remains only truly appreciable by those who share that context. "Not a country, not a people, not a natural history, not a state, are like one another," he wrote in *Another Philosophy of History for the Education of Mankind* [1774]. "Hence the True, the Good, the Beautiful in them are not similar either. If one does not search for this, if one blindly takes another nation as a model, everything is extinguished" (Herder 1877–1913: 4:472).

The alleged sources of national particularism vary. Herder stressed language. To be sure, he acknowledged other factors: "The original character of a nation is derived from its family traits, its climate, its type of life, its education, its first efforts and its habitual occupations" (quoted in Sternhell 2010: 201). But among these specifically interconnected factors none was more important than language: "Has a nation anything more precious than the language of its fathers? In it dwell its entire world of tradition, history, religion, principles of existence; its whole heart and soul" (Herder 1877–1913: 17:58). Language formed the core of what Herder (1877–1913: 8:392) termed the *Volksgeist*, literally a "people's soul," its "inner character," its particular "genius" (Herder 1877–1913: 25:10). The Volksgeist represented a people's "center of gravity" (Herder 1877–1913: 5:509), the ultimately inscrutable and even ineffable something that made one person Italian, another German, and, moreover, enabled both of them automatically to recognize the difference. Herder deemed it tragic to lose or, worse, to abandon one's mother tongue, the "dictionary of the soul" (quoted in Gillies 1945: 37). For example, he heaped scorn on the pronounced Francophilia of the court of Frederick the Great, where only French was spoken. Germans, he believed, could never amount to more than second-class Frenchmen and therefore should not endeavor to emulate them no matter how great they seemed. "Nations evolve in accordance with the place, the time, and their inner character. Each one bears within itself the harmony of its perfection, not comparable to any others" (Herder 1984: 3:759).

Montesquieu underscored climate. In the *Spirit of the Laws* [1748], he maintained that laws

> should be so adapted to the people for which they are created, that it should be a great coincidence if the laws of one nation suit another. . . . They ought to be fitted to the *physical conditions* of a country, to its climate, whether cold, hot or temperate; to the nature of its

soil, to its situation and extent, and to the way of life of its people whether it is agricultural or pastoral or that of hunters. (Montesquieu 1950–1955: 1:8–9)

It should be noted, however, that the French baron, like other *philosophes*, did believe in natural law, knowable through reason and whose moral principles needed to be customized to fit particular national settings.

Religion represented the critical bonding agent for the French patriot (of the France of Louis XIV rather than 1789) Joseph de Maistre. In *Considérations sur la France* [1796], he pilloried the Revolution for its secularizing tendencies. Acts such as the Constitution of the Clergy, he contended, dangerously diluted Roman Catholicism, whose unadulterated version he took to be an integral part of French identity. "A man must have lost his senses to believe that God has commissioned academies to tell us what He is and what is our duty to Him. . . . Those who speak or write in such a way as to rob a people of its natural dogma should be hanged like burglars" (Maistre 1884–1887: 5:108). The *comte* cast aspersions on the idea of a civic religion whose universal secular principles could apply to all mankind. He dismissed the Enlightenment axiom of a single human nature with a notorious quip: "I have seen in my life French, Italians, Russians, etc. I even know, thanks to Montesquieu, that *one can be Persian;* but as for *man,* I declare I have never met him in my life" (Maistre 1989: 145). He insisted that "nations, like individuals, have their character and even their *mission.* . . . Each of them reveals to the observer an unalterable character" (Maistre 1989: 71).

For Edmund Burke, it was the incremental unfolding of a shared history that stamped a people. He viewed a nation as inhering in a kind of quasi-sacred pact or "partnership . . . obtained in many generations . . . between those who are living, those who are dead, and those who are to be born" to honor the nation's achievements of the past, cherish those of the present, and make possible those of the future (Burke 1973: 110). The Irish-born representative to the British House of Commons abhorred the French Revolution for trying to invent a polity and people from scratch.

A nation is not an idea only of a local extent, an individual momentary aggression, but it is an idea of continuity, which extends in time as well as in numbers, and in space. And it is not the choice of one day, or one set of people, not a tumultuary or giddy choice; it is a deliberate election of ages and generation, it is a Constitution made by what is ten thousand times better than choice. (Burke 1803–1827: 10:96–97)

Homogeneity

It takes no clairvoyant to discern a proclivity for national homogeneity among nationalist thinkers. They tend to fear foreign elements as a dilution of the national character. For instance, Fichte (1968: 215), in his famous *Addresses to the German Nation* in French-occupied Berlin during the winter of 1807/1808, maintained:

> Those who speak the same language are joined to each other by a multitude of invisible bonds by nature herself. . . . They belong together and are by nature one and an inseparable whole. Such a whole, if it wishes to absorb and mingle with itself any other people of different descent and language, cannot do so without itself becoming confused, in the beginning at any rate, and violently disturbing the even progress of its culture.

Similarly, de Maistre (Maistre 1989: 270) warned that "the excessive introduction of foreign words . . . is one of the surest signs of a people's degradation." Montesquieu (1989: 310) advised readers to be "careful not to change the general spirit of the nation." "If the character is generally good, what difference do a few faults make?"

The faults might be prejudices against nonnatives. The founding fathers of particularism not only defended national prejudice; they lionized it. In prejudices lay embedded the collected and bequeathed wisdom of a people—not wisdom in an erudite, bookish form but in the form of "common sense" palatable to ordinary folks, what Vico (1948: para. 142) described as "judgment without reflection felt in common by the whole of a people, order, nation, or the whole human race." In a thought that is often echoed with regard to Islam in Europe today, Herder noted that "the introduction of any foreign religion is very dangerous. It always destroys the national character and honorable prejudices" (quoted in Sternhell 2010: 309). Burke too celebrated prejudice: "Instead of casting away all our old prejudices, we cherish them to a very considerable degree, and . . . we cherish them because they are prejudices; and the longer they have lasted and the more generally they have prevailed, the more we cherish them" (Burke 1973: 100).

Nation-state

Prejudice constituted an important element of the collective but unique wisdom of a people that made it imperative that each nation have its own state. In a slogan often uttered by European nationalists striving throughout the nineteenth century for national self-determination against empires like the Austro-Hungarian, Ottoman, and Russian, the Italian nation-builder Giuseppe Mazzini proclaimed "every nation a state, only one state for the entire nation" (quoted in Glover 1997: 12). If each nation is truly unique, has its own "soul," then it follows (in nationalist logic) that only it can govern itself aright. "Wherever a separate language is found, there a separate nation exists, which has the right to take independent charge of its affairs and to govern itself" (Fichte 1968: 184). Only natives can understand the singular needs of their nation; foreign rulers or rules will ultimately destroy a nation. Nationalism further postulates that the individual can experience the fullest richness and felicity of human life only as part of a national community— that is, as a communal "We" as opposed to an isolated "I" (Hegel 1953: 110). The nation binds its individual members to a reassuring community beyond the immediate family and grants them a kind of immortality by antedating and outlasting their own physical existence. Liberalism's freedom for the individual alone is incomplete at best and chimerical at worst. True freedom can, from the nationalist perspective, be enjoyed only collectively as a member of a nation living with co-nationals in sovereign control of "our" nation-state. No one developed this idea of collective national freedom more thoroughly and systematically than Georg Wilhelm Friedrich Hegel, who called its realization "the divine Idea as it exists on earth."

> What counts in a state is the practice of acting according to a common will. . . . This spiritual content then constitutes the essence of the individual as well as that of the people. It is one life in all, a grand object, a great purpose and content on which depend all individual happiness and all private decisions. The state does not exist for the citizens; on the contrary, one could say that the state is the end and they are its means. But the means-end relation is not fitting here. For the state is not the abstract confronting the citizens; they are parts of it, like members of an organic body, where no member is end and none is means. (Hegel 1953: 50–52)

Egalitarian Nationalism

Hegel's vision represents the core aspiration of egalitarian nationalism. Though they did not all articulate as intricate, systematic, and dialectical a philosophy as the great savant of Jena, most important nationalist thinkers and activists of the late eighteenth and first half of the nineteenth centuries subscribed to some version of this ideal in which each nation gains genuine independence over its own affairs. They were optimistic that peoples afforded self-determination would be content and therefore live together in international harmony. Herder painted the vision of a grand international garden of humanity, with each independent nation symbolizing one of the beautifully blossoming flowers. Egalitarian nationalists tended to denounce all forms of cultural or political chauvinism, chief among them imperialism. Burke, to his credit, deplored his own beloved Britain's empire, and not only for its mistreatment of his Irish brethren but also the peoples of Asia and Africa whom it subjugated. Herder poured vitriol not only on French expansionism but also on the European colonies around the world that wrongly quashed different peoples' right to self-determination. Egalitarian nationalism arguably reached its political highpoint (in Europe) during the revolutions of 1848, the "springtime of the peoples," when many *Kulturnationen* (nations without a state) sought to form democratic nation-states independent of various empires and kingdoms, the so-called "prisons of the peoples" (see Alter 1994: 39–65).

Antagonistic Nationalism

Many students of nationalism note a transformation to a more chauvinistic variety of nationalism after 1848, ultimately culminating in the two world wars (Kohn 1955: 50–80; Hayes 1931: 164–231). Variously labeled as "integral nationalism" (Hayes 1931: 164), "primordialism" (Sutherland 2012: 132), "jingoism" (Heywood 2012: 188), "biological nationalism" (Kohn 1955: 73), "ethnic nationalism" (Smith 1991: 82), or simply (proto)"fascism" (Kohn 1955: 78), I prefer "antagonistic nationalism" to describe the view of "our nation" as in a kind of Darwinian survival-of-the-fittest competition with all other nations (Darwin's *Origin of the Species* appeared in 1859). It lays equal if not greater stress on identifying, neutralizing, and even eliminating perceived external *and* internal enemies of the nation rather than merely nourishing and celebrating the national character. While some claim that antagonistic nationalism was more prominent in central and eastern Europe (Smith 1991: 81–82; Kohn 1946: 329–454; also see Marx 2003 against this thesis), I read egalitarian and antagonistic nationalism as poles between which nationalists across Europe move. Both poles belong to a single ideological orbit philosophically rooted in metaphysical particularism. Both variants share the particularistic notions that the world is divided into unique nations, that the nations represent for their members their most meaningful association or community (beyond the family) without which their lives are less than complete, and that for this reason it is critical to protect and nurture the national culture or character—to wit, maintain homogeneity. The antagonistic variant injects into an otherwise naively idealistic nationalism a dose of sober realism by maintaining that in a world populated by distinct peoples, nations and nation-states will inevitably collide and conflict. It adds the sociopolitical insight that such enmity tends to reinforce national solidarity.

Antagonistic nationalism arguably received its most philosophically profound and sociopolitically incisive articulation by Carl Schmitt (1976), especially in *Der Begriff des Politischen* (*The Concept of the Political*) from 1927. Schmitt did not originate the outlook, however. Hints of it turn up in numerous conservative and nationalist thinkers and activists, such as Fichte, Ernest Renan, Hippolyte Taine, Charles Maurras, Giovanni Gentile, Paul de Man, Ezra Pound, W. B. Yeats, Robert Brasillach, Pierre Drieu La Rochelle, Maurice Barrés, Ernst Jünger, Otto and Gregor Strasser, Georges Valois, Oswald Mosley, and Oswald Spengler. Long discredited after World War II due to the author's membership in the Nazi Party, Schmitt's work has experienced a deserved reassessment in recent decades (Tralau 2010; Agamben 2005; Mouffe 2000). Not only are his interpretations based on rigorous philosophizing about the shortcomings and contradictions of liberalism and democracy but are also now validated by a virtual mountain of social scientific research into how persons view and treat those whom they deem different from themselves (Kosic and Phalet 2006; Stolz 2000; Taguieff 1988; Lévi-Straus 1985; Horowitz 1985; Tajfel 1982).

Schmitt rejected the Enlightenment notion of a common ethics that could unite all peoples. He referred to the political world as a "pluriverse rather than a universe," in which war between nations was likely if not inevitable (Schmitt 1996: 53). In fact, for the Berlin professor politics ultimately boiled down to a relationship between friend and enemy (*Freund und Feind*): "The specific political distinction to which political actions and motives can be reduced is that between friend and enemy" and "Were this distinction to vanish then political life would vanish altogether" (Schmitt 1996: 26). In order to prevail against the enemy and avoid annihilation, a people had to be homogeneous and its members loyal to the state (ultimately to the point of dying for it). Schmitt abhorred the divisive politics of parliamentary democracy and postulated that only the threat (real or imagined) of an enemy (external and internal) could overcome the divisiveness of interest-group politics:

The endeavour of a normal state consists above all in assuring total peace within the state and its territory. . . . As long as the state is a political entity the requirement for internal peace compels it in critical situations to decide also upon the domestic enemy. Every state provides, therefore, some kind of formula for the declaration of an internal enemy. (Schmitt 1996: 46)

Indeed, Schmitt believed that denying or appeasing the enemy amounted to treason, such that "if a part of the population declares that it no longer recognizes enemies, then, depending on the circumstance, it joins their side and aids them. Such a declaration does not abolish the reality of the friend-and-enemy distinction" (Schmitt 1996: 51). A nation that tolerated internal diversity and discord was doomed to extinction: "If a people no longer possesses the energy or the will to maintain itself in the sphere of politics, the latter will not thereby vanish from the world. Only a weak people will disappear" (Schmitt 1996: 53).

Nativism

The ideological progeny of antagonistic nationalism, what I term "nativism," lay largely dormant in Western Europe and marginalized to the political fringe for a generation following World War II due to its association with fascism and the Holocaust. It was in opposition to large-scale postwar immigration that nativism revived (in the domestic politics of Western European polities) and began its gradual but steady rise into the legitimate, mainstream public philosophy it represents today. The earliest nativist arguments to reach the political limelight after World War II likely fell from the lips of British Conservative MP Enoch Powell. On 20 April 1968 in Birmingham, he delivered his "River of Blood" speech in which he presaged massive civil unrest in Britain "of American proportions" if immigration was not curbed. Supported (according to Gallup) by 74 percent of Britons, many of whom marched in protest against his immediate sacking as shadow defense secretary by Edward Heath, the address by the intellectual-turned-politician was built on classic particularist presuppositions: "The West Indian or Asian does not, by being born in England become an Englishman. In law he becomes a United Kingdom citizen by birth; in fact he is a West Indian or an Asian still" (quoted in Hansen 2000: 188). Across the English Channel, it was Jean-Marie Le Pen who brought the argument against "unassimilated" immigrants into mainstream French politics: "As a general rule, we believe populations should live in their own territories, within their own historical borders. When cultural and ethnic identities are mixed, it makes for an explosive combination" (quoted in Holmes 2000: 67, 70). In Germany, it was the fifteen German professors who in 1982 published the *Heidelberg Manifesto*, which warned:

Peoples are . . . living systems of a high order, each with its own systematic characteristics which are transmitted genetically and through tradition. For this reason the integration of large masses of non-German foreigners is impossible for the simultaneous preservation of our people, and leads to the well-known ethnic catastrophes of multicultural societies. (Quoted in Chin 2007: 148)

Analysts choose different labels for this outlook, such as "integralism" (Holmes 2000: 6), "cultural racism" (Wieviorka 2002: 141), or the "new racism" (Barker 1981), but they all tend to discern a transformation from an older form of racial discrimination based on biological differences and claims of racial inferiority and superiority to a newer differentialist form emphasizing allegedly unbridgeable cultural differences that purportedly necessitate the separation of ethnic cultural communities (Wieviorka 2002: 143).

We err, however, if we associate nativism exclusively with the Far Right. A large number of reputable contemporary scholars voice concern that cultural heterogeneity and multiculturalism erode national well-being. Although Alain de Benoist has been accused of supporting the radical Right, he has openly rejected Le Pen and the National Front. Nevertheless, the director of the influential Nouvelle Droite think-tank Groupement de recherche et d'études pour la civilisation européenne (GRECE) opposes immigration on grounds that it threatens to transform France into the United States, a "mere agglomeration of men and women from all countries" that as a result has no culture, only a "lack of culture" (Benoist 1979: 398). He prefers "the affirmation of collective singularities, the spiritual reappropriation of heritages, the clear awareness of roots and specific cultures" (Benoist 1977: 19; see also Champetier and de Benoist 1999). Dominique Schnapper (1998: 112, 80) too dislikes "multiculturalism," because it can degenerate into "Lebanon." The daughter of Raymond Aron contends that only a homogenous national culture can transcend the divisive conflicts of local and regional identifications (*"ethnies"*). Moreover, she rejects as insufficiently binding the abstract universalism of Kant's cosmopolitanism or Habermas's constitutional patriotism in favor of a "cultural homogeneity" forged through commonly lived experiences, such as serving in the same military force, speaking the same language, practicing the same religion, and living according to the same customs and mores (Schnapper 1998: 30, 116).

> Historical experience has demonstrated that the minimization of cultural and historical difference has been the most economical, and probably the most effective means of transcending ethnic identities. Objective homogeneity of population is not enough to create a nation, but it is true that it favors the interaction of social life and of political society. That is why the formation of the nation was always accompanied by policies aimed at reducing particularisms, not only political but cultural. (Schnapper 1998: 116)

Although Schnapper insists on labeling her variety "civic nationalism" in contradistinction to "ethno-nationalism" (76), it is nigh impossible to read

Community of Citizens: On the Modern Idea of Nationality and escape the impression that the author believes her beloved France was much better off before the onslaught of large-scale postwar immigration (see, for instance, 155–69).

Likewise, the eminent German legal philosopher Ernst-Wolfgang Börkenförde sides with cultural homogeneity over abstract universalism:

> A relative homogenization in a shared culture is needed . . . if the society which tends to become atomized is to be reunited into a unity capable of concerted action, in spite of being differentiated into a multiplicity of parts. This task is performed by the nation and its attendant national consciousness along with, and in succession to, religion. . . . Thus the ultimate goal cannot be to overtake national identity and replace it with something else, not even with a universalism of human rights. (Börkenförde 1995)

British political philosopher David Miller worries about the negative impact of cultural diversity on social solidarity. Social justice, he postulates, has a real chance of emerging and persisting only in societies "whose members acknowledge ties of solidarity" (Miller 1995: 93). Furthermore, "without a common national identity, there is nothing to hold citizens together" (Miller 1992: 94). "National character," he explains,

> will include political principles such as belief in democracy and the rule of law . . . [including] social norms such as filling in your income tax return or queuing as a way of deciding who gets on the bus first. It may also embrace certain cultural ideals, for instance religious beliefs or a commitment to preserve the purity of the national language. (Miller 1995: 25–26)

Indeed, empirical studies have shown a strong correlation between social homogeneity and generous redistributive welfare policies (Alesina and Glaeser 2006; Putnam 2007). For Miller (2000: 27), this is how things should be, for "nations are ethical communities. . . . The duties we owe to our fellow-nationals are different from, and more extensive than, the duties we owe to humans as such."

Though hardly as chauvinistic as Schmitt, or Far Right politicians like Le Pen for that matter, these more respectable scholars nevertheless view unassimilated immigrants as detrimental to the receiving society. They are, therefore, in some fashion enemies simply by virtue of not conforming to the national character of the majority. It should come as no surprise, then, that Schmitt's "friend-enemy" realism turns up in their scholarship. Thus,

Schnapper (1994: 183) underscores that "collective attachments are always affirmed in opposition to others," while Miller (1989: 67–68) contends "that communities just are particularistic. In seeing myself as a member of a community, I see myself as participating in a particular way of life marked off from other communities by its distinctive characteristics." The consequences for Muslim immigrants (examined in detail in subsequent chapters) are unmistakable: assimilate, depart, or remain as unwelcome, marginalized residents.

Communitarianism

As far as immigration is concerned, communitarianism represents the ideological progeny of egalitarian nationalism. Contemporary communitarianism maintains, however, that each bona fide community ought to be able to preserve and practice the norms and values that make it distinct regardless of where the physical frontiers of nation-states fall (Walzer 1983: 314). Communities of immigrants should be neither expected nor compelled to forsake their language, religion, manners, or anything else integral to their distinct identity as a result of having immigrated to a new homeland. While what I term "communitarianism" is often dubbed "multiculturalism," by detractors and proponents alike, I prefer the former label because there are liberal and postmodern varieties of multiculturalism that are philosophically distinct from communitarianism. The latter prizes the good over the right—not, however, the universal good postulated in liberal perfectionism, but rather the particular good envisaged differently by distinct communities (MacIntyre 1984: 220). Contemporary communitarianism reimagines Herder's particularistic claim (quoted previously) that "the True, the Good, the Beautiful in them [nations] are not similar" to fit a transnational age of migration in which it is not possible or even perhaps desirable for an entire nation to inhabit the same territory that it calls its own.

Before his death at the age of 102 in 2002, Hans-Georg Gadamer articulated the arguably most philosophically sophisticated version of modern-day Herderism. Richly and creatively borrowing from philosophical traditions such as Edmund Husserl's phenomenology, Friedrich Schleiermacher's and Wilhelm Dilthey's hermeneutics, and Ferdinand de Sassure's semiotics, Gadamer developed his influential notion of distinct "horizons of experience." Each significant community lives within its own horizon of understanding that defines its world, or how the members collectively experience it. A common language constitutes an important, to be sure, but not the sole ingredient of the horizon. "All human knowledge of the world is linguistically mediated. Our first orientation to the world fulfills itself in the learning of language. But not only this. The linguistic nature [*Sprachlichkeit*] of our being-in-the-world articulates in the end the whole realm of our experience" (Gadamer 2007: 65). A horizon is, furthermore, not something we choose. Rather, it represents a collection of shared experiences and outlooks that we inherit and share as part of a persisting community.

> For we live in what has been handed down to us, and this is not just a specific region of our experience of the world that we call the "cultural tradition," which only consists of texts and monuments and which are able to pass on to us a linguistically constituted and historically documented sense. No, it is *the world itself* which is communicatively experienced and continuously entrusted to us as an infinitely open task to pass on. It is never the world as it was on its first day but the world as it has come down to us. (Gadamer 2007: 26)

The author of *Truth and Method* [1960] and public debating opponent of liberal icon Habermas, Gadamer readily admitted that horizons amounted to prejudices, but like many metaphysical particularists before him, he adjudged these as neither avoidable nor deplorable: "It is not so much our judgments as it is our prejudices that constitute our being." These "pre-understandings," as he preferred to label them, "constitute the initial directedness of our whole ability to experience . . . whereby what we encounter says something to us" (Gadamer 2007: 74, 9). Prejudice and other aspects of our horizon, if properly valued, held out for the German hermeneutist the promise to make possible firmer bonds of solidarity among members of a community than are possible through instrumental consent. Gadamer understood himself to be rehabilitating and modernizing Aristotle's notion of *ethos*—political solidarity and unity of purpose built on *philia* (friendship) as opposed to *facturm* (arrived at via reason).

> "Friendship" in a philosophical reflection is a term for solidarity. But solidarity is a form of experiencing the world and social reality which one cannot bring about and make possible through objectivistic plans to overcome this solidarity through artificial institutions. On the contrary, solidarity exists before all possible overt acceptance and before the working of institutions, economic orders, legal orders, or social customs. It carries them and makes them possible. (Gadamer 2007: 271)

Like Herder, Gadamer deemed a world of profound, even ultimately insurmountable diversity richer and healthier for the human soul than a world standardized through and through according to the dictates of pure reason. Like Herder, he refused to ditch the vision of diverse communities living in harmony with one another, appreciating and embracing rather than deprecating and loathing their differences. He urged his admirers to work toward a "fusion of horizons" (1975: 289–90) by opening their minds to the perspectives of other horizons in ways that could broaden their own. Gadamer warned that a final, absolute fusion would forever elude us, but seeking it nonetheless would provide a much more intriguing philosophical journey than rationalist monism. Gadamer's was a deeply humane message admonishing his fellow humans to cherish that which made their specific community invaluable to them, to appreciate that other communities cherished their common values equally as strongly, and to embrace that diversity rather than recoil from it.

For Charles Taylor (1995: 256), an avid admirer of Gadamer, the only way to encourage human diversity, rather than asphyxiate it through the imposition of an artificial universalism, is to organize diverse societies according to the principle of "the presumption of equal worth." "As a presumption, the claim is that all human cultures that have animated whole societies over some considerable stretch of time have something important to say to all human beings . . . so all should enjoy the presumption that their traditional culture has value" (Taylor 1995: 252–53). The principle translates into what the Canadian philosopher calls the "politics of recognition," which is distinct from and not infrequently in conflict with "the politics of equal dignity." The latter, founded on liberalism, presumes that all humans are fundamentally the same (in the abstract) and therefore prizes equal or identical treatment regardless of differences in race, creed, nationality, gender, and so on. By contrast, the politics of recognition foregrounds communities' particularities and therefore prizes recognizing and encouraging them. As Taylor (1994: 43) explains,

> The reproach the first makes to the second is just that it violates the principle of nondiscrimination. The reproach the second makes to the first is that it negates identity by forcing people into a homogeneous mold that is untrue to them. This would be bad enough if the mold were itself neutral—nobody's mold in particular. But the complaint generally goes further. The claim is that the supposedly neutral set of difference-blind principles of the politics of equal dignity is in fact a reflection of one hegemonic culture. As it turns out, then, only the minority or suppressed cultures are being forced to take alien form. Consequently, the supposedly fair and difference-blind society is not only inhuman (because suppressing identities) but also, in a subtle and unconscious way, itself highly discriminatory.

No community should have to live according to standards alien to it. For Walzer (1983: 314), "justice is rooted in the distinct understandings of places, honors, jobs, things of all sorts that constitute a shared way of life. To override those understandings is (always) to act unjustly."

Postmodernism

Like nationalism, postmodernism rejects liberalism's universalism. However, whereas nationalism has been in many ways antirational, for instance in its celebration of prejudice, postmodernism has tended to be hyperrational. Postmodernism employs the Enlightenment's sharpest tool, reason, but utilizes it to interrogate rationalism itself. In this way, postmodernism represents less an anti-Enlightenment movement, like nationalism, and more an extension, or better, even a culmination of the Enlightenment tradition. For postmodernism maintains that the human intellect has developed to a state of such penetrating perspicacity in late modernity as to render belief in universal truths and values intellectually unsophisticated (Vattimo 2006: 165). The truth about truthfulness, to invoke Nietzsche's remark at the head of the chapter, is that apodictic or Absolute Truth does not exist. Rather, "truths are illusions which we have forgotten are illusions" (Nietzsche 1954: 47). In place of illusory timeless truth, postmodernism discerns infinite interpretations—that is, competing truth claims none of which can indubitably demonstrate its validity over and above rivals. The irreducible multiplicity of perspectives—perspectivism—ultimately undermines all attempts to form a metaphysical bedrock on which firmly to build our lives individually or collectively—nihilism.

Postmodern perspectivism and nihilism thus differ markedly from nationalism's particularism. The latter posits a particular but *single* culture or character for each nation (or community) that provides its members a mostly taken-for-granted, inscrutable-but-secure, lasting, holistic sense of who they are and what they stand for. By contrast, postmodernism reads our societies and ourselves as sites of a hurly burly, even schizophrenic and constantly morphing patchwork of meanings that generate hybrid and fluid identities and values that make final closure or certainty elusive. The resulting impermanence, furthermore, renders overarching political consensus, whether liberal or national, chimerical and impossible.

Perspectivism

Nietzsche (1968: 267), arguably the intellectual father of postmodernism, originated the notion of "perspectivism." He rejected positivism's postulate of unequivocal facts with a now famous aphorism: "No, facts is precisely what there is not, only interpretations" (1968: 267)—to wit, "There are many kinds of eyes . . . and consequently there are many kinds of 'truths,' and consequently there is no truth" (Nietzsche 1968: 291). Nietzsche averred that the epistemological notion of truthfulness was philosophically indefensible despite millennia of presupposing it in the Western tradition, whether in ancient Greek thought, monotheism, or modern science, all of which, for Nietzsche, were of a piece in their inveterate monism. The formally trained philologist interpreted language as the starting point of the yearning for apodictic truth. Language depicts a world that we quite understandably want to believe is "true" or actually "out there" in a way that corresponds to how our language describes it. But wishing something to be true does not make it so. Indeed, Nietzsche contended that serious scrutiny eventually exposes every truth claim, including the belief in God, to be a self-soothing illusion (1968: 45). "The 'apparent' world," he scribbled in *Twilight of the Idols*, "is the only one: the 'true' world is merely added by a lie" (Nietzsche 1967–1977: 4:481). The "first perfect nihilist of Europe" (Nietzsche 1968: 3) chastised his readers' immature yearning for truth and implored them to confront both the constructed and contested nature of knowledge:

> But I should think that today we are at least far from the ridiculous immodesty that would be involved in decreeing from our corner that perspectives are permitted only from this corner. Rather has the world become "infinite" for us all over again, inasmuch as we cannot reject the possibility that *it may include infinite interpretations*. (Nietzsche 1974: para. 374)

Subsequent thinkers in the postmodern tradition have augmented Nietzsche's seminal insights. (Late) Wittgenstein, for instance, argued that language, rather than representing more or less accurately the independent essence of objective things, actually assigns meaning to things. Moreover, "the meaning of a word is its use in the language" (Wittgenstein 1958: sec. 43). Needless to say, usage varies from one linguistic context to the next depending on the specific rules and understandings of the language application (understood loosely as "grammar"). "*Essence* is expressed by grammar. . . . Grammar tells what object anything is. (Theology as grammar)" (Wittgenstein 1958: sec. 371, 373). Different grammars or "language games" can therefore impart very different meanings to the "same" object. Competing interpretations are neither valid nor invalid, merely different.

> Was Augustine in error, then, when he called upon God on every page of the *Confessions*? But—one might say—if he was not in error, surely the Buddhist holy man was—or anyone else—whose religion

gives expression to completely new views. But *none* of them was in error, except when he set forth a theory. (Wittgenstein 1993: 119)

The Austrian school teacher turned Cambridge don conceded that most humans do not perceive the ongoing subtle changes to their language game that to them appears stable (Wittgenstein 1958: sec. 18; 1969: sec. 99). Nonetheless, the illusion of stability cannot ultimately shield one from potentially upsetting alterations in the language game or from coming into contact with different language games altogether. Despite originally setting out to provide perfect philosophical certainty in *Tractatus Logico-Philosophicus* (1922), Wittgenstein wound up asserting that philosophy can offer no comfortable escape from "the groundlessness of our believing" (Wittgenstein 1969: sec 166), "cannot give it any foundation" (Wittgenstein 1958: sec. 124).

Wittgenstein's contemporaries were drawing equally arresting conclusions, albeit from different angles. Max Weber (1922: 154), for example, argued that our enhanced ability to reason led us further from rather than closer to certainty:

> It is the destiny of a cultural epoch which has tasted of the tree of knowledge to know that we cannot decipher the meaning of world events, regardless of how completely we may study them. We must, rather, be prepared to create them ourselves and to know that worldviews can never be the product of factual knowledge. Thus the highest ideals, those which move us most powerfully, can become valid only by being in combat with the ideals of other men, which are as sacred to them as ours are to us.

His compatriot Martin Heidegger maintained that what persons take as reality ("being in the world" or *Dasein*) is a product of "Enframing" (*Ge-stell*). The latter is more of an occlusion of than an opening to the fullness of being (*Sein*) that enframed persons forget has happened (*Seinsvergessenheit*).

> World picture, when understood essentially, does not mean a picture of the world but the world conceived and grasped as picture. What is, in its entirety, is now taken in such a way that it first is in being and only is in being to the extent that it is set up by man, who represents and sets forth. (Heidegger 1977: 129–30)

Maurice Merleau-Ponty, who was deeply influenced by Heidegger, preferred to see the body as the most important frame of reference. All experience, he argued, must needs take place through and in the body. "Our constant aim," he explained in the *Phenomenology of Perception,* "is to elucidate the primary function whereby we bring into existence, for ourselves, or take hold upon a space, the object or the instrument, and to describe the body as the place where this appropriation occurs" (Merleau-Ponty 1962: 154). The French philosopher thus rejected the Cartesian distinction between mind and body ("I think, therefore, I am") and with it the quest for a purely abstract perception of the world that, because it was thought to be disembodied, was reputed to be objective. Nor did Merleau-Ponty advance a version of biological determinism whereby the body as the identical physiological configuration in all humans generates identical experience for all. On the contrary, he interpreted the body as the complex and indeterminate site not only of physiological and psychological structures but also of accumulated experiences that, all taken together, made possible an infinite array of lived meanings even within a single embodied person.

A generation later, Jacques Derrida (1991) further enriched perspectivism with his influential notion of *différance.* Untranslatable due its intended double meaning (in French) of deferral and difference, the neologism conveys the claim that any word (and by extension any concept) only acquires meaning in relation to other words, words that are not only anterior to and concurrent with it, but also words that will emerge in the future. Thus, for any word there can be no fixed or permanent meaning (final or correct interpretation); it is infinitely deferred and therefore potentially different from one moment to the next. "There is nothing outside the text" with which to (in)validate the text's meaning (Derrida 1976: 158). The ineluctable and interminable intertextuality of language is tantamount for Derrida to "the deconstruction of the transcendental signified, which at one time or another, would place a reassuring end to the reference from sign to sign" (Derrida 1976: 49). Because we can comprehend and experience the world only through language, our understandings of it have to be forever indeterminate, mutable, and plural (Derrida 1992). Ours is a world of "infinite *variabilities*" (Deleuze and Guattari 1994: 201).

Will to Power

Postmodernist insistence on the constructed nature of truth begs the ultimately political question of how some representations of truth come to prevail (even if temporarily) over others. Needless to say, Nietzsche had an answer. In *The Will to Power,* he asked:

> *By which means does a virtue come to power?* By exactly the same means as a political party: the slandering, inculpation, undermining of virtues that oppose it and are already in power, by rebaptizing

them, by systematic persecution and mockery. Therefore: through sheer "immorality." (Nietzsche 1968: 172)

Nietzsche discerned an intrinsic and mutually reinforcing relationship between knowledge and power. At the root of every truth claim, he argued, lay an often unconscious drive to dominate others, to force them to live by one's own interpretation of the world. "It is our needs that interpret the world; our drives and the For and Against. Every drive is a kind of lust to rule; each one has its perspective that it would like to compel all the other drives to accept as the norm" (1968: 267). For example, the self-declared anti-Christ contended that Christianity was a perspective that was motivated by the mediocre masses to constrain the brilliant and gifted few. The critical insight bequeathed to postmodernism was that knowledge and power cannot be decoupled. The former is always implicated in ultimately political relations of power.

Michel Foucault has arguably done more than any other postmodern analyst to deepen the understanding of the interconnected relationship between power and knowledge.

"Truth" is to be understood as a system of ordered procedures for the production, regulation, distribution, circulation, and operation of statements. . . . It is linked in a circular relation with systems of power which produce and sustain it, and to effects of power which it induces and which extend it. (1984: 74)

The crux of the Frenchman's exploration of the "microphysics of power" is that knowledge is constructed by an interlocking, mutually reinforcing nexus of resources, institutions, administrators, and experts that becomes strategically positioned in such a way as to establish its representation of reality (both normative and empirical) as "objective." This form of "governmentality" operates through normalization. The dominant discourse and the institutions and actors that produce and administer it form a definition of "normal" and therewith simultaneously establish, diagnose, sequester, and discipline the "abnormal." Furthermore, the "normalizing gaze" not only defines and spotlights the negative Other but also conveniently projects back a positive and reinforcing image of the "normal ones" who live the dominant discourse's representation as objective truth.

Besides Foucault's (1978; 1979; 1988) own case studies into sexual, criminal, and psychological deviance, Edward Said's *Orientalism* (1978) rightfully stands as one of the most celebrated Foucauldian analyses of how a power-knowledge discourse actually functions in all its complexity. The discourse of Orientalism, according to Said, enables and legitimizes European domination of the "Orient."

> Taking the late eighteenth century as a very roughly defined starting point Orientalism can be discussed and analyzed as the corporate institution for dealing with the Orient—dealing with it by making statements about it, authorizing views of it, describing it, teaching it, selling it, ruling over it: in short, Orientalism as a Western style for dominating, restructuring, and having authority over the Orient. (Said 1978: 3)

The Palestinian American scholar contended that "European culture gained in strength and identity by setting itself off against the Orient as a sort of surrogate and even underground self" (Said 1978: 3). Furthermore, following both Nietzsche's and Foucault's insistence on the constructed and imposed nature of knowledge, Said (1978: 6) cautioned:

> One ought never to assume that the structure of Orientalism is nothing more than a structure of lies or of myths which, were the truth about them to be told, would simply blow away. . . . What we must respect and try to grasp is the sheer knitted-together strength of Orientalist discourse, its very close ties to the enabling socio-economic and political institutions, and its redoubtable durability.

Said's work profoundly contributed to Postcolonial Studies, which interrogates Eurocentrism past and present and, as we shall see in subsequent chapters, has had a considerable impact on the politics of immigration in Europe.

Hobbesian Postmodernism

Both Foucault and Said have come under criticism for exaggerating the power of a single discourse to dominate over all others. Jean-François Lyotard (1984), for example, maintains that the "postmodern condition" is such that no "meta-narrative" can remain beyond suspicion and contestation. Similarly, Giorgio Agamben (2005: 83) observes that "contemporary politics . . . all over the planet unhinges and empties traditions and beliefs, ideologies and religions, identities and communities." The erstwhile liberal turned postmodernist John Gray (1995: 85) has something similar in mind when expressing grave doubt about the prospects for a political consensus rooted in liberalism, noting "the intellectual foundations of the Enlightenment project have fallen away; but liberal theory, for the most part, proceeds as if nothing has happened." Likewise, Bhikhu Parekh (2000: 13) argues that

> liberalism is a substantive doctrine advocating a specific view of man, society and the world and embedded in and giving rise to a distinct way of life. As such it represents a particular cultural perspective and cannot provide a broad and impartial enough framework to conceptualise other cultures or their relations with it.

Truth claims of all sorts are regularly recognized as and challenged for being implicated in political power relations. "Today," observes Gianni Vattimo (2006: 128),

> we all know that television lies and that the media do not in the least supply disinterested and objective representations of the world, and . . . even what we call "nature" is only accessible to us through scientific paradigms fraught with historicity and loaded with theory, hence with "prejudice."

Alluding to Hobbes's notorious "Leviathan," a state so awesomely powerful that it alone can keep the peace among otherwise warring factions whose worldviews know no common ground, Etienne Balibar (2004: 201) insists:

> There can be no new "Leviathan" that would regulate belief and officialize knowledge ("institute the truth," as the modern state has done through its schools and universities), and there is even less possibility for a new "civic religion" that would relativize "traditional" or "revealed" religions and relegate them to private choice.

"Hobbesian postmodernism" (meaning, like Balibar, *sans* Leviathan) is the shorthand label I give to this outlook, according to which overlapping political consensus, ethical or procedural, is impossible, and bald political contestation remains the final arbiter among vying adherents of competing worldviews. Stanley Fish (1999: 14, 12), for instance, dismisses the efforts of prominent contemporary liberal philosophers like Rawls and Habermas to anchor consensual politics in universally reasonable and fair procedures: there can be "no hope of a procedural republic from which divisive issues have been banished and in which we can all just get along. . . . Conflict is always just around the corner (Hobbes was right)." This is because competing groups enter politics today informed by firmly held worldviews that are not only incompatible but incommensurable, each representing "an orthodoxy to itself, fully equipped with dogma, criteria for evidence, founding texts, exemplary achievements, heroes, villains, goals, agenda, and all the rest" (Fish 1999: 218). In the absence of commonly recognized standards or principles by which to evaluate competing outlooks, political struggle becomes the final arbiter. "Everything is politics," declares Fish (1999: 9). There is no escaping "the political game." "Play it (the lesson is superfluous; what else could you do?) and play it to win" (Fish 1999: 7, 240). One does this by taking whatever political and rhetorical steps are deemed necessary to make one's preferred outlook the "prestige discourse" and one's opponents' the stigmatized discourse. Gray (1995: 90) likewise recommends abandoning idealistic quests for harmony and settling for a postmodern "*modus vivendi.*" Such an arrangement does not even constitute the proverbial "agreeing to disagree." Rather, conflicting, though perhaps parleying parties come to the realization that it is more convenient, less disruptive, to permit one another variously constructed and understood zones of discretion in which their particular mores predominate. The borders of such zones will inevitably be contested, and opposing parties will from time to time vehemently and even violently clash. Though perhaps unsettling, this is simply the Hobbesean reality of postmodern life and society.

Although both advocate a separatism of sorts, Hobbesian postmodernism and communitarianism should not be confounded. The latter reposes on ethical consensus—namely, on the principle of the presumption of equal worth. Different communities recognize and respect the borders separating them. The better metaphor for grasping Hobbesian postmodernism is the turf war where the borders themselves are contested and fluid. To be sure, vying parties might reach a stalemate or even a truce, but neither represents an agreement regarding overall principles or procedures of mutual governance. The parties never fully relinquish the effort to expand their sphere of influence because they view politics as a zero-sum game in which one either dominates or is dominated. Chantal Mouffe (2000: 45) claims that "no final resolution or equilibrium . . . is ever possible, and there can be only temporary, pragmatic, unstable and precarious negotiations of the tension." What is necessary is a "constant process of negotiation and renegotiation— through different hegemonic articulations."

As far as immigration is concerned, Hobbesian postmodernism casts doubt and suspicion on the notion, let alone actual achievement, of genuine community held together by common norms and values respected by all or most members. The only real community, claims Jean-Luc Nancy (1991), is "the inoperative community." Gray (1995: 911–92), for example, pours cold water over the smug confidence that immigrants will eventually adopt Western individualism on account of its allegedly unequivocal superiority, arguing that "the evidence of recent Asian immigrant groups, who do as well or better on all measures of well being in the absence of any commitment to an idea of autonomy, and perhaps because they have no such commitment, are compelling counter examples." Similarly, Parekh (1999: 71) points to many "adult, sane, and educated women" who "freely" undergo clitoridectomy or engage in polygamy because in their worldview these practices make perfectly good sense. The confidence of decidedly anti-Western Islamists to resist Westernization both outside and inside Europe has been mounting since the Iranian Revolution of 1979 (Göle 2011). Germany's foremost expert on German Islamism, Werner Schiffauer (2007: 79), contends that Islamists are so firmly entrenched and well organized that relations between them and their opponents "must almost by necessity lead to an agonising conflict-oriented *fight for recognition*." With similar Hobbesian postmodern candor did Tariq Modood (1990: 144) refer to Britain's Muslims as "the group that British society is currently being forced to adjust to or defeat." Parekh (2000: 238) mirthlessly notes that diverse "political communities are exceedingly difficult to hold together and, as history shows, there is no means of knowing what might precipitate their break up." If a multicultural society's effort to cohere "proves inadequate, it should avoid repressive violence and accept its misfortune as part of the inescapable frailty of all human institutions."

Hospitable Postmodernism

Hobbesian postmodernism can seem frightfully grim. One thinks of Foucault's (1980: 90) oft-cited inversion of Carl von Clausewitz's famous dictum: politics is the continuation of war by other means. But postmodern politics does not necessarily have to degenerate into rampant "mixophobia"; there are opportunities for "mixophilia" as well (Bauman 2003: 27). Certainly in the global cities of today, "groups of different backgrounds, ethnic and otherwise, cannot help but enter into relations with each other, no matter how great the desire for separateness and the attempt to maintain cultural purity" (Ang 2001: 89–90). What I dub "hospitable postmodernism" seeks to conceptualize such relations in ways that can prove cooperative and mutually beneficial to actors taking radically different positions—a "*modus covivendi*" rather than a mere modus vivendi (Bauman 2003: 32). What is necessary for constructive as opposed to destructive relations to have a chance of emerging is, according to Derrida (2001: 22–23), "unconditional hospitality, offered *a priori* to every other, to all newcomers, *whoever they may be*." Similarly, in his analysis of what ought to be done *When Faiths Collide*, Martin Marty invokes the metaphor of "risky hospitality," inviting "strangers" to one's table without the guarantee that the encounter will turn out to be agreeable. The best one can hope for is a thickening of the discourse. It will not produce anything so near as a straight-arrow secular rational approach. It will eventuate in a thicket, a bramble, of entangled and sometimes not completely un-entangleable strands, mixed with branches or other growths. But is it likely to reflect not only the messiness of a pluralist society but also repositories of options that would not have been contemplated in the world of the Rawlsians. (Marty 2005: 121)

Marty succinctly enunciates the essential spirit of hospitable postmodernism. It neither promises nor even aspires to anything remotely as harmonious or as stable as nationalist homogeneity, or liberal consensus for that matter. Though hospitable postmodernism does not foreclose cooperation, it nonetheless acknowledges that the unexampled and interminable diversity of postmodernity makes firm certainty and lasting accord unlikely, if not impossible. We do well, therefore, not to exaggerate the differences between Hobbesian and hospitable postmodernism. They represent poles between which postmodern theorists gravitate. Often the same thinker expresses elements of both, hospitable postmodernism typically emerging in gentler moments when the writer is trying to reassure readers that embracing postmodernism does not have to entail a headlong leap off the precipice of moral absolutism into a relativistic abyss of anarchic turmoil. Take Mouffe, for instance. Although she invokes Schmitt to underscore the inescapably antagonistic dimension of politics, in the end she articulates her own theory of "agonistic pluralism." Hers is a vision in which differing parties come to see themselves not as Schmitt's enemies, but as "adversaries, adversaries being defined in a paradoxical way as 'friendly enemies,' that is, persons who are friends because they share a common symbolic space but also enemies because they want to organize this common symbolic space in a different way" (Mouffe 2000: 9). Fish (1999: 15) claims "that conflict is manageable only in the short run and that structures of conciliation and harmony are forever fragile and must always be shored up, with uncertain success." For his part, Parekh (2008: 2) outlines a "new politics of identity" rooted in the "spirit of human solidarity." But by his lights such solidarity can only emerge through recognizing and embracing the infinite differentness of fellow humans and not through ignoring or suppressing particularities through abstract universalism. "Particularity or difference is valued, but not particularism, which absolutizes it. The universal is valued, but not universalism, at least not of the kind that sets itself in opposition to and despises the particular" (Parekh 2008: 3). Modood (2007: 150) goes so far as to maintain that a common "national identity" is "necessary to make a success of a multicultural society." However, he immediately qualifies: "Not assimilation into an undifferentiated national identity; that is unrealistic and oppressive as a policy. An inclusive national identity is respectful of and builds upon the identities that people value and does not trample upon them." Furthermore, it "should be woven in debate and discussion, not reduced to a list" (Modood 2007: 153).

Hospitable postmodernism seeks to transform strangeness into something to welcome rather than fear, "from a threat to an opportunity" (Mavelli 2012: 137). Kristeva (1991), for instance, argues that deep down we are each of us strangers to ourselves—an unavoidable state of the human condition that, however, can be tapped to ease and encourage openness vis-à-vis foreigners. Similarly, Bonnie Honig (2001: 4) urges reframing the conventional question of "What problems do foreigners pose for us?" to "What problems does foreignness solve for us?" Foreigners often transgress convention in ways that annoy natives. Honig (2001: 99) recommends reconceptualizing such disturbances as invigorating reminders that democracy itself originated in challenges to convention. These authors do not preach engaging otherness in order to emulate adversaries, but rather as a vehicle for expanded self-understanding. This is what Agamben (1993: 68) means when he writes: "The *outside* is not another space that resides beyond a determinate space, but rather, it is the passage, the exteriority that gives it access."

Hospitable postmodernism especially prizes hybridity. Exploring rather than avoiding alterity, it is argued, yields hybrid perspectives, experiences, and identities that, even when initially uncomfortable, can prove to be salutary. Salman Rushdie, for instance, encourages readers to celebrate "hybridity, impurity, intermingling, the transformation that comes from new and unexpected combinations of human beings, cultures, ideas, politics, movies, songs" (quoted in Joppke 1996: 488). Parekh (2008: 28) contends that hybridity enhances tolerance, for persons exposed to hybridity are less likely to fixate on a single identity and demand its defense or imposition on others. Homi Bhabha (1994: 226, 37) likewise welcomes the "hybridity as heresy" that surfaces in what he calls the "third space of enunciation." The latter is "the 'inter'—the cutting edge of translation and negotiation, the *in-between* space"—that can generate hitherto unimagined and unexperienced outlooks and perhaps even solutions to intractable conflicts. "And by exploring this Third Space," he adds, "we may elude the politics of polarity and emerge as others of ourselves" (Bhabha 1994: 38). Balibar (2004: 178) also champions the experience of "translation." Building off the ideas of Umberto Eco, the French philosopher reminds readers that Europe, due to its enduring multilingual experience, has traditionally excelled in the art of translation, repeatedly making comprehensible to nonnative speakers ideas originally crafted in alien tongues. This noble tradition should be tapped and expanded to welcome non-European newcomers rather than jettisoned in favor of a fortress Europe attitude. Similarly, Derrida (1992: 29) urges his fellow Europeans to be "the guardians of an idea of Europe . . . but of a Europe that consists precisely in not closing itself off in its own identity and in advancing itself in an exemplary way toward what it is not." This would also seem to be the tenet of a brand of postmodern cosmopolitanism advocated by thinkers such as Ulrich Beck (2000), who want to untie cosmopolitanism from its tight moorings to Kantian universalism and make it a looser public philosophy that welcomes and celebrates difference while at the same time seeking to forge "political dialogs that cut across boundaries" (Radtke 2011).

Such dialogues should be totally open-ended and free of strict taboos. The conditions and conclusions should never be preordained. Claude Lefort (1988: 39), for example, favors "a regime founded upon *the legitimacy of a debate as to what is legitimate and what is illegitimate*—a debate which is necessarily without any guarantor and without any end." Stuart Hall (2000: 235) adds:

> A process of final political adjudication between rival definitions of 'the good' would be inimical to the whole multi-cultural project, since its effect would be to constitute every political space as a "war of manoeuvre" between entrenched and absolutized particular differences.

Open-endedness necessitates the relaxation of firm principle in favor of flexible, context-specific pragmatism. Solutions to conflicts that work will likely be local and last only temporarily before they need to be renegotiated. Modood (2007: 134), for example, warns that "there is no general remedy." He recommends instead of a general principle to follow a "pragmatic, case-by-case, negotiated approach to dealing with controversy and conflict: not an ideological, 'drawing a line in the sand' mentality" (Modood 2009: 180).

It is worth reiterating that hospitable postmodernism "comes without guarantees" of success (Amin 2002: 973). This "means constant exposure to ambivalence—that is, to a situation with no decidable solution, with no foolproof choice, no unreflective knowledge of 'how to go on'" (Bauman 1993: 245–46). It is more akin to an experiment, even a venture or gamble, that engaging difference will yield more agreeable results than limiting or suppressing it. Thus, Honig (2009: 38) encourages "an embrace of the perpetuity of political contestation." Doing so can facilitate a

> self-overcoming [that] may take the form of civic commitments to practices of agonistic respect and to an ethos of pluralization that acknowledges the remainders of all forms of life by actively but not uncritically supporting the efforts of new identities to come into

being without prior guarantees about the rightness or justice of their claims.

Hospitable postmodernism is motivated by a sense that alternatives to it have proven themselves unable to manage the postmodern condition of un-precedented and unending difference.

> The point of the dialogue is to deepen mutual understanding, ex-pand sympathy and imagination, exchange not only arguments but also sensibilities, to get both parties to take a critical look at them-selves, build up mutual trust, and to arrive at a more just and bal-anced view of both the contentious issues and their wider context. It must be robust, frank and critical, telling the truth as each party sees it, but always in the knowledge that it cannot be allowed to fail, because the only alternative to it is the vicious cycle of hatred and violence. (Parekh 2008: 170)

Conclusion

I have so far treated liberalism, nationalism, and postmodernism as separate public philosophies. I did note slipperiness between poles within each public philosophy. It remains in this conclusion to adumbrate ways in which borrow-ing and blending between public philosophies transpires. Such intermingling is symptomatic of the mutual fragilization spawned from a spreading aware-ness of the plurality of normative persuasiveness. Many thinkers fuse ele-ments from more than one public philosophy because they seem compelling.

Take liberal nationalism, for example. Its expositors contend that lib-eral democracy functions best in a homogeneous national culture such as the putative European nation-state (before mass immigration). In this vein, Margaret Canovan (1996: 80) calls nationalism the "battery that makes lib-eral democracy run." Yael Tamir (1993: 139) goes so far as to claim that "most liberals are liberal nationalists" because they typically conceive of liberalism as functioning within nation-states. Thus, although Laborde's (2002: 610) "civic patriotism" is mainly rooted in shared liberal values, she concedes that within any given national setting

> a variety of "ethnic" practices will be maintained, because they are deemed innocuous (e.g., most street names), convenient (e.g., Chris-tian calendar), or open to re-interpretation and deconstruction (e.g., aspects of national history). Civic patriotism . . . demands . . . that they [immigrants] feel "at home" with what must be a genuinely shared national identity.

Gravitating in the other direction, there can be no gainsaying that Miller (1995) or Schnapper (1998) both want to press their prized national homogeneity into service toward liberal democratic ends among nationals. Similarly, Taylor (1985: 187–210) hopes and believes that communitarianism can enhance rather than restrict personal autonomy.

As appealing or even as natural as liberal nationalism might seem, it cannot in the end avoid contradiction when confronted with large-scale immigration. If the goal of homogeneity is pursued in earnest, illiberal policies will have to be enacted that penalize or marginalize those who refuse or fail to conform. Inversely, if liberal equality is taken seriously, the equal treatment of nonconforming citizens is bound to erode national homogeneity (Tonkiss 2013: 22; Müller 2007: 9).

Border crossings with postmodernism are also discernible. We already saw, for example, that Mouffe's (2000) postmodern theory of "agonistic pluralism" borrows heavily from Schmitt's (1996) reading of the ineluctable friend-enemy relations among nation-states. Or listen to Bauman (1997: 57) laud liberalism's moral centerpiece of individual autonomy:

There is a true emancipatory chance in postmodernity . . . through revealing conditions of individual freedom which transcend both national and ethnic/tribal limitations; through focusing on the right to choose as the sole human universality; on the ultimate, inalienable individual responsibility for that choice, and on the complex State- or tribe-managed mechanisms aimed at depriving the individual of the freedom of choice and that responsibility.

Liberal theories of deliberative democracy take a page from hospitable postmodernism when they call for open-ended dialogue. Jan Werner Müller's (2007: 69) version of constitutional patriotism, for example, is "one that does not see constitutional cultures as fully 'achieved' and closed to self-critical learning, but rather views them as an ongoing project of realizing certain norms and values in an 'ever more perfect' way." He furthermore takes inspiration from postmodernism's idea of fluid, hybrid, negotiated identities when he envisages the "integration [of immigrants] not as something done to 'them,' but something accomplished in common through mutual deliberative engagement . . . in such a way that a reconstituted 'we' emerges" (Müller 2007: 89). Likewise, Gadamer's (1975: 289–90) striving for a "fusion of horizons," which, however, can never be fully realized, would seem to embrace both hybridity and open-endedness.

Again, however, borrowing and blending cannot fully avoid normative trouble spots. If liberalism declares equality and liberty for all inviolable, then the deliberative dialogue is not truly open-ended and free of foregone conclusions. Relatedly, if postmodernism insists that the values by which humans live are ultimately the result of political struggle, it cannot guarantee that liberty and equality for all will prevail.

There is furthermore an unmistakable normative affinity among liberal, communitarian, and (hospitable) postmodern endorsements of multiculturalism. All three prefer a thin conception of citizenship that does not demand that immigrants identify so strongly with the receiving country that they wind up fully relinquishing the affiliations and values with which they emigrated. Additionally, all three wish to see different cultural communities cohabitate in mutually beneficial relations. However, normatively speaking, liberal multiculturalism cannot tolerate communities that violate the liberty and equality of members—a criticism, as we shall see, that is often leveled against some Islamic organizations, particularly regarding their attitudes toward women. For its part, communitarianism, because of its central tenet of the presumption of equal worth, is normatively obligated to tolerate communities whose long-standing traditions and teachings prize other values (for example, obedience to God or to parents) over individual liberty. And not even the hospitable variety of postmodernism can guarantee a given cultural community that it will survive intact and not succumb to the corrosive forces of proliferating and intersecting worldviews.

We can also discern normative alliance among liberal assimilationism, nativism, and Hobbesian postmodernism. If one insists that immigrants should be required to assimilate to the national culture of the receiving society, but additionally maintains that the national culture is a liberal one, then liberal perfectionism and nativism obviously overlap. Indeed, we will frequently encounter just this argument in the case study chapters to follow. If one prefers a more preemptive, exclusionary, and aggressive strategy based on the claim that "our" liberal culture finds itself in an existential battle with "their" illiberal culture that can only be won in "our" favor by neutralizing and dominating "them," then the potential alliance between nativism and Hobbesian postmodernism comes into sharp relief. Indeed, this is the essential logic of the popular "clash of civilizations" thesis (Huntington 1996), which, as we shall see, has found considerable purchase in Europe. But it should be and will be noted that such aggression toward Muslims casts grave doubt on the liberal credentials of its supporters. Furthermore, relentless aggression toward Islam can prompt a backlash from (some) Muslims that can endanger the security of the receiving nation in the form of so-called "terrorism."

3

Citizenship

No single question is more likely to test the capacity of European nations to address the issue of multiple "belongings," exclusive or incompatible "loyalties," the growing uncertainty of boundaries between "insiders" and "outsiders" (or, rather, the increasing number of "citizens" who are neither simply inside nor simply outside), than the status and the importance of Islam within the European space.
—ETIENNE BALIBAR, *European Anti-discrimination and the Politics of Citizenship*

I t is hard to think of an issue that has shifted more decidedly from low to high politics than citizenship for immigrants. "No issue," writes Marc Howard (2006: 450) in his comparative survey, "has been more sensitive, explosive, or politically effective than immigration and citizenship." Benhabib (2004: 150) describes them as "time bombs . . . ready to explode at very short notice." While the issue figured prominently in European politics in the second quarter of the twentieth century through the creation of stateless peoples or what amounted to the denaturalization (including disenfranchisement, expropriation, sequestration, and elimination) of Jews and other "undesirables" in fascist regimes as well as mistreatment of "former fascists" by vengeful anti-fascist states following victory in World War II (Arendt 1966), during the third quarter the issue faded from center stage as most Europeans came to take for granted the idea that each person should be a citizen of one country in the traditional sense of possessing a single passport (the express goal actually of the 1930 Hague Convention that "every person should have a nationality and should have one nationality only" as well as the Council of Europe's 1963 Convention on the Reduction of Cases of Multiple Nationality). Because most economically burgeoning West European states recruited foreign workers to alleviate labor shortages in the 1950s and 1960s, there existed a growing number of migrants, but their naturalization—easier in some places and harder in others—garnered very little political attention.

This low profile for immigration began to alter in the 1970s when in response to persistent recession West European governments halted the recruitment of foreign laborers. The cessation spawned a profound unintended consequence. Fearing that by leaving they could never return to jobs more lucrative than ones available in their homelands, the migrants remained (some legally, some illegally). Moreover, with a long-term stay now anticipated, the mostly young men brought their families to their side (some legally, some illegally). These family unifications drastically expanded both the number and diversity of the migrant population in West Europe, creating permanent immigrant communities with the full range of demographic complexity and accompanying needs from infancy to old age. Already in 1971, the Swiss author Max Frisch (1983: 416) had characterized the extraordinary transformation with his terse observation that "we called for workers and human beings showed up."

With the steadily growing number and permanent settlement of immigrant families and entire transnational communities, the questions of how many of these alien residents to naturalize and under what conditions have gained since the 1980s ever greater political salience. Virtually every national government has revisited and revamped its immigration and naturalization laws—some toward greater exclusivity (such as France's Loi Pasqua-Méhaignerie of 1993 or Loi Besson/Guéant of 2011), others toward greater inclusivity (such as Germany's Nationality Law of 2000). In fact, most governments have moved in both directions, as will become clear below. Furthermore, significant change is also transpiring at the international, supranational, and subnational levels as well. Benhabib (2005: 676) discerns "epochal change" stemming from the "disaggregation of citizenship and the disaggregation of sovereignty." Indeed, it no longer makes sense to employ the concept of citizenship without a modifying adjective such as "ancillary" (Goodman 2014: 66), "plastic" (Konsta and Lazaridis 2010), "flexible" (Ong 1999), "incipient" (Isin and Nyers 2014: 9), "post-territorial" (Ragazzi 2014: 490), "multi-layered" (Yuval-Davis 1999: 120), or "multilevel" (Maas 2013b). The fact is that in all countries of Europe we now find many different, coexisting kinds or degrees of citizenship. This "graduated sovereignty" (Ong 1999: 21) ranges from plural citizenship (multiple passports) to conventional citizenship (single passport), to various permanent and temporary visas for resident aliens (that often entail considerable civil, social, and political rights of conventional citizenship), to accepted and pending refugees, to the undocumented (Ataç and Rosenberger 2013; Maas 2013b; Sainsbury 2012; Boswell and Geddes 2011, Joppke 2010; Bohman 2007; Schierup, Hansen, and Castles 2006).

The current chapter explores how normative discord contributes to the "deep policy contradictions" observable in European immigration and naturalization policies (Triandafyllidou 2010d: 2). From the liberal tradition come contentions that rampant immigration and other forces of unbuttoned globalization have ushered in a peerless postnational era in which international cosmopolitan norms should apply for all persons and in all nation-states (Carens 2013; Tonkiss 2013; Delanty 2009; Beck and Grande 2007; Benhabib 2004; Habermas 2003; Rubio-Marin 2000; Held 1995; Soysal 1994). Defenders of the nation-state retort that a national state governing a homogeneous nation remains the most influential, effectual, and ethical way of organizing citizens within a polity (Villiers 2006; Huntington 2004; Thaa 2001; Schnabel 1999; Schnapper 1998; Jacobson 1996; Miller 1995; Börkenförde 1995). The postmodern perspective discerns such thoroughgoing alterity and hybridity that living according to commonly observed norms, whether international, national, or local, becomes neither possible nor desirable (Isin and Nyers 2014; Cohen 2009; Ang 2001; Nancy 2000; Hall 1992; Kristeva 1991). As Will Kymlicka and Wayne Norman (2000: 41) conclude, no perspective has managed to gain normative supremacy when it comes to citizenship (see also Bertossi 2012: 262). Once we appreciate the high degree of fragmentation and mutual fragilization in this discordant normative atmosphere, the "bewildering complexity of rules and regulation" (Baubőck et al. 2006: 20), "contradictory trends" (Sainsbury 2012: 282), "paradoxical picture" (Hansen and Hager 2010: 11), and "messy and muddling practices" (Bertossi and Duyvendak 2012: 238) become less surprising, if not necessarily less unsettling.

Liberal Cosmopolitanism

Hope springs eternal that Europe will one day acknowledge and embrace itself as a continent of and for immigrants. To do so, European states must work to realize the cosmopolitan norm that all (long-term) residents should enjoy full rights of citizenship regardless of their race, ethnicity, nationality, language, culture, and religion. In the first place, European states are signatories to several international declarations, including the UN Universal Declaration of Human Rights (1948), the European Convention for the Protection of Human Rights (1950), the UN Convention on the Elimination of all Forms of Racial Discrimination (1965), the UN Declaration on the Elimination of all Forms of Intolerance and Discrimination Based on Religion and Belief (1981), the UN Convention on the Protection of the Rights of Migrant Workers (1990), and the UN Declaration of the Rights of Persons Belonging to Minorities (1992). All declare some version of the lofty liberal ideal that rights should be attached to personhood alone. Article 2 of the Universal Declaration of Human Rights stipulates:

> Everyone is entitled to all the rights and freedoms set forth in this Declaration, without distinction of any kind, such as race, colour, sex, language, religion, political or other opinion, national or social origin, property, birth or other status.

To the extent that European states honor such international norms, they establish what Hollifield (1992: 26–28) termed "embedded liberalism."

The European Union (EU) has pressed its burgeoning political clout into the service of cosmopolitanism. Since its founding in 1951 (as the European Coal and Steel Community), the EU has placed itself on a steady, if slow, course of realizing equal civil, political, and social rights for citizens of member states regardless of where they reside within the EU (Boswell and Geddes 2011: 177–78; Joppke 2010: 161–72; Maas 2007). As far as migrants from nonmember states, so-called "third-country nationals" (TCNs), were concerned, however, appeals to cosmopolitan openness remained largely symbolic until 1999 (Besson and Etzinger 2007: 574). Article 13 of the Amsterdam Treaty of that year bestowed on the EU the prerogative to pass binding legislation to counter discrimination. The Tampere European Council of 1999 swiftly demonstrated that it would not shy away from the enhanced power. The council proclaimed that "a more vigorous integration policy" should work toward securing for TCNs "rights and obligations comparable to those of EU citizens." In 2000, the council issued the Racial Equality Directive dedicated to "Implementing the Principle of Equal Treatment between Persons Irrespective of Racial or Ethnic Origin" (Council of the EU 2000a). Among other things, the directive mandated the establishment of an anti-discrimination agency in each member country, such as the United Kingdom's Commission for Equality and Human Rights (2004), France's Haute Authorité de Lutte contre la Discriminations et pour l'Egalité (2005, renamed Défenseur des Droits in 2011), or Germany's Antidiskriminierungsstelle des Bundes (2006). The directive was followed up in 2000 with the council's highly detailed six-year Community Action Programme to Combat Discrimination (Council of the EU 2000b). Realizing it had its hands full, the commission announced that successful implementation of the new initiative would "require strong political leadership to help shape public opinion" and to "avoid language which could incite racism or aggravate tensions between communities" (Commission of the European Communities 2000: 22). These efforts led to adoption of the Common Basic Principles for Immigration and Integration Policy in the European Union in the Hague Program of 2004. The principles, meant to guide immigration policy in all member states, include the following:

> Access for immigrants to institutions, as well as to public and private goods and services, on a basis equal to national citizens and in a nondiscriminatory way, is a critical foundation for better integration.
>
> The participation of immigrants in the democratic process and in the formulation of integration policies and measures, especially at

the local level, supports their integration. (Council of the EU, Justice and Home Affairs 2004: 19–24)

In 2011, the EU issued the Single Permit Directive, aiming to harmonize and simplify residency and work visas into one process that accords holders of the permits equal rights to EU nationals in work and education. The EU also established in 1997 the European Monitoring Centre for Racism and Xenophobia (in 2007 renamed the EU Agency for Fundamental Rights) and charged it with documenting and denouncing racism throughout the EU. Andrew Geddes (2000) rightly draws attention to a "thin Europeanisation" of rights for TCNs in that they are guaranteed at the EU level irrespective of whether or not the individual country in which they reside grants those rights in its domestic laws. Joppke (2011: 226) discerns decided movement toward "a kind of quasi-European citizenship for immigrants, without the need for acquiring a member state nationality first." What seems obvious is that "any consideration of state-level trends must first draw the EU framework that constrains, triggers or gives shape to state-level trends" (Joppke 2011: 225; see also Faist and Ette 2007).

Furthermore, nation-states face a constantly accumulating corpus of international jurisprudence generated by benches such as the European Court of Human Rights (ECHR) and the European Court of Justice (ECJ) that enforce these laws "beyond the state" (Slaughter 2004; see also Besson and Etzinger 2007). As far back as 1985, for instance, the ECHR ruled in *Abdulaziz, Cabales and Balkandali vs. UK* that Britain's practice of barring foreign husbands from joining their immigrant wives in the United Kingdom violated Articles 8 and 14 of the European Convention on Human Rights. In 2008 in the groundbreaking *Metock* case, the ECJ ruled that every EU citizen has the unconditional right to bring his or her spouse to any member country in the EU even if the spouse is not an EU citizen or even a legal resident of a member state. Such rulings and the cosmopolitan conventions and treaties that they interpret and enforce have been gradually establishing a "postnational" form of citizenship that "confers upon every person the right and duty of participation in the authority structures and public life of a polity, regardless of their historical or cultural ties to that community" (Soysal 1994: 3). States that violate this international regime of human rights increasingly find themselves as losing defendants hauled before international tribunals by nonstate individuals and organizations (Benhabib 2007: 33). In order to avoid the same fate, many other states have preemptively altered practices and amended statutes to bring them into conformity with international law (Boswell and Geddes 2011: 228). Though, for reasons detailed below, it seems an exaggeration to maintain that the nation-state "is in the process of becoming a territorial administrative unit of a supranational legal and political order based on human rights" (Jacobson 1996: 133), there can be no gainsaying the liberalizing impact of international law on citizenship in Europe (Sassen 1996).

Many European governments needed little or no nudging on behalf of cosmopolitanism. Well before the EU Race Directive of 2000, for instance, Sweden (1986), Belgium (1993), the Netherlands (1994), and Denmark (1994) each instituted anti-discrimination laws and/or commissions. Similarly, well before the Tampere Council of 1999, many European states made citizenship automatic or easy for nonnatives. As early as 1947, France conferred full French citizenship on Arab men from Algeria, a status those born before independence in 1962 retained thereafter. In the British Nationality Act of 1948, the United Kingdom guaranteed fully equal rights of citizenship to all members of the Commonwealth. Home Secretary James Ede defended the bill by saying it would "give the coloured races of the Empire the idea that . . . they are the equals of the people in this country" (quoted in Schain 2008: 164). The Netherlands emulated the British example in 1954 for the inhabitants of Surinam and the Dutch Antilles.

Furthermore, many governments granted aliens partial if not full rights of citizenship. For example, Sweden, the Netherlands, Belgium, Denmark, Norway, Finland, Ireland, Spain, Portugal, the United Kingdom, and the Swiss cantons of Neuchatel and Jura permit all or some TCNs to vote in at least local elections. Of course, all European Community (EC) citizens may (according to Article 17 of the Maastricht Treaty of 1992) cast ballots in local elections as well as elections for the European Parliament. Moreover, since Tampere the EU has urged member states to fully enfranchise both EC citizens and TCNs. Local voting rights for TCNs have been introduced in some cities in France, Austria, Italy, and Germany but have been either rescinded or ruled unconstitutional. As early as 1975, France's secretary of state for immigration, Paul Dijoud, enunciated his "government's dedication to assuring the equality of social rights between foreign and French workers" (quoted in Schain 2008: 51). Three years later the Conseil d'État issued a decision endorsing the position (Schain 2008: 110). Likewise, Italy's Turco-Napolitano Law of 1998 gave long-term resident aliens equal access to the Italian welfare state, though some aspects of the law were effectively repealed by the subsequent Bossi-Fini Law of 2002 (Schierup, Hansen, and Castles 2006: 189–91). Across Europe, legal (and in some cases illegal) aliens have gained broad if not fully equal access to the welfare state (Sainsbury 2012; Boswell and Geddes 2011: 173, 178; Ferrera 2005: 144; Ireland 2004; Bommes and Geddes 2000; Bauböck 1994; Hollifield 1992: 222–23). Indeed, the extent and speed with which immigrants have acquired social rights in Europe led Guiraudon (2000) incisively to contend that, as far as aliens are concerned, social rights tend to be granted before rather than after political rights, as was famously theorized in T. H. Marshall's *Citizenship and Social Class* of 1950. As far as civil liberties are concerned, most European constitutions can be and have been interpreted by courts to guarantee them to all persons rather than exclusively to citizens. To cite but one example, in 1973 when the German government still obstinately insisted that "Germany is not a land of immigration" (*kein Einwanderungsland*), the Federal Constitutional Court ruled that the "free development of one's personality" guaranteed in Article 2 of the Basic Law applied to both citizens and aliens (O'Brien 1996: 54). Freedom from extradition, needless to say, represents a gravely consequential exception to protected civil rights (Joppke 2010: 84), although even here the courts have often blocked deportations (for example in keeping with the *non-refoulement* clause in Article 33 of the 1951 UN Convention Relating to the Status of Refugees) or governments have proven unwilling or unable to deport (Hollifield 2014: 181; Hampshire 2013: 49–50; Rosenberger and Winkler 2013; Freedman 2011; Boswell and Geddes 2011: 171–72; Ellermann 2008). Generally speaking, courts have tended to defend immigrants' rights when legislative and executive branches have tried to curtail or transgress them (Hollifield 2014: 180–81; Kneip 2008; Joppke 2001; Guiraudon 1998). Aliens enjoy so many, if not all the rights of citizens that it is not outlandish to posit the seemingly contradictory notion of "alien citizenship" (Bosniak 2006). Call it "alien" or "postnational" citizenship or "citizenship light" (Joppke 2010: 145) or even "self-limited sovereignty" (Hampshire 2013: 47), Europe has taken significant strides in the direction of the universal hospitality and world citizenship envisaged by Kant in *Toward Perpetual Peace*.

Though traditionally associated with "classic lands of immigration" such as the United States, Canada, and Australia, the principle of *jus soli* (citizenship for all born in country) is hardly foreign to Europe. France enacted it into law in 1889. Britain formally codified jus soli in 1914 (Janoski 2010: 69–71). Denmark adopted jus soli in the 1983 Aliens Law but rescinded it in 2004 for children born of non-Nordic parents (Vink and de Groot 2010: 719). Belgium not only adopted jus soli in the Code of Belgian Nationality of 1984 but also considerably reduced naturalization requirements for those born outside Belgium in the so-called "quickly Belgian law" of 2000 (Foblets and Loones 2006: 71). In defending the latter the Belgian Justice Ministry contended "a foreigner wishing to acquire Belgian nationality is seen as a citizen of the world, with a positive attitude to a variety of cultures and ready to co-invest in the future of the multicultural society" (quoted in Foblets and Loones 2006: 78). Article 2 of Ireland's Constitution was amended in 1998 to read: "It is the entitlement and birthright of every person born in the island of Ireland . . . to be part of the Irish nation." Double jus soli (citizenship for those born in the country with at least one parent also born there) was adopted by the Netherlands in 1953 and by Spain in 1982. Although Germany did not adopt conditional jus soli (for children of aliens resident eight or more years) until 2000 under the government of Social Democratic chancellor Gerhard Schröder, Helmut Kohl's conservative regime had introduced a right of naturalization for second-generation immigrants born in Germany in the Aliens Law of 1990 and had significantly restricted *jus sanguinis* (citizenship based on ethnic ancestry) in 1992 for ethnic Germans from the former Soviet Union (O'Brien 1996: 89–95, 113). Schröder captured the general cosmopolitan spirit in 1998:

> For far too long those who have come to work here, who pay their taxes and abide by our laws have been told they are just "guests." But in truth they have for years been part of German society.... We will reach out a hand to those who live and work here and pay their taxes so they may be encouraged to participate fully in the life of our democracy. This is responding positively to the realities of Europe. (Quoted in Howard 2009: 133)

Indeed, a host of countries—Sweden (2001), Finland (2003), Portugal (2006), Luxembourg (2009), Czech Republic (2012)—have recently adopted some form of jus soli such as facilitated naturalization for aliens born in the settlement country or double jus soli (Vink and de Groot 2010: 718–19: Joppke 2010: 43–50; Howard 2009: 73–93). Italy's Prodi government introduced jus soli legislation in 2006 but could not push it through parliament before Berlusconi's coalition (including the xenophobic Lega Nord) replaced it, and in 2013 Greece's high court overturned the jus soli law of 2010. In sum, nineteen European governments (Honohan 2010: 9) have long ago or more recently moved their citizenship laws closer to the normative ideal that persons who spend all or most of their lives in a country ought to be citizens of that country regardless of their parents' nationality. Though it seems overstated to announce a "convergence toward more liberal citizenship laws and policies in Europe" (Joppke 2010: 50), "within the EU-15 as a whole, recent liberalization of citizenship policies is undeniable" (Howard 2009: 30; see also Koopmans, Michalowski, and Waibel 2012: 1233).

I would be remiss, of course, not to add that despite these trends toward greater equality, Muslim immigrants in particular tend to experience higher levels of exclusivist discrimination when applying for citizenship or visas (Hainmueller and Hangartner 2013; Weil 2004: 377–87; Hagedorn 2007). Furthermore, Muslims in the aggregate tend to register rates of unemployment, poverty, high-school dropout, incarceration, and other undesirable social indicators twice that of non-Muslim natives across Europe (Alba and Holdaway 2013; Sainsbury 2012: 113–34; Algan and Aleksynska

2012: 322–26; Dancygier 2010: 282–83; Open Society Institute 2010; Hellyer 2009: 154–55; Karich 2007; Heath, Rothon, and Kilpi 2007). To take one dramatic example of persistent underprivilege, 18 percent of all people in France, compared to 50 percent of North African and 36 percent of Turkish immigrants, reside in squalid HLM projects (*habitations à loyer modéré* or *cités*) of the kind that garnered so much attention in the notorious riots of 2005 and 2007 in Paris's *banlieues* (Bowen 2010: 19).

The struggle for full equality for Europe's immigrants will doubtless persist, for they have numerous political advocates. What Benhabib (2007: 33) calls an "interlocking network of local and global activists" working for nongovernmental organizations (NGOs), such as Amnesty International, Human Rights Watch, the European Network against Racism, France Plus, Proasyl (Germany), the German Institute for Human Rights, the Human Rights League in Belgium, the Catholic charity Caritas, the UK Forum against Islamophobia and Racism (FAIR), No One Is Illegal (U.K.), Sin-Papeles (Spain), Zivilcourage und Anti-Rassismus-Arbeit (ZARA) in Austria, tirelessly keeps highly focused pressure on governments to improve migrants' rights. Let us take as typical of such political strivings the 2010 report of the Open Society Institute, with offices in London, Budapest, and New York. After laying out its empirical findings of widespread discrimination against Muslims, *Muslims in Europe: A Report on 11 EU Cities* recommends the ethnic and religious integration of boroughs; the elimination of housing discrimination against Muslims; the enhanced integration of Muslim and ethnic organizations in schools, workplaces, and other public associations; the development of municipal campaigns that "promote a common and integrative identity of the city in order effectively to strengthen unity and solidarity"; the liberalization of naturalization requirements for TCNs; the allowance of dual citizenship; and the right to vote for resident aliens at all levels, not just municipal (Open Society Institute 2010). Through repeated web posts, pamphlets, demonstrations, editorials, and sponsored events they channel into the public arena a steady stream of cosmopolitan slogans (what I call "philosophical fragments"), such as "same ground, same right, same voice" (from Mouvement contre le racism et l'amitie des peoples) or "fairness and equality for all" (from the U.K.'s Antiracist Alliance). Even the Fédération Internationale de Football Association sponsors its annual FIFA Day against Discrimination, which features prominent soccer stars condemning ethnic and racial prejudice. Moreover, soccer fans around the world could read the slogan "Say No to Racism" during World Cup 2014 games in Brazil.

It is the undeniably far-reaching normative sway of such liberal universalism that in part moves governments at various levels regularly to issue conspicuous public service announcements propagating cosmopolitanism

(Berg and Sigona 2013: 352). To cite but three examples, the German government's Du bist Deutschland (You are Germany), Oslo's OXLO (Oslo Extra Large), or media blitzes like London's campaign to win the Summer Olympics deliberately spotlighted persons of easily recognizable ethnic, racial, and religious difference from the majority culture to celebrate multiculturalism as a plus for the city and country. In 1998, Jacques Chirac awarded the multicultural (so-called *Black-Blanc-Beur*) French World Cup champion team (with its Algerian French captain Zinedine Zidane) the Legion d'honneur. Tony Blair captured the essence of the Europe-wide movement to eliminate discrimination with his much quoted phrase "racists are the only minority" (quoted in Koopmans et al. 2005: 243). With equally effective pith, Angela Merkel, while defending her government's policy of hosting increasing numbers of refugees in 2015, retorted: "If we had not shown a friendly face, that's not my country" (*Guardian* 15 September 2015).

Many scholars interpret the increasing legalization or toleration of dual citizenship as an important dimension of the broader liberalization of citizenship laws (Joppke 2010: 47–49; Howard 2009: 24–26). A large and expanding number of European states, including the United Kingdom, France, Belgium, Ireland, Sweden, Finland, Luxembourg, Greece, Bulgaria, Germany, Denmark, and Hungary, have legalized dual citizenship for immigrants. In its European Convention on Nationality of 1997, the Council of Europe ended its strict prohibition (from 1963) of dual nationality. Furthermore, states that have resisted formal legalization of dual nationality, such as Spain, the Netherlands, and Austria, increasingly tolerate it (Sainsbury 2012: 109; Vink and de Groot 2010: 721–25; Faist 2009: 184–85; Kezjar 2009: 137–38; Hansen 2003: 95; Joppke and Morawska 2003: 18–19; Freeman and Ögelman 1998: 777). For example, four-fifths of the naturalizations in the Netherlands make exceptions for dual nationality on grounds (in accordance with Article 16 of the European Nationality Convention) that renunciation of the original nationality would produce undue hardship for the applicant (*MiGAZIN* 25 April 2012; Faist and Ette 2007: 927; see also Dumbrava 2014: 37; Joppke 2010: 47–50). In that both de jure and de facto acceptance of dual nationality make easier the naturalization of immigrants, the practices serve the cosmopolitan ideal of facilitating the acquisition of full rights of citizenship wherever one resides.

Communitarianism

But dual nationality also serves the normative ideal of nationalism, particularly its communitarian variant. Dual nationality can be interpreted as Herderian egalitarian nationalism adapted to fit the age of migration.

The German philosopher theorized a people (*Volk* or *Kulturnation*) whose cultural homogeneity justified its acquisition of a sovereign state. In the age of migration, the integrity of nations that possess nation-states is threatened by the myriad push and pull factors that motivate or compel many members of the nation to reside outside the territorial boundaries of their nation's state. Dual nationality facilitates the maintenance of a variety of integral ties to the nation (as well as nation-state) even though millions of its members have been dispersed into distant diasporas. It aids the nation in transnationally cohering as a *Kulturnation* across borders by promoting the notion that one can "take the migrant out of his homeland but not the homeland out of the migrant." In Herderian language, dual nationality helps to defend the "soul" of a people against the fissiparous forces of a relentlessly globalizing world.

In this light, it should come as no surprise that origin states turn out to be among the most assiduous proponents of dual nationality and other communitarian privileges for "their" emigrants. In the first place, there is a long tradition stretching back to colonial times of European powers insisting on the creation and preservation of ethnic enclaves replete with separate churches, schools, hospitals, neighborhoods, and so on for their expatriates. Most of these enclaves survived colonialism and continue to thrive in some form for expatriate communities around the world. Indeed, in what Joppke (2010: 63) terms "re-ethnicizing citizenship," increasing numbers of European states—twenty, including seven of the EU-15 and all of the later succession states in Eastern Europe (Boswell and Geddes 2011: 197)—offer automatic or privileged access to citizenship for their emigrants and their progeny (jus sanguinis).

But our focus is Muslim migrants. Their homeland states have lobbied long and hard for dual nationality as well as other communitarian rights. Governments like Algeria, Morocco, Tunisia, Turkey, Pakistan, and Bangladesh exert formidable diplomatic pressure to facilitate all manner of links—familial, recreational, burial, commercial, financial, political, and cultural—between their respective countries and their emigrant diasporas in Europe. In visits to Germany in 2008 and 2010, for instance, Turkish prime minister Recep Tayyip Erdoğan came under sharp criticism, including from his German counterpart, for allegedly undermining the goal of integration when he urged Turkish emigrants to preserve their Turkish identity by founding and sending their children to Turkish schools. In a very public example of what I theorize as "fragilization" (acknowledging the partial validity of one's opponent's view), Merkel was moved to soften her criticism when Erdoğan stole her thunder with a remonstrating communitarian fragment: "If we have German high schools in Turkey why shouldn't there be Turkish high schools in Germany?" (quoted in *Migration und Bevölkerung* April 2010). In another fine example of fragilization, Morocco's minister for the Moroccan diaspora in France sought to juggle the ideals of liberal integration and nationalist communitarianism: "Integration is an objective, but it must not constitute a rupture with the mother country" (quoted in Laurence 2012: 219).

Sending-country governments have many compelling reasons for preventing rupture, not all of which are normative. Remittances, valued in the billions of dollars annually, typically constitute the second or third largest single contributor to GDP in sending countries, amounting to 2–3 percent of GDP in Algeria and Turkey and 8–10 percent in Morocco (Laurence 2012: 33; Ahmed 2012; Sassen 2003; Freeman and Ögelman 1998). Furthermore, for the economies of these countries their emigrants in Europe, often numbering in the millions, represent sizable, lucrative markets for products peculiar to and produced in the sending countries (travel packages, entertainment and news in the native language, specialty foods, Islamic services and accessories, etc.). Arabic, for instance, is the second most transmitted language in the world after English (Allievi and Nielsen 2003; Faist 2000). Officials believe, rightly or wrongly, that this steady economic fillip from Europe contributes to regime durability (Ahmed 2012). Relatedly, sending governments endeavor to monitor and mold the political opinions and activities of their expatriates. Ruling and opposition parties endeavor to sway the votes (and donations) of the many absentee voters that can in tight elections make *the* difference. For instance, it seems unlikely that Turkey's Welfare (Refah) Party, the predecessor to the currently ruling Justice and Development (Adelet ve Kalkınma) Party, would have risen to electoral victory in 1995 without the votes and funds raised in Germany by its leader, Necmettin Erbakan, himself an erstwhile migrant to Germany (Kaya 2012: 53). Dual citizenship keeps this critical political support accessible even when émigrés naturalize in receiving countries.

It is important to underscore, however, that, despite their rhetoric and measures promoting integration, the governments of destination countries have for decades encouraged communitarian separatism. Moreover, this holds true for all major destination lands in Europe, not exclusively for those with official policies of "multiculturalism" such as Sweden, Belgium, the Netherlands, and the United Kingdom. Policies promoting physical and cultural separatism were common in receiving countries from the start of postwar immigration in the 1950s and 1960s. Most recruiting countries officially declared that the laborers were temporary workers summoned to fill labor shortages, who would "rotate" back to their homelands within a few years. The foreign workers were typically employed in national or ethnic teams at the workplace, boarded in segregated housing units, and generally encouraged to remain among themselves. After all, they were supposed to return home (Fredette 2014: 128–30; Duyvendek and Scholten 2012: 272; Abadan-Unat 2011: 9–13; Castles and Miller 2009: 97–103; Schain 2008: 46–48, 128–33; Ceylan 2006: 246–48; O'Brien 1996: 44–46; Castles and Kosack 1973).

When their families started arriving in the 1970s, the segregation tended to persist in the form of ethnic neighborhoods (ghettos). Various officials in the destination countries who had to deal with migrants—social workers, healthcare providers, educators, police—faced the dilemma of how to serve clients whose language and cultural ways they did not know (well). The officials typically turned to the embassies of the sending countries that, for reasons suggested above, eagerly provided materials, programs, and personnel. Eventually, governments at various levels, particularly municipal ones facing dense concentrations of migrants, also commissioned and funded ethnic and religious organizations independent of the embassies to provide mother-tongue classes, non-Christian and non-Jewish religious services, and other ethnically specific programs and activities. Whether through embassies or NGOs, the point to stress is that European governments have played a significant role in encouraging transnational connections and identities among separate immigrant communities (O'Brien 2013a: 75–77; Laurence 2012: 30–104; Kaya 2012: 40–44, 63–67, 103–4, 120–29; Schain 2010: 140–41; Gest 2010: 87–92; Mohr 2006: 268; Fadil 2006: 57).

In 1977, the European Community issued a directive that member states should offer to migrant pupils mother-tongue classes sponsored by sending governments (Laurence 2012: 39). Already in 1969, a report commissioned for the Economic and Social Council in France had recommended "repatriation" for "inassimilable islands" of migrants (quoted in Schain 2008: 92). The French adopted a two-pronged policy of "adaptation [to France] or return" and negotiated agreements with Maghrebi embassies to administer the second prong to the *étrangers,* as migrants were labeled (Laurence 2012: 39). In 1981, the Mitterand government abolished a wartime law that prohibited equal funding for French and non-French associations. Francs from the Social Action Funds (Fonds d'Action Sociale) were channeled to ethnically distinct cultural and religious organizations whose number proliferated to 4,000 by the end of the decade (Withol de Wenden 1992; see also Schain 2008: 107–9; Guiraudon 2006: 137–40). As Jocelyn Cesari (1994: 250–51) observed, this communitarian pattern of funding that targeted ethnically specific associations actually discouraged efforts to organize interethnic and interreligious associations and programs. The 2005 Loi Sarkozy also encouraged return migration (Castles and Miller 2009: 257). Until the Minorities Law of 1983, the Dutch stressed reintegration alone, but thereafter adopted a "dual policy" (*tweesporenbeleid*) that sought to "simultaneously create opportunities for a successful reintegration of immigrants who decided to return, and to equip those who decided to stay with a strong and positive sense of identity" (Maussen 2009: 127; see also Kaya 2012: 129–33; Vink 2007: 340, 345). Likewise in Germany, where immigrants were tellingly referred to as "guestworkers" (*Gastarbeiter*), the federal government published its first report calling for integration in 1972 and appointed a commissioner for integration in 1978 (O'Brien 1996: 53–57). But these liberal measures added to rather than replaced preexisting communitarian policies such as the "Bavarian Model" of segregating pupils according to ethnicity into mother-tongue classes (Joppke 1996: 469; Radtke 1997). "Reintegration" became the officially recognized goal of the federal government (again alongside rather than in place of integration) in 1983 with passage of the Law to Promote the Willingness of Foreigners to Return Home, which earmarked millions of marks to subsidize programs helping foreigners maintain their homeland culture in Germany (O'Brien 1996: 81, 99–101). The British adapted their customary policy of "indirect rule" in the empire to deal with the immigrants streaming into the British Isles from the former colonies. Prominent elders were identified for distinct ethnic groups and then given the discretion and resources to care for their co-ethnics in exchange for promoting their docility (Bowen 2012b: 159; Gest 2010: 87–92; Rex 1996: 58; Joppke 1996: 480).

Whether official or "de facto multiculturalism" (Joppke and Morawska 2003: 19), communitarian policies have persisted. Indeed, its welcoming, cosmopolitan rhetoric notwithstanding, the European Commission (2000: 8, 10) has breathed new life into the communitarian dimension of dual nationality by calling for a "reintegration framework" "to assist returning migrants to re-settle in their countries of origin." Lest we consign them to some bygone era before Europe "woke up" to the permanent nature of postwar immigration, research at Queens University ("Multiculturalism Policy Index" 2012) found that multiculturalist policies increased not only from 1980 to 2000 but also from 2000 to 2010 across Europe and "more than offset" the high-profile rescinding of such policies in places such as the Netherlands since 9/11. Indeed, numerous studies spanning several decades and countries have repeatedly demonstrated (and typically derided) the separatist and segregationist impact of government-sponsored policies of multiculturalism (Ranstorp and Dos Santos 2009; Ateş 2008; Sniderman and Hagendoorn 2007; Rogstad 2007; Koopmans et al. 2005; Bundesamt für Verfassungsschutz 2005; Brenner 2002; Cantle Report 2001; Spinner-Halev 1999; Haut Conseil à l'Intégration 1997; 1995; Wetenschappelijke Raad 1989; also see Wright and Bloemraad 2012 for counter-argument). The complex or messy truth is that in most European countries multicultural policies coexist intertangled with exclusionary and assimilative policies (Banting and Kymlicka 2013).

Postmodern Citizenship

From the postmodern perspective, dual nationality represents but one of multiple alternatives to single citizenship. The same holds for the binary distinction between citizen and noncitizen stressed by both liberalism and nationalism. The latter seeks to preserve the distinction in ways that privilege citizens. Liberalism ultimately aims to abolish noncitizenship by making all persons citizens of the world in some fundamentally equal sense. Postmodernism, by contrast, reads citizenship as a constructed legal and political status that is protean, plural, and contested (Maas 2013a; Sassen 2002).

De Jure and De Facto Citizenship

Once one begins to analyze citizenship as numerous legal political statuses that confer rights and entitlements on some and deny them to others, the many differing degrees of what amounts to one's de facto citizenship in Europe become readily apparent. As intimated in the introductory section, the variety and gradation of statuses are vast and appear to be expanding rather than contracting. We can distinguish four categories, noting considerable variety within each: (1) conventional citizen, (2) legal resident alien, (3) "illegal" resident, and (4) denied or deported nonresident.

Conventional citizens are citizens in the sense of possessing a passport. We must immediately add the qualification, however, that many citizens have multiple passports. Possession of multiple passports typically brings with it considerable advantages (for example, in entering or residing in the countries that issued the passports) but can in countries that forbid multiple citizenship force the abandonment of all but one passport (Heisler 1998: 577–78). However, not all citizens are equal. For example, when seeking to live together as a family unit, citizens with family members who are nonnationals often face greater obstacles (for instance, maximum age requirements for children or proof of authentic marriage for spouses) and obligations (such as assuming financial responsibility for dependents denied access to the welfare state) (Ruffer 2011; Howard 2009: 152). Some stigmatized groups, especially Muslims, even after naturalizing suffer informal discrimination in many walks of life to such an extent that they experience citizenship differently from unstigmatized "co-citizens" (Chebel d'Apollonnia 2015: 43–44; Midtbøen 2014; Fredette 2014: 42–46; Bertossi 2014; Organisation for Economic Cooperation and Development 2013: 191–230; Cesari 2013: 80–138; Antidiskriminierungsstelle des Bundes 2013; Amnesty International 2012; Ansari and Hafez 2012; Zick, Küpper, and Hövermann 2011; Open Society Institute 2010; 2002; European Union Agency for Fundamental Rights 2009;

Peucker 2010; European Union Monitoring Centre 2006; Runnymede Trust 1997; see also Islamophobia Watch at www.islamophobia-watch.com). There also exists an undeniable hierarchy of passports, at least as far as Europe is concerned. Those holding passports from other EU countries may enter, reside, and work anywhere in the EU without a visa. Passports from favored countries such as the United States, Canada, Australia, and Japan generally entitle holders to visa-free entry into Europe but only as a tourist for a short period (typically ninety days). Holders of passports from most other (less affluent) countries require a visa to enter Europe. Moreover, long-term work and residence visas are typically much harder to come by for persons from these nations than for those from the favored countries (Hampshire 2013: 66; Castles 2012: 69–70).

The mention of visas brings us to the category of legal resident alien, which is enormously complex and ranges from the highly privileged to the highly precarious. We have already noted the privileged status of resident aliens from EU member states. Persons possessing certain high skills deemed in great demand (in, say, information technology or engineering) or plentiful funds for investment typically receive expedited visa processing through various "blue" (EU since 2009) or "green" card schemes (Germany since 2000) or "investor visas" (in Austria, the United Kingdom, Switzerland, and Germany) designed to attract the best, brightest, and richest (Dzankic 2012). Though they may have waited long and paid much to acquire permanent visas, those who hold them typically have very secure statuses that can be revoked only as a result of being convicted of a crime. They can, however, have less equal access to the welfare state than citizens enjoy and in most places have neither full voting rights nor freedom from extradition (Sainsbury 2012: 113–31; Joppke 2010: 89–91). Furthermore, some visas permit gainful employment while others forbid it (Sainsbury 2012: 281; Sigona 2012; Wilpert and Laacher 1999: 53). Temporary visas can range from several years (for instance, in the process of applying for the permanent visa) or several weeks (in the case of seasonal workers). Temporary visas too can come with severe restrictions. Spouses allowed entry are often denied work permits either permanently or temporarily during a period of probation (Afonso 2013: 30–32; Staver 2013: 61–79; Ruffer 2011). Student visas usually prohibit working in paid jobs and expire upon completion or termination of study (frequently with a brief grace period). Seasonal and other short-term workers' visas are often limited to a specific branch of industry (for example, health services, tourism, agriculture) and sometimes even to a specific employer (for instance, with au pairs). Refugees typically not only have restricted access to social welfare but are usually forbidden to work or else permitted to seek employment only in narrowly stipulated types of work. Furthermore, refugees are often compelled to reside in specified areas and thus do not enjoy freedom of movement (Sainsbury 2012: 281; Sigona 2012). Asylum seekers inhabit a veritable no-man's land between legality and illegality. They are neither fully legal nor fully illegal pending a definitive ruling on their application. While waiting (often for years) they are typically denied the right to work and to move freely (Hampshire 2013: 69–76; Craig 2013; Sigona 2012; Hatton 2009).

The category of "illegal" alien might seem unambiguous at first thought. In fact, it too is varied and complex (Cross 2012; Triandafyllidou 2010e; Schierup, Hansen, and Castles 2006). Accurate accounts of undocumented migrants in Europe, needless to say, elude us. The European Commission (2008: 6) estimates eight million. Anna Triandafyllidou and Dita Vogel (2010: 298) estimate four million. Others claim one in ten migrants resides illegally (Bloemraad et al. 2008: 166). Despite the sensational media's spotlight on undocumented migrants who cross the border clandestinely with or without the help of traffickers, this stereotypical illegal alien represents a small proportion of total "irregular" migration. According to Franck Düvell (2011), 80 percent of irregular migrants enter with a valid visa of some sort and only later become illegal by remaining beyond the expiration date (see also Sigona and Hughes 2012: viii; Triandafyllidou 2010d: 4–5; Engbersen 2001: 222). As Bridget Anderson (2013: 124) perceptively stresses, large numbers of illegals are actually semi-illegal because they are in semi-compliance rather than full noncompliance with the law (most commonly by residing legally but working illegally). Their statuses can and do change frequently. Consider that in 2011 the countless East Europeans of the so-called EU-8 (states that acceded in 2004) who were residing or working illegally in the EU-15 states became legal overnight. The frequent declarations of amnesty, especially common in southern Europe in Spain (1985, 1986, 1991, 1996, and 2005), Italy (1986, 1990, 1995, 1998, and 2002), Greece (1998, 2001, 2005, and 2011), and Portugal (2001, 2004, and 2005) have not only legalized "illegals" (typically only temporarily) but also unofficially encouraged irregular migrants to come or stay in the hope of one day being regularized (Gest 2010: 135; Fasani 2010; Triandafyllidou 2010c: 203–5; Castles and Miller 2009: 113). France permits *sans papiers* to acquire legal papers after ten years of demonstrated residence (Schain 2008: 70). Needless to say, there exists a critical difference both in quantity and consequence between undocumented residents in the custody of the state and those at large. However, not all apprehended "illegal" aliens are deported. Many remain for long periods in detention centers, while others who are notified of an impending deportation abscond before it is carried out (Anderson 2013: 131–35; Boswell and Geddes 2011: 171–72).

The overwhelming number of undocumented migrants comprise those who never set foot in Europe (Cross 2012). European governments devote considerable resources and energy to denying would-be migrants entry to "Fortress Europe." For example, many governments, including the Netherlands (2006), Germany (2007), France (2007), Britain (2010), Denmark (2010), and Austria (2011), have not only increased the level of language proficiency required for family reunification but have transplanted the site of taking the language classes and exams from the receiving country to sending countries (Goodman 2014: 205). Those who fail to meet the requirements are never allowed to reach the destination country, thus avoiding altogether the often unpleasant and expensive deportations. Following the example of the United Kingdom and Germany in 1987, most European states exact steep fines on private passenger carriers (for instance, airlines or cruise ships) that bring inadequately documented persons onto their national territory (Hampshire 2013: 67). The EU annually budgets over €100 million for Frontex "to reduce the number of irregular migrants entering the EU undetected" (http://frontex.europa.eu/about-frontex/mission-and-tasks/). Frontex, of course, coordinates but does not replace the member states' own extensive border-control actions, agencies, and agents. Migrants who make it to Europe "illegally" come under the Schengen Convention. Originally signed in 1985 in Schengen, Luxembourg, by five countries (Belgium, France, the Netherlands, West Germany, and Luxembourg), the convention now has twenty-six mostly contiguous signatory countries (excluding Ireland and the United Kingdom) and stipulates that travelers denied entry into the territory of any signatory country are thereby automatically denied entry into the other twenty-five territories (the so-called "Schengen area," spanning 4.3 million square kilometers). All too frequent tragedies, such as the shipwrecks in 2013 and 2015 between the coast of North Africa and the Italian island of Lampedusa that cost hundreds of lives, or the abandoned lorry found full of corpses outside Vienna in 2015, dreadfully remind us of the thousands of migrants who perish or suffer severe injury endeavoring to reach Europe. Of course, this is not to mention the unfathomable number of human beings who have effectively lost what Ayelet Shachar (2009) calls the "birthright lottery" by being born in countries of the impoverished global South and who wish to migrate to Europe but do not because they deem the obstacles insurmountable.

The multidimensional and polymorphous quality of de facto citizenship reveals fragilization toward and fragmentation from postmodernism. Citizenship is increasingly viewed instrumentally by migrants, citizens, and officials alike. Instrumentalization, furthermore, reflects relaxed commitment to the normative goals of solidarity, either inclusively with all humans (liberalism) or exclusively with native nationals (nationalism). Less insistence on realizing normative ideals facilitates expanding acceptance of nonuniform and inconsistent citizenship policies that result from the vagaries of political contestation rather than from an unambiguous ethical doctrine (Isin and Nyers 2014: 8).

Instrumental Citizenship

Many analysts observe the instrumentalization of citizenship (Vink and de Groot 2010: 714; Joppke 2010: 157–61; Gest 2010: 175). This can mean individuals who apply for, acquire, and utilize their citizenship status(es) as a way of addressing largely pragmatic challenges of securing genial living conditions. They might neither seek nor feel a "thick" identification with or deep loyalty to the nation-state of which they are citizens. At this juncture, however, and employing the less conventional understanding of plural de facto citizenship developed above, I want to underscore instrumentalism on the part of the state. Here I have in mind the tendency on the part of officials publicly and unashamedly to describe migration and migrants as mere means for enhancing the domestic economy. George Menz (2009: 29–30) writes of the "European competition state, which perceives of migration . . . as a valuable opportunity to avail oneself of attractive human resources with desirable skill portfolios." Austria actually sells citizenship for $300,000 to anyone who invests more than $2.5 million in its economy. Since 2013, Germany's Ministry of Labor and Social Affairs maintains Jobmonitor, which systematically identifies sectors sorely in need of foreign workers (Organisation for Economic Cooperation and Development 2013: 45). Justifying in 2005 his government's "green card" program (since 2000) for certain highly skilled migrants, Schröder crassly opined "there are people we need and there are people who need us," the implication being that Germany should attract the former and repel the latter (quoted in O'Brien 2013b: 143). A year later, Sarkozy contrasted preferred *immigration choisie* with unwanted *immigration subie* (a proposal actually first put forth by Socialists in 1998). The French introduced the Carte de Competences et Talents for skilled foreign workers in 2006. In that same year, the Swiss enabled expedited visas for skilled TCNs. Britain has had a Highly Skilled Migrant Programme since 2002 (Corvalho 2013). It uses a "point-based system" (PBS) introduced by the Labour government to rank migrants' skills so as to sift out those Britain wants (officially) from those it does not want (Anderson 2013: 59). The Netherlands, Denmark, and Austria subsequently introduced PBS (Hampshire 2013: 61), though Denmark abolished its program in 2012 after ten months in force (Goodman 2014: 113). In 2011, David Cameron explained that Britain seeks "good immigration, not mass immigration" (*New Statesman* 14 April 2011), while his Home Office (2011: 12) officially strives to "allow . . .

only the brightest and the best to stay permanently." In 2008, EU Commission president José Manuel Barosso announced that "with the [newly introduced] European blue card, we send a clear signal. Highly skilled workers are welcome in the EU" (quoted in Rudolph 2010: 51). The EU's Stockholm Programme of 2009, which set the EU's migration agenda until 2014, called for "a flexible admission system . . . to adapt to increased mobility and the needs of national labour markets" (quoted in Boswell and Geddes 2011: 76).

Readers should keep in mind that West European governments initiated postwar immigration in the 1950s and 1960s primarily in an effort to fill labor shortages, at that time mostly in unskilled jobs (Castles and Kosack 1973). Moreover, Anthony Messina (2007) demonstrates that, all the clamor regarding unchecked immigration notwithstanding, European nation-states have continued into the twenty-first century their adept control of migration to serve perceived economic interests. This includes turning a blind eye to much illegal immigration that supplies the labor market with cheap workers desired by many industries (Anderson 2013; van den Anke and van Liempt 2012; Boswell and Geddes 2011: 135–36; Schierup, Hansen, and Castles 2006; Verstraete 2003; Engbersen 2001).

On initial consideration, instrumental use and abuse of alien workers would seem to accord with nationalism's favoritism for nationals. However, this is only partially true, for migrants (legal and illegal) can undermine nationals' interests. Programs designed to recruit highly skilled aliens channel them into typically well-paid, desirable jobs. The European Centre for the Development of Vocational Training estimates a need for sixteen million highly skilled workers by 2020 (http://www.cedefop.europa.eu/en/news-and-press/newsletters/cedefop-newsletter-no-14-julyaugust-2011?view=full). It is true that such positions may not be filled by TCNs if EU citizens are available. However, businesses that are keen to swiftly fill indispensable positions rarely look very far or long for nationals or EU members (Hampshire 2013: 41–44; Anderson 2013: 71). More importantly, recruitment of foreigners alleviates pressure on governments to commit the resources needed to attract nationals to and train them in the highly skilled professions where shortages abound. Similarly, both regular and especially irregular migrants often take low-paying, undesirable, so-called 3-D (dirty, difficult, dangerous) or 3-C (cooking, caring, cleaning) jobs that nationals tend to spurn. Moreover, the steady supply of cheap labor eases pressure on employers and regulators to improve the wages and conditions of such positions to levels that would attract nationals (Castles and Miller 2009: 222). Meanwhile, large numbers of nationals remain indefinitely unemployed across Europe. To quote ultranationalist Jean Marie Le Pen, "We have six million migrants in France, and six million unemployed" (quoted in Koopmans et al. 2005: 213).

Instrumentalism can contravene liberalism's ethical ideal of equal treatment for all. Undocumented aliens in particular are vulnerable to exploitation by employers, landlords, and even family members who threaten to expose the migrants' illegality if they protest iniquitous conditions (Mantouvalou 2014: 52–58; Anderson 2013: 159–76; Sainsbury 2012: 13–31; Schierup, Hansen, and Castles 2006: 209–10; Calavita 2005; Andall 2003; Anderson 2000; Rubery, Smith, and Fagan 1999). For fear of exposure and deportation, many irregulars forego welfare assistance to which they or their dependents are entitled (Sainsbury 2012; Triandafyllidou 2010e). Needless to say, governments denounce both "illegal" migration and the exploitation of "illegals" and announce high-profile campaigns to eliminate both repugnant phenomena (Afonso 2013: 32; Boswell and Geddes 2011: 135–36; Triandafyllidou 2010d: 11). Thus, François Hollande, while campaigning for president in 2012, pledged: "I shall lead a merciless struggle against illegal immigration and the clandestine work networks" (quoted in Daguzan 2013: 107). But both phenomena persist across Europe. Moreover, they not only persist but also flourish to such an extent that they cannot be explained as rare exceptions to an otherwise uniform and prevailing regularity (Boswell and Geddes 2011: 131–32; Koser 2008; Schierup, Hansen, and Castles 2006: 30; Düvell 2006). "The danger with tough enforcement is that it can never be tough enough. The tougher the enforcement, the bigger the 'problem' it uncovers" (Anderson 2013: 136).

Indeed, we can discern the regularization of irregularity, or what Agamben (1998: 7) calls "inclusive exclusion." I have in mind official and unofficial government actions that encourage or enable the normalization of irregular migration, contributing to its emergence or persistence as an integral as opposed to aberrational feature of receiving societies. In the first place, the state creates the category of illegal alien. We most often think of the state as conferring citizenship. But it also confers illegality. Illegal migrants would neither exist without the state's laws that illegalize them nor be as readily exploitable without the state's threat to deport them (Hampshire 2013: 63–64; Anderson 2013: 86–90; Khosravi 2012: 62; Vivar 2012: 116; Karakayali 2008; Bauder 2006). Moreover, Europe's economies depend on a constant pipeline of undocumented workers that the state not only creates but tolerates. Neoliberal trends have been transforming European societies into "post-Fordist" economies that function with an increasing number of precarious ("flexible") forms of employment (especially in the expanding service industries) that provide neither living wages nor benefits for jobholders (Munck, Schierup, and Wise 2012; Schierup, Hansen, and Castles 2006; Sassen 1998; Wacquant 1996; Harvey 1989). Concurrently with the emergence of the dual labor market, "post-social" welfare states trim entitlements and increasingly foist the responsibility for one's socioeconomic security onto the individual (Rosanvallon 2013: 209–54; Sainsbury 2012: 113–31; Castles 2012; O'Malley 1996; Rose 1996). Both trends combine to spawn a growing minority underclass—a "precariat" (Munck, Schierup, and Wise 2012: 9) or "shadow side" (Castles and Miller 2009: 310)—that is forced permanently to endure "new social risks" or, in other words, living and working conditions systematically and significantly inferior to those of the middle-class majority (Bauman 2011; Esping-Anderson et al. 2002; Balibar and Wallerstein 1991). Migrants, legal and illegal, so disproportionately fill the ranks of this underclass of "the new poverty in the European Community" (Room, Lawson, and Laczko 1989) that some authors speak of "an incipient ethno-racial stratification" (Schierup, Hansen, and Castles 2006: 81) or even a "European apartheid" (Balibar 2004: 121). Just as lawmakers know perfectly well from demographers (Organisation for Economic Cooperation and Development 2013; 2011; Eurostat 2008; United Nations 2000) that Europe depends on immigrants to replace its aging and dwindling population with its low birthrate, they know equally well from political economists and sociologists that their economies, if they are to remain globally competitive, depend on an underclass of modern day "helots" (Cohen 2006: 152) comprising migrants with varying degrees of (il)legal status.

It is a well-established fact that southern European economies function through systematic reliance on large numbers of illegal and semi-legal migrants to fill informal but critical niches in secondary labor markets such as construction, domestic service, hotels, restaurants, agriculture, and retail trade. Because the workers are typically paid in cash and have no written contracts, employers can intimidate them into accepting salaries and conditions below legal minimums. These practices are so extensive in southern Europe that analysts argue that illegal laborers should be understood as a cause rather than effect of large-scale migration. The frequent amnesties attest to the integral and regular nature of this labor force, for they not only legalize (often only temporarily) undocumented workers, but, as already mentioned, attract additional undocumented migrants (Maroukis 2010; Fasani 2010; Gonzalez-Enriquez 2010; Sciortini 2004; Reyneri 2003; King 2000; Anthias and Lazaridis 1999; Baldwin-Edwards and Arango 1999). In 2009, Italy's public service and innovation minister Renato Brunetta candidly admitted that the underground economy "plays an important role, especially during an economic crisis" (quoted in Fasani 2010: 183).

In what might be termed a process of the "southernization" of the North, illegal and semi-legal work is expanding in northern Europe (Anderson 2013: 159–76; Sigona and Hughes 2012; Withol de Wenden 2010; Cyrus and Kovacheva 2010; Castles and Miller 2009: 238; Schierup, Hansen, and Castles, 2006: 23; Düvell 2006; Anderson 2000; Rubery, Smith, and Fagan 1999). Lest one think, however, that illegal migration is a completely new phenomenon in northern Europe, consider that as early as 1966 the French Minister of Affairs, Jean Marie Jeanney, remarked that "illegal immigration has its uses. [Without it] we would perhaps be short of labour (quoted in Geddes 2003: 53). Though the French amnesty in response to the *sans papier* movement of 1997 was ostensibly designed to legalize illegal migrants, Schain (2008: 54) insists that officials deliberately made the mandatory period of documented residency in France prohibitively long (ten years) so as to guarantee that the vast majority of the undocumented would remain so. In 2003, the Swedish government estimated that a surprisingly high percentage (8–9 percent) of youths between the ages of sixteen to twenty-four resided in Sweden without proper papers and had no legal employment or course of study (Statens-offentliga-utredningar 2003). Similarly, a British report on irregular migration warns "of producing a generation of disenfranchised youth" (Sigona and Hughes 2012: vii). Christian Joppke (2011: 230) observes that increasing numbers of TCNs are coming to the realization that it is easier to migrate to the EU illegally and avoid or contest deportation than it is to acquire legal visas. Germany has become envied and emulated across Europe for cleverly legalizing what normally would be considered illegal work. In the late 1990s and early 2000s, lawmakers and employers devised highly flexible laws and practices that made it legal for German firms to pay foreign subcontractors to supply laborers to work at sites in Germany but under terms of employment established in the country in which the subcontracting company is incorporated (Schierup, Hansen, and Castles 2006: 34, 152). In the 2000 decision to jettison its zero-immigration policy for TCNs, the European Commission (2000: 17–18) had given the green light to such "special arrangements" for "certain types of workers, e.g. seasonal workers, transfrontier workers, and intra-corporate transferees" that facilitate "the efficient management of migration flows."

Such proclivity for flexibility reflects fragilization toward a postmodern interpretation of citizenship, which reads citizenship as a political construct that is mutable and plural rather than firm and unitary. Moreover, types of citizenships are constantly being worked out by vying and allying political actors who wield asymmetrical political power (Isin and Nyers 2014: 8–9; Maas 2013a: 3; Neveu 2013: 205; Ataç and Rosenberger 2013; Cohen 2009: 14; Sassen 2002). This is precisely the point that many scholars seek to underscore with their often clever but still unconventional-sounding neologisms such as "alien citizens" (Bosniak 2006), "digital citizens" (Isin and Nyers 2014: 9), "hybrid citizens" (Stasiulis 2004), "fragmented" citizens (Wiener and Della Sala 1997), "semi-citizens" (Cohen 2009), "denizens" (Hammar 1990), or "margizens" (Castles and Davidson 2000). Such examples manifest a willingness on the part of many officials to experiment with the plasticity of citizenship to address pragmatically the varied political situations that confront them. Thus, for privileged and powerful noncitizens, conditions and conveniences similar or even superior to those enjoyed by the formal citizen can be swiftly made possible without forcing the welcomed "super citizens" (Chimienti and Solomos 2012: 96) to wade through the thicket of red tape characteristic of the formal naturalization process (Organisation for Economic Cooperation and Development 2013: 48–49). By contrast, powerless and politically vulnerable migrants can be effectively made to endure miserable living and working conditions that are unacceptable or illegal for the conventional citizen. Such exploitation occurs not only indirectly through the unacknowledged toleration by officials of illegal employers, traffickers, and landlords, but directly through the denial of rights and benefits to migrants to which they are legally entitled—a practice well documented across Europe and particularly pronounced in regard to Muslims (Hebling 2013; Anderson 2013: 122–25; van den Anke and van Liempt 2012; Sainsbury 2012: 251; Alonso 2012: 485; Cyrus and Kovacheva 2010: 133; Verkaaik 2010; Human Rights Watch 2008; Hagedorn 2007; Mouritsen 2006; Triandafyllidou 2006; Green 2005: 921; Klausen 2005: 21; Weil 2004: 377–87; Guiraudon 2003; Koopmans 1999: 630). Christina Boswell and Andrew Geddes (2011: 137) speak of the "deliberate malintegration" of foreigners on the part of officials. Such practices reflect an openness to tolerating or facilitating third-world conditions in Europe, including stratified statuses of legal membership that resemble those of former European colonies. We can also conceptualize these plural modes of citizenship as a kind of re-medievalization of the modern European state and society in which a quasi-legal hierarchy of ranks is allowed to erode the normative ideal of equality before the law for all citizens that is intrinsic to the Westphalian model of the unified nation-state. Countless European citizens daily interact with migrants who have precarious legal statuses. The former work with or alongside semi-legals and illegals in their places of employment. They hire irregular migrants to clean their homes or care for their children or elderly parents. They dine in restaurants or sleep in hotels staffed by persons with substantially inferior legal statuses, not to mention living conditions (Mantouvalou 2014; van den Anke and van Liempt 2012; Sassen 1998). A study of domestic workers in the U.K., for example, found that 67 percent of those surveyed in 2010 worked seven days per week and 48 percent worked no less than sixteen hours per day, 56 percent earned £50 or less per week, 60 percent were not allowed in public unaccompanied, 65 percent had their passport withheld, and 49 percent did not have their own room (Lalani 2011). Indeed, lest they lose a politically advantageous issue, the very politicians who rail against illegal immigration both enable and rely on its continuation (Maas 2013c: 14; Schierup, Hansen, and Castles 2006: 79). Just as in colonial and medieval times, inequalities and asymmetries occasion varying degrees of political identification and loyalty among subjects (more in this regard in subsequent chapters). They also spark resistance and protest on the part of the underprivileged and their advocates of the kind already noted above. Citizenship (actually a montage of citizenships) is, thus, very much in flux in Europe (Hansen and Hager 2010).

Contra Immigration

Most of the same countries that have encouraged immigration and naturalization have also adopted policies to discourage them as well. All of the Western European countries that actively recruited foreign laborers in the 1950s and 1960s have ceased doing so since the recession of the 1970s, with some limited exceptions regarding seasonal and highly skilled workers (Castles and Miller 2009: 108). A number of countries with open naturalization laws tightened them. In 1962, under a Conservative government, Britain targeted "coloureds" by revoking the unconditional right to reside in Britain for citizens of the United Kingdom whose passports were issued in the colonies, including those already residing in the U.K. In 1964, a Labour-controlled Parliament targeted white settlers in the colonies by passing the Nationality Act, which gave unconditional right of entry and residence to the U.K. to those with colonial passports who had a parent or grandparent born in the U.K. ("the Natal Formula"). The Immigration Act of 1971 and the British Nationality Act of 1981 refined these legal distinctions between those with ancestral connections to the British nation ("patrials") and those without, the overall effect being to introduce a strong jus sanguinis dimension into what had been a cosmopolitan jus soli policy for the entire Commonwealth (Schain 2008: 130–35). Likewise, in the Loi Pasqua-Méhaignerie of 1993, France shrewdly dismantled automatic jus soli for Maghrebians by devising cumbersome bureaucratic requirements for naturalization that could only be fulfilled between the ages of sixteen and twenty-one. The Debré Law of 1997 further tightened restrictions. Although some of the restrictions were rescinded in 1998 under the premiership of Socialist Lionel Jospin (Goodman 2014: 190), the 1999 census recorded roughly 500,000 eligible Maghrebians who failed to naturalize (Schain 2008: 75–78). Soon-to-be interior minister Charles Pasqua bluntly averred that "France has been an immigration country, but she wants to be one no longer" (quoted in Hollifield 2014: 171). In 2004, Denmark abolished jus soli for children born of non-Nordic parents (Vink and de Groot 2010: 719). Spain denies dual citizenship to Moroccans, whence the lion's share of its approximately one million Muslims originate, while permitting it for naturalizing immigrants from former colonial states in Latin America (Janoski 2010: 83). As mentioned, all the Eastern European countries adopted strict jus sanguinis naturalization regimes after abandoning the Soviet Bloc (Dumbrava 2014: 56–58; Bauböck, Perching, and Wiebke 2007; Howard 2009: 169–92), thereby emulating Austria, Switzerland, Greece, Italy, Finland, and Luxembourg in Western Europe (Howard 2009: 21). Although Germany dismantled (most of) its jus sanguinis citizenship law from 1913 with the introduction of conditional jus soli in the Nationality Law of 2000, the same law nonetheless simultaneously discouraged naturalization by making dual nationality *verboten*. The Bundestag further deliberately diluted jus soli in 2004 by raising residency requirements for TCN parents with children born in Germany (Vink and de Groot 2010: 719). In Ireland 80 percent of voters supported a national referendum in 2004 to deny jus soli to children born of parents who had not resided in the British Isles for at least three years. Several countries have made it more difficult for foreigners applying for citizenship after birth (that is, without jus soli entitlements) by lengthening residency requirements or raising the language proficiency bar (Italy in 1992, Greece in 1993, Denmark in 2002, France in 2003, Finland in 2003, Britain in 2009, and Belgium in 2012) (Organisation for Economic Cooperation and Development 2013: 103; Vink and de Groot 2010: 725–26; Howard 2009: 94–168). Following the lead of the Netherlands in 1998 (Civic Integration for Newcomers Act) and formally encouraged by the European Council Tampere Conclusions of October 1999, Denmark (2004), Austria (2004), Germany (2007), France (2007), the United Kingdom (2007), and Spain (2012) have introduced mandatory civics classes and exams for naturalization (Klekowski von Koppenfels 2013; Mourão Permoser 2013; Goodman 2010; Groot, Kuipers, and Weber 2009; Michalowski 2009). It should be noted, however, that in light of the exemptions made for EU citizens as well as other "Westerners" (via bilateral agreements), the courses and exams clearly target non-Westerners, in particular applicants from Muslim-majority countries (Goodman 2014: 214–20; Michalowski 2014; Cesari 2013: 88; Ersbøll, Kostakopoulou, and Van Oers 2011; Ruffer 2011: 947; Joppke 2010: 1137–42; Saharso 2007). We should also not overlook the discouraging impact of naturalization fees that can run in the hundreds and sometimes thousands of euros for applicants who typically possess limited means (Vink and de Groot 2010: 727).

Numerous countries have, especially since 9/11, made it harder for aliens to reside legally. Commonly implemented measures include lengthening the number of years of legal residency required for permanent visas or citizenship, raising language proficiency requirements, increasing the duration of marriage for spousal reunification as well as decreasing the maximum age for offspring reunification, introducing or increasing the minimum income (allegedly to prevent reliance on noncontributory welfare benefits), and making it easier to deport foreigners convicted of a crime. Some or all of these measures have been adopted by, among others, Austria (2002, 2005, 2011), Denmark (1992, 2002, 2005, 2012), France (2003, 2006, 2011), Germany (2004, 2007), Switzerland (2006), Italy (2002, 2009), Spain (2012), the Netherlands (1998, 2002, 2004, 2012), and the United Kingdom (2004, 2009, 2012) (Organisation for Economic Cooperation and Development 2013: 56–57; Hampshire 2013: 76–80; Koopmans, Michalowski, and Waibel 2012: 1223; Sainsbury 2012; Janoski 2010: 153, 179; Vink and de Groot 2010; Kraler 2010; Howard 2009: 101–3; Schain 2008; Messina 2007; Schierup, Hansen, and Castles 2006; Aleinikoff and Klusmeyer 2002). Moreover, most of the obligatory courses and exams apply to visa applicants as well. Once an important ideological weapon in the Cold War, lenient asylum laws have been tightened virtually everywhere in Europe. An "architecture of exclusion" (Gibney 2004: 3) has been erected, especially since the civil wars in the former Yugoslavia sent hundreds of thousands of refugees fleeing to Western Europe (Hampshire 2013: 69–76; Boswell 2005: 28–30). In particular, the Schengen Agreements, combined with the Dublin Convention (1990) and Dublin Regulation (2003 and 2014), have propelled something of a race among European states to restrict asylum. In 2015, Hungary announced plans to build a fence along its entire border with Serbia (*The Telegraph* 17 June 2015). Most of the signatory countries want to gain a reputation as the most lenient, lest they, like Germany, attract untold numbers of asylum seekers who have only "one shot" at applying in the entire Schengen area (Hampshire 2013: 101–5; Hatton 2009; Schierup, Hansen, and Castles 2006: 65–80). Tony Blair's comment from 2003 is typical of this "get-tough" posture:

> We have cut asylum applications by half. But we must go further. We should cut back the ludicrously complicated appeal process, derail the gravy train of legal aid, fast track those from democratic countries, and remove those who fail in their claims without further judicial interference. (*Guardian* 30 September 2003)

David Cameron was curter, calling refugees a "swarm" trying to enter Britain (*Telegraph* 15 August 2015). In response to Silvio Berlusconi's threat to legalize and send packing northward the "human tsunami" of refugees reaching Italy's shores as a result of the Arab Spring, the Danish government enraged the European Commission in 2011 by reinstating passport control for travelers from other Schengen lands. Germany followed suit in 2015 as tens of thousands of asylum-seekers were being "released" northward by Macedonia, Greece, Hungary, and Italy in blatant violation of the Dublin Regulation. In the same year Slovakia said it would accept Christian but not Muslim refugees. Swiss citizens went even further, voting in 2014 with a razor-thin majority in favor of a referendum placed on the ballot by the radical Right Swiss People's Party to impose quotas on the number of foreigners entering the land, including EU citizens. In the face of lost votes to the surging United Kingdom Independence Party, David Cameron too has said that limiting the number of EU foreigners into Britain might be necessary (*Die Zeit* 15 May 2014).

Despite its rhetoric and action in favor of equal rights for TCNs alluded to above, the EU hardly qualifies as an unequivocal voice in favor of cosmopolitan openness. Until 2000, the European Commission endorsed a zero-immigration policy and thereafter open borders only for highly skilled TCNs. The European Commission (1994: 32) all but officially supported xenoskeptic concerns that migrants pose a threat when it stated: "Society's willingness to accept the inflow of new migrant groups depends on how it perceives government to be in control of the phenomenon." Furthermore, one has to wonder just how far the EU can go in supporting multiculturalism for TCNs when Article 6.3 of the Treaty of European Union (1992) states: "The Union shall respect the national identities of its Member states." Small wonder, then, that the EU's Family Directive of 2003 authorizes member states to deny family reunification to immigrants who are not well integrated (Goodman 2014: 208).

Backlash against Multiculturalism

Behind much anti-immigrant policy making lies a harsh critique of multiculturalism. Although we should not discount the postmodern instrumentalism that justifies exploiting migrants for no other reason than that they are vulnerable, there can be no denying the emergence of a "multicultural backlash" (Vertovec and Wessendorf 2010) or "retreat of multiculturalism" (Joppke 2004) across Europe (also Boswell and Geddes 2011: 202; Bukow et al. 2007: 13; Brubaker 2001). The strongest purveyors and greatest beneficiaries of this "backlash against diversity" (Grillo 2005: 38) have been radical Right political parties and politicians, the marked improvement in whose political fortunes arguably represents the most significant novel development in European politics over the past three decades. No European polity has remained immune from sporadic spikes in the electoral success of extreme Right parties; they represent formidable fixtures on the political spectrum in many countries where they regularly garner between 10 and 15 percent of the popular vote; they have negotiated their way into ruling coalitions in Austria, Denmark, Switzerland, Norway, the Netherlands, Italy, Estonia, Romania, Poland, and Slovakia. They shrewdly deploy xenophobic slogans that directly appeal to many voters: "Keep Sweden Swedish" (Sweden Democrats), "Give us Denmark back" (Danish People's Party), "Shake off the creeping tyranny of Islamization" (Dutch Party for Freedom), "Islam out of Britain" (British National Party), "Stop the Foreigners" (Austrian Freedom Party), "Rescue Hungarians" (Jobbik), "Masters in our own house" (Northern League in Italy), "Greece belongs to Greeks" (Golden Dawn). These clever rallying cries of the "politics of closure" (Hampshire 2013: 16) represent ideological fragments of Schmitt's sophisticated friend-enemy philosophy of nationalism: "A nationally homogeneous state then appears normal; a state that lacks this homogeneity is abnormal, a threat to peace" (Schmitt 1983: 231).

Only at their peril can mainstream political parties ignore or dismiss this "resurgence of nationalist thinking" (Bukow et al. 2007: 13). Many have registered it and endorsed or adopted aspects of the Far Right's platform, generating an unmistakable "restrictive turn" in immigration policy making (Koopmans, Michalowski, and Waibel 2012: 1234; also see Hampshire 2013: 16–35; Art 2011; Howard 2009: 11–12; Berezin 2009; Givens and Luedtke 2005; Norris 2005). For example, a study by the European Commission against Racism and Intolerance (2011: 7) bemoaned "the increasing use of xenophobic and anti-Muslim arguments by mainstream political leaders." In a much discussed article from 2000, the prominent Labor Party member and publicist Paul Scheffer bemoaned the "ethnic underclass" in the Netherlands that does not identify with Dutch culture as irrefutable evidence of the "multicultural disaster" (*NRC Handelsblad* 29 January 2000). In 2004, Pope Benedict XVI denounced multiculturalism as a Western pathology born of self-loathing (Pera and Ratzinger 2004). In 2010, Angela Merkel maintained that "multiculturalism has failed, and failed utterly" (*Das Bild* 17 October 2010). Sarkozy echoed her in the same year, deriding multiculturalism as a "failed concept" (quoted in Kaya 2012: 216). Both Gordon Brown and David Cameron disavowed multiculturalism as an explicit goal of their respective governments. The Tory leader complained in 2011 that "under the doctrine of state multiculturalism we have encouraged different cultures to live separate lives apart from each other and the mainstream" (quoted in Mavelli 2012: 139). Governments at various levels around Europe have commissioned studies that document and denounce the desultory impact of multiculturalist policies and lifestyles. Typical of their conclusions is Britain's Cantle Report, whose compilers were

> particularly struck by the depth of polarization of our towns and cities. . . . Separate educational arrangements, community and voluntary bodies, places of worship, language, social and cultural networks, means that many communities operate on the basis of a series of parallel lives. These lives do not seem to touch at any point,

let alone overlap and promote any meaningful interchanges. (Cantle Report 2001: 9)

Indeed, the notion of the "parallel society" has throughout Europe taken on the pejorative connotation of a society so thoroughly divided into separate cultural communities that it lacks the common bonds required for social cohesion (Ranstorp and Dos Santos 2009; Netherlands Ministry of the Interior 2007; Bundesamt für Verfassungsschutz 2005; Cantle Report 2001; Haut Conseil à l'Intégration 1997, 1995; Wetenschappelijke Raad 1989; but also see Wright and Bloemraad 2012 for counter-argument).

Earned Citizenship

One prominently prescribed remedy for the allegedly disintegrative effects of the multicultural society is the reinvigoration of citizenship. On this view, citizenship should reflect common values that bind citizens together in a profound manner. The defenders of a more robust, thicker citizenship insist that it must be earned rather than merely granted, prized rather than merely possessed. The U.K. Home Office (2008: 11), for instance, stipulates that "citizenship must be earned." Blair and other "Third Way" Social Democrats were wont to speak of "no rights without responsibilities" (quoted in Kuisma 2013: 101). In 2006 during an interview on prime-time television, Sarkozy averred that would-be citizens must master French and "learn to respect the country [and accept] French laws, even if they don't understand them," because "it is up to them to adapt, not France" (quoted in Cesari 2013: 7). His presidential rival, Jean Marie Le Pen, stated simply: *Etre Français, cela se mérite* (You must deserve to be French) (quoted in Kaya 2012: 71). This same sense of deservedness is cleverly captured in the German government's catchy slogan *Fördern und Fordern* (promote and require) to characterize its immigration and naturalization strategy (quoted in Bahners 2011: 36). On this view, successful applicants for citizenship (as well as permanent residency) ought to be expected to demonstrate an earnest identification with and commitment to the host society—that they have made it their "home" as opposed to their current place of residence. They ought, that is, to have assimilated to some significant degree.

But what exactly are migrants expected to assimilate in this widespread "return of assimilation" (Brubaker 2001)? When we analyze what political actors pressing for assimilation include and propose to include as requirements for naturalization, we discover fragments of both nativist nationalism and liberal perfectionism. The resulting mixture manifests mutual fragilization between the two. Philosophically, the differing demands of nativist nationalism and liberal perfectionism exclude one another but politically they can make quite comfortable bedfellows.

Nativist Nationalism

Demands for ethnonational assimilation can be heard around Europe. In a direct rebuff to Habermas's liberal alternative to ethnonationalism, Interior Minister Wolfgang Schäuble averred that "constitutional patriotism, as a matter of reason (and not of emotion), is not sufficient. . . . If we want to feel part of a collectivity, then there must be something that connects us at a deeper level, at the level of religion and culture, values and identity" (*Frankfurter Allgemeine Zeitung* 27 September 2006). In 2006, he called on Muslims to identify with the "German value community" (*deutsche Wertgemeinschaft*) (quoted in Amir-Moazami 2009: 203). In 2014, the Christian Social Union went so far as to propose mandating that German be spoken in immigrants' homes (*Die Tagesschau* 7 December 2014). Several prominent German politicians have used the term *Leitkultur* (leading culture) in the same assimilative vein (Green 2005: 942). Christian Democratic Union (CDU) general secretary Laurence Meyer, for example, claimed "there should be no doubt who has the rights of a house owner and who is the guest" (quoted in Leiken 2012: 248). For its part, the German government has long demanded as a requirement for naturalization a "voluntary and lasting orientation toward Germany" (quoted in Hansen 2003: 91) and was wont to deny citizenship to applicants who joined immigrant ethnic or religious associations (Koopmans 1999: 630). Though the 2000 Citizenship Law amended the language to "sufficient oral and written German language skills" (quoted in Goodman 2014: 127), Green (2005: 944–48) argues that through bureaucratic discretion and clever political stonewalling by Christian Democrats ethnonationalist bias persisted nevertheless. The civics exam required since 2007 requires extensive knowledge of German history (Klekowski von Koppenfels 2013: 149).

In Italy, successful applicants for naturalization must demonstrate not only knowledge of the "Italian language," but also of "the essential elements of the national history and culture" (quoted in Spena 2010: 175). In order to pass Austria's citizenship test, applicants must correctly answer culturally specific questions such as "In which Upper Austrian town are there two famous winged altars?" (quoted in Jenkins 2007: 274). In 2012, Mariano Rajoy's government introduced a "Spanish identity" test as a requirement for naturalization, while Catalonia's integration contract requires immigrants to prove "an adequate knowledge of Catalan civil life" (quoted in Hazán 2014: 384).

According to the national models paradigm, such ethnonationalist inflection should be expected in these countries based on their long-standing ethnonationalist traditions (Koopmans, Michalowski, and Waibel 2012; Koopmans et al. 2005; Brochmann and Hammar 1999; Favell 1998; Joppke 1996; Brubaker 1992). But similar "neo-assimilationist" (Hansen and Hager 2010: 169) pressure turns up in countries that the paradigm does not categorize as ethnonationalist. British law, for instance, requires unmistakable attributes of "Britishness" (quoted in Ryan 2009: 290–91) and "a clear primary loyalty to this Nation" (Home Office 2001: 20). Home Secretary David Blunkett explained in 2001 that "we have norms of acceptability and those who come into our home—for that is what it is—should accept those norms" (quoted in Joppke 2004: 250). In unmistakably Burkean language, Minister of Education Michel Grove said of the citizenship test in 2013: "If we can develop a better understanding of our past—how institutions have evolved and changed—then we'll have a better understanding . . . of how *institutions* can give expression to our shared sense of identity" (quoted in Goodman 2014: 154). The Netherlands requires "feeling Dutch" (quoted in Van Oers 2009: 128), one reason why Integration Minister Rita Verdonk argued in 2006 that the mandatory naturalization ceremonies should celebrate "our history that has formed our identity" (quoted in Verkaaik 2010: 73). She also endorsed the idea that migrants should be required to speak Dutch in public, a suggestion that the city of Rotterdam wrote into law (Kaya 2012: 134). Similarly, Amsterdam launched a major campaign in 2006 to teach the city's history so that immigrants could be helped to "feel themselves Amsterdammers" (quoted in Duyvendak 2011: 102). Indeed, the very Minderhedennota of 1983, which established the Netherlands' official policy of multiculturalism, plainly stressed the dominance of Dutch culture: "It [integration] is a confrontation between unequal partners. The majority culture is after all anchored in Dutch society" (quoted in Vink 2007: 345). In neighboring Belgium, Filip Dewinter (2000: 10), leader of the nationalist Flemish movement Vlaams Belang, says immigrants should have a simple choice: "Assimilation or return." In 2006, Sarkozy rephrased Jean Marie Le Pen's favorite patriotic exclamation—*La France, aimez-la ou quittez-la* (France, Love it or leave it): "If there are people who are not comfortable in France, they should feel free to leave a country which they do not love" (quoted in Kaya 2012: 70). Showing that nationalism is not limited to the political Right, Socialist interior minister Manuel Valls claimed that "you have to be proud to be a Frenchman to be part of this nation" (*Spiegelonline* 29 October 2013). At least since François Mitterand introduced the campaign for "the right to be different" (*droit à la différence*) in 1981, prominent opponents of multiculturalism proudly dubbing themselves "national republicans," such as Philippe de Villiers (2006), Dominique Schnapper

(1998), Jacqueline Costa-Lascoux (1989), Emmanuel Todd (1994), Pierre-André Taguieff (1987), and Michèle Tribalat (1996), among others (Laborde 2008: 196), have urged a policy of deliberate francofication.

The French, of course, purport that their requirement of *assimilation à la communauté française* is based on the universal republican principles of the French Revolution and not on ethnic origins. Yet the web page of the Ministry of Justice instructs prospective applicants that they need to be "well assimilated to the French customs and manners." As early as 1988, France's Nationality Commission stipulated that immigrants worthy of French citizenship should manifest "clear adhesion to the essential common values of French society," which entails "speaking *the same language*, sharing the *same* culture and patriotic *values*, participating in the national life like the others" (quoted in Laborde 2008: 196, 191). The current civics course underscores that "French and Frenchmen are attached to a history, a culture and fundamental values. . . . It is necessary to know them, understand them and respect them" (quoted in Michalowski 2014: 182). Small wonder, then, that in practice French officials are known automatically to deny naturalization to Muslims who observe the pious duty to pray five times daily at prescribed moments (Klausen 2005: 21) or who wear Islamic garb (Goodman 2014: 198), a practice documented elsewhere (for Denmark, see Mouritsen 2006; for Italy, Triandafyllidou 2006). In 2011, France went so far as to prohibit Muslims from praying on the street, while permitting Catholic religious processions through the same streets (Vakulenko 2012: 22).

Even the EU has lent support to this "renationalization of citizenship" (Modood and Meer 2012: 34). Its Hague Program of 2004 claims that migrants should be expected to "acquire" the "culture of the host society," including "basic knowledge of the host society's language, history and institutions" (quoted in Hansen and Hager 2010: 166). Finally, we should not overlook the effect of what Michael Billig (1995) terms "banal nationalism." He means the saturation of everyday life by myriad signs, symbols, and meanings, which taken together strongly reinforce the idea that identifying with the majority culture is "normal" while resisting such identification is "abnormal."

Such policies and attitudes discriminate against migrants for not belonging to the nation. They are deemed undeserving of equal citizenship rights and privileges because they purportedly do not command the national language, respect the national history, or observe the national norms in the same degree as nationals. Following Schmitt's friend-enemy logic (if only in fragmentary rather than comprehensive fashion), the differences manifested by unassimilated migrants are made to render them potential or real threats to the well-being of the citizenry. The citizenship courses, exams, and oaths, of course, ostensibly seek to encourage assimilation. However, in light of the fact that practically everywhere they have been introduced naturalization rates have declined (Anderson 2013; *MiGAZIN* 25 April 2012, http://www.migazin.de/2012/04/25/amnesty-international-kritisiert-diskriminierung-von-muslimen/; Löwenheim and Gazit 2009: 160), the courses, exams, and oaths wind up functioning as exclusionary measures that deny full citizenship to far more ethnic minorities than they certify for naturalization. Whether on the actual or symbolic level, they work to accentuate and perpetuate rather than eliminate difference and differential treatment (Mourão Permoser 2013; Hampshire 2013: 127; Boswell and Geddes 2011: 120; Verkaaik 2010: 77).

Liberal Perfectionism

The courses, exams, and oaths also reveal what one author labels "Schmittian liberalism" (Triadafilopolous 2011: 863). On this view, the defect that disqualifies applicants for citizenship (renders them potential foes) is their alleged unfamiliarity with or even disrespect for the liberal values that purportedly undergird democracy. Consider the decision of France's high court (Conseil d'Etat) in 2008 to uphold the denial of French citizenship to a burqa-wearing Moroccan woman married to a French national on grounds that she exhibited an "assimilation defect" (*défaut d'assimilation*). However, according to the court, the defect lay in her "adoption of a radical practice of her religion, incompatible with the essential values of the French community, especially the principle of the equality of the sexes" (quoted in Joppke 2010: 139). Likewise, in 2010 a Moroccan man was denied citizenship because, in the words of Immigration Minister Eric Besson, he "forced his wife to wear the full veil . . . and rejected the principles of secularism and the equality between men and women" (*Guardian* 2 February 2010). Both Moroccans were not denied citizenship simply for being Muslim in the sense of not being Roman Catholic like the majority of the French nation. Rather, their (admittedly Muslim) practice allegedly violated the liberal universal principle of gender equality. Some might object that they nevertheless were discriminated against based on their religion. I in no way discount the possibility that religious (or for that matter racial or gender) prejudice was covertly or even subconsciously at play in these decisions. However, it is not insignificant that the *official* justification is ultimately rooted in liberal universalism rather than nationalist particularism, for a strict application of the latter would rule out the idea of French Muslims altogether. France, of course, is home to millions of French citizens who practice Islam.

Yet we should not overlook the court's particularist allusion to the "*French* community." It exemplifies the fragmentation and fragilization common in political practice in contrast to pure theory. Thus, a fragment of nationalist thinking ("the French community") detached from the broader theory of nationalism (which would theorize that French values are unique rather than universal) becomes married with a liberal fragment ("equality of the sexes") detached from the philosophy of liberalism (which would reject the idea that gender equality can be "French" precisely because it is a universal principle). Such practical overlaying of theoretically incompatible fragments makes good political sense because both nationalism and liberalism resonate positively with fragilized European publics for whom the philosophical inconsistency is irrelevant. Thus, when asked in 2004 to define "Britishness," Gordon Brown replied a "passion for liberty anchored in a sense of duty and an intrinsic commitment to tolerance and fair play" (quoted in Joppke 2009: 84). Tony Blair (2006) mentioned "belief in democracy, the rule of law, tolerance, and equal treatment for all, respect for this country and its shared heritage." Rita Verdonk said that to qualify as Dutch one must respect the "fundamental constitutional rights" of the Netherlands, especially gender equality and freedom of religion (quoted in Verkaaik 2010: 73). Retired Dutch Labor Party leader Wouter Bos (2005) averred that all Dutch citizens must "accept civil liberties—including freedom of expression, the equal treatment of men, women, heterosexuals and homosexuals, the separation of church and state, the principle of democratic government and the rule of law." Since 2011, France requires for citizenship "adherence to the principles and essential values of the Republic" (quoted in Goodman 2014: 187).

The national models paradigm, again, predicts such statements from countries with a multicultural tradition. But listen to former Danish prime minister Anders Rasmussen: "Danish society has been built on some fundamental values, which must be accepted, if you are to live here. In Denmark, politics and religion are separated. In Denmark, there is inviolable respect for human life. In Denmark . . . women are equal to men" (quoted in Mouritsen 2006: 82). Austria's integration contract requires knowledge of "European values and core democratic values" (quoted in Mourrão Permoser 2013: 165). In Germany, Bundestag president Norbet Lammert urged his fellow Christian Democrats to replace the notion of *deutsche Leitkultur* with a *Leitkultur für Deutschland*. The latter revolves around the "inviolability of human dignity, the free development of the personality, the equality of men and women, the freedom of science, art and culture, as well as the free religious expression" (*Süddeutsche Zeitung* 20 December 2007). With this suggestion Lammert escaped nationalist particularism but not a (slightly) wider civilizational or Eurocentric particularism, for in the same article he made the common assertion that such principles form the "Western community of values."

Such statements purport to defend universal values but they employ a particularistic logic and strategy. Nationals (and Westerners) are presumed to respect liberal values, while nonnationals (more precisely, non-Westerners) are presumed not to respect them and to need mandatory training to learn to internalize them. Thus, the British handbook for integration courses simply states that "the fundamental principles of British life include: democracy, the rule of law, individual liberty, tolerance of those with different faiths and beliefs, participation in community life" (Home Office 2013: 7–8). Joppke (2010: 137) labels this line of thinking "particular universalism" and "the main form in which Western states practice exclusion today." As Per Mouritsen (2009: 29) observes, "An identitarian civic-liberalism-as-national culture is politicized and essentialized against Islam." Or more broadly, "our" Western culture purportedly based on liberalism is juxtaposed against "their" presumably illiberal and therefore threatening Islamic culture (Cesari 2013: 142). Mouritsen, Cesari, and many others are right to stress Islam (O'Brien 2013b 133–34; Hampshire 2013: 150–54; Kaya 2012: 211; Göle 2011: 155; Amiraux 2010: 145; Sayyid 2009: 198–99; Ewing 2008: 28; Schiffauer 2006: 111; Muñoz 1994: 219). As mentioned, the courses, exams, and oaths are for all intents and purposes designed for Muslims (and some other non-Westerners). Exemptions are typically made for Westerners. No one in Europe is seriously suggesting that, say, non-Muslim Germans residing in France should be trained and tested in respect for gender equality. Likewise, no one is suggesting that, say, non-Muslim French nationals in Denmark should be compelled to prove their commitment to the freedom of religion. Rather, the courses and requirements teach and test the "correct" liberal answers to questions regarding the kind of topics, such as polygamy, gender equality, homosexuality, and apostasy, toward which Muslims are presumed to have illiberal attitudes (Michalowski 2014; Ersbøll, Kostakopoulou, and Van Oers 2011) . The Dutch test goes so far as to ask test-takers how they react to scenes of kissing men and topless women shown during the exam (Jenkins 2007: 274–75).

There is, then, an unmistakable liberal perfectionist element that endeavors to mold Muslims into trustworthy liberals. Thus did Minister for Immigration Maria Böhmer defend the tests as an effective way to "shape politically mature subjects" (*Süddeutsche Zeitung* 9 July 2008). The liberal perfectionist goal, however, augments rather than replaces the nativist dimension. The French exam, for example, is designed as "an evaluation of language goals and the values of the Republic" (quoted in Schain 2008: 57). Likewise, the Integration Policy New Style of 2002 demands "that people speak Dutch, and that one abides to [*sic*] basic Dutch norms" (quoted in Duyvendak and Scholten 2012: 274). The U.K.'s Home Office (2008: 5) stipulates that "all who live here should learn our language, play by the rules, obey the law and contribute to the community." In addition to recommending that the courses impart "basic knowledge of the host society's language, history and institutions," the European Council's 2004 Hague Programme recommendations additionally stipulate that newcomers should be made to "understand [and] respect . . . the full scope of values, rights, responsibilities, and privileges established by the EU and member state laws" (Council of the EU, Justice and Home Affairs 2004: CBP 4.2 and CBP 2). Home Secretary Charles Clark called in 2006 for a legally binding integration contract to ensure that "new immigrants live up to the values of our society" (quoted in Schain 2008: 158). In 2010, David Cameron referred to such insistence on liberal rectitude as "muscular liberalism" that is "unambiguous and hard-nosed about the defence of our liberty" (quoted in Joppke and Torpey 2013: 153).

Critics of liberal perfectionism claim the courses and requirements are too intrusive. Timothy Garton Ash (2006), for instance, anathematizes them as "enlightenment fundamentalism," while Bauböck (2002: 176) rejects them as overbearing "liberal assimilationism" and Liav Orgad (2010: 53) as "illiberal liberalism." Labeling the courses, exams, and oaths "repressive liberalism," Joppke derides them as "the imposition of virtuous citizenship" and likens them to overbearing efforts at social engineering in the Soviet Bloc (Joppke 2010: 62, 141–42). Bridget Anderson (2013: 109) speaks of "super-citizenship" that holds immigrants to much higher standards than natives. Indeed, with the Borders, Citizenship and Immigration Act of 2009 the United Kingdom introduced a probationary year of citizenship in which the newly naturalized must demonstrate "active citizenship" through "civic activities" that "benefit the local community"—a kind of compulsory civic activism (Home Office 2008: 50). Imagine how many native Britons would have their citizenships revoked if held to this standard? It deserves mention that the Cameron government decided to cease implementation of the measure (Goodman 2014: 151–52). Since 2007, the French government reserves the right to withdraw welfare benefits from immigrant parents who fail to fulfill the obligation to integrate their children into French society (Sainsbury 2012: 191). The *Land* government of Baden-Württemberg requires its naturalization officials to employ specified interview guidelines (*Gesprächsleitfaden*) to test whether the applicants' required oath to uphold the German constitution is sincere. The questions are designed to certify a genuine "inner disposition" to honor the constitution as opposed to a mere outward pledge, and this despite the fact that the Constitutional Court had ruled in 2000 that citizens are "legally not required personally to share the values of the Constitution" (quoted in Joppke 2010: 140–42).

As these examples suggest, the defense of liberalism can exclude immigrants as much or more than it includes them. Their alleged illiberalism marks them with a kind of scarlet letter that ostracizes them from partaking equally of the privileges of mainstream society. Liberal exclusion, however, operates alongside or in combination with nativist exclusion. It is widespread normative fragilization that, in part at least, makes simultaneously appearing to defend the nation and to embrace liberal values politically prudent, even if philosophically inconsistent.

Conclusion

Comparative scholars of citizenship and immigration policy painstakingly search for patterns. One group of analysts seeks order in the convergence of policy across Europe, typically, though not always (Hollifield, Martin, and Orreneus 2014b), in a more liberal, open direction (Joppke 2010: 143; Hansen and Weil 2001; Beck 1998; Jacobson 1996; Held 1995; Soysal 1994). A competing school of researchers, as mentioned, discerns distinct and persistent national styles anchored in past tradition and path dependency (Goodman 2014; Koopmans, Michalowski, and Waibel 2012; Koopmans et al. 2005; Brochmann and Hammar 1999; Favell 1998; Joppke 1996; Brubaker 1992). These otherwise laudable studies tend to exaggerate the order and coherence of citizenship and immigration policies. In reality, the latter are "contradictory and polyvalent" (Joppke 2010: 67), "fragmented" (Wiener and Della Sala 1997: 605), "multilayered and complex" (Maas 2013b: vii), with "new policies added on top of previous ones" (Garbaye 2010: 166) in a "blended approach" (Banting and Kymlicka 2013: 577) or "dizzyingly" "complex assemblage" (Hampshire 2013: 132, 54) that is "incoherent" and riddled with "inconsistencies and double standards" (Fasani 2010: 178), not to mention constantly "in flux" (Boswell 2003: 1). Likewise, while some optimistic ethicists such as Habermas (1987b: 170) would like to believe that "all alternatives to a universalistic broadening of moral consciousness are being decimated," analysis of the normative discussion of citizenship and immigration does not find imminent consensus, but rather a "multiplicity of frames" (Duyvendak and Scholten 2012: 276) and "a variety of often contradictory sets of public ideas and theories about citizenship" in a "discursive and normative field of struggles for legitimacy . . . [that] vary all the time" (Bertossi 2012: 249, 262). As Hampshire (2013: 12) incisively observes, "Few studies have sought to examine how these factors interact to produce conflicting policy outputs."

This chapter has advanced normative fragmentation and fragilization as a *partial* explanation of policy incoherence or messiness. In the statements of policy makers and other political activists I have highlighted abundant normative fragments employed trying to legitimize policies and policy recommendations. These selected philosophical tidbits can be traced back to the more comprehensive public philosophies of liberalism, nationalism, and postmodernism that I outlined in the previous chapter, although political actors exhibit little concern for philosophical consistency. Rather, like bricoleurs (Carstensen 2011: 148), they pragmatically deploy and even clump together multiple fragments from the three public philosophies (and their variants) in an effort to legitimize a broad variety of policies to a broad variety of audiences. This opportunistic political strategy makes sense or "works" due in part at least to the mutual fragilization or interpenetration among the three public philosophies. As discussed in the previous chapter, because none of the three has been able definitively to discredit its two rivals, fragments emanating from all three can and often do sound convincing to philosophical laypersons. Thus, to put it in lay terms, standing up for equal rights (liberalism), defending the integrity of the nation (nationalism), or eschewing solidarity in favor of instrumental selfish gain (postmodernism) can each seem like compelling causes in certain contexts despite their ethical incompatibility. While the resulting moral pluralism and laxity may prove unsettling to philosophers reared on monism and exactitude, they turn out to be an enabling opportunity for political actors who need not confine either their rhetoric or their policies to a normative straitjacket. Rather, fragilization and fragmentation enable political flexibility and opportunity that few politicians can afford not to exploit. The result, I have underscored, are immigration and citizenship policies that across Europe tend to lack coherence and defy neat classification.

4

Veil

Wives . . . submit yourselves to your own husbands so that, if any
of them do not believe the word, they may be won over without
words by the behavior of their wives, when they see the purity
and reverence of your lives. Your beauty should not come from
outward adornment, such as elaborate hairstyles and the wearing
of gold jewelry or fine clothes. Rather, it should be that of your
inner self, the unfading beauty of a gentle and quiet spirit, which
is of great worth in God's sight. For this is the way the holy women
of the past who put their hope in God used to adorn themselves.
They submitted themselves to their own husbands, like Sarah, who
obeyed Abraham and called him her lord.
—I Peter 3:1–5

Men are the maintainers of women. . . . So the good women are
obedient, guarding the unseen as Allah has guarded. . . . And say
to the believing women that they lower their gaze and restrain
their sexual passions and do not display their adornment except
what appears thereof. And let them wear their head-coverings over
their bosoms. And they should not display their adornment except
to their husbands or their fathers, or the fathers of their husbands,
or their sons, or the sons of their husbands, or their brothers, or
their brothers' sons, or their sisters' sons, or their women, or those
whom their right hands possess, or guileless male servants, or the
children who know not women's nakedness.
—Qur'an, 4:34, 24:31

Scholarship on policies regulating Islamic veiling in Europe exhibits the
propensity to impose order on what is actually a messy reality. Christian
Joppke (2009: vii), for instance, points to distinct national approaches
in "Republican France," "Christian-Occidental Germany," and "Multicultural Britain." Similarly, Schirin Amir-Moazami (2007: 35–38) insists on the
critical differences between a discourse based on "abstract universalism" in
France compared to an "ethnic-cultural" idiom in Germany. Sawitri Saharso (2007: 527) differentiates between the Netherlands' "multicultural" and

Germany's "ethno-cultural" model (also see Collet 2004). Anna Korteweg and Gökçe Yurdakul (2014) contend that France, Turkey, Germany, the Netherlands, and the United Kingdom each has a unique national narrative of belonging to which veiled Muslims must conform or be stigmatized as outsiders. From a different but no less orderly perspective, Sabine Berghahn (2012) contends that governments with strict separation of church and state tend to be intolerant vis-à-vis veiling while states having formal relations with religious organizations tend to be tolerant. The rich detail provided in these otherwise superb studies tends to belie the neat ordering proffered by the authors. In actuality, the politics of veiling in Europe is fraught with controversy. As a result, policies are polymorphous, indeed messy. In their ambitious cross-national study, for example, Sieglinde Rosenberger and Birgit Sauer (2012a: 12, 3) found a "multifaceted spectrum of approaches to headscarf policies" that "is much more complex than a . . . typology can cover" (Rosenberger and Sauer 2012a: 12). Likewise, Sevgi Kiliç, Saharso, and Sauer (2008: 403) find that national models cannot explain the full complexity of policies regulating the head scarf (see also Siim 2014).

At first thought, veiling policy would seem to be unambiguous; governments either permit or prohibit the Islamic practice. The reality, however, is far more fluid and complex. France likely jumps first to mind when the topic of veiling in the European context crops up. The French National Assembly voted in 2004 to ban the veil (and all other "ostentatious" expressions of religious affiliation) from public schools (though not universities). In 2011, a law took effect proscribing in public the full-length burqa covering the face (*niqab*), which the European Court of Human Rights upheld in 2014. Proscribing veiling supposedly originated in Creil in 1989 when three pupils of Moroccan heritage who refused to unveil were expelled by administrators of Gabriel Havez Secondary School for violating the 1905 law separating religion and state (even though the same school had allowed veiled students in 1988). In 1989, two veiled girls were also expelled from Altrincham Girls' Grammar School in the United Kingdom. The Muslim pupils were eventually readmitted on condition that the veils conformed to school uniform colors. However, four years earlier, the authorities of the Dutch town of Alphen aan de Rijn had banned the *hijab* (headscarf), though their policy was later overturned by the lower house of parliament. Yet, in supposedly intolerant France, the Conseil d'Etat, in the vast majority of cases (forty-one of forty-nine) regarding covering that came before it between 1989 and 2004, struck down prohibitions in the name of guaranteeing female students' (though not female teachers') "freedom of conscience" (Haut Conseil à l'Intégration 2000: 56)—a stance prominently supported by first lady Danielle Mitterand, who insisted on the girls' "right to be different." The court cases helped to fuel a national debate that raged in, among other places, the nation's newspapers throughout the 1990s, laying the ground for the 2004 law, which itself was, like the 2011 law, opposed in conspicuous public demonstrations of covered protesters and their allies (such as *Le Monde* itself). The burqa ban also drew criticism from the Conseil d'Etat (2010) for raising "strong constitutional and statutory uncertainties." The heated discord, refueled in 2013 by the controversial recommendation of the Haut Conseil à l'Intégration to ban the veil from universities (Fredette 2014: 164), is presumably why the French characterize the issue as "*la guerre des voiles*" (war of the veils) as opposed to, say, the "national consensus regarding veiling" (Bertossi 2012).

In the supposedly tolerant, multicultural Netherlands, dozens of women sacked for veiling have sought justice before the Equal Treatment Commission. Though the commission has ruled in favor of the coverer in all but one of its rulings, the quantity and frequency of the cases cast doubt on a firm and widespread Dutch consensus in the matter. Indeed, anti-veiling legislators have tirelessly sought to finesse a French-like ban through parliament. In 2005, they managed to push through a burqa ban, though the law was subsequently withdrawn when the Council of State deemed it unconstitutional. Roughly the same fate befell the 2007 parliamentary initiative to proscribe the niqab from public. Buoyed by the success of his Party for Freedom (PVV) in the 2010 elections, Geert Wilders made proscription of the hijab for all public employees a major bargaining chip for any coalition involving his party. The cabinet of the coalition eventually formed with the PVV approved a burqa ban but dissolved in 2012 before it could implement the policy. In fact, state officials have possessed since 2002 the legal authority to ban the niqab in state institutions, have exercised it, and have been vindicated in 2005 by the Equal Treatment Commission. Furthermore, judges and police officers are forbidden to don Islamic garb.

The situation in Germany has been very fluid. In 1998, education officials in Baden-Württemberg dismissed Fershta Ludin for refusing to unveil when teaching in public school. In 2003, the Constitutional Court nullified the ban but left a legal loophole by maintaining that the firing would have been constitutional had it been stipulated in statutory law, which in the case of education is the jurisdiction of individual *Länder*. Seven Christian Democratic *Land* governments swiftly legislated laws that forbade public school teachers to don the hijab (but not the Christian habit or Jewish yarmulke). The Berlin Law on the Ideological Neutrality of the State, passed by a coalition of Social Democrats and the Left Party in 2004, proscribed the outward manifestation of all religious symbols by teachers (but not students), as did Bremen and Lower Saxony. However, North Rhine-Westphalia, so long as it was run by Social Democrats, refused to outlaw the headscarf despite the fact that fifteen veiled teachers were employed in its schools. When the Christian Democratic Union (CDU) took control in Düsseldorf in 2006, however, it quickly legislated a ban on Islamic but not Christian or Jewish covering. Needless to say, each of these laws has occasioned stiff opposition, and it should be noted that attempts to extend the ban beyond the schools to private businesses were ruled unconstitutional in 2002 by the Federal Labor Court for violating the right to religious freedom. Despite evidence from pollsters of overwhelming support among the masses for a burqa ban in 2011, German mainstream politicians tabled the discussion (Bowen and Rohe 2014: 158). Then in 2015 the Constitutional Court reversed its 2003 decision, ruling that a general ban of the headscarf for teachers violated the religious freedom guaranteed in the Constitution.

The United Kingdom too has a variety of regulations. Preferring to resolve disagreements through pragmatic mediation on a case-by-case basis, British officials have not established a uniform policy in the law books. However, we should not misinterpret the absence of a formal legal ban on veiling in public schools as national consensus. First, some schools ban Islamic coverings and some do not. Second, there would be no need for case-by-case mediation if there were no deadlocks between proponents and opponents of covering. Third, though in the vast majority of mediated cases a way is found to permit veiling, the compromise often nevertheless involves restrictions, for instance, as to the color or design of the hijab. Female Muslim judges, for example, may cover themselves but it must be with the wig traditionally worn in British courts. The topic of veiling has long been salient and controversial. The case of Shabina Begum drew national attention in 2005 in part because Tony Blair's wife, Cherie Booth, successfully argued before the Court of Appeal for Begum's right to wear the *jilbab* (a floor-length dress coat) to the school that had banned it. Foreign Minister Jack Straw stirred up controversy in 2006 when he publicly stated that niqab-wearing women made him feel uncomfortable because he could not see their facial expressions. Since 2007, when the government granted public schools the authority to ban the niqab, it is more likely forbidden than allowed in British schools.

The situation is equally fluid elsewhere. Like the U.K., Austria has no blanket bans. There, where Islam has been officially recognized and supported by the state since 1912, teachers and pupils alike are permitted to cover. In 1995, however, the government rejected the proposal of the officially recognized Islamic Religious Community to mandate veiling for female students during Islamic religious education classes in public schools. In 2005, Interior Minister Liese Prokop announced her objection to veiled teachers, and, since 2006, the Freedom Party has endorsed a ban on veiling in the public schools. Fervor over the headscarf erupted in Denmark in 2006 (the year following the Muhammad cartoon controversy) when Asmaa Abdol-Hamid began co-hosting a TV talk show. The Palestinian refugee wore a hijab and refused to shake hands with male guests, preferring to raise her hand to her heart as an alternative greeting. After the Danish People's Party (DPP) failed to win parliamentary approval for its proposed ban on veiling in state-supported institutions, Anders Fogh Rasmussen's center-right government in 2009 passed legislation to ban veils for judges. In 2003, the High Court had already permitted proscription of veiling in private companies if part of a general dress code. The Swedish Board of Education upheld a ban on the burqa in schools but not the hijab, while the Equality Ombudsman annulled a niqab prohibition at the Västerort Adult High School. In 2010, Norway maintained its ban on the hijab for officers of the court and police despite the ruling of the Anti-Discrimination Tribunal that the 2009 ban violated the Anti-Discrimination and Gender Equality Acts. Belgium, a state that has officially recognized Islam since 1974, banned the burqa from public in 2011; several municipalities, such as Maaseik (2004) and Antwerp (2005), had done so several years earlier. Yet dozens of women refused identity papers because they would not unveil for photos fought successfully in court to acquire the documents. In 2011, the Constitutional Commission of Italy cleared the way for the burqa ban proposed by Berlusconi's Popolo della Libertà party (PDL), but the embattled prime minister resigned before he could make it law. Similarly, the Spanish Cortes appeared poised in 2010 to legislate a burqa ban, but in the end the bill failed by a narrow margin of twenty-one votes. In 2013, the Spanish Supreme Court nullified a municipal burqa ban in Lleida (and therewith bans in several cities across Catalonia). Swiss policies vary from canton to canton. Sixty-five percent of the voters of Ticino voted in 2013 to ban the burqa in public. In Turkey, where veiling has been prohibited in all government institutions since 1923, Prime Minister Recep Tayyip Erdoğan's Justice and Development Party government in 2008 moved to relax the ban at state universities and then for state employees in 2013 (except judges, police, and military officers). The 2008 amendment touched off a firestorm among Kemalist protesters who demonstrated by the tens of thousands against the relaxation as the first step down the slippery slope to an Islamic Republic of Turkey. In the same year, the Constitutional Court declared the amendment null and void (for country-to-country details see VEIL at www.veil-project.eu; Islamaphobia Watch at http;//www.islamophobia.watch.com/islamophobiz-watch/category/hijab; or Siim 2014; Rosenberger and Sauer 2012b; Nielsen 2009).

International bodies are also not marching in lock step. While the European Court of Human Rights in the 2004 case *Şahin v. Turkey* upheld the prerogative of a state to ban veiling in the interest of public order, the European Council in 2010 spoke out against general prohibitions like those against the burqa. The United Nations Commission on Human Rights ruled in 2005 against proscribing the veil (though in a case from Uzbekistan).

FIFA disqualified Iran's female footballers from the 2012 Olympic Games because their uniform included the hijab but issued new rules in 2014 permitting head coverings.

This brief overview stressing controversy and fluidity treats only official policies. Countless female Muslims encounter de facto regulations. Abundant credible sources document the widespread harassment of and discrimination against covered women and girls at work, in school, or on the street (Antidiskriminierungsstelle 2013; Amnesty International 2012; Ansari and Hafez 2012; Gauci 2012; Zick, Küpper, and Hövermann 2011; Zivilcourage und Anti-Rassismus Arbeit 2011; Peucker 2010; Commission on British Muslims and Islamophobia 2004; Forum against Islamophobia and Racism 2002; Runnymede Trust 1997). With the relatively rare exception of those possessing the time, fortitude, and means to endure arduous, lengthy, and expensive legal action in court, such mistreatment represents their lived reality, regardless of what formal law stipulates. The same holds true for female Muslims who are bullied or pressured to cover against their will (Alonso 2012: 479; Ranstorp and Dos Santos 2009; Brouwer 2004: 52; Amara 2003; Macey 1999; Ashfar 1994). Such de facto constraints add to the polymorphous and contradictory character of veiling regulations. Thus, the informal climate regarding Islamic garments can vary between diametrically opposite extremes within the space and time it takes to ride the subway or bus to one's destination.

There is, then, nothing remotely resembling the stable consensus tolerating the outward display of garments and symbols of Christian or Jewish devotion that has long prevailed across Europe. This might incline some to want to conclude that Muslims "brought" the controversy to Europe and that the controversy pits Muslims against non-Muslims. Close examination, however, reveals no firm divide between the two groups. Rather, what can be identified as fragments of liberal, nationalist, and postmodern reasoning turn up among both Muslims and non-Muslims. Furthermore, frequent fragilization occasions blurring of the purely theoretical lines distinguishing the three public philosophies and breeds tolerance of discourses and policies that are "messy . . . [and full of] tensions and contradictions" (Korteweg and Yurdakul 2014: 4). There exists "a range of legal approaches . . . to the handling of the issue by courts, legislatures, human rights activists, the media and within the public debate more generally" (Vakulenko 2012: 55).

Unfree Veil

Many arguments against veiling have a feminist flavor. However, in that they typically object to female heteronomy, most fall within the ethical ambit of liberalism with its insistence on the autonomy of the individual. Furthermore, bans on veiling are often driven by perfectionist reasoning. They are meant to compel women and girls to adorn themselves against their will in the name of liberating them from the alleged error of their ways. Removing the veil is seen as but the first step in a larger process of education and self-reflection that is supposed to culminate in genuine, enlightened rather than illusory, benighted volition on the part of female Muslims. Like Rousseau's Émile, it is presumed, they will one day be grateful for being forced to be free.

Voices condemning veiling as the subjugation of women are many and can be heard across Europe. In her book *The Caged Virgin*, the prominent Dutch feminist Ayaan Hirsi Ali (2006: xi) excoriates the hijab as a "constant reminder to the outside world of a stifling morality that makes Muslim men the owners of women." In Britain, Yasmin Alibhai-Brown, journalist and chairwoman of British Muslims for Secular Democracy, condemns the veil as a "physical manifestation of the pernicious idea of women as carriers of Original Sin" (*Independent* 9 October 2006), while feminist columnist Polly Toynbee maintains that "the ideology of the veil" is "covering and controlling women" (quoted in Cesari 2013: 9). Similarly, The Turkish Federation of Berlin-Brandenburg deplores both the hijab and burqa as "instruments for the oppression of women" (quoted in Yurdakul 2006: 161). Necla Kelek (2007: 114), the author of the 2005 bestseller *Die fremde Braut* (*The Foreign Bride*), alleges that "political Islam wants . . . to establish an Apartheid of the sexes in free European societies," whereby "women in public don't have the right to be human" (quoted in Cesari 2013: 9). Sixty-seven eminent French women signed a petition, originally published in *Le Monde* (7 December 2003) and reprinted in the feminist magazine *Elle* (8 December 2003), that called on Jacques Chirac to pass the law banning the headscarf, arguing that "the Islamic veil . . . subjects all women, Muslim and non-Muslim, to an intolerable discrimination. Any accommodation in this regard would be perceived by every woman in this country as a personal affront on her dignity and liberty." "Remember," beseeches Fadela Amara (2006: 93), the leader of the French association Ni Putes Ni Soumises (Neither Sluts Nor Slaves) and organizer of a national march in 2003 under that slogan, "the headscarf is not simply a religious matter. . . . It is foremost a means of oppression, of alienation, of discrimination, an instrument of power over women used by men." Her successor, Sihem Habchi, maintained that "the burqa is the most violent symbol of the oppression of women and has nothing to do with the Muslim religion, my religion" (quoted in Joppke and Torpey 2013: 25).

Similar liberal fragments frequently fall from the lips of lawmakers. When proposing the ban for public school teachers in Baden-Württemberg in 2004, for example, the *Land*'s (and Germany's future) minister of education, Christian Democrat Annette Schavan, averred that

the headscarf constitutes a political symbol [that is] a part of a female oppressive history. It can symbolize an interpretation of Political Islamism, which conflicts with the principle of equality between
men and women. In that sense, it is also incompatible with a fundamental value embedded in our constitution. (Quoted in Andreassen
and Lettinga 2012: 25)

The Social Democratic president of the German parliament, Wolfgang
Thierse, condemned the headscarf as "a symbol of oppression" (*Frankfurter Allgemeine Zeitung* 4 January 2004). Across the Rhine, Bernard
Stasi, who headed the presidential commission that recommended the
French ban in 2004, referred to the hijab as a "sign of the alienation of
women," while the government's official mediator for helping to resolve
headscarf disputes in schools, Hanifa Cherifi, claimed that the veil represents a "restriction of mixity, of individual liberty, and of gender equality"
(quoted in Laborde 2008: 115). In his defense of the burqa ban of 2011,
President Sarkozy, who had earlier publicly opposed the ban, insisted that
the garment is "not a religious symbol, but a sign of subjugation and degradation" (*Le Monde* 24 June 2009). Demonstrating that opposition to the
burqa is not confined to the political Right, Communist Party member
André Gerin, who introduced in the National Assembly the bill to ban the
burqa, claimed that this "walking prison" subjects women to "an unbear-
able situation of reclusion, exclusion and humiliation. Her very existence
is denied" (*Le Monde* 19 June 2009). Likewise, the legislator who introduced Italy's bill, the Moroccan-born member of Premier Silvio Berlusconi's PDL, Souad Sbai, justified the bill on grounds that "we have to help
women get out of this segregation . . . to get out of this submission. I want
to speak for those who don't have a voice, who don't have the strength to
yell and say, 'I am not doing well'" (*Huffington Post* 2 August 2011). Geert
Wilders, who proposed the burqa ban to the Dutch parliament, derided
the niqab as "an insult to everyone who believes in equal rights" (quoted
in Jenkins 2007: 196). "The Islamic head scarf is a symbol of women's submission," claims the Danish People's Party (quoted in Siim 2014: 225). The
2001 ruling of the European Court of Human Rights in *Lucia Dahlab v.
Switzerland,* which upheld a ban on the headscarf, maintained that the
garment "appears to be imposed on women by a precept that is laid down
in the Koran and which . . . is hard to square with the principle of gender
equality" (quoted in Vakulenko 2012: 46).

Fragments of liberal perfectionism's insistence on informed over merely
free choice invariably crop up in response to complaints that the bans violate the autonomy of Muslim women who freely choose to cover. Thus, Hirsi
Ali (2006: 31–32) retorts:

Because they have internalized their subordination, they no longer experience it as an oppression by an external force but as a strong internal shield. . . . They are like prisoners suffering from Stockholm syndrome, in which hostages fall in love with the hostage takers and establish a deep intimate contact with them.

Likewise, the chairwoman of the Turkish Women's International Network in the Netherlands argues that "restrictions such as wearing headscarves are made up by men who are using women as marionettes. Women . . . maintain that their scarves are a purely voluntary affair, for they do not want to be repudiated by their family and community" (*De Volkskrant* 22 March 2001). Lale Akgün, Bundestag member for the Social Democratic Party (SPD) and its spokesperson on issues related to Islam, dismissed the idea that voluntarily donning a headscarf could represent authentic liberty: "It is absurd to declare clear subordination under a symbol of gender separation as emancipation" (*Tageszeitung* 26 January 2004). A few weeks later, a group of roughly 100 prominent women, many of whom were of Turkish background, reinforced Akgün by contending in an open letter that veiling was rarely voluntary even if women and girls claimed otherwise (*Tageszeitung* 14–15 February 2004). In France, Anne Vigerie of the Cercle d'Etude de Reformes Feministes and Anne Zelensky, president of the Ligue du Droit de Femmes, co-published an editorial insisting that the veil symbolizes "submission to men. The fact that women choose to wear it does nothing to change its meaning. . . . There is no surer oppression than self-oppression" (*Le Monde* 30 May 2003). Following this perfectionist line of thinking, the Stasi Commission refused to hear public testimony from veiled women on grounds that their views could not possibly be autonomous. Likewise, the Conseil Constitutionnel upheld the burqa ban, arguing that those who don it "misrecognize the minimal requirements of living in society" by being unaware that they "find themselves placed in a situation of exclusion and inferiority clearly incompatible with the constitutional principles of freedom and equality" (quoted in Bowen and Rohe 2014: 155).

Liberal perfectionism defends compulsion in the name of emancipating those unwilling to liberate themselves. Thus, French minister of immigration Eric Besson endorsed the burqa ban with the argument that "public authority is founded on protecting the dignity of the person, if necessary against the person herself" (quoted in Joppke and Torpey 2013: 34). Ciska Dresselhuys, chief editor of the Dutch feminist magazine *Opzij*, who refuses to hire veiled reporters, maintains that tolerating the Islamic sartorial practice amounts to "justifying and submitting to an error" (quoted in Andreassen and Lettinga 2012: 19). Although it was not in conjunction with a burqa ban per se, even the Home Office (2002: para. 2.3) foresaw that "it will sometimes be necessary to confront some cultural practices which conflict with these basic [liberal] values—such as those that deny women the right to participate as equal citizens." With similar perfectionist zeal, Article 5 of the UN Convention on the Elimination of all Forms of Discrimination against Women endorses the "modification of social and cultural patterns of conduct of men and women" in an effort to "eliminate prejudices of female inferiority." As Joan Scott (2007: 131) incisively observes, it is only the autonomy of "those who had made the right choice" that is protected.

From the perspective of liberal perfectionism, there is no more appropriate place for the liberal state to force citizens to be free than the public schools. Unsurprisingly, bans apply mostly, though not exclusively, to schools. In the first place, schools rear young and therefore impressionable minds that can supposedly be more easily molded or resocialized away from the illiberal ideas inculcated in the home. The Stasi Commission (Stasi 2004: 128), for example, justified France's 2004 ban with the following reasoning:

> There are pressures constraining young girls to wear religious signs. Their family and social environment impose on them a choice that is not their own. The Republic cannot remain deaf to these girls' cry of distress. The space of the school must remain for them a place of liberty and emancipation.

Across the channel in the Begum case, Baroness Hale approvingly quoted Raday (2003: 709): a "mandatory policy that rejects veiling in state educational institutions may provide a crucial opportunity for girls to choose the feminist freedom of state education over the patriarchal dominance of their families." Similarly, German feminist Alice Schwarzer (2010: 17) has supported a ban on veiling in German schools with the argument that compulsory uncovering exposes the girls to an invaluable critique of their parents' values.

Second, the liberal democratic state, because it is ruled by its citizenry, has an especially acute, even existential interest in fostering liberal citizens. The Stasi Commission (2003: 56), for example, recommended the ban as necessary to fulfill the schools' responsibility to produce "enlightened citizens." It follows in liberal perfectionist logic that the liberal state should permit neither symbols nor acts of repression and subjugation in its schools. In the open letter to President Chirac mentioned above, the sixty-seven signatories averred: "To accept the Muslim headscarf in schools and public administration is to legitimize a symbol of the submission of women in places where the State should guarantee a strict equality of the sexes" (quoted in Cesari 2013: 9). Again, Baroness Hale voiced a similar argument:

Like it or not, this is a society committed, in principle and in law, to equal freedom for men and women to choose how they will lead their lives within the law. Young girls from ethnic, cultural or religious minorities growing up here face particularly difficult choices: how far to adopt or to distance themselves from the dominant culture. A good school will enable and support them. (Quoted in Joppke 2009: 99)

As Hale implies, public schools in liberal democracies should promote open-mindedness and critical thought, including self-reflection, so that their graduates can mature into citizens capable of rational deliberation. Thus, schools must stand as "a privileged locus for the inculcation of the habit of independence through the exercise of critical judgment" (Kintzler 1996: 33). As an allegedly obstinate and obscurantist commitment to Islamic orthodoxy, veiling is said to foreclose dialogue. For instance, Necla Kelek, in supporting a ban on headscarves in German primary schools, contended that the sartorial custom sends the closed-minded message that there is but one form of proper femininity: "This is not compatible with our society, which needs equal, self-assertive, and responsible citizens" (quoted in Deutsche Islam Konferenz 2009). Likewise, Alice Schwarzer (2010: 13) argues that to exempt Muslim girls from co-educational swimming classes because they refuse to don immodest swimwear in the presence of boys is to reinforce rather than challenge gender stereotypes. In the United Kingdom, Dr. Taj Hargey, an imam and chairman of the Muslim Educational Centre of Oxford, endorsed prohibiting the burqa and niqab in public schools because the religious practice "means that Muslim children are being brainwashed into thinking they must segregate and separate themselves from mainstream society" (*Telegraph* 2 October 2010). Something similar seems to be what Tony Blair had in mind when he denounced the garments as "a marker of separation" (*Guardian* 6 October 2006).

Veiling is also objected to with the allegation that it amounts to proselytizing. Furthermore, the long-standing liberal suspicion of religion manifests itself in the insistence that proselytizing should have no place in a school committed to open dialogue and critical examination. Thus, in *Lucia Dahlab v. Switzerland* of 2001, the European Court of Human Rights upheld a school's refusal to let a public school teacher veil in the classroom with the claim that "it cannot be denied outright that the wearing of the headscarf might have some kind of proselytizing effect" (quoted in Vakulenko 2012: 45). An interesting dimension of this fragment of perfectionist logic is the contention that veiling constitutes unwarranted proselytizing *whether or not the veiled Muslim intends it as such*. Such reasoning figured prominently in *Ludin v. Land Baden-Württemberg* of 2003, which legally paved the way for the bans on veiled public school teachers in eight of Germany's sixteen *Länder*. Ludin swore that she covered not in order to proselytize, but to fulfill a purely personal commitment to Islamic piety. The Constitutional Court conceded as much but ruled that the "objective reception" (*objektiver Empfängerhorizont*) of the headscarf among her colleagues and pupils was more significant than her subjective intentions and, therefore, trumped her right to freedom of religion (quoted in Vakulenko 2012: 119). Indeed, the court contended that the mere possibility that the hijab could be perceived as proselytizing merited "precautionary neutrality" (quoted in Saharso 2007: 17). Chancellor Gerhard Schröder defended the ruling by claiming that the German state had no business telling private citizens how to dress, but with teachers acting as public servants in schools, "there we expect another way to dress" (*Frankfurter Allgemeine Zeitung* 24 November 2004).

In France, the veil, even when worn by students, represents what President Chirac termed "an aggressive sign of religious proselytism" (*BBC Online News* 17 December 2003). Likewise, Prime Minister Jean-Pierre Raffarin defended the 2004 ban, maintaining that "religion cannot be a political project as was clearly the case with the wearing of the Islamic veil" (*New York Times* 4 February 2004). Whereas the German justices made the case for "precautionary neutrality," the French National Assembly discerned a need for "reinforced protection" against proselytizing (quoted in Joppke and Torpey 2013: 29). The British House of Lords, in its decision to uphold the ban on the niqab, declared it legal for school officials to "wish to avoid clothes which were perceived by some Muslims (rightly or wrongly) as signifying adherence to an extremist vision of the Muslim religion and to protect girls against external pressures" (quoted in Vakulenko 2012: 122). The High Court agreed in 2007 that "many girls might become subject to pressure to wear the niqab" (quoted in Vakulenko 2012: 63).

Foreign Veil

Fragilization in the direction of nationalism becomes detectible when the entity to be protected by the veiling ban switches from female Muslims to the receiving society. Islamic veiling is objected to less because it subjugates Muslim women and more because it represents an unwanted foreign practice that purportedly disturbs or even imperils the native majority's culture and "way of life." Listen, for instance, to Wilders's animus voiced before parliament in 2007:

Dutch citizens . . . have had enough of burkas, headscarves, the ritual slaughter of animals, so-called honour revenge, blaring minarets, female circumcision, hymen restoration operations, abuse of homosexuals, Turkish and Arabic on the buses and trains as well as on town hall leaflets." (Quoted in Hampshire 2013: 33–34)

The Vlaams Blok calls for the "repatriation of those who reject, deny or combat our culture and certain European values," with one party leader adding that the veil amounts to a "'contract' signed by Muslim women to be deported" (quoted in Bleich 2011: 96).

Grave concern for the well-being of the receiving nation is hardly confined to the Far Right. Prime Minister Raffarin, for instance, argued that the 2004 ban would help to ensure "the permanence of our values" that are "constitutive of our collective history" and the "principal factor of the moral or spiritual unity of our nation" (quoted in Joppke 2009: 50). Likewise, Immigration Minister Besson asserted that "the burka is unacceptable and contrary to the values of the national identity" (*Le Monde* 25 October 2009). In the United Kingdom, shadow Home Minister David Davis maintained that the issue of Islamic veiling raises "the question of the very unity of our nation" (*Sunday Telegraph* 15 October 2006). Self-described "leftie" journalist Yasmin Alibhai-Brown asserted that the niqab so deeply offends British sensibilities that it ought to be proscribed for that reason alone. "There is such a thing as British society," she maintained, implying something like the stance "when in Rome do as the Romans do" (*International Herald Tribune* 23 October 2006). Similarly, Gudrun Krämer (2011), an eminent German scholar of Islam and respected public intellectual, argues that banning the niqab is "legitimate" because the garment is "a demarcation, which in the context of my culture, of German culture, is an expression of latent aggression. That doesn't have to be the case everywhere, above all not in places where most women wear veils; but this is how I perceive it here." Similarly, Dominique Schnapper threw her support behind the burqa ban because "France is the country where everyone says '*bonjour*'" face to face (quoted in Joppke and Torpey 2013: 44).

In political rhetoric nationalist and liberal fragments often fall from the same lips. Thus, Wilders, Alibhai-Brown, Besson, and Raffarin were each quoted above denouncing the veil as a violation of women's individual liberty. Consider Sarkozy's statement that the burqa is

not a religious symbol, but a sign of subservience and debasement. I want to say solemnly, the burka is not welcome in France. In our country, we can't accept women prisoners behind a screen, cut off from all social life, deprived of all identity. This does not conform to our idea of a woman's dignity. (*Le Monde* 24 June 2009)

The concern for the autonomy of the women who wear the burqa is plain. But equally unmistakable is the president's indignation that the act transgresses the French ("our") idea of a woman's dignity. It is hard not to be left with the impression that the indignity is somehow graver because it is happening in "our country" rather than just in any country. We hear similar combining of or fragilization between nationalist and liberal reasoning in the support of banning veiling put forth by Peter Skaarup, a member of parliament representing the Danish People's Party:

> According to Danish norms it is discriminatory to veil. The fact that women must hide their sexuality, cover their hair, that is, in a Danish context, an expression of the devaluation of the woman . . . and that is what we have fought against with our struggle for gender equality, and therefore the veil is a problem for our society. . . . The right thing is therefore to ban the headscarf and live accordingly [sic] to our customs here in Denmark. (Quoted in Andreassen and Lettinga 2012: 22)

We can also read in Skaarup's remark the common complaint that veiling forces the host nation to regress—that is, to reexperience objectionable practices that it had allegedly purged from its ranks. Thus, the populist Dutch politician Pim Fortuyn opined: "I don't feel like having to go through the emancipation of women and homosexuals all over again" (*Volkskrant* 9 February 2002; see also Scheffer 2011: 3). Similarly, British journalist Minette Marrin complained: "A woman shrouded in veils represents . . . a pre-Enlightenment religion and a view of relations between the sexes that the mainstream of this country can no longer accept" (*Sunday Times* 22 October 2006). Again, here, the indignity to the nation caused by veiling would seem to be equal if not greater than that to the female Muslims. Or in Theo Sarrazin's angry words, "I don't have to accept anyone who lives off the state, rejects this same state . . . and constantly produces new little headscarf girls" (quoted in Bahners 2011: 279).

In terms of actual policy, nativism is typically said to have its greatest impact where Islamic veiling is proscribed or circumscribed while sartorial practices more commonly and longer associated with the majority culture are permitted. The country most often spotlighted for such blatant nationalist favoritism is Germany, where public teachers could not (until 2015) don the hijab but could teach in a Christian habit or a Jewish yarmulke (Joppke 2009; Saharso 2007; Amir-Moazami 2007). For example, sentence one of Baden-Württemberg's 2004 statute reads: "Teachers are not allowed . . . [to] give external statements [*äussere Bekundungen*] of a political, religious or ideological nature which could endanger or disturb the neutrality of the *Land* towards pupils or parents or . . . the political, religious or ideological peace of the school." However, sentence three further stipulates: "The representation of Christian or occidental values or traditions corresponds to the educational mandate of the [regional] constitution and does not contradict the behavior required [*Verhaltensgebot*] according to sentence 1" (quoted in Joppke 2009: 72). Unsurprisingly, the Catholic Bishops Conference of Germany (Saharso 2007: 16) and the Jewish Community of Germany (*Spiegelonline* 2 April 2004) endorsed the law. Both reasoned that due to their far deeper heritage in Germany, neither Christian nor Jewish symbols (respectively) should be put on a par with Islamic imagery.

Some qualifications deserve mention. First, eight of sixteen *Länder* proscribed the hijab (as of 2015) but not Jewish or Christian outward symbols. Half of the *Länder* hardly constitutes a national consensus of ethnonationalism. Furthermore, governments that do not formally favor Judeo-Christian symbols do so informally. Take France for example. The 2004 ban does, in keeping with liberal universalism, prohibit all "ostentatious" religious symbols. However, Chirac assured his compatriots that the law was designed to target the "Islamist veil" (*BBC Online News* 17 December 2003) and would only outlaw "manifestly over-sized crosses" and not ones that adorn conventional jewelry such as necklaces or rings (quoted in Hargreaves 2007: 114). In fact, the governmental *circulaire* with instructions on how to implement the 2004 ban gives prerogative to headmasters to proscribe the religious "signs [that are] ostensible in intent," including when the students deny any proselytizing intent. Because most headmasters view neither Jewish nor Christian symbols as intentional proselytizing, Muslim students wind up being the primary target of administrative discretion (Laborde 2008: 65). Indeed, the UN Human Rights Commission's special rapporteur chided the French government for "selective interpretation and rigid application" of the ban as well as for "abuses that provoked feelings of humiliation, in particular amongst young Muslim women" (United Nations 2005). As for the 2011 (burqa) ban on full facial covering in public, it formally exempts facial coverings "in the context of festivities (disguise for a carnival or as Father Christmas) or traditional expressions (processions, particularly religious)" (quoted in Vakulenko 2012: 22).

The point to stress, again, is that the policy reality in France is no more purely republican than it is consistently ethnonationalist in Germany. As for countries that do not proscribe veiling, their public schools either formally or informally tolerate myriad Christian symbols to such an extent that the latter far outnumber Islamic veils in the overwhelming majority of classrooms. Nativist particularism thus proves difficult to eradicate even in states with a formally liberal policy.

Hyperbolic Veil

Fragilization toward postmodernism turns up among the opponents of the veil through hyperbolic exaggeration of the threat it poses. Deliberate hyperbole manifests an appreciation, whether acknowledged or not, of the postmodern postulate that truth is constructed rather than discovered, subjective rather than objective. Like the postmodern icon Andy Warhol's remark that "art is what you can get away with" (originally uttered by Marshall McLuhan), many opponents of veiling seem keen to expand the limits of credulity. In the public letter that arguably elevated the headscarf debate from low to high politics, from political oblivion to "political hysteria" (Terray 2004), five prominent French intellectuals—Alain Finkielkraut, Elisabeth Badinter, Régis Debray, Elisabeth de Fontenay, and Catherine Kintzler—likened Creil in 1989 to Munich in 1938 (the "Munich of the republican school") and beseeched French educators not to repeat the fateful error of appeasement committed by Neville Chamberlain with Hitler (*Le Nouvel Observateur* 2 November 1989). Thus were three teen-aged girls (and no more than an estimated 2,000 veiled pupils in the whole of France) equated with the bellicose chancellor of a mighty nation-state poised to invade and occupy France. The analogy to the Nazis is common. For instance, Chahadortt Djavann (2004), an Iranian novelist domiciled in Paris, has compared the veil to the yellow star forced upon Jews under the Nazi regime; so too has Alice Schwarzer (*Frankfurter Allgemeine Zeitung* 4 July 2006). Likewise, Sarkozy's eventual minister for urban renewal, Fadela Amara, described the hijab as "an instrument of oppression that is imposed by the green [meaning Islamist] fascists" (quoted in Jenkins 2007: 196–97).

Another gross distortion comes in associating the veil with terrorism. Likely the cleverest and most effective wheedling emanated from the Swiss committee Yes to the Ban on Minarets, whose 2009 poster depicted a woman wearing a burqa treading on a Swiss flag from which arose numerous minarets fashioned to resemble missiles. The cover of Melanie Phillips's 2007 bestseller *Londonistan* shows a woman on whose hijab are etched the words "I love Al-Qaeda." The Stasi Commission (2003: sec. 3.2.2) inveighed against veiling as "permanent guerilla war." Regarding a different kind of terrorization, a Spanish government minister likened veiling to "the practice of female genital circumcision. These cannot be understood as a cultural or religious concept, but only as savagery" (quoted in *The Observer* 1 February 2004).

With even greater frequency the veil is equated with cultural annihilation. The reader should keep in mind that of the more than five hundred million persons living in the EU, only between two and three million of them regularly wear Islamic covering in public. For example, Dutch politicians pushing the burqa ban have outlandishly warned that the Netherlands is teetering on the brink of turning into Afghanistan. They deliberately refer to all covered Muslims as burqa-wearers when in fact no more than 400 women wear the black *chador* associated with the Taliban (Moors 2009: 18). The same applies to Vlaams Belang in Belgium, where an estimated thirty women don the chador (Tyrer 2013: 45). Similarly, André Gerin promoted the French burqa ban as a necessary step to halt the "Talibanization" of France (quoted in Joppke and Torpey 2013: 22). As early as 1989, *Le Figaro* had featured a front page depicting Marianne, the historic symbol of the republic, wearing a chador with the headline "Will the French Ever Be French Again?" Likewise, the Danish People's Party (DPP), in a 2009 advertisement, vituperated: "The Islamic head scarf . . . is not only about '30 grams of cloth.' It is about tyranny and submission. . . . Give us back Denmark" (quoted in Siim 2014: 225). As mentioned, Anders Fogh Rasmussen's center-right government in 2009 banned the hijab for judges, though there neither had been nor was at the time a single veiled judge in the Nordic country. Without going so far as to imply, like the DPP, that his homeland actually lay in the possession of veiled Muslims, Siv Jensen, leader of Norway's Progress Party, nevertheless pointed to veiling as evidence of "sneak-Islamization" (*snikislamisiering*) "through the backdoor" (quoted in Siim 2014: 226–27). In 2012, Vlaams Belang politician Filip Dewinter organized a campaign for "women . . . fighting against the Islamization of society" with a poster that depicted his daughter An-Sofie clad in a burqa opened to reveal a bikini. The caption read: "Freedom or Islam? Dare to choose" (*De Standaard* 5 February 2012). Similarly, David Sexton, a columnist for the *Evening Standard* (16 June 2007), hurled invective at the veiled women of the United Kingdom as a "walking rejection of *all* our freedoms" (emphasis mine). For Bernhard Henri Lévy, the very "soul of Europe [is] at stake" (*Libération* 11 February 2008).

"Systematic exaggeration" (Bahners 2011: 154) has extended beyond veiling to other issues affecting female Muslims. So-called "honor killings" of Muslim women who have allegedly disgraced their family by consorting with non-Muslims—for example, Fadime Sahindal (Sweden, 2002), Ghazal Khan (Denmark, 2003), Schijman Kuashi (Netherlands, 2005), Hatan Sürücü (Germany, 2005), and Banaz Mahmod Babakir Agha (Britain, 2007)—have frequently become sensationalized flashpoints (Korteweg and Yurdakul 2014; Fredette 2014: 132). In the case of Sürücü, experts on gender and Islam published an open letter criticizing Islam critics Serap Çileli, Seyran Ateş, and Necla Kelek for deliberately exaggerating and exploiting the case in an effort to advance their personal Islamophobic agendas (Terkessidis and Karakaşoğlu 2006; see also Schneiders 2010b). The film *La Squale* (2000) and the book *Dans l'enfer des tournantes* (translated into English as *To Hell and Back*) by Samira Bellil (2002) focused French national attention on the arresting problem of gang rape among Muslims in the banlieues, when, in fact, the despicable act transpires in non-Muslim circles as well (Muchielli 2005). *Burned Alive*, the 2005 best-selling French memoir of a woman who survived being doused with gasoline and set ablaze by her brother, appears to have been largely fabricated with the assistance of writer and promoter Marie-Thérèse Cuny, who "assisted" at least two other women in similar fashion (Abu-Lughod 2013: 124). So-called "forced marriages" have also garnered much sensationalized attention in widely circulated books such as *Brick Lane* (Ali 2004), *Die Fremde Braut* (Kelek 2005), and *The Caged Virgin* (Hirsi Ali 2006), which depict real or fictional accounts of young women dragooned into marrying men whom they despise (Chin 2010; Surkis 2010). In reality, however, the overwhelming majority of arranged marriages result from negotiations freely entered into by the bride and groom with their parents (Roy 2007: 89). Theo van Gogh and Ayaan Hirsi Ali's *Submission* [2004] provokingly brings all these issues together in a short film shot in English (with Dutch subtitles) that received wide distribution via YouTube. In it, a lone woman narrates the tale of the injustices committed against her by her father, uncle, and husband. Each of the injustices, she claims, is sanctioned by verses in the Qur'an, which she cites and which appear tattooed on her naked body made visible by the sheer, see-through burqa that she wears. The film caused a sensation that culminated in van Gogh's murder at the hand of an incensed Moroccan Dutchman and Hirsi Ali's flight from the Netherlands due to death threats. Perhaps the most incongruous allegation regarding female Muslims fell from the lips of Silvio Berlusconi, who in 2011 tried to justify his relationship with a seventeen-year-old Moroccan prostitute on grounds that he was liberating the damsel from a life of repeated rape and abuse inflicted on her by a misogynistic Islamic culture (Cousin and Vitali 2012: 60).

Gross distortion is not confined to the opponents of veiling. More than a few Islamist organizations seek to reverse the stigmatization of veiling by demonizing the uncovered. I employ the admittedly imperfect term "Islamism" loosely and broadly to envelop the beliefs of all those who strive toward a society in which Islamic precepts and laws—typically understood as those enunciated in the Qur'an and Sunna—predominate. Among those I label "Islamists" the general idea tends to prevail that God revealed through the Prophet Muhammad (and by some accounts certain subsequent Hadith as well) sufficient guidelines for leading a morally upstanding life as an individual and as a community in all times and places. Islamists tend in various ways to see Islam as integral rather than antithetical to modern life and believe that the latter needs to conform to the former rather than vice versa (Göle 2004: 14–15). They view and practice "Islam as a way of life" (a

common slogan among Islamists) rather than a private spiritual confession
(Maréchal 2008: 204–7). Due to limited space, I gloss over the significant
differences in strategy for achieving the Islamist goal—differences ranging
from pietist personal conversion stressed by such groups as Tablighi Jamaat
(Association for the Propagation of Islam), Jamaat Nur, the Süleymanli, and
the Gülen Movement, to nonviolent political action practiced by the Muslim Brotherhood and its European affiliate, the Union of Islamic Organizations in Europe (UOIE), the Islamische Gemeinde Milli Görüş (IGMG), the
Muslim Council of Britain (MCB), or the Jama'at-i Islami, to violent jihadist
militant organizations such as Hizb ut-Tahrir (arguably), Al-Muhajiroun,
Supporters of Shariah, Islamic Cultural Institute of Milan, Al-Jama'a Al-
Islamiya, and Groupe Islamique Armé. The connections between these Islamist organizations are typically informal and often strained, though they
all tend to see themselves working in the service of the international Islamic
community or *umma* (Ceylan and Kiefer 2013: 82–88; Pargeter 2008: 65).
As a leader of the United Kingdom Islamic Mission (UKIM) remarked, "We
belong to the international Islamic movement, neither to *Jama'at*, nor to *Ikh-
wan* [Muslim Brotherhood] nor to the [Islamist] *Refah* party in Turkey—but
all of them are our friends" (quoted in Vidino 2006). "Notwithstanding their
variations," observes one analyst, "Islamists in general deploy a religious
language and conceptual frame, favor conservative social mores and an exclusive social order, espouse a patriarchal disposition, and adopt broadly
intolerant attitudes toward different ideas and lifestyles" (Bayat 2013b: 7).
Furthermore, despite adhering to distinct schools of Islamic jurisprudence
(*fiqh*), such as the Mâliki (North Africa), Hanafî (Turkey, India), Hanbalî
(Saudi Arabia), and Shâfi'î (Egypt), what I am calling "Islamist" organizations typically interpret some form of veiling outside the exclusive presence
of family as a religious obligation (Hellyer 2006: 340). But let the reader be
forewarned that Islamist (not to mention Islamic) doctrine and practice are
highly complex and evolving phenomena, full treatment of which would demand a separate volume (Mandaville 2014; Cesari 2013; Leiken 2012; Laurence 2012; Yükleyen 2012; Göle 2011; Vidino 2010b; Bowen 2010; Roy 2007;
2005; Abu Zayd 2006; Nielsen 2003; Schiffauer 2000).

To reiterate, Islamist organizations and personalities frequently employ
distorting images and claims in their effort to defend and encourage veiling. Non-Muslim European women are often depicted as sinfully unchaste,
indeed wantonly oversexed and sexualized. Thus, the Union for Islamic
Development and Culture in Bulgaria laments that "women can be seen in
the streets dressed in clothes that barely cover their underwear (and this
is taken as normal) . . . [trying] to appear as sexually attractive as possible
. . . and disappointed if no one turns their head to look at them" (quoted in
Ghodsee 2012: 119). Al-Muhajiroun claims that in British secular schools

"children are taught to conform to a code of dress that shows their nakedness. . . . Children grow up idolizing pop-stars and footballers rather than
appreciating the Messengers from their creator and worshiping God alone"
(quoted in Wiktorowicz 2005: 169). The preoccupation with women and
girls as sex objects is typically made to mushroom into myriad additional
problems that plague Western women's lives. In her study of the Swedish
journal *Salaam*, for instance, Jonas Otterbeck (2000: 259) found that

> Swedish (or Western) women is a recurrent theme. The Swedish
> woman . . . is described as a victim of several powers. She is exploited
> by commercialism, especially by the fashion industry. She is over-
> worked and underpaid, has a full-time job and all the housework.
> She never has time for her children who will end up on the streets
> which will lead them to self-destruction, drugs, crimes and a high
> suicide rate. Her marriage will eventually break down and lead to
> divorce due to unrealistic hopes built on the first moments of love
> and passion in the relationship.

By contrast, the veil is implausibly exalted as a foolproof safeguard
against perilous Westernization. Fereshta Ludin, the woman at the center
of Germany's headscarf controversy, insisted that her veil ensured "protection against Western decadence" (quoted in Oestreich 2004: 116). Inversely,
Muslims are warned at websites such as "The Choice between the Burka and
the Bikini" that removing the veil in public represents the first capricious
step down a treacherous path ineluctably leading to mundane profanity
and eternal damnation (www.allaahuakbar.net/womens/choice_between_
burka_and_bikini.htm). Likewise, at the website "Islam: Die Wahre Religion," German Salafist Ibrahim Abou-Nagie warns that unveiled women
will land in hell (www.diewahrereligion.de). One internet meme that has
found wide distribution depicts a veiled woman ascending a staircase to
heaven and an unveiled, secularly clad woman descending a staircase into
hell. Unveiling is further said to invite certain harassment from lascivious
Western men, which will either lead to rape or, worse, consorting and fornicating with them which, in turn, will alienate the wayward women from
their true family and community. Typically, verses from the Qur'an will be
cited to emphasize divine injunction: "O Prophet! Tell thy wives and daughters, and the believing women, that they should cast their outer garments
over their persons (when outside): that they should be known (as such) and
not molested" (Qur'an 33:59). Such purported Qur'anic approbation is reinforced by an abundance of popular film and fiction widely distributed
among Muslim immigrants that dramatize stories of unsuspecting Muslim
daughters and wives lured from chastity and piety into depravity and ruin

by mischievous European playboys (Gerlach 2006: 58–59). So great appeared the danger that Sheikh Mohamad Kamal Mostafá of Fuengirola, Spain, published the book *Women in Islam,* which instructed Muslim men to beat their wives and daughters if necessary to keep them from straying from Islamic virtue. When it was learned that the book was widely circulated by major Islamist institutions in Madrid and Barcelona, a national furor erupted that culminated in criminal prosecution of the author (Jenkins 2007: 184–85). Similarly, Swedes were riled in 2012 when an undercover camera team from Swedish Television taped imams in several (state-funded) mosques advising wives to tolerate beatings from and unwanted sex with their husbands (Yilner 2012). France deported Tunisian imam Mohamed Hammami in the same year for advocating corporal punishment of wayward wives and daughters (*Al Jazeera,* 31 October 2012), just as it had done with Abdelkader Bouziane in 2004 (*Le Monde* 6 October 2004). An uproar was ignited in 2001 when Khalil El-Moumni, a conservative imam from Rotterdam, asserted in a television interview that un-Islamic sexual impropriety can lead to rampant homosexuality, as evidenced by the legalization of same-sex marriage in the Netherlands. This "sin," he added, if not stopped "will lead to extinction," "for who will make children when men and women can marry each other?" (quoted in Uitermark, Mepschen, and Duyvendak 2014: 243).

I do not aim to bombard the reader with outlandish allegations. I wish rather to point out fragilization toward postmodernism's tenet that truth is whatever passes for truth. These anti-European allegations are no less essentializing distortions of Europeans than are the anti-Islamic insinuations that Muslims are misogynist. The former too blatantly ignore conspicuous counter-evidence of non-Muslim European men and women who do not fit the stereotype. Furthermore, the preposterous notion that veil-lessness leads to certain ruin engages no less in fear-mongering than the claims of the impending Islamization of Europe. Just as the Islam-bashers gloss over the fact that an extremely small proportion of women in Europe cover, the defenders of strict Islamic orthodoxy equally glaringly overlook the thousands upon thousands of devout Muslim women who regularly attend mosque but who choose to cover only there in the sacred sanctuary (Mandel 2008: 306). Like the Islamophobes, the Islamists spotlight extreme and typically rare cases and pass them off as the norm. They also conveniently neglect the more nuanced dialogue and debate among sophisticated exegetes of the Qur'an regarding what the holy writ does and does not require women to wear (for example, Kaddor 2010; Hamidi 2009; Mohr 2006; Safi 2003; Barlas 2002).

Islamists' rejection of modern European society does not have to mean that they are unaffected by it. Keep in mind that they must regularly witness their adversaries shrewdly and effectively producing and circulating gross distortions of the veiling phenomenon. They cannot be unaware that for vast numbers of Europeans such distortions pass for truth. In a You-Tube video spotlighting the conversion of women to Islam, the imam of the video's sponsor, the Central Mosque of Birmingham, explains to watchers that rampant Islamophobia spreads apocryphal slander regarding the status and treatment of women in Islam (https://www.youtube.com/watch?v=Cx37WaHDwuc). Nor can Islamists be unaware that the images inform policy makers and policy. Islamists, then, hardly need to read Nietzsche or Foucault to conclude that, in politics at least, knowledge is constructed to serve partial interests and agendas. Likewise, they do not need to steep themselves in Stanley Fish's (1999: 273) postmodern analysis to recognize that political actors who confine their pronouncements and programs to what is objectively true more likely hamper than help their political fortunes. The theory of fragilization does not necessitate the total conversion to postmodernism and rejection of Islam. The theory posits only a softening or opening toward some fragmentary aspects of a public philosophy with which one does not explicitly identify.

Postcolonial Veil

Another postmodern fragment that Islamists often invoke to oppose bans on veiling is the postcolonial trope. Postcolonial analysis of anti-veiling rhetoric and regulation abounds. All take a page from Edward Said's influential *Orientalism*, which, as discussed in Chapter 2, analyzed the phenomenon as a power-knowledge discourse enabling and legitimizing European domination of the Orient. During colonial times, asserts Leyla Ahmed (1992: 152), the veil represented "the most visible marker of the differentness and inferiority of Islamic societies." The French, for instance, publicly and forcibly unveiled Muslim women during the war of independence in Algeria to demonstrate the necessity of French colonial rule for the liberation of women (Vakulenko 2012: 97; Mas 2006; Bouteldja 2004). The "civilizing mission" (Vergès 2011) is said to be resurrected through a "neocolonial attitude" (Amiraux 2006: 30) and "post-colonial discourse" (Freedman 2006: 181) that represents veiled Muslims in Europe as benighted and subjugated. In the "subalternization" of the headscarf controversy (Berghahn 2009: 61), "leaders, intellectuals and feminists all speak for Muslim women, thereby infantilizing them and reinscribing colonial binary oppositions—secular/religious, free/oppressed, liberal/illiberal and the like—that further deprive them of agency" (Cesari 2013: 143). Needless to say, "the hegemonic policy of representation dominated by the logic of speaking about and not with the Other" (Amir-Moazami and Salvatore 2003: 73) self-servingly projects a flattering image of non-Muslim European women (as well as their men who do not force them to veil) as enlightened and liberated (Mavelli 2012: 68;

Göle 2011: 94; Mandel 2008: 294–310; Scott 2007: 161–62; Freedman 2006: 181; Guénif-Souilamas 2006; Terray 2004). "Muslims are constructed as the 'other' to modern European democracies and the boundaries of 'belonging' are renegotiated within the context of the headscarf debates" (Gresch, Rostock, and Kiliç 2012: 56). Sarkozy is said to have subconsciously acknowledged the ultimately ideological and political nature of the neo-Orientalist discourse in his remark "If I enter a mosque, I take off my shoes. If a young Muslim enters school, she has to take off her veil" (*Le Figaro* 12 September 2003). *Laïcité* is thus exposed as no less a particular faith than Islam and unveiling as no less politically imposed than the proscription on shoes in mosques (Vakulenko 2012: 118).

It goes without saying that Islamists are familiar with Said's *Orientalism*. But Islamists appear to be familiar with and keen to exploit postcolonial analysis far beyond the pioneering classic (Kersten 2011: 12–25). For example, Houria Bouteldja (2004) of the European Muslim Network denounces the "neo-colonial instrumentalization of the cause of women." She avers that "the media frenzy over the full-face veil ban in France is the latest political maneuver by the Sarkozy government looking to frame the presence and visibility of . . . Muslims . . . as a threat to national identity" (Bouteldja 2011). Iqbal Sacranie, erstwhile head of the Muslim Council of Britain, discerned in the French ban of 2004 "an institutionalized Islamophobia that is unfortunately taking root in several parts of Europe. . . . Banning *hijab* will send a strong signal throughout the Muslim world that the French government is intent on revisiting its dark and brutal days in North and West Africa" (quoted in Baran 2011: 145).Those Anna Piela (2010: 429) dubs "Islamist feminists" are wont to complain of a double stigmatization of female Muslims through neo-Orientalist discourse: first for simply being Muslims and second for being the pious adherents of a faith that particularly oppresses women. Rather than being seriously asked why they cover, veiled Muslim women are presumed to have no autonomous opinion of their own. Albeit a male, an imam with the L'union des Organisations Islamique de France (UOIF) complained on behalf of his confessional sisters: "Muslim women who wear a *foulard* are still asking themselves why our French co-citizens feel ill at ease with them, and they have no satisfactory answer" (*Le Monde* 5 September 2004). Samy Debah, head of the French Collective against Islamophobia, deploys a postcolonial fragment in his critique of the burqa ban: "The niqab law is a pretext to reduce the visibility of Muslims in public spaces. It exposes an old French colonial reflex, that 'Arabs and blacks' only understand force and you can't talk to them" (*Guardian* 12 April 2011). Although the "colonial reflex" would, of course, not be appropriate in the German case, we can still discern the tone of stigmatization and domination in the opposition of the IGMG to the German ban for school teachers: it "cultivates prejudices against Muslims, encourages continued discrimination against Muslims in all social spheres, and negatively affects the integration efforts of Muslims" (quoted in Yurdakul 2006: 151). Similarly, Sacranie responded to Salman Rushdie's assertion that the veil "sucks" by saying, "Islamophobes are currently doing all they can to attack Islam" (*Telegraph* 11 October 2006). Massoud Shadjareh, chair of the Islamic Human Rights Commission in London, reproved the 2014 ruling of the European Court of Human Rights upholding the French burqa ban:

> This judgment is indicative of the structural marginalisation of Muslims. . . . This judgment is yet another that has refused to uphold core human rights values for some of the most oppressed within European society, in particular, Muslims targeted by discriminatory national laws. (The Islamic Human Rights Commission, 4 September, 2014, www.ihrc.org.uk)

Fatima, one of the three girls originally expelled in Creil in 1989, simply exclaimed regarding the French authorities: "They have taken revenge on us" (quoted in Collet 2004: 135).

From this perspective, veiling becomes an act of real and symbolic resistance to Western demonization and domination of Muslims. An imam with the Union of French Islamic Organizations (UOIF), for example, implored Muslims to defy the 2004 ban (*Le Monde* 5 September 2004). Similarly, Mohamad Achamlane, leader of the Islamist organization Forsane Alizza (Knights of Pride), which was outlawed by the French Interior Ministry in 2012, publicly burned the French civil code to demonstrate his organization's defiance of the burqa ban (*BBC News* 30 March 2012). In response to the Dutch Equal Treatment Commission's 2005 ruling that the Islamic College in Amsterdam could not fire Samira Hadad for wishing to teach without a hijab, the college's administration stated its intent not to comply with the decision (Vakulenko 2012: 39–40). The Munich-based hip-hop star Ammar implores female Muslims to "never give up": "Even if they continue to spread lies/Allah will stand by you" (quoted in Gerlach 2006: 92–93; my translation from the German).

It is hard not to detect in such rebellious words and deeds the influence of Frantz Fanon's (1965a) *The Wretched of the Earth*. The anticolonial celebrity wrote:

> In the beginning the veil was a mechanism of resistance, but its value for the social group remained very strong. The veil was worn because tradition demanded a rigid separation of the sexes but also because the occupier was bent on unveiling Algeria. (Fanon 1965b: 63)

Nor can it be lost on any committed Islamist that the uproar over veiling in Europe began only in the wake of and in response to the Iranian Revolution and its resistance to Western domination. Needless to say, nowhere in Europe are Islamists leading a war of independence on the scale of Algeria in the 1950s or a revolution like Iran's in 1979, but in those corners of Europe where veiling is mandatory Islamists have effected what we can call "micro-rebellions." In 2011, for example, Anjem Choudary, leader of the banned Islam4UK, created a stir when he announced a campaign to establish in several British cities "Shariah-controlled zones" in which, among other things, uncovered women would be proscribed. Choudary himself seems to have had little success (*Daily Mail* 28 July 2011), and, of course, public veiling is de jure mandatory nowhere in Europe.

However, there are areas—some small, others rather expansive—where veiling is for all intents and purposes de facto law. There female Muslims beyond the age of puberty are placed under so much pressure to cover in public that for them the de facto law of the street trumps formal law. Women, Muslim and non-Muslim, who fail or refuse to observe the mandate are harassed and even driven out of the area, which can be a single street, apartment complex, or entire neighborhood (Alonso 2012: 479; Gest 2010: 103; Ranstorp and Dos Santos 2009; Roy 2007: 85; Jenkins 2007: 182, 252; Obin 2004; Brouwer 2004: 50–51; Kepel 2004: 51; Amara 2003; Macey 1999; Ashfar 1994). For example, in the Band of Gold campaign in both Birmingham and Bradford during 1995 young Muslim men harassed and eventually expelled prostitutes from their neighborhoods (Samad 2007: 166). Salafi associations often organize campaigns to denounce unveiled women and girls in neighborhoods and schools where their members are highly concentrated (Kepel 2004: 51). With considerable financial resources at hand due to Saudi ties, Salafi foundations are known to deny grants to applying organizations that tolerate uncovered female members (Bowen 2010: 117). When in 2003 Interior Minister Sarkozy told an audience of the UOIF (with ties to the Muslim Brotherhood movement) that women would have to unveil for their official ID photos, he was literally booed off the stage. Indeed, the French press's spotlighting of the event figured significantly in the subsequent legislating of the 2004 ban (Joppke 2009: 46).

We should take pains not to exaggerate the intimidation of Islamist resistance. In the first place, harassment of veiled women surely exceeds that of unveiled women in both frequency and intensity. In the second place, more than a few women pressured to cover simply remove the hijab once they have exited the "*sharia* zone," or they move out of the zone altogether (Roy 2007: 86–87). As Roy (2007: 97) sagely observes, Islamic fundamentalists, like Christian and Jewish—or even atheist fundamentalists for that matter—would not be true to their beliefs if they did not try to realize them in practice. Thus, Islamist entrepreneurs have opened women-only Islamic gyms (for instance, Al-Hayat in Cologne and Orty in Paris) where female Muslims can exercise without violating *sharia*. Because Islamic fundamentalists tend to view going out uncovered in public as a sin, they would be impious if they were not to oppose and resist statutes banning the veil. It should be, then, in a liberal democracy neither surprising nor alarming that Islamist organizations such as the UOIF and IGMG sponsor the legal endeavors of women and girls sacked or expelled for veiling to overturn the bans. It should shock no one that the deputy head of the Muslim Council of Britain, Inayat Bunglawala, chastised British Muslims for Secular Democracy in 2002 for permitting female members of its organization to unveil (Baran 2011: 133). Nor should it be considered unusual or untoward that Islamists proselytize. Jusuf al-Qaradawi, leader of the European Council for Fatwa and Research (ECFR), tells his millions of followers on television and the internet that all Muslims "should keep up in mind that calling others to Islam is not only restricted to scholars and sheikhs, but it goes far to encompass every committed Muslim," including female Muslims, who should seek to convince their non-Muslim sisters of the virtue of dressing modestly (quoted in Shavit 2007: 16). Or as Nadeem Elyas, chairman of the Zentralrat (Central Council) der Muslime in Deutschland put the matter, his organization would observe German laws even if they violate Islamic precepts "as long as Muslims are in the minority" (quoted in Joppke 2009: 114). Likewise, Abdallah ben Mansour, former secretary-general of the UOIF, stated that "a law once forced Jews to wear yellow stars, and was eliminated. . . . As long as the law prohibits the veil, we will respect it, but we will try to get it changed" (*Le Figaro* 6 May 2003). It should also be noted with regard to the allegation that Islamists want to impose veiling that when two French reporters were kidnapped in Iraq in 2004 and held as ransom in exchange for rescinding the ban in France, all major French Islamist organizations denounced the deed and implored the French state not to accede to the demands. The UIOF spokeswoman said she would readily replace one of the journalists rather than have her veil "tainted with the hostages' blood" (quoted in openDemocracy 11 November 2004; https://www.opendemocracy.net/faith-europe_islam/article_2216.jsp).

Voluntary Veil

Once European Muslims begin to seek rather than spurn the approbation of the state, they drift (or fragilize) away from Hobbesian postmodernism into the normative orbit of either liberal multiculturalism or communitarianism. Hobbesian postmodernism interprets European states as instruments of domination in the hands of non-Muslim majorities for whom the

demonization of Muslims is constitutive of their very identity. Here beneficial state assistance for Muslims is by definition impossible. The only sensible position is resistance and revolution.

For many Muslims, usurping the European state is neither possible nor
desirable. They want the state's support for their religious practices and
therefore work either to prevent or to rescind veiling bans. An obvious place
to turn for normative backing is to liberal multiculturalism. They contend
that Muslims should enjoy the same rights as non-Muslims. IGMG, for example, frequently argues that women should be no less free to don the hijab
than to wear a miniskirt (Amiraux 2007: 138). Needless to say, the Islamist
organization does not condone miniskirts. However, in a normative milieu
with a venerable liberal tradition of defending individual liberties it makes
political sense to offer the analogy. Thus, the Islamic Human Rights Commission (in the U.K.) has "urged people to be supportive for [sic] a woman's
right to wear the veil as this complies with the values upon which western
civilization was founded—the protection of human and religious rights"
(quoted in Hadj-Abdou and Woodhead 2012: 192). The association Critical Muslims in Denmark claims veiling is justified by the "freedom of religion and self-definition" (quoted in Gresch, Rostock, and Kiliç 2012: 66).
Many Muslim organizations opposed to veiling bans invoke, like the UIOF
(Hervieu-Léger 2007: 213), Article 9 of the European Convention on Human
Rights, which stipulates that "everyone has the right to freedom of thought,
conscience and religion . . . either alone or in community with others and
in public or private, to manifest his religion or belief, in worship, teaching,
practice and observance." "The way forward," argues the Polder Moslima
Headscarf Brigade, the Dutch association of professional Muslim women
formed in 2009,

> is not to insist on social, let alone theological, conformity, but on
> observance of the law and the basic rules of democratic society. As
> long as people play by the rules of free speech, free expression, inde-
> pendent judiciaries, and free elections, they are democratic citizens,
> whatever they choose to wear on their heads. (Quoted in Buruma
> 2010: 114–15)

French Muslims have cleverly expressed this liberal normative fragment
by wearing hijabs made from the French tricolors to their public demonstrations against the bans (Strassburger 2000). The British organization
Protect Hijab campaigns with the slogan "Our Choice, Our Freedom, Our
Right" (quoted in Hadj-Abdou and Woodhead 2012: 192), while the fashion
company StyleIslam sells thousands of tote bags inscribed with "Hijab, My

Right, My Choice, My Life" (http://www.styleislam.eu/?ActionCall=WebAc tionArticleSearch&Params%5BSearchParam%5D=hijab).

Ample scholarship exists demonstrating that covering can enhance rather than undermine personal autonomy. The reader will remember from Chapter 2 the tenet of liberal multiculturalism whereby robust affiliation with a religious or ethnic community can fortify rather than endanger self-determination. Regarding the headscarf, the pioneering study was conducted by Françoise Gaspard and Farhad Khosrokhavar (1995: 47), who concluded that many of their subjects "desire to be French and Muslim, modern and veiled, autonomous and dressed in the Islamic way" (see also Abu-Lughod 2013; Göle 2011: 134–36; Haug, Müssig, and Stichs 2010; Jessen and Wilamowitz-Moellendorff 2006; Karakaşoğlu-Aydin 2000; Klinkhammer 2000; El Guindi 1999). Subsequent studies have found that while veiling can exemplify mass conformity in Muslim majority societies where the sartorial habit is commonplace, in Europe it often represents a "mark of bold individualism" (Favell 1998: 178). Shabina Begum, the girl at the center of the jilbab controversy in the United Kingdom, complained to *BBC Online News* (22 March 2006; http://news.bbc.co.uk/2/hi/4832072.stm): "I don't see why I was told to go home from school when I was just practicing my religion. I'm just a teenager—not many teenagers go out there and challenge the system." Indeed, Anastasia Vakulenko (2012: 124) reports that in practically all of the high-profile court cases involving veiling, lawyers for covered girls and women have emphasized the courage and independence demanded to swim against the tide of secular mass conformity. Researchers also find that veiling frequently expresses an admirable statement against discrimination and symbolizes praiseworthy solidarity with the oppressed that under other circumstances most people would approvingly associate with human rights activists (Göle 2003: 820–24). On a personal level, the decision to veil can open up opportunities for significant growth and independence. For example, female Muslims can appease or outmaneuver conservative family members who might attempt to impede their wives, daughters, or sisters from taking a job outside the home or pursuing a diploma if they were to insist on doing so without the veil. Similarly, young Muslims can and do subtly challenge and change tradition by choosing different styles of hijab not worn, for example, by the older generation (Bowen 2012b: 71–74; Dwyer 1999: 5). Piela (2010: 429) identifies "Muslim feminists" who outspokenly condemn patriarchal practices of compulsory veiling that have no credible justification in the Qur'an. Indeed, they equate patriarchy with blasphemy because it exalts men rather than reserving exaltation for God alone (Piela 2010: 431; see also Ali 2014). These free-thinking Muslims tend to insist that the holy script is open to multiple plausible interpretations and that, therefore, each pious woman should decide herself when, where, how, and whether God obligates her to cover (Piela 2010: 426).

Prominent Muslims echo these academic findings and thereby distribute them beyond the confines of the academy. Lord Bhikhu Parekh (1999: 73), who served as chairman of the Commission on the Future of Multi-Ethnic Britain from 1998 to 2000, explains that covering can be "a highly complex autonomous act intended both to remain within the tradition and to challenge it. . . . To see it merely as a symbol of their subordination . . . is to miss the subtle dialectic of cultural contestation." In 2010, Baroness Sayeeda Warsi, the first Muslim cabinet minister in the U.K., weighed in on the burqa controversy in favor of free choice, claiming "just because a woman wears the burqa, it doesn't mean she can't engage in everyday life" (quoted in Chesler 2010: 42). Ayten Kiliçarslan (2014), member of the executive committee of the Turkish-Islamic Union for Religious Affairs and the only veiled member of the Deutsche Islam Konferenz sponsored by the Federal Ministry of the Interior, contends that only those who wish to ban the veil see it (mistakenly) as unwanted subjugation: "No woman who wears the headscarf of her own free will sees it as a symbol of oppression." "The state should remain neutral regarding the different interpretations of the headscarf." As mentioned, Asmaa Abdol-Hamid caused a stir in 2006 when she became the first veiled woman to host a talk show (*Adam og Asmaa*) on Danish TV. She went on to become a candidate for parliament with the Red-Green Alliance. "Wearing a headscarf does not mean that I'm oppressed or deprived," she insisted. "Otherwise I wouldn't have got so far as I have today" (*KVINFO* 16 May 2007; http://kvinfo.dk/search?filter=Asmaa+Abdol-Hamid+). Islamic women's organizations such Al Nisa (Netherlands), trendy magazines for female Muslims such as *Sisters* (U.K.) or *Ala* (Turkey) or upscale on-line fashion studios such as New Hijab in Geneva (www.newhijab.com) or MuslimGear (www.muslimgear.com) widely distribute images and stories of veiled women leading modern, independent lifestyles. These "hijabistas," as they are sometimes labeled, want to look and feel as fashionable and "together" as non-Muslim "fashionistas." In Germany, the younger ones are called *Frauleinwunder,* veiled girls who creatively dress themselves in ways that express eroticism more cleverly than their unveiled counterparts (Mandel 2008: 309).

The freedom to choose to cover or not resonates with many influential non-Muslims. "We are a free country," declared David Cameron. "People should be free to wear whatever clothes they like in public or in private." He added, however, that the niqab should be proscribed in court because "a jury needs to be able to look at someone's face" (*Reuters* 29 September 2013.) Tony Blair had said of the veiling debate in 2006: "Issues such as these are matters of personal views, not government policies" (quoted in Joppke 2009:

24). Similarly, Interior Minister Sarkozy opposed the proposed 2004 ban because veiling "is a personal decision that belongs to the private sphere. As for the question of the veil in schools, the Conseil d'Etat has already made a decision [to permit veiling]" (*Libération* 21 February 2003). In 2005, a group of sixty-eight members of the European Parliament signed and published a *Written Declaration on Religious Rights and Freedoms in France and throughout the European Union*, which berated the French ban as a violation of the religious freedom that the EU should guarantee in all its member countries. German president Johannes Rau, warning in 2003 against the slippery slope, said that "banning the headscarf is the first step toward the creation of a secular state that bans religious signs and symbols from public life" (quoted in Klausen 2005: 153). In that same year, three German politicians renowned for their involvement with immigration issues, Rita Süssmuth (CDU), Barbara John (CDU), and Marieluise Beck (Greens), opposed the ban for school teachers in an open letter published in *Die Tageszeitung* (15 December 2003):

> The equal treatment of all religions is mandated by the constitution. A different treatment of Islamic symbols as opposed to Christian or Jewish ones is problematic from the viewpoint of integration and exacerbates conflicts instead of reducing them. (Quoted in Yurdakul 2006: 160)

German cardinal Ratzinger (the future Pope Benedict XVI) opined that "I would not prohibit a Muslim woman from wearing the headscarf," though he added in particularist language, "but even less are we prepared to accept prohibition of the cross" (quoted in Joppke 2009: 71). The archbishop of Canterbury also defended veiling, arguing that "the ideal of a society where no visible public signs of religion would be seen . . . is a politically dangerous one" (*Jurist* 23 October 2006). Add to these high-profile individuals outspoken NGOs such as Human Rights Watch, Human Rights without Frontiers, and International and Minority Rights Group, all of which condemn France's bans (Vakulenko 2012: 19). Amnesty International, for example, denounces the ban as a violation of women's "rights to freedom of expression and religion" (*BBC News* 27 November 2013).

Freedom to don the Islamic veil is well established in much European statute. Despite the many polls, parties, and politicians opposed to veiling, the practice is permitted in Europe much more than it is prohibited. Furthermore, where bans exist, they typically face formidable battles in local, regional, national, or international courts that more often than not decide against the proscriptions (for instance, Germany in 2015). As Joppke (2009: 20) concludes, through "(mostly) silent and highly legalistic ways . . . the

Islamic headscarf has made mighty inroads into western societies." As far as veiling is concerned, dire warnings that Europe lies poised to repeat with its Muslim citizens the abominable persecution it once committed against Jews are overblown. They are better understood as deliberate political hyperbole designed to construct rather than reflect truth.

Mandated Veil

When Muslims seek state authority to mandate rather than simply wear the veil, they tend to employ fragments of communitarian logic. They contend that non-Muslims cannot grasp the persistent and profound importance of veiling within Islam. For these (mostly Islamist) Muslims, covering is a plainly divine commandment, and piety lies in submitting to God's will. From this perspective, the right to choose to cover or not is itself a sin. It transfers the authority to determine right and wrong from God to the individual, which represents the unholiest of blasphemies. The religious obligation of the believing Muslim is to obey, not to judge God (Asad 2003: 197). Listen to the reasoning in an open letter to President Chirac published in 2003 by the ECFR, led, as mentioned, by Jusuf al-Qaradawi, whose books such as *The Lawful and the Prohibited in Islam* and *On the Jurisprudence of Muslim Minorities* are translated into multiple languages and distributed widely throughout Muslim communities in Europe:

> Wearing the headscarf is a devotional commandment and a duty prescribed by the Islamic Law, and not merely a religious or political symbol. Islamic women consider this to be an important part of their practising of the teachings of their religion. This adherence is a commandment that has not been made conditional on any (specific) public place, regardless whether this is a place for religious service or an official or non-official institution. By their very nature, the teachings of Islam do not know any contradiction or division in the life of a Muslim practising his religion. This is a matter upon which all Islamic schools in past and present have agreed and which has been confirmed by specialised Muslim scholars in all parts of the world. (Quoted in Shadid and van Koningsveld 2005: 36–37)

Ali Kizilkaya, longtime IGMG activist and chair of the Koordinierungsrat (Coordination Council) der Muslime in Deutschland (KRM), which itself acts as the officially recognized representative of Islam in the North Rhine-Westphalia, caused a stir in 2006 when he insisted that veiling is an unconditional "religious commandment" that "cannot be contextualised according to different countries and places" (quoted in *Qantara.de* 19 October 2012).

The inconveniences of veiling are not lost on pious Muslim women. However, they view the practice differently than secular individualists. Those Piela (2010: 433) labels "non-feminist traditionalists" interpret the hardships of abiding by traditional gender precepts, like veiling, polygamy, or docile obedience to husbands, as tests designed by God that if passed will result in eternal salvation—a far greater joy than, say, unveiling on a hot day. In this same vein the Union for Islamic Development and Culture in Bulgaria contends that the

> hijab is not an attribute of fake modesty. It delivers a certain message to people. First, the message is that the woman has decided to submit all aspects of her life to the will of God; and second, that she wants to be judged on the basis of her virtues and deeds and not her beauty, elegance and sex appeal. (Quoted in Ghodsee 2012: 120)

Actually, however, the communitarian stance is not that non-Muslim officials should comprehend, let alone agree with this line of pious thinking. Rather, precisely because it strikes them as alien, they ought not to meddle. They ought to grant Islamic organizations the presumption of equal worth and that they have compelling reasons unique to their own tradition and community for mandating veiling. After all, Islam antedates secular European states and will likely outlive them. The wisdom of Islam—a world religion—is well established and should stand beyond reproachful second-guessing on the part of non-Muslim lawmakers. Thus, Qawadawi's ECFR insists that it alone has the authority to prescribe what is proper Islamic attire for female Muslims residing in Europe (Islamophile Ressources Islamiques en langue française; http://www.islamophile.org/spip/spip.php?page=recherche&recherche=voile). Similarly, Nadeem Elyas exclaimed in 2004: "We want to keep our identity as Muslims in Germany, as German Muslims. . . . Society does not have a right to decide for us what parts of Islam are acceptable and which are not. That step has to come from us" (quoted in Klausen 2005: 30). Although the Austrian government refused its request to mandate veiling in Islamic religion classes in public schools, the officially recognized Islamic Religious Community in Austria (Islamische Glaubensgemeinde in Österreich) continued to insist, when facing demands of the Freedom Party in 2003 to ban veiling, that the sartorial practice represents an internal matter for the Muslim community alone to determine (Avramopoulou, Çorbacioğlu, and Sanna 2012: 40). Likewise, declaring that only Muslims should determine proper practice, the Muslim Council of Britain (2007) also urged that veiling should be mandatory in Islamic education classes. The Islamic Council of Norway (Islamsk Råd Norge) agreed with Oslo's 2006 proscription of the niqab in secondary schools because "the niqab is not obligatory in Islam." However, the organization harshly criticized the government for not consulting with the council first, arguing it alone should determine what is obligatory in Islam (quoted in Vakulenko 2012: 42). Even the prime minister of a secular state, Recep Tayyip Erdoğan, in response to *Şahin v. Turkey*, said that "the Court [the European Court of Human Rights] has nothing to say on this issue, we have to ask the Ulama" (*Hürriyet* 16 November 2005).

Sympathy for the communitarian outlook can be heard from non-Muslim Europeans as well. In 2004, for instance, the pope, archbishop of Canterbury, and vice-president of the World Jewish Congress each criticized the French ban and warned secular states in general about interfering in the internal matters of religious organizations (Vakulenko 2012: 19). Manifesting the philosophical kinship between nationalism and communitarianism, a number of Far Right nationalist parties such as France's National Front, the Vlaams Blok, and Austria's Freedom Party have endorsed the idea of separate Islamic schools with the discretion to choose whatever dress code they deem appropriate (Fillitz 2006: 112; Wieviorka 2002: 144). The same holds for the French New Right think tank GRECE and its German sister organization the Thule Seminar. Jean Marie Le Pen went so far as to claim that he prefers veiling because it makes it easier to distinguish clearly between Muslims and non-Muslims (Tyrer 2013: 48).

European states do tolerate and even support Islamic organizations that mandate veiling. Most mosques, many of which receive public subsidies of one sort or the other, mandate veiling for female Muslims and non-Muslims alike. Islamists organizations whose members must cover count among the many organizations that European governments at various levels financially assist to offer services to immigrant communities (more about these in the next chapter). In 2000 when deciding to annul a municipal ban on veiling, a Belgian judge consulted the Islamic and Cultural Centre of Belgium, which explained that it was a religious duty to cover in public (Shadid and van Koningsveld 2005: 45). In 1993, the Federal Administrative Court of Germany, in what would become an important precedent-setting decision, sided with the Muslim parents of a twelve-year-old Turkish girl who sought an exemption from mandatory co-educational swimming classes because her veil might slip off in front of boys (Joppke 2009: 55). Indeed, many schools and municipalities throughout Europe now provide single-sex swimming hours to accommodate female Muslims (Shavit and Wiesenbach 2012: 53–54; Baran 2011: 138). Nor should we forget that European governments tolerate hundreds of Islamic organizations that mandate veiling simply by virtue of the fact that they are allowed to operate legally without state subsidies. Keep in mind too that far more discretion and money are granted to Roman

Catholic churches, all of which forbid women from serving in the most significant ecclesiastical offices.

Pragmatic Veil

The seemingly intractable controversy over the practice of compulsory veiling garners much public attention. In actuality, however, on a daily basis across Europe, thousands of Muslims and non-Muslims forge pragmatic resolutions of the conflicts by bending principle, engaging ambiguity, and tolerating inconsistency. These pragmatists tend to be ordinary citizens tasked with fulfilling concrete responsibilities—teaching students, parenting kids, providing social services, hiring able employees, keeping jobs—who simply cannot afford to paralyze their immediate efforts by becoming bogged down in stubborn disagreement over incompatible principles. In such situations, observes Anne Norton (2013: 226), "the 'clash of civilizations' has given way to conviviality in popular practice. The opposition of 'us vs. them' has given way to the complex demands and possibilities of ordinary life together." Without necessarily being either able or willing to articulate a coherent doctrine of hospitable postmodernism, these everyday problem-solvers regularly follow fragmentary precepts of the public philosophy, such as relaxing principle, attending to context, probing alterity, and embracing hybrid solutions.

Concrete cases are too numerous to detail in full; a few outstanding examples will have to suffice. As mentioned in the introduction, although Altrincham Girls' Grammar School expelled two pupils for veiling in 1989, they were allowed to return so long as the veils conformed to the colors of the school's uniform. Since then, many schools in the U.K. require and many Muslims agree to wear veils that match the school uniforms. In 1993, for example, Shabina Begum's school (Denbigh High) had consulted with both Muslims and non-Muslims to devise a design of the *shalwar kameeze* in school uniform colors (Joppke 2009: 97). Indeed, when the controversy over Begum's jilbab broke out in 2004, Denbigh offered Begum free daily transportation to nearby schools that permitted the garment. Begum obstinately refused, took the school to court, eventually lost, spent two years without classroom instruction, and ultimately enrolled in one of the schools to which Denbigh had offered to transport her (*BBC News* 22 March 2006). In the case of Aishah Azmi, who was sacked for refusing to shed the niqab when teaching, a solution was found in 2006 whereby the state-controlled Anglican junior high school permitted Azmi to wear the niqab when not teaching, including "when she was moving to different parts of the school" (quoted in Joppke 2009: 102).

Pragmatic solutions can be found beyond the shores of "multicultural" Britain. The Dutch state allowed policewomen to wear blue hijabs until 2001, when veils were proscribed. As intimated, the 1993 ruling by Germany's Federal Administrative Court, whereby girls may not be forced to unveil in physical education classes, has prompted numerous pragmatic adjustments. Some schools simply exempt the girls from swimming classes. In others where parents and teachers alike do not want the girls to forego swimming instruction, gender-segregated instruction takes place or the burkini is required. Veiled girls have also been integrated into co-educational classes, like volleyball, where the hijab does not appear to pose any danger to the wearer (Collet 2004: 121–22). A 2007 study conducted by the Intercultural Council of the Ministries of Culture of the *Länder* found that in the vast majority of cases a mutually agreeable solution is reached by parents, teachers, and pupils (reported in *Migration und Bevölkerung* October 2007; http:// www.migration-info.de/ausgabe/oktobernovember-2007-807). We should always keep in mind as well that the number of cases is typically small; in the entire school system of Berlin in 2004/2005, for instance, there were only fifteen girls who sought exemption (Bahners 2011: 254).

Private-sector businesses in particular have proven imaginatively flexible. More interested in profit than stalemate, employers and employees have devised numerous ways to keep female Muslims on the job, to a point where Veit Bader (2007: 164) reports that the headscarf issue has proven easier to resolve than others, such as excused absences for religious holidays or daily prayer. The Dutch department store Vroom and Dressman and the supermarket chain Albert Heijn have designed special headscarves with the respective business logos in the store's brand colors (Saharso 2007). Switzerland's largest supermarket chain, Migros, employs a case-by-case approach that emphasizes the need to respect "differentness" (*Neue Zürcher Zeitung* 20 July 2007).

These approaches would appear far more flexible and accommodating than those of the French. For example, the school whose ban on the veil in physical education was upheld by the European Court of Human Rights in *Dogru v. France* (2008) expelled Dogru despite the fact that she proposed wearing a hat or a balaclava (Vakulenko 2012: 115). Other evidence, however, points to much more flexible pragmatism, even in France. For example, of the 639 cases between 2004 and 2011 in which female pupils defied the French ban, 550 disputes were solved through what the Education Ministry termed "dialogue" (Leiken 2012: 32). Most resolutions involve striking a compromise such as a bandana that covers the hair but not the entire head and neck like the hijab (Bertossi and Bowen 2014). In another example, the Driving Standards Agency does compel women applying for licenses to unveil for their photo but only in a private room in the presence of a female examiner (Joppke 2009: 105). Arguing that arrests for violating the burqa ban of 2011 would be a waste of time, the French police union announced that gendarmes would not arrest women for wearing the burqa in public. Likewise, boutique owners on and near the Champs Élysées made it known that they intended neither to turn away nor to report burqa-clad patrons (*Guardian* 12 April 2011).

More than a few Islamist organizations have also exhibited flexibility. The UOIF, for instance, endorsed the aforementioned bandana compromise but added that turtleneck sweaters should be permitted to cover the neck (Hellyer 2009: 183). The UOIF also agreed in 2004 to sign the statement of the Conseil français du culte musulman (CFCM) that declared veiling a "religious prescription" as opposed to a "religious obligation," but only on condition that the CFCM would call for recognition of "interested third parties" to consult with officials in particularly difficult cases. As long as state officials were open to negotiations, the UOIF agreed not to encourage its members to defy the 2004 ban. As one of the organization's imams put the matter, "The only Muslims who will survive spiritually are those who know how to moderate, adapt and negotiate their practices with the reality of French society" (quoted in Laurence 2012: 214, 215). Similar conciliation issued forth from the Unione della Comunità Organizzazioni Islamiche in Italia (UCOII) in regard to a 2009 proposal to proscribe the niqab in public schools: "The niqab is against the law, which requires everyone's faces to be recognizable." At the same time, however, the UCOII upbraided the proposal, alleging that there were no niqab-wearing students in Italian schools (quoted in Laurence 2012: 215). Similarly, the general secretary of MCB, Farooq Murad, has said "it is wrong to force anyone to wear the veil" but also added that it is equally wrong for government to force anyone to discard it (*BBC News* 4 November 2013). With regard to swimming classes in German schools, the female deputy director of IGMG's legal department, Gülüzar Keskin, has pleaded for each pupil's right to "decency," leaving to case-by-case negotiation, however, exactly how decency is to be realized (Amir-Moazami 2011: 11).

The practical wisdom emerging from these pragmatic compromises would seem to emphasize open-ended negotiations with all interested parties as well as context-specific rulings and statutes subject to trial and open to renegotiation. Drafting the opinion of the House of Lords, Lord Bingham of Cornhill (2006: §34) argued that conflicts regarding veiling should always be considered as matters pertaining to "a particular pupil and a particular school in a particular place at a particular time." "The House," he insisted, "is not, and could not be, invited to rule whether Islamic dress . . . should or should not be permitted in the schools of this country" (§2). In the same year, the spokesman for the Department of Education and Skills stressed the same kind of contextual specificity: "What an individual pupil should or should not wear in school is a matter for individual schools in consultation with parents" (*BBC News* 22 March 2006). Similar advice was recommended by three of the four constitutional experts summoned for testimony by the *Landtag* of Baden-Württemberg, though their counsel was not heeded (Joppke 2009: 74). The SPD, however, has endorsed the case-by-case strategy (Andreassen and Lettinga 2012: 26), and *Länder* such as Hamburg, Schleswig-Holstein, and Saxony have implemented it (von Blumenthal 2009). This was the same approach prescribed by the Conseil d'Etat in 1989, endorsed by Interior Minister Sarkozy (*Le Monde* 10 May 2003), and carried out by state-appointed mediator Hanifa Cherifi before (and even after) the blanket ban of 2004 (Korteweg and Yurdakul 2014: 24–25). Resolutions seem to work best when involved parties suspend the stubborn attitude that compromising one's principles must needs constitute failure. Thus the French section of Milli Görüş urged that "we should find a 'modus vivendi' which will permit each one not to lose face in front of the others" (quoted in Strassburger 2000: 136). Malika Hamidi (2009) of the European Muslim Network beseeches all involved to keep an open mind by posing "audacious questions that help in changing mentalities." Through "bypassing fears and stereotypes" negotiators open themselves to resolutions neither sanctioned nor imagined by rigid adherence to principle.

Nilüfer Göle (2011: 137) advises "mature multiculturalism." Mature multiculturalism embraces diversity but without the naïve presumption that all forms of difference are salutary. Traditional Muslim women, for example, can learn much from exposure to Western-style feminism, but they should not be impervious to its imperious dismissal of all forms of Islamic veiling as subjugation (see also Balibar 2004: 156–57). Relatedly, conventional secular feminists can sensitize themselves to their own narrow-mindedness through encounter with the Islamist critique of liberal feminism's simplistic equation of women's liberation with having the same rights and opportunities as men. But this should not mean that Islamist teaching and practice regarding women should be beyond reproach. Indeed, vigorous resistance to unchecked patriarchy can be heard from within Islamist circles. For example, IGMG, as part of its campaign to encourage girls and women to pursue higher degrees and professional careers, offers classes, workshops, and support groups designed to equip pious female Muslims with Qur'an-based objections to traditional patriarchal customs and mores that impede female flourishing (Joppke 2009: 61; Ewing 2008: 79). Rather than rejecting and eschewing their religious tradition, these (mostly but not exclusively female) Islamist activists are competing within their organizations for leadership positions from which they can redefine and reshape that tradition (Piela 2012: 33–39; Schiffauer 2008a:

126; Laborde 2008: 144–46; Amir-Moazami and Salvatore 2003: 60–70). According to Hamidi (2009), these efforts manifest a "new way of thinking: feminist in its demands and deeply rooted in the Muslim tradition." The Islamist activist discerns a new, hybrid "model/profile of European Muslim women [that] is half-way between the western model of emancipation and the traditional model of the Muslim woman." Mature multiculturalism would shy away from neither including Hamidi and others like her in the policy-making process nor exploiting their insights to determine on a case-by-case basis when and where state intervention is needed to stop veiling (or other) practices truly harmful to girls and women.

Conclusion

The present chapter, like the previous one, demonstrates how in practical politics fragments from all three public philosophies—liberalism, nationalism, and postmodernism—become combined in efforts to advance and legitimize a particular political agenda. Thus, opponents of the veil curse it as an intolerable violation of female individual liberty with one breath and as an affront or even threat to "our" national way of life with the other. Moreover, few opponents can resist the postmodern temptation to exaggerate the desultory consequences of veiling by likening it to savagery or slavery. For their part, proponents of veiling hail it as an expression of bold and brave individualism while also pronouncing it a communal prerogative that Islamic organizations should be allowed to mandate for individual members. As far as postmodern-inspired manipulation of the truth is concerned, proponents of the veil outlandishly equate its banning (that usually affects only a few hundred or thousand persons at most) with the Christian Crusades or European imperialism.

Such practical political bricolage or montage manifests more than mere philosophical laxity and imprecision on the part of political practitioners. It reflects, normatively speaking, expanding mutual fragilization in the protracted *Kulturkampf* among liberalism, nationalism, and postmodernism. It reflects diffuse, if not fully conscious appreciation that liberal, nationalist, and postmodern forms of normative reasoning, while different and conflicting, nonetheless prove persuasive to voters. In an increasingly fragilized normative atmosphere political activists who confine their moral justifications to a single public philosophy run the risk of handicapping their prospects of political success. Consistently principled strategizing is an academic luxury (or burden) that is simply too costly in practical politics.

Furthermore, examining the headscarf controversy from the vantage point of fragilization and fragmentation helps to avoid two common oversimplifications. First, the controversy does not pivot around Muslim versus non-Muslim perspectives, as the clash-of-civilization thesis posits. The chapter provided ample examples of persons of both Muslim and non-Muslim heritage who oppose veiling by invoking fragments of liberal, nationalist, and postmodern reasoning. Likewise, both Muslims and non-Muslims work to permit veiling and also deploy crisscrossing fragments of liberal, nationalist, and postmodern logic.

Second, differences from one country to the next are neither as distinct nor as firm as the national models paradigm postulates. In the first place, the chapter showed that the debates about whether to proscribe or permit veiling share much in common across Europe. There does not appear, for instance, to be an unmistakable preponderance of liberal perfectionism in the French debate, liberal multiculturalism in the British discussion, or nativist nationalism in the German context, as the national models paradigm implies. Rather, strains of each as well as of communitarianism and Hobbesian and hospitable postmodernism are discernable across European countries. The discordant yet increasingly fragilized discourse is truly Europe-wide.

As far as actual policies are concerned, the national differences appear starker at first glance but begin to blur when viewed through the lens of fragmentation and fragilization. France's ban on all ostentatious religious symbols in public schools would seem to be normatively motivated by unadulterated liberal perfectionism. However, by attuning to fragilization toward nativism we were able to realize that the ban, both in design and in implementation, actually targets Islamic symbolism. This means that in actuality the French policy differs far less from the statutes of the CDU-controlled German *Länder* that, until the 2015 ruling of the Constitutional Court, proscribed the hijab (for teachers) but permitted the yarmulke and habit. As for the sway of nativism in Germany, half of the *Länder* followed policies that accorded with liberalism until the court decided squarely in favor of individual autonomy in 2015. Attention to fragilization toward communitarianism and especially Hobbesian postmodernism helped to shed light on the de facto mandatory veiling transpiring regularly in numerous corners of European countries, though none of the latter formally sanctions the practice. And focus on hospitable postmodernism revealed that pragmatic problem-solvers (again Muslim and non-Muslim) in both places that ban veiling and those that allow it contrive makeshift compromises that eliminate or alleviate real human suffering caused either by veiling or unveiling.

Both the policies and conditions under which (un)veiling takes place are in flux. They alter because they are contested. Across Europe we encounter "opposed answers to the same question" (Bowen and Rohe 2014: 155). "No agreement exists on the meaning of . . . terms, nor about the strategies they entail" (Andreassen and Lettinga 2012: 18). The national models paradigm does not exclude the possibility of change but, with its emphasis on path dependency and national accord, it inclines toward accentuating constancy and consensus as opposed to fluctuation and contestation. The paradigm foregrounds the winners in the political process, whereas the approach taken in this chapter spotlights winners and losers. But today's losers can swiftly become tomorrow's victors. In countries like France, Belgium, and Germany, veiling bans are being contested in the courts, legislatures, and on the streets. No one should be surprised if the bans are circumvented, nullified, or rescinded, as, in fact, took place in Germany in 2015. Nor should one (or, hopefully after reading the current chapter, could one) consider countries without bans such as Austria, the Netherlands, or the United Kingdom immune to anti-veiling strivings, for they exist in those countries as well. Finally, regardless of whatever formal laws are registered on the books, informal discrimination both in favor of and against veiled female Muslims will surely persist.

5

Secularism

A new religious pluralism is shaking up Atlantic democracies.
—THOMAS BANCHOFF, *Democracy and the New Religious Pluralism*

The comparative study of church-state relations has generated its fair share of tidy models. Bader's (2007: 203) impressive study, for example, delineates five models: strong establishment (Greece, Serbia, Israel), weak establishment (England, Scotland, Norway, Denmark), plural establishment (Finland), nonestablishment combined with public institutionalization of religious pluralism (Netherlands, Sweden, Germany, Austria, Belgium, Spain), and strict separation (France, United States). Triandafyllidou (2010b: 11) distinguishes between "Absolute secularism" (France), "Moderate secularism" (Sweden, Netherlands), "Moderate religious pluralism" (Britain, Germany, Spain, Italy, Greece), and "Absolute religious pluralism" (no European land yet) (also see Monsma and Soper 2009; Casanova 2007). This national models paradigm has been extended to analyze mosque-state relations in Europe, yielding the claim of, say, a distinctly French style of handling Islam clearly demarcated from a German, British, or Swedish approach (Joppke and Torpey 2013; Fetzer and Soper 2005). Scrupulous comparativists never fail to offer the obligatory caveat that no country perfectly fits any one ideal type but proceed nonetheless to assign countries to typology cells to yield the kind of tidy contrasts and comparisons just mentioned (Bader 2007: 201–5). Faced with muddle or model, in other words, the analysts prefer the latter.

I resist this urge and instead employ a deliberately disordering tack that emphasizes policy muddle born of normative diversity and discord. Now diversity and discord over the role of religion in politics represent rather recent phenomena in Europe during the postwar era. Many scholars concur that during the generation following World War II, something close to a political consensus formed in Europe that religion should be a private matter with virtually no role to play in politics outside of innocuous tokenism (such as a prayer to open a session of parliament). Most Europeans fell into the category of "believing without belonging" (Davie 1994) or "belonging without believing" (Hervieu-Léger 2004). José Casanova (2007: 63) rightly characterizes the period as "the triumph of the knowledge regime of secularism." This consensus has evanesced. To be sure, many remain confident, even superciliously so, that European-style secularism represents a model that others should copy. But this position no longer goes unchallenged. As Habermas (2006: 2) remarks, "divisive political moods [are] crystallizing around" secularism as we move into the "post-secular" age. Grace Davie (2007: 238) observes that "religion has become an increasingly salient factor in public debate." Göle (2004: 151, 14) discerns a "sacralization of public opinion" and postulates that "the conspicuous way in which Islam is appearing in the national public spheres is destabilizing homogenous structures and conventional principles of consensus." Similarly, Casanova (2006: 77) notes that Muslims are causing a stir "not only because of their religious otherness as a non-Christian and non-European religion, but more importantly because of their religiousness itself as the 'other' of European secularity."

However, I want to resist the temptation to assert that the growing discord in Europe regarding secularism pits antisecular Muslims against secular non-Muslims, as several popular books contend (Fallaci 2006; Ye'or 2005; Schwarzer 2002a). Against this binary reading I submit that viewing the politics of secularism through the normative prism of liberalism, nationalism, and postmodernism offers a more nuanced interpretation. Warnings that fundamentalist zealots must be prevented from injecting religious and even theocratic tendencies into politics stem from the liberal tradition. Claims that European nations must insist on and even strengthen their Judeo-Christian character against the diluting effects of "Islamization" echo nationalist thinking. Postmodernism yields the notion that liberal secularism is itself a faith like both Christianity and Islam in the sense of ultimately being based on arbitrary axioms and contingent beliefs that must be imposed in one way or the other on believers and unbelievers alike. Acting like pragmatic bricoleurs, political actors, both Muslim and non-Muslim, regularly deploy these and other fragments of liberal, nationalist, and postmodern thinking, creating a highly fragmented and, we shall see, fragilized normative atmosphere that contributes to "messy empirical data" (Laurence 2012: 28) revealing "contradictory policies" and "inconsistent institutional arrangements" of "stunning complexity" (Bader 2007: 53, 276).

Liberal Neutrality

Every European government formally honors in some way the liberal secular ideal of neutrality. According to this norm, the state should neither determine the religion of its citizens nor discriminate among them on the basis of the religion they do (not) choose to follow. In addition, the state must see to it that nonreligious organizations do not coerce or discriminate on the basis of creed. Most European constitutions enshrine this principle. Article 16 of Spain's Constitution is standard:

> Freedom of ideology, religion and worship of individuals and communities is guaranteed, with no other restriction on their expression than may be necessary to maintain public order as protected by law. No one may be compelled to make statements regarding his or her ideology, religion or beliefs.

Furthermore, European states typically pledge to honor various international conventions and treaties that also guarantee religious freedom, such as Article 9 of the European Convention on Human Rights or Article 4 of the United Nations' Declaration on the Elimination of All Forms of Intolerance and of Discrimination Based on Religion or Belief.

As regards Muslims, European governments have regularly transgressed this liberal tenet or have tolerated its transgression by others. Numerous organizations and reports have documented pervasive discrimination against European Muslims in practically all walks of life (Hafez 2014; Organisation for Economic Cooperation and Development 2013: 191–230; Antidiskriminierungsstelle 2013; Amnesty International 2012; Ansari and Hafez 2012; Zick, Küpper, and Hövermann 2011; Peucker 2010; Open Society Institute 2010; 2002; European Union Agency for Fundamental Rights 2009; European Union Monitoring Centre 2006; see also www.islamophobia-watch.com). Such analyses draw conclusions regarding Islamophobia for numerous European lands similar to those arrived at by the Runnymede Trust (1997) for Britain: "In twenty years it has become more explicit, more extreme, more pernicious and more dangerous . . . [and] is part of the fabric of everyday life in modern Britain, in much the same way that anti-Semitic discourse was taken for granted earlier in this century" (quoted in Joppke 2009: 90).

Shamed by such illiberal practices, many European governments have taken steps to redress the abuses. The EU's so-called "Framework Directive" "establishing a general framework for equal treatment in employment and occupation," issued in conjunction with the 2000 Race Directive, explicitly denounces discrimination on the grounds of religion or belief and calls on member states to take concrete steps against both direct and indirect discrimination with the aim of "ensuring full equality in practice" (Article 7). Many member states have passed laws and established governmental agencies to combat discrimination such as the Netherlands' Equal Treatment

Law (1994), the Commission for Equality and Human Rights in the United Kingdom (2004), the Haute Authorité de Lutte contre la Discriminations et pour l'Egalité in France (2005; since 2011 Défenseur des Droits), and the Antidiskriminierungsstelle des Bundes in Germany (2006). Going a step further, most European governments have sought to counterbalance inherited institutional favoritism by establishing formal, high-profile relations with Islam that aim to parallel and (eventually) emulate those already in place between the state and Christianity (and often Judaism) in most European countries. While some states, such as Austria, Belgium, Spain, Greece, Sweden, and the Netherlands, already had close ties with Islamic representatives long before 9/11, others deliberately moved to form them thereafter. Thus did France found the Conseil Français du Culte Musulman in 2003, Britain the Mosques and Imams National Advisory Board in 2005, Italy the Consulta per l'Islam Italiano in 2005, and Germany the Deutsche Islam Konferenz in 2006.

These relations are highly complex and protean. In the first place, countries have intricate and varying existing relations between church and state into which Islam is expected to fit—already a problematic endeavor given significant differences between Christianity and Islam, such as the latter's general lack of centralized authority to represent the creed before the state (Laurence 2012; Pēdziwiatr 2007; Godard 2007; Warner and Wenner 2006; Fetzer and Soper 2005). Second, as we shall see as the chapter unfolds, mosque-state relations turn out to be sites of vehement normative discord, although far less over the finer points of theology than over the competing stances of secularism spawned by liberalism, nationalism, and postmodernism.

We must enter this normative thicket from somewhere. Liberal multiculturalism represents a good starting point, for it prima facie informs the state's gesture to reach out to Islam and Muslims. According to liberal multiculturalism, the state should be neutral. It should treat all (significant) religions equally, on condition, however, that their adherents eschew theocracy and recognize the supreme sovereignty of manmade law in mundane affairs (Habermas 2008a; Bader 2007: 112; Casanova 1994: 211). Furthermore, believers and unbelievers alike are expected to respect personal autonomy— that is, the right of each individual freely to choose which faith(s) he or she wishes to embrace, abandon, or ignore. In the European context, this means extending to Islam and Muslims similar if not identical benefits (such as tax breaks for mosque construction; subsidies for private religious schools; religious education in public schools; marriage and burial rights; pastoral clerical services in hospitals, prisons, and the armed services; and public access TV time) to those long granted Christian (and other) denominations in most if not all European societies. The Austrian political philosopher Rainer Bauböck (2002: 170) writes:

The state can live up to its obligation of equal concern and respect for all citizens by, on the one hand, extending whatever historical privileges the dominant religion has enjoyed to the minority congregations and, on the other hand, abolishing those that involuntarily subject non-believers to some religious authority. (see also Modood 2003: 164; Hervieu-Léger 2001: 101–3)

Something like this moral vision has received typically sententious endorsement at the highest political levels. As early as 1993, French interior minister Charles Pasqua posited: "It is no longer enough to talk of Islam in France. There has to be a French Islam" (quoted in Schain 1999: 216). This new engagement with Islam subsequent interior minister Nicolas Sarkozy would label "positive secularism"—the state's encouragement of rather than separation from religious communities. In 2009 in an editorial in *Le Monde* (9 December), President Sarkozy voiced his desire to "put the Muslim religion on an equal footing with all other great religions." German interior minister Wolfgang Schäuble also expressed his wish that the "Muslims in Germany" become "German Muslims" (*Frankfurter Allgemeine Zeitung* 26 September 2006), while Angela Merkel has exclaimed that "Islam belongs in Germany" (*Deutsche Welle* 12 January 2015). Tony Blair first visited a mosque at the outset of Ramadan in 1999, Her Majesty ordered a prayer room built at Windsor Castle for her lone Muslim servant in 2004, and Prince Charles has voiced his wish to be crowned "Defender of Faiths" rather than "Defender of the Faith" (*The Independent* 22 March 2014). Furthermore, the EU's draft constitution of 2004 did not (after much debate however) refer to Europe's Christian roots, and the criteria for membership stipulated in the European Council Summit in Copenhagen of 1993 do not include Christian heritage. The applications for membership from predominantly Muslim Turkey and Morocco are currently being negotiated (if amidst objections). The official message is unmistakable: Muslims are welcome and should not have to quit their creed as a consequence of residing in traditionally Christian Europe. As the founder of the Muslim Council of Britain, Iqbal Sacranie, approvingly noted, "There is now an open door to the government" (quoted in Lewis 2002: 133).

The warm welcome, however, usually comes accompanied by the liberal quid pro quo demanding allegiance to the constitution and commitment to the secular values it enshrines. For example, the Italian interior minister, Giuseppi Pisanu, maintained in 2002: "Italian Islam must harmonize with . . . Italian rules" (quoted in Laurence 2012: 107). In the very same editorial mentioned above, Sarkozy averred that integration for Muslims "means accepting gender equality, secularism and separation of the temporal and spiritual." Across the Rhine, Chancellor Angela Merkel urged that "anyone coming here must respect our constitution and tolerate our Western and Christian roots" (*Financial Post* 17 February 2006). "In Germany only the constitution is valid, not Sharia" (*Frankfurter Allgemeine Zeitung* 8 October 2010). Tony Blair, while averring that the only sure strategy for defeating Islamist extremism had to embrace Islam, nonetheless emphatically added: "There has to be a shared acceptance that some things we believe in and we do together: obedience to certain values like democracy, rule of law, equality between men and women. . . . This common space cannot be left to chance or individual decsion. It has to be accepted as mandatory" (*Wall Street Journal* 9 November 2010).

Euro-Islam

The desired end of such outreach is "Euro-Islam," a neologism as telling as it is fashionable. It is telling because Euro-Islam is not only conceived as an Islam befitting life in Europe, but also as a Europeanized Islam—that is, an Islam that has been subjected to a similar self-scrutiny and self-reform as the Christian denominations are alleged to have undergone in the modern age (Roy 2004: 29). In the notion of Euro-Islam we can detect the blurry line between liberal perfectionism and voluntarism. To the extent that the state resolves to shape Euro-Islam and actively recruit Muslims to it, as we shall see below, liberal perfectionist logic weighs in. However, if the state leaves it to Muslims themselves to articulate, preach, and practice Euro-Islam, liberal voluntarism prevails.

It just so happens that Muslim reformers abound in Europe. Prominent Egyptian-born Italian journalist Magdi Allam, for example, long insisted that "Islam is a faith which, in a moderate interpretation, is absolutely compatible with the values shared by the Italian civil society and the Italian Constitution" (*Il Grillo* 2 April 2001). Advocates of Euro-Islam, self-appointed modernizers like Naser Khader (Denmark), Baroness Kishwer Falkner, Ziauddin Sardar, Maajid Nawaz, Shahid Malik (U.K.), Bassam Tahhan, Dounia Bouzar, Mohammad Arkoun, Malek Cheleb, Samia Labidi (France), Lamya Kaddor, Seyran Ateş, Bassam Tibi (Germany), Ehsan Jami, the late Nasr Hamid Abu Zayd (Netherlands), Mansur Escudero (Spain), and Sadiq Jalal al-Azm (Belgium), tend to start from the assumption that the conventional practice of Islam in the sending countries has over the centuries taken on countless cultural and ethnic accretions that are not integral to the pristine faith. As envisaged by its proponents, Euro-Islam would abrogate, for example, any theocratic ambitions and embrace democracy. It would tolerate all other creeds, including atheism, and recognize the right of each individual to choose or craft his or her own faith. The prohibition of apostasy would have to be excised from Islamic doctrine. Furthermore, this "liberal Islam" (Bouzar 2004) would purge from conventional Islam all precepts and rituals that offend modern democratic sensibilities, such as eye-for-eye justice, the subordination of women to men, or homophobia (Marcouch 2008). Likewise, this "enlightened Islam [which] is compatible with world civilization, with Europe, and with the spirit of the Republic" (Cheleb 2004) would systematically disavow Qur'anic interpretations of nature belied by modern science and underscore the many passages in congruence with current science. Most importantly, it would entail subjecting the Qur'an to the same kind of rational scrutiny applied in biblical criticism since the nineteenth century. The sacred text would be read not as the inerrant and literal word of God, but as the words of specific men formulated in specific times—indeed, times very different from our own (Abu Zayd 1996: 68). Bassam Tahhan writes:

> The tradition regards the Koran as one-dimensional and fixed. This approach is not rationalist. To be a rationalist is to accept that each era, with its [particular] methods and discoveries, presents its own reading of the Koran, and this is the way it will be until the end of days. (Quoted in Jenkins 2007: 140)

Once European Muslims understand that there exists no real alternative to interpreting the Qur'an, it is believed they will become more comfortable customizing the creed to better jibe with modern rationalism, including democracy and pluralism. A thorough "rethinking [of] Islam" (Arkoun 1994) harbors the potential to bring forth an Islam based on independent judgment (*ijtihad*) rather than on slavish obedience to authority. This Euro-Islam, its proponents contend, is likelier to survive and thrive in a culture such as Europe's that prizes free choice (Bencheikh 1998). The self-acknowledged Habermasian and Euro-Muslim Bassam Tibi (2002: 37–38) summarizes:

> By acknowledging cultural and religious pluralism, Euro-Islam would give up the claim of Islamic dominance. Thus defined, Euro-Islam would be compatible with liberal democracy, individual human rights, and the requirements of a civil society. It would also contrast sharply with the communitarian politics that result in ghettoization. To be sure, the politics of Euro-Islam would not allow complete assimilation of Muslims. Yet it could enable the adoption of forms of civil society leading to an enlightened, open-minded Islamic identity compatible with European civic culture.

Dozens if not hundreds of Islamic organizations in Europe have endorsed some version of Euro-Islam. For instance, the Islamic Charter drafted by the Zentralrat der Muslime in Deutschland in 2002 explicitly renounces the goal of creating a theocracy and declares that "Muslims affirm the liberal democratic order of the Federal Republic of Germany, including party pluralism, women's right to vote, and religious liberty." Furthermore, "Muslims accept the right to change one's religion, to have another religion or no religion at all" (quoted in Joppke 2009: 113). Similarly, Denmark's Demokratiske muslimer (www.demokratiskemuslimer.dk), formed in 2006 in the wake of the cartoon controversy by Social Liberal MP Naser Khader, dedicates itself to "furthering the understanding that Islam is compatible with democracy" (trikkefrihed.dk at http://www.trykkefrihed.dk/de-demokratiske-muslimer-hvor-blev-de-af.htm). A like message resounds from Islamic political parties, such as the Islamic Party of Britain or the Muslim Democratic Party in Belgium, which seek to elect more Muslims to public office.

Perhaps the most persuasive case for an Islam compatible with European secular ways and norms issues forth from millions of European Muslims, who daily choose to live in this way. A bevy of survey studies documents among European Muslims widespread support for liberal democratic values in general and secularism in particular (Cesari 2013: 21–80; Algan and Aleksynska 2012: 312–13; Kaya 2012: 86; Saunders 2012: 62–68; Haug, Müssig, and Stichs 2010; Inglehart and Norris 2009; Pew Global Attitudes Project 2006; Peter 2006; Diehl and Schnell 2006; Klausen 2005; Lucasson 2005; Tribalat 1996). The Scientific Council for Government Policy of the Netherlands (2006: 198), for instance, urged readers to keep in mind that "the overwhelming majority of Muslims, of course, fully comply to [sic] the rules of the democratic constitutional state." If we are to believe the polling of the Pew Global Attitudes Survey of 2006, between half and three-quarters of European Muslims, depending on the country, see no problem with remaining pious in modern secular society. It is actually non-Muslim Europeans who in far greater numbers discern a profound conflict between Islam and secularism (Pew Global Attitudes Project 2006). Jocelyn Cesari (2007: 114) argues that most Muslims in Europe "resemble the 'pickers and choosers' of other religions in the West. Like 'consumers,' they tailor their religious practice and tradition to their own subjective specifications." This "personalization" (LeVine 2003: 102) of religion yields a "patchwork quilt" (Wuthnow 2005) or "bricolage" of "experienced Islams" with "quasi unlimited itineraries of belief identification" (Hervieu-Léger 2007: 203, 216; see also Yükleyen 2012: 145–51). Individualized Islamic practice helps to explain the immense popularity among European Muslims of several televangelist-like imams such as Amr Khaled (3.5 million Facebook "likes"), Mustafa Hosny (1.65 million "likes"), Ahmad al-Shugairi, Moez Masoud, and Fethulla Gülen (*Economist* 29 October 2011; Gerlach 2006: 29–31). These purveyors of "popular Islam" (Mandaville 2014: 392) send a steady message over television and computer screens imploring Muslims to interpret and practice Islam in ways that fit their personal lives, independent of the precepts emanating from traditional Islamic authorities. "We should decide our own lifestyles," preaches Khaled (quoted in Gerlach 2006: 40). Though hardliners deride this as "Islam light," there is not much they can do to diminish the prominence of these clerical mavericks, because Islam lacks a central authority like the Vatican to certify bona fide preachers (Hervieu-Léger 2007: 209; Warner and Wenner 2006; Roy 2000). The result is the prevalence of "Pop-Islam," "cool Islam," or even "Cola Quran" customized to fit into a quotidian consumer culture that bedazzles Muslims no less than non-Muslims (Foroutan and Schäfer 2009; Gerlach 2006: 109; Boubekeur 2005: 12). Olivier Roy (2004: 124–25) contends that consumerism has so diluted Islamic belief and practice that the term "Muslim" now connotes no more than a loose affiliation ("neo-ethnicity") with Islam that includes millions of persons who seldom observe the creed's doctrine. These are "cultural Muslims" (Akbarzadeh and Roose 2011: 320) who are no more religious in any "thick" sense than the "Christian" Europeans who "believ[e] without belonging" (Davie 1994) or "belong . . . without believing" (Hervieu-Léger 2004; also see Gest 2010: 106; Brettfeld and Wetzels 2007; Allievi 2003: 23–24; Dassetto 2000).

This would all seem to be good news for liberal secularism, and it is. Most European governments seek to integrate Islam into the secular order, and most European Muslims appear to be integrating. Yet it is premature to predict victory for liberal secularism, as does Laurence (2012: 245); for opponents (both Muslim and non-Muslim) of the liberal multicultural vision of secularism are many, and their voices too have swayed increasingly fragilized policy makers.

Communitarian Secularism

Let us begin with Muslim opponents who chide European governments for their insistence on Euro-Islam. The critics discern an imperious effort to dictate to Muslims how they should worship—a kind of thinly veiled "churchification" of Islam (Roy 2004: 29). They do not oppose secularism per se; rather, they work with a different normative conception of state neutrality informed by communitarian reasoning. Briefly recalling from Chapter 2, communitarianism posits that any genuine community, including a small diaspora, should be permitted to determine itself the chief values and standards according to which it lives. It should not be compelled to observe or honor norms and values foreign to itself. The ethical core of communitarianism resides in what Charles Taylor (1994: 66) calls "the presumption of equal worth." In our case, this means that mosques and their related organizations should be presumed to have good reasons for organizing and governing themselves the way they do, including when their measures appear objectionable to "outside" officials or to the majority population. From this differentialist perspective, individuals are said to gain greater satisfaction from organizations in which they can recognize themselves and their values—in which, in other words, they experience a sense of ownership and authorship. Furthermore, such self-governing organizations of persons who recognize themselves as a community tend to be more attuned to members' particular needs and can customize programs to meet them, making more productive and effective use of resources than "outsiders" (Walzer 2004: 56).

Embassy Islam

The most influential advocates of a communitarian approach to Islam in Europe have arguably been the governments of sending countries with large numbers of Muslim émigrés. The European embassies and consulates of countries such as Pakistan, Morocco, Algeria, Tunisia, and Turkey have steadfastly and often successfully applied diplomatic pressure on European governments to be permitted to superintend the everyday practice of Islam for their émigrés in Europe. Not long after they signed bilateral agreements with receiving countries in the 1960s to send workers, the foreign ministries of the sending countries negotiated additional bilateral accords to provide cultural centers (for instance, the Maghrebi *amicales*), radio and television programs, prayer rooms, and imams to service the particular cultural and religious needs of expatriates (Brand 2006: 14). As the number of immigrants grew, and especially once the families of what had been mostly male laborers and students joined them in the 1970s and 1980s, their governments expanded the outsourcing agreements to include teachers, curricula, and textbooks for "mother-tongue" classes in the public schools providing instruction in the language, culture, and religion of the immigrant pupils' respective homelands. The embassies erected their own "official" mosques and associated Islamic organizations and federations, such as the Diyanet İşleri İslam Birliği (Turkish-Islamic Union for Religious Affairs) or La Fondation Hassan II pour les Marocains Résidant à l'etranger (Hassan II Foundation for Moroccans Living Abroad) and the related Féderation nationale des musulmans de France. Algeria exercised its influence by gaining control of the Grande Mosquée de Paris, whose chief imam has long been appointed by Algiers. The Saudis underwrote and thereby controlled the Islamic Council of Europe based in London, the Munich Islamic Center, the Islamic Cultural Center (ICC) of Brussels (recognized by the Belgian government as the official representative of Islam in Belgium since 1974), and the Centro Islamico Culturale d'Italia (CICI) in Rome. These organizations have aspired and in many cases managed to become hubs of religious activities for their expatriates and their descendants in Europe, coordinating and overseeing intricate transnational networks of Islamic services ranging from Friday worship to after-school religious education (Qur'an schools) to provision of *halal* foods, proper Islamic burial (often back in the homeland), or travel accommodations for the *haj* to and from Mecca (Cesari 2013: 245–54; Laurence 2012: 30–69; Pargeter 2008: 16–31).

The European embassies of the sending countries have waged vociferous campaigns against the assimilation of their émigrés, underscoring adherence to Islam as an indelible marker of difference. What observers label "embassy Islam" promotes interpretation and practice of the creed in the diaspora identical to the officially sanctioned Islam of the sending countries (Laurence 2012: 30; Gould 2009: 62). The secretary general of the Saudi-sponsored Organisation of the Islamic Conference, which has worked closely with the Islamic Council of Europe established in 1973, maintained: "The most serious problem that can face a minority is social absorption by the majority. Such an absorption is usually the result of a long assimilation process that nibbles at the Islamic characteristics of the minority until it disappears altogether" (quoted in Laurence 2012: 38–39). The Pakistani minister for religious affairs was more hopeful, asserting in 1980 that adherence to Islam made Muslims in Europe like "sand in water—they cannot possibly get dissolved and be assimilated" (Brohi 1980: 31). According to its mission statement, the Hassan II Foundation "strives to maintain and develop fundamental ties between Moroccans living abroad with their home country" (quoted in Laurence 2012: 66). The Turkish-Islamic Union for Religious Affairs (DITIB), whose official mission since 1971 has been to "instill love of fatherland, flag and religion," obliges the approximately 900 mosques it sponsors in Germany to observe the laws and statutes of the Turkish Republic (quoted in Dere 2008: 292–93). The embassy-sponsored organizations not only preach and teach almost exclusively in the languages of their respective homelands and thereby encourage separatist congregations of mainly native speakers; they also in their sermons, pamphlets, curricula, and classes are known directly or indirectly to reinforce jingoistic, misogynistic, homophobic, authoritarian, and other illiberal norms and values that, while perhaps commonplace in the sending countries, conflict with the allegedly predominant values of the liberal democratic receiving countries (Laurence 2012: 68–69; Gest 2010: 121; Mohr 2006: 38, 267; Zeeuw 1998). Employing classic Herderian logic, embassy representatives contend that their citizens abroad will identify only with an Islam they can recognize, and that is the Islam of the homeland: "Once an immigrant encounters another society which is new to him . . . he starts to ask questions of identity and he finds that the first response that comes to him is religion and nation. . . . Belonging to a nation, belonging to a religion can give comfort" (quoted in Laurence

2012: 221). Indeed, the embassies have stubbornly resisted cooperation with nongovernmental Islamic organizations in Europe, arguing that sending country governments should be granted exclusive control over the provision of Islamic services to their respective diasporas (Laurence 2012: 55, 68, 159–62, 218–22; Steinberg 2010: 151–56; Bowen 2010: 26–60). Turkish prime minister Erdoğan went so far as to aver in 2004 that DITIB, which answers to his government, should "be accepted as the EU's only partner on related issues" in recognition of the "leading role played by Turkey in the Islamic world" (quoted in Laurence 2012: 230–32). CICI proclaims itself "the only credible interlocutor for Italian authorities," while the ICC has been recognized as the "*interlocuteur privilegie*" in Belgium since 1978 (quoted in Laurence 2012: 68).

Communitarianism serves the concrete interests of the embassies. As mentioned in Chapter 3, they are keen to keep ties to the homeland robust so as to encourage the remittances that are so important to economic prosperity and arguably regime stability. Embassies further have sought to marginalize, indeed squelch, nongovernmental Islamic associations in Europe, many of which have been led by radical and exiled dissidents associated with Islamist movements, such as the Egyptian Muslim Brotherhood, the Turkish Milli Görüş (National Vision), the Algerian Islamic Salvation Front, the Moroccan Justice and Spirituality Movement, and the Tunisian Islamic Tendency Movement. No comfortably ensconced governmental official can easily erase the memory of the Iranian Revolution of 1979, which was originally fomented by cassette tapes smuggled in from France, where Ayatollah Khomeini resided in exile. If anyone needed a reminder, Rachid al-Ghannouchi, after twenty-two years of exile in the United Kingdom, returned triumphantly to his native Tunisia following the ouster of President Zine el-Abidne Ben Ali in 2011. The embassies have long argued that without the availability of their "moderate Islam" the exiled radicals will win the hearts and loyalties of the Muslims in Europe (Laurence 2012: 37, 55).

Communitarianism has also dovetailed nicely with the interests of receiving governments, who have tended to prefer embassy Islam as the lesser of two evils and more likely to encourage docility among immigrants than radical Islamism, whose political mobilizing occasionally turned violent in European streets during the 1980s and 1990s (Laurence 2012: 35–38). As one French official remarked, "Algeria, Morocco, and Turkey were able to offer France a common front that was perhaps not pro-Western but at least anti-terrorist" (quoted in Laurence 2012: 37). Favoring embassy Islam also pleased governments with which European states wanted to maintain cordial relations for geopolitical reasons. Erstwhile Italian prime minister Guilio Andreotti explained regarding oil-rich Saudi Arabia: "All the mosques the Saudis have built around the world became elements of propaganda. I am not naïve. But the important thing is to try to have a relationship with them" (quoted in Laurence 2012: 54). More importantly still, communitarianism has aided receiving governments in placating their publics. Tolerating and even fostering an essentially separatist Islam oriented to the homeland has reinforced the convenient though illusory notion that the Muslims were temporary guestworkers who would one day repatriate. Naturally, the degree of communitarianism has varied from country to country. France went so far as to instruct judges in the 1980s to apply Islamic law (for example, polygamy and unilateral husband divorce) in family matters for first-generation migrants, though this policy was halted in 1993 (Bowen 2010: 175). Since the Treaty of Lausanne in 1923, Greece has permitted *sharia* law in family matters for the Turkish Muslim minority in Western Thrace (Triandafyllidou 2010c: 202). However, as Laurence (2012: 32) incisively concludes, "Every European government, whether overtly 'multicultural' or not, accepted outside funds and allowed outside authorities—from Algeria, Morocco, and Turkey to Saudi Arabia, Libya, and beyond—to influence its local Muslim population." In this way, the very same governments that have endorsed the liberal goal of integration and today vilify "multiculturalism" for encouraging Muslim separatism have long fostered the latter. But that is precisely the kind of policy messiness that we should expect in a fragmented and fragilized normative milieu.

NGO Islam

In similarly messy fashion, the liberal policy of guaranteeing freedom of religion and association has made possible, if largely unintentionally, a form of communitarianism practiced by nongovernmental Islamic associations in Europe. From the time of their first arrival on European soil, Muslim migrants who did not wish to affiliate with the worship centers overseen by their governments have established independent mosques and Islamic organizations. In the early years, these were typically very small-scale operations housed in abandoned warehouses or other undesirable, low-rent commercial spaces and financed through meager budgets patched together with tiny donations, principally from indigent migrants. These independent mosques too tended to orient to the homeland—however, not to the official Islam sanctioned by their homeland governments, but rather to the actually practiced Islam of the villages from which most migrants originated. As migrants followed fellow villagers who migrated before them in a process of "chain migration," they sought to recreate in the receiving country the conditions of the village back home. It was common, for instance, to recruit an imam from the village of origin to run the community's mosque in the settlement land. Islam was thus pivotal to establishing this comforting *"ersatz home*" in a threatening foreign environment (Schiffauer 2010: 46), but it was an Islam characterized by a very high degree of "ideological inflexibility" (Ansari 2004: 346; see also Macey 1999). The recruited imams as well as their flocks often exhibited "frozen clock syndrome": nothing should change in their religious practice from the moment they left the village, even if cultural life in the village continued to evolve (Pickles 1995: 107; see also Leiken 2012: 62, 244). This "guestworker Islam" (Ceylan 2006: 177) has tended to be a largely "defensive religion" at the cultural epicenter of an insular community life that has rarely extended much beyond the confined "triangle of flat, work, and mosque" (Schiffauer 2010: 47)—what Justin Gest (2010: 79) labels the "square mile mentality." These tiny congregations of faithful Muslims were "rarely heard and even more rarely recognised and listened to beyond their own communities" (Werbner 2002: 6–7; see also Simonsen 2000: 148–50). Well over three-quarters of imams in Europe neither are citizens of the destination country in which they reside nor speak its dominant language proficiently (Laurence 2012: 144). Though they have never received nearly as much aid from receiving governments, when the latter did allot financial aid (often at the municipal level) to the independent mosques, it was almost always given along with maximum discretion to mosque leaders to use the aid as they deemed necessary (Laurence 2012: 74–75; Leiken 2012: 213–14; Schain 2010: 140–41; Gest 2010: 87–92; Mohr 2006: 268; Fadil 2006: 57). Whether simply tolerated as part of guaranteeing freedom of religion and association or directly funded with little or no oversight in a policy of multiculturalism, nongovernmental Islamic associations were also able to practice and preach norms and values profoundly at odds with those officially espoused by the receiving governments and allegedly embraced by their majority publics (O'Brien 2013a: 75–77; Frampton and Maher 2013: 40–51; Abadan-Unat 2011: 128; Bowen 2010: 30; Gest 2010: 121; Otterbeck 2010: 112; Briggs, Fieschi, and Lownsbrough 2006: 27; Ceylan 2006: 249–51; Mohr 2006: 38; Werbner 2002: 6–7; Shaw 2000; Gardner 1995).

In the late 1970s and 1980s, many of the small mosques began organizing into federations. The most adept of the organizers have turned out to be Islamists, many of whom took refuge in Europe as political exiles persecuted by homeland governments for alleged radicalization of Islam—for example, in Nasser's Egypt of the 1960s and 1970s as well as under Mubarak in the 1990s, in Turkey with the recurrent party bans and coups during the 1980s and 1990s, in Morocco with Hassan II's campaigns against the Justice and Spirituality Movement, or the cancelled elections in Algeria in 1991 won by the subsequently ousted Islamic Salvation Front (Laurence 2012: 77). In this way, major Islamist movements across the Islamic world, such as the Muslim Brotherhood, Milli Görüş, Jama'at-i Islami (Islamic Community), and Deobandi, came to have European counterparts—respectively, the Union of Islamic Organisations in Europe (with national branches in most lands such as the L'union des Organisations Islamique de France or L'Unione delle Comunità e Organizzazioni Islamiche in Italia), the Islamische Gesellschaft Deutschland and the Islamische Gemeinde Milli Görüş (with affiliated branches beyond Germany, for instance, in the Netherlands, France, and Belgium), the United Kingdom Islamic Mission, and Tablighi Jamaat (for details see Laurence 2012: 85–97; Meijer and Bakker 2012; Baran 2011: 73–83; Boubekeur and Amghar 2006; Amin 2002: 965; Grillo 1998: 198).

The nongovernmental activists have sought to distinguish themselves from and vie with the embassies for the allegiance of European Muslims. This the former have accomplished by increasingly directing their energies and resources away from the homeland to the situation in Europe. In particular, they have focused their efforts on pragmatically addressing the real-life problems of pious Muslims striving to practice their faith in a European environment not especially conducive to doing so. Doctrinally this has involved establishing a novel school of Islamic jurisprudence—*fiqh al-aqalliyyat*—to issue rulings on what constitutes pious behavior for Muslims living in the non-Muslim majority societies of Europe. There now exist dozens of books (Qaradawi 1999), websites, hotlines, radio and television call-in talk shows, such as *Al-Shari'ah wal-Hayat* (Islamic Law and Life) carried on the Al Jazeera network or found at www.Islamonline.net, and sponsored by the hugely popular Jusuf al-Qaradawi and his organization, the European Council for Fatwa and Research (ECFR), formed in 1997 by the Union of Islamic Organisations in Europe (UOIE). From these sources devout Muslims can seek helpful advice on how to work, date, marry, educate, dress, eat, fast, pray, and even die piously in Europe (Mandaville 2014: 380–82; Parray 2012; Gerlach 2006: 60–67)—what the ECFR labels "integration without assimilation" (quoted in Joppke and Torpey 2013: 148). Institutionally, these nongovernmental Islamic federations have sponsored most of the legal battles to win exemptions for Muslims whose religiously required behavior transgresses statutes and regulations of European governments and businesses. Thus, L'union des Organisations Islamique de France (UOIF) funded the legal battle of the three girls from Creil to attend school wearing the hijab (Laurence 2012: 208); the Islamische Gemeinde Milli Görüş (IGMG), which warns of the "rising danger of assimilation," sponsored Fershta Ludin's court case in Baden-Württemberg (quoted in Bundesministerium des Innern 2008: 252). The IGMG was also behind the successful effort in 2002 to legalize *halal* butchering in Germany over the remonstrations of animal rights activists who deem the ritual slaughter without anesthetic cruel (Joppke and Torpey 2013: 65). Various forms of halal slaughtering are permitted in France, Italy, Spain, Finland, Denmark, the United Kingdom, and Belgium, although the Dutch parliament banned the practice in 2011

(*Financial Times* 3 August 2011). The IGMG also steered the endeavor to exempt Muslim girls from mandatory mixed-gender swimming classes in public schools because their parents "do not wish their daughter[s] to be emancipated as Westerners understand that term" (quoted in Joppke and Torpey 2013: 59; Rohe 2004: 92). The nongovernmental organizations have led the campaigns, in Germany, the United Kingdom, the Netherlands, and to a lesser extent in France and Switzerland, to allow Muslims to be buried separately from non-Muslims and facing Mecca (Bader 2007: 18; Koopmans et al. 2005: 55–56). The same generally holds true for efforts to gain from non-Muslim employers special prayer spaces and break periods for Muslims keen to meet the Islamic requirement to pray toward Mecca at designated moments five times per day or, for instance, not to be required to handle pork products or alcohol (Maréchal 2008: 36–37; Bader 2007: 18; Hervieu-Léger 2007: 204; Koopmans et al. 2005: 55–56). Indeed, Ruud Koopmans and colleagues (2005: 155) found that in Europe Muslims seek exemptions from statute and convention more than any other minority community (also see Shavit and Wiesenbach 2012: 49; Pêdziwiatr 2007; Yurdakul 2006: 157; Lewis 2006: 170).

To justify such exemptions they frequently deploy fragments of communitarian logic. For example, the Institut Européen des Sciences Humaines in Château-Chinon, which has strong ties to the UOIF, has long offered to supply French schools with its graduates to teach Islamic instruction, but only on condition that it and it alone determine the content of the training (Khosrokhavar 2010: 138). In 2001 after a protracted political and legal struggle, the IGMG-affiliated Islamic Federation of Berlin scored a major communitarian victory by winning the privilege to write and implement the curriculum for Islamic religious education in Berlin schools (Yurdakul 2009: 98–99). However, after a few years in operation city officials terminated the program by replacing all denominationally specific religious instruction with a generic religious studies curriculum (Schiffauer 2006). Longtime Milli Görüş activist Ali Kizilkaya, who heads the Koordinierungsrat der Muslime in Deutschland (Coordinating Council of Muslims in Germany), which offers religious education for the schools of North Rhine-Westphalia, insists that only his organization can and should determine what constitutes "correct belief." "People will have to get used to that," he adds, "something that should not be that difficult since this same prerogative Christian churches have long enjoyed" (quoted in *Qantara.de* 19 October 2012; https://en.qantara.de/content/islamic-religious-education-in-germany-allah-or-the-advisory-council). Indeed, several other German *Länder* (Lower Saxony, Hesse) have recently contracted with Islamic organizations to offer Islamic instruction in public schools (Ceylan and Kiefer 2013: 154). Approvingly citing the example of separate Christian and Jewish courts in the

Ottoman Empire, Abdullah Bin Bayyah (2002) of the ECFR advocates the establishment in contemporary Europe of *fiqh* courts (tribunals of Islamic jurisprudence) staffed by Muslim judges appointed by the ECFR but with the backing of the secular state. Indeed, in the United Kingdom several Islamic tribunals, such as London's Islamic Sharia Council, the Muslim Arbitrational Tribunal in Nuneaton, or the (all-female) council in Birmingham's Central Mosque, are currently operating (Griffith-Jones 2013; Bowen 2012a: 82–83). The Arbitration Act of 1996 recognized the rulings of such Christian, Jewish, and Islamic tribunals as legally binding in civil matters so long as both parties voluntarily submit to the arbitration (Saunders 2012: 91). As mentioned, something roughly similar has existed in Greece for the Turkish Muslim minority in Western Thrace since the Treaty of Lausanne in 1923 (Triandafyllidou 2010c: 202).

Many non-Muslims endorse differentialist exemptions for Muslim Europeans. Erstwhile archbishop of Canterbury Rowan Williams touched off a great row in 2008 when he asserted that aspects of sharia dealing with private matters (for example, divorce) should be "recognised" by British law, a position seconded later that year by the country's highest justice, Lord Phillips (Bowen 2012a: 72–73). Prominent legal experts and officials in other lands have announced their interest in something similar, for example, Norwegian Prime Minister Erna Solberg (*Drammens Tidende* 6 November 2003; see also Cesari 2013: 115–20; Bowen 2010: 176; *Migration und Bevölkerung* February 2012; *Radio Netherlands Worldwide* 3 September 2009). In 2002, while mayor of Amsterdam, subsequent Labour Party leader Job Cohen advocated state subsidies to Islamic organizations even when some of their practices (for example, subordinating women) offend the sensibilities of most Dutch citizens (Buruma 2006: 245). When conceding in 1999 that North African immigrants were not likely to disappear from French soil in the foreseeable future, French New Right guru Alain de Benoist maintained

> that ethnocultural identity should no longer be relegated to the private domain, but should be acknowledged and recognized in the public sphere. The New Right proposes, then, a communitarian model which would spare individuals from being cut off from their cultural roots and which would permit them to keep alive the structures of their collective cultural lives. (Benoist and Champetier 2012: 3:2)

I in no way wish to imply that communitarianism is upstaging liberal multiculturalism. For instance, a German judge in 2007, claiming that the Qur'an permits wife battery and that it is not unusual in Moroccan cultural circles, denied divorce to a Moroccan Muslim wife complaining of physical abuse at the hands of her husband. The decision caused a national scandal and was swiftly nullified. Virtually the same thing recurred in 2008 with the decision of a court in Lille that granted a divorce to a Muslim husband on grounds that his wife was not a virgin at the time of their marriage (Surkis 2010). My point is that governments allow and European Muslims encounter at once both integrative and separatist policies and opportunities—a conclusion that several studies have drawn (O'Brien 2013a; Scholten 2011; Otterbeck 2010: 112; Sunier 2010: 125; Spena 2010: 169; Schiffauer 2002: 15). There is no consistent and uniform policy toward Islam, just as there is no overarching ethical consensus favoring liberal multiculturalism over communitarianism.

Hobbesian Postmodernism

A conspicuous number of Muslim persons and organizations have severed or spurned relations with European governments (Roy 2007: 49; Boender 2006: 107; Scientific Council 2006: 202; Klausen 2005: 87; Bielefeldt and Bahmanpour 2002; Modood 1994). For example, Martin Muñoz and colleagues (2003: 119) found that roughly one-third of the Islamic organizations in Spain eschew state funds and prefer to remain independent and separate. Jonas Otterbeck (2010: 107) estimates the number in Sweden at 25 percent. Hizb ut-Tahrir (Liberation Party) maintains that

> the hopeless track record of the current Muslim MPs is clear proof of how they must abandon our communities and Islamic values to remain within those parties. The path for voting for, and participating in, these secular parties will no doubt bring harm rather than any good to our community. (Quoted in Akbarzadeh and Roose 2011: 314)

As distrust of the state intensifies, the sway of Hobbesian postmodernism comes into play. Communitarianism nurses the hope for a neutral state in the application of the presumption-of-equal-worth principal to Islam. By contrast, Hobbesian postmodernism rejects the possibility of neutrality and conceives the state as an integral part of a complex array of powerful persons and forces for which the demonization and domination of Islam are constitutive. Thus, anything approaching a more level playing field can only be achieved by eluding and resisting state authorities—to wit, by building pockets of resistance and autonomy among Muslim diasporas amidst the surrounding *dar al-harb* (abode of war) (Boubekeur 2007). Göle (2011) argues that Islamists have since the Iranian Revolution of 1979 become increasingly emboldened about resisting Western secularization (see also Pargeter 2008: 16). As the prominent Islamist leader Rachid al-Ghannouchi has opined, "One day, we will be able to influence the West as much as it has influenced our countries" (quoted in Maréchal 2008: 263).

I hasten to add, however, that in real politics the boundaries between Hobbesian postmodernism and communitarianism are as shifting and porous as those between the latter and liberal multiculturalism. As will be demonstrated below through an analysis of consultative bodies established of late in many European lands between the state and Islam, some organizations make overtures to the state despite distrusting it. Others trust the state initially but begin to doubt after frustrating experiences. In many organizations the leaders and the rank-and-file alike are divided on what is the best strategy to pursue: enthusiastic support, cautious cooperation, or obstinate rejection. Some pursue all three at one time or the other depending on the context. Precisely such fluidness and polyvalence—that is, messiness—should be expected in a normative landscape rife with fragmentation and fragilization.

Islamism

With that caveat registered, we can nonetheless discern the sway of Hobbesian postmodernism among Muslim organizations, particularly Islamist ones. I emphatically reiterate that Islamists and their supporting organizations are not monolithic. Critical differences in doctrine and strategy divide them, but they all tend to concur on the ultimate superiority of God's law as they interpret it, especially in the Qur'an, Sunna, and Hadith. In the context of this chapter on secularism *in Europe*, it makes sense to lump the differing groups and beliefs together under a single category. Islamists, like Christian and Jewish fundamentalists, who, by the way, outnumber Islamic fundamentalists in Europe by a factor of two to one (Jenkins 2007: 75), pose a challenge to the secular European state's demand, in theory at least, that all its citizens eschew theocracy and submit to man-made law (Roy 2007: 23).

For Islamists, resisting European-style secularism means much more than simply maintaining a particular identity; it is about defending their access to eternal salvation. They resolutely believe that the majority of European Christian and Jewish denominations have, in submitting to the conditions of Western secularism, made a tragic mistake, with grave consequences for all humanity. By subordinating themselves to man-made law, they have forfeited the role of moral leadership, thereby opening the way for unbuttoned hedonism to become the ersatz religion of the masses and leaving morally unguided and unchecked an economic and political elite that has ravaged the planet and its peoples through wanton pursuit of this-worldly profit and power. Secularism, for Islamists, is synonymous with the triumph of sin over morality, evil over good. They resolve to resist it, which they believe they do best by endeavoring to live by Islamic precepts as much as possible in all aspects of their lives, private and public. IGMG's website (www.igmg.de), for instance, claims the organization is committed to "the application of Islamic principles to the public sphere." In an interview in 2003, UOIF leader, Lhaj Thami Brèze, repeated the tenet of the Muslim Brotherhood that "the Qur'an is our constitution," though he later denied it (Laurence 2012: 72). This theocratic philosophy was profoundly inspired by Sayyid Qutb's *Milestones*, still a widely read and praised book among Islamists, in which the venerated martyr denounces all man-made laws as the product of ignorance (*jahilyya*) and calls on his brethren to defy, depose, and replace them with Islamic law wherever possible (Qutb 2007: 1–2). Hassan al-Banna, founder of the Muslim Brotherhood, spoke of Islam as a "comprehensive order" (quoted in Rosen 2008: 118). Likewise, Jama'at-i Islami's founder, Abul Ala Maududi, envisaged an Islamic union based on sharia that would "supersede all other ties" (quoted in Landau 1990: 227). The UKIM website (www.ukim.org) claims the organization strives for "a caring and sharing society . . . based on the ideals, values, and principles of Islam." Similarly, Hizb ut-Tahrir maintains that "Islam is a complete way of life that provides guidance for man in all aspects of life . . . the truth revealed by the creator of man, life and the universe" (quoted in Akbarzadeh and Roose 2011: 313). The website IslamQA declares that swearing allegiance to a non-Muslim state is impious (Cesari 2013: 136).

In the context of such avowedly theocratic statements, it might seem like the height of folly to posit influence from Godless postmodernism on God-fearing Islamists. To be sure, I argue neither that Islamists produce no independent thought nor that they are secret disciples of, say, Nietzsche or Heidegger. I do contend, however, that common postmodern tropes or fragments often turn up in Islamists' stances, if for no other reason than that they persuade audiences and thereby advance Islamist agendas. Here I concur with Roy (2005), who refutes the putative portrayal of Islamists as proverbial ostriches with their heads sunk deep in the sands of a medieval outlook. The French scholar prefers to read Islamist activists as fully integrated into a single global political discourse whose successful ideas and tactics they keenly study and dexterously exploit (see also Weimann 2015; Vidino 2010a: 11; Bunt 2009; Wiktorowicz 2005: 12–25; LeVine 2003; Gray 2003). Moreover, in the context of Europe, in good part because postmodernism enjoys there a respected tradition, postmodern arguments strike many as persuasive.

European Islamists encounter experiences that often resonate strongly with postmodern interpretations. Take, for example, the arguably central postmodern tenet that truth is constructed rather than found and, therefore, that truth is whatever passes for truth. European Muslims are daily inundated with distorting images of their creed and their practices that they know all too well many non-Muslims accept as the truth. There now exists a plethora of studies that find in practically every European country that images of Islam and of Muslims tend to be monolithic, negative, and reductionist (Pollack and Müller 2013; Cesari 2013: 7–20; Commission Nationale 2008; Moore, Mason, and Lewis 2008; Navarro 2008; Poole 2002; see also islamophobiawatch.com); moreover, they tend to attribute disagreeable behavior (such as higher rates of crime, of high school dropout, of joblessness, or of extremism) among persons of Muslim heritage to their purported socialization to the "culture of Islam" (Fredette 2014; Rommelspacher 2010: 445; Gest 2010: 56; Roy 2007: 88). The negative images tend to be widely cited by politicians and in media (print and electronic), and they strongly weigh upon public opinion (on politics, see Amnesty International 2012; Ansari and Hafez 2012; Morgan and Poynting 2012a; European Commission against Racism and Intolerance 2011; Sayyid 2009; Ansari 2004; on media, Meijer 2013; Schneiders 2010a; Zapata-Barrero and Qasem 2008; Deltombe 2005; Geissler and Pöttker 2005; Poole 2002). Not surprisingly, then, the 2011 Pew Global Attitudes Survey found that 36 percent of those polled in Britain and France, 55 percent in Germany, and 63 percent in Spain have an "unfavorable" attitude toward Muslims in general (Pew 2012). Indeed, many of these studies have been conducted by scholars with postmodernist and postcolonial leanings, profoundly informed, as already noted, by Said's (1978) *Orientalism*. Gest (2010: 56) is representative:

> Interpretations of Islam that portray it as irreducible, impenetrable, undifferentiated and immune to processes of change have long obscured the complexities of the historical experience of Muslims across different societies. Today, these perceptions persist, overlooking the complicated process of acculturation and mutual adaptation by Muslims and institutions of Western Europe. They ignore Islam's plasticity and diversity, and instead allow exaggerated misimages—stemming from exotica or invented in a narrow historical context and augmented by selective episodic details—to constitute Muslim history and tradition. And by considering Islam as an undifferentiated whole, essentialist discourse is able to broad-brush Muslims as a threat to the equally undifferentiated "good" societies of the West. (see also Cesari 2013: 139–45; Kaya 2012: 211; Göle 2011: 155; Amiraux 2010: 145; Sayyid 2009: 198–99; Ewing 2008: 28; Schiffauer 2006: 111; O'Brien 1996: 43–104; Muñoz 1994: 219)

Islamists often echo such postmodern readings. That is, they go beyond the liberal claim that the distortions are inaccurate and in need of correction (Hafez 2011) and endorse the postmodern assertion that they are constitutive of European identity itself. In this reading, Europeans have long relied on a negative image of Islam to project and sustain their supercilious self-understanding. Tariq Ramadan, the grandson of the Muslim Brotherhood founder, Hasan al Banna, and arguably the poster child of the Brotherhood movement in Europe, says of the avidly secularist Left in Europe who vilify Islam:

> Convinced that they are progressive, they give themselves the arbitrary right to proclaim the definitively reactionary nature of religions. . . . The possibility that Islam could engender resistance is not even imagined . . . unless it's to modernity. In the end, only a handful of "Muslims-who-think-like-us" are accepted, while the others are denied the possibility of being genuinely progressive fighters armed with their own set of values. By doing this, the dialogue with Islam is transformed into an interactive monologue which massages "our ideological certainties" just as Huntington wanted to ensure "our strategic interests." (Ramadan 2009)

But one does not, like Ramadan, have to be an Oxford don who wrote his dissertation on Nietzsche to have "fragilized" toward postmodernism. Thus, a speaker at a Hizb ut-Tahrir meeting in London in 2008 maintained that "the West needs hatred for Islam to support its interventions in the Muslim world" (quoted in Gest 2010: 112). "The ones who are behind this negative propaganda," writes the Swedish journal *Salaam*, deliberately set out to "make Islam look like a weird, horrible and strange faith so that no one ever should come to think of taking an interest in or convert to that faith" (quoted in Otterbeck 2000: 261). The imprint of Said's *Orientalism* is unmistakable: "The Orient has helped to define Europe (or the West) as its contrasting image, idea, personality, experience. . . . European culture gained its strength and identity by setting itself off against the Orient" (Said 1978: 1–3). Again, I do not suggest that, say, Hizb ut-Tahrir supporters admire, like Said, Nietzsche or Foucault, though they might. Rather their anti-European rhetoric would not resonate as well if it were not for Nietzsche's, Foucault's, and Said's contribution to postmodern thought.

Said (1978: 3), of course, famously contended that Orientalist discourse made up a critical part of "a Western style for dominating, restructuring, and having authority over the Orient." Whether or not Said himself was influenced by Qutb and other Islamists, will-to-power fragments frequently find their way into Islamist propaganda in Europe. It should come as no surprise that Islamist organizations regularly excoriate "western foreign policy" as wanton humiliation and devastation of Muslim lands and peoples. While the United States and Israel come in for the greatest criticism in the present age, European governments earn Islamist scorn for allying with the oppressors as well as for initiating the protracted domination of Muslims in the medieval Crusades and in modern colonialism. Hizb ut-Tahrir, for instance, contended that the Boston Marathon bombing of 2013 had to be understood in a wider context in which

> the USA and its allies have committed numerous heinous crimes against Muslims . . . [w]hether . . . Guantanamo Bay, the deaths of Iraqis on false pretences [sic], the systematic destruction of Afghanistan since 2002, the drone attacks in Pakistan, Yemen and Somalia . . . overt support for Israel's crimes in Palestine. (Hizb ut-Tahrir, 23 April 2013, www.hizb.org.uk/current-affairs/boston-bombings)

In his 2002 book *Naal bou la France* (Damn France), Farid Abdelkrim, president of Jeunes Musulmans de France, denounced France as a neocolonial power that conspired with the West to commit the 9/11 atrocities and pin them on Osama Bin Laden (also see Leiken 2012: 232; Schiffauer 2010: 183; Wiktorowicz 2005: 68, 12; Werbner 2004: 463). IGMG alleged that Salman Rushdie's *Satanic Verses* was actually published by the CIA (Laurence 2012: 207).

Islamists decry demonization and domination of Muslims within Europe as well. Britain's Islamchannel, for instance, advertises itself as the "Voice of the Voiceless, Voice of the Oppressed." IGMG too presents itself as "supporting the socially disadvantaged and oppressed" (Das islamische Portal, www.igmg.de/gemeinschaft/wir-ueber-uns). In response to France's veil ban, Abdullah Ben Masour, general secretary of the UOIF, criticized the French state for portraying "a twelve-year-old child . . . like an enemy . . . just because she wants to do her own thing" (quoted in Koopmans et al. 2005: 170). Kalim Siddiqui, who founded the Muslim Parliament UK in 1989, charged that "post-Christian secular society," including "the British Government," seeks "to destroy our values" (quoted in Kepel 1997: 143). Similarly, Abdul Wahid, chairman of Hizb ut-Tahrir Britain, claims "the government's long-term objective is to manufacture a compliant, subdued, secular Muslim community in Britain" (quoted in Akbarzadeh and Roose 2011: 314). *Al-Islam*, the journal of the Munich Islamic Center, charges "in a society where the majority of the population—and nearly all politicians—are critical of or reject Islam, one cannot expect Muslims to enjoy real freedom" (quoted in Meining 2012: 228). Abou Jahjah, leader of the Antwerp-based Arab-European League, talks of "Flemish cultural terrorism" against the Islamic community of Belgium (*Telegraph* 29 November 2002). Complaints about the relentless and systematic oppression of European Muslims have for at least two decades represented a major theme in the lyrics of famous Islamist hip-hop and rap artists such as IAM (Imperial Asiatic Men), Lala

Man, 3ème CEil, Fun-Da-Mental, Mecca2Medina, Poetic Pilgrimage, Salah Eddin, Pearls of Islam, or Yazid. The latter sings: "I'm the Arab, stopping oppression is my mission" (quoted in Jenkins 2007: 172; also see Aidi 2014).

In such critique we can discern the postmodern notion of the "negative other." Muslims are the "new Jews," the latest group Europeans love (need) to hate. Social scientists may explain such Europe bashing as an "escape from the oppressive tedium of being constantly identified in negative terms" (Gardner and Shuker 1994: 164), "inverted othering" (O'Brien 2013a: 72), "adversarial assimilation" (Leiken 2012: 47), or "apartism" (Gest 2010: 49). Journalists declare it the new "coolness" (Jenkins 2007: 127). Regardless of the label or explanation, the critical rhetoric borrows fragments from scholarship on immigration with postmodern and postcolonial leanings whose findings are now widely disseminated. Thus, to take but a small sampling, Göle (2011: 155) spotlights the "'alterizing,' orientalizing, Islamizing, or even barbarizing" of European Muslims, Valérie Amiraux (2010: 145) "the continuity between pre- and post-colonial imagination, discourse and practice in handling Muslim otherness in France," Gerdien Jonker (2006: 126) "the old binary construction of 'Oriental (Muslim) culture' versus 'Western enlightenment,'" and Ricard Zapata-Barrero (2006: 145) the protracted history of "Maurophobia" in Spain. To repeat, I do not aim to paint Islamists as postmodernists. Rather, I contend that postmodern fragments are so pronounced and compelling that Islamists would be foolish not to exploit them simply because they originate with or are augmented by many non-Muslim thinkers. Fragilization occurs, in part at least, because it proves politically useful.

Nor do Islamists draw exclusively on postmodern arguments, though they tend to predominate. Islamists can be heard deploying classic liberal arguments against oppression that inveigh against the alleged hypocrisy of European governments that fail to live up to their own standards. IGMG, for instance, "reminds that the majority of Muslims in Europe are excluded from direct democratic participation" and claims that "political participation must be independent of social differences such as immigrant background or ethnic heritage" (Das islamische Portal, www.igmg. de/gemeinschaft/wir-ueber-uns). Here Islamists sing in unison with human rights NGOs like SOS-Racisme—or the European Commission itself, for that matter. And why not? Oppressed people have for centuries played the hypocrisy card to shame explicitly liberal states into quitting or correcting their illiberal practices.

As intimated above, fragilization toward postmodernism manifests itself when Islamists reject the possibility of a neutral state that treats Muslims and non-Muslims equally and fairly. The postmodern reading of secularism theorizes it, like liberalism more generally, as a modern Western construct or discourse whose very presuppositions exclude the possibility of a rational critique of secular tenets. To oppose secularism is to be irrational, to be under the spell of religious enthusiasm (Asad 2003). Those Muslims, Islamists or not, who believe that God's revealed truths should be taken seriously in the public sphere are a priori conceived of as lunatics and zealots with their heads clouded by a premodern and prerational outlook. Needless to say, this dualist reading conveniently projects as progressive and rational all those who accept the secular condition to relegate religion to private life. Again, so standard is this postmodern interpretation of secularism that one need but eyes to find it swiftly (Mavelli 2012; Amir-Moazami 2011; Asad 2006; Connolly 2005; Nordmann and Vidal 2004). The analysis understandably resonates with Islamists. They are daily surrounded by images of Muslims that depict them as backward and benighted. Moreover, the vast majority of non-Muslims (and many credulous Muslims) accept these images as truth, despite, from Islamist perspective, their blatant inaccuracy. What more obvious conclusion to draw in their shoes than that European governments and publics cannot and will not abandon or amend these prejudices because to do so would undermine their own positive image? And to boot, the very same argument is corroborated by the hippest cutting-edge research!

The savvy political response is resistance, for to conform to the secular order is to help perpetuate one's own domination. The fight-the-power message resounds in Islamist rap and hip-hop. Fun-da-Mental sing: "I'M the soldier in the name of Allah. . . . So watch out now I'm comin' at ya." (Quoted in Samad 2007: 165).

Here again the imprint of widely dispersed postcolonial thought, such as Frantz Fanon's *The Wretched of the Earth*, is unmistakable (see also Aidi 2014; Majid 2000; Said 1993; Nandy 1988). What Jørgen Nielsen (1999: 95) has labeled "resistance Islam" takes many forms. The next chapter treats violent resistance or what many term "terrorism." At this juncture, I want to focus on (for the most part) nonviolent resistance. In pure theory (remembering that no actual humans correspond to pure theory), Islamist resistance occurs whenever Muslims put God's laws in front or in place of secular laws. That is, one permits and embraces (as much as possible) only those practices of the secular order that do not contravene one's understanding of God's precepts—for instance, sharia. This is the stated goal, for example, of the Sharia4 movement with branches in many European countries. Such acts of Islamist defiance include, but are hardly limited to, taking multiple wives and arranging marriages (often not recognized by the state) (Bowen 2010: 156–65); eating only halal food and imbibing no alcohol; dressing modestly, including pressuring others to do so (Alonso 2012: 478–79; Gest 2010: 109; Jenkins 2007: 182, 252; Kepel 2004: 51; Amara 2003; Macey 1999; Ashfar 1994); sending children to private Qur'an schools or summer camps to "unlearn" the secular teachings of the public schools (Leiken 2012: 53; Bowen 2010: 125; Schiffauer 2008a: 59–70; Pargeter 2008: 142; Lewis 1994: 141); shooing homosexuals, sex workers, drug dealers, and other purveyors of Western "decadence" out of the neighborhood (Leiken 2012: 195; Schiffauer 2008a: 105; Pargeter 2008: 143; Taheri 2005); protesting books (*Satanic Verses*, Irshad Manji's *Islam, Liberty and Love*), newspapers (*Jyllands-Posten*), films (*Submission*), and performances (Voltaire's *Mahomet*, Mozart's *Idomeneo*) that "insult" Islam (Pargeter 2008: 187–203; Jenkins 2007: 280); cyberattacking hostile broadcasts (*TV5Monde*); and, of course, conventional proselytizing such as handing out Qur'ans on street corners (Khosrokhavar 2010: 139; Schiffauer 2010: 222; Shavit and Wiesenbach 2009; Jonker 2006: 141–45; Nielsen 2003: 34).

Motivating such acts is the desire and attempt to create spheres of Islamist autonomy in which Islamic laws and practices prevail, including when they transgress secular laws. Other scholars prefer different labels such as "protection zones" (Schiffauer 2008a: 69), "zones of exclusion" (Kastoryano 2006: 66–67), or domains of "Islamic ambiance" (Bowen 2010: 105), but they all document the same general phenomenon of enclaves where Islamist practices represent the expected norm rather than the ridiculed exception (see also Alonso 2012: 478–79; Roy 2004: 281–82). These "Islamist milieux" (Laurence 2012: 101) often amount to no more than the four walls of a flat or mosque but in some cases can envelop broad swaths of neighborhoods and boroughs where large numbers of Muslims concentrate, such as East London, Amsterdam's Slotervaart, Brussels' Sint-Jans-Molenbeek, Paris's banlieues, or Berlin's Kreuzberg (Metcalf 1996). In 2011, for example, in the London neighborhoods of Waltham Forest, Tower Hamlets, and Newham there appeared daubed on traffic signs and lampposts bright yellow posters reading "You are entering a Sharia-controlled zone—Islamic rules enforced" (*Daily Mail* 28 July 2011). In 2014, Salafists organized the "sharia police" to patrol the streets of Wuppertal, discouraging young Muslims from drinking, gambling, or fornicating (*Deutsche Welle* 7 September 2014). Indeed, some such districts receive quasi-governmental recognition when police treat them as "no-go areas" where formal law either need not or cannot be rigorously enforced (Leiken 2012: 38).

Naturally, illegal acts transpire. So-called "honor killings," for instance, have garnered inordinate and sensationalized attention within European society, despite the fact that their numbers are rare and pale in comparison to "standard" domestic violence homicides (Altinbaş 2013; Korteweg and Yurdakul 2014). The overwhelming majority of acts of "self-imposed apartheid" (Kepel 2004: 253) are perfectly legal. Moreover, they are legally protected by freedom of religion, speech, and association clauses anchored in European constitutions and inspired by fundamental liberal principles safeguarding the autonomy of the individual. In no few cases, furthermore, formally liberal secular governments provide monetary or institutional support to vehemently antisecular organizations that have successfully made the case for state aid using the classic communitarian logic of the presumption of equal worth. This is what I mean by "policy messiness." This thicket of crisscrossing, overlayering, and contradictory policies and realities—secularisms instead of secularism—results, at least in part, from vibrant but vying public philosophies, none of which is able definitively to smite rivals due to a protracted *Kulturkampf* (O'Brien 2013a).

Liberal Perfectionist Secularism

Let us not, however, underestimate the resolve of those who consider Islam a threat. As the perceived threat grows, so too does the apparent appropriateness of liberal perfectionism. In Chapter 2, we already encountered the blurred—that is, fragilized—line between liberal voluntarism and perfectionism. Habermas (2008b), for instance, observes:

> It is a well-known fact that the Catholic Church first pinned its colors to the mast of liberalism and democracy with the Second Vaticanum in 1965. And in Germany, the Protestant churches did not act differently. Many Muslim communities still have this painful learning process before them.

But the German liberal adds that "the state can only encourage rather than impose the learning process of self-reflection that leads to questioning one's own religion enough to tolerate others and non-believers and realize that doing so is the most rational approach." But encouragement, especially strong encouragement, already starts one down the slippery slope toward perfectionism. No doctrine that posits absolute universal principles, as does liberalism, can fully elude the temptation of perfectionism. It becomes unsettling not to correct blatant ignorance and injustice, even when they appear to be voluntarily willed or tolerated (Bader 2007: 124–25). Many in Europe are convinced that the errors, both empirical and ethical, committed by pious Muslims are too grave to leave uncorrected. They implore the state assiduously to defend the secular democratic order against Muslims, who are presumed to reject and imperil it. The state, then, should be anything but neutral toward Muslims. Rather, it should rigorously test their loyalty to liberal democratic principles and resocialize or repress those who fail. "*Laïcité* must be a [shared] culture, or it will not be" (Debray 2003: 43).

In this context, some version of the "clash of civilizations" argument tends to surface. In a widely read book, former German chancellor Helmut Schmidt (2011: 71) argued that the fact that roughly a quarter of the world's governments are Islamist-leaning and none is a democracy should occasion profound skepticism and caution regarding the prospects for a Euro-Islam compatible with Western democratic values and laws. Frits Bolkenstein (1991), as leader of the People's Party for Freedom and Democracy, had two decades earlier made a similar argument that attained great salience in the Netherlands. We already encountered the claim in the previous chapter that Islam is inherently misogynistic. Another common charge is that the Qur'an, as well as the example of Muhammad, teaches Muslims to be intolerant of unbelievers and even to convert them with the sword if necessary (insinuated, for instance, by Benedict XVI in his notorious Regensburg speech in 2006). Although the pontiff spoke of the distant past, Italian journalist Oriana Fallaci perceived a much more immediate threat in her second best-selling rant against Islam, *The Force of Reason* (2006): "Europe becomes more and more a province of Islam, a colony of Islam. In each of our cities lies a second city: a Muslim city, a city run by the Koran. A stage in the Islamic expansionism" (quoted in Jenkins 2007: 244). An international chorus of prominent opinion leaders, including, from France, André Gerin, Samira Bellil, Pascal Bruckner, André Glucksmann, Emmanuell Todd, Chadortt Djavann, and Caroline Fourest; from the Netherlands, Ayaan Hirsi Ali, Hafid Bouazza, Frits Bolkestein, Paul Scheffer, Herman Philipse, and Hans Jensen; from Germany, Henryk Broder, Hans-Peter Raddatz, Thilo Sarrazin, Ralph Giordano, Seyran Ateş, Alice Schwarzer, and Necla Kelek; from Norway, Shabana Rehman Gaarder and Bruce Bawer; from the United Kingdom, Bat Ye'or, Melanie Phillips, Farrukh Dhondy, Roy Jenkins, and Niall Ferguson; and from Italy, Magdi Allam, Giovanni Sartori, and Galli della Logia, has sounded the alarm. Though the verses of the individual authors, like their political affiliations, may vary, their common refrain is in unison: Islam is illiberal and antidemocratic and, therefore, pious Muslims and the organizations that represent them threaten democracy, indeed Western Civilization itself. Accompanying these voices are the clarion sounds of mostly sensationalized, best-selling books and articles as well as widely viewed documentaries and reportage spotlighting alarming practices of forced marriage, honor killings, genital mutilation, anti-Western indoctrination, and terrorist plotting on European soil (Dirie 1999; Bellil 2002; Kelek 2005; Çileli 2002; Phillips 2007). All of these warnings against a threatening Islam revivify inveterate Orientalist readings of Islamic civilization such as Ernest Renan's from 1883 (and thereby provide evidence for the postcolonial reading mentioned above):

Any person with a bit of education about current affairs clearly discerns the actual inferiority of Muslim countries, the decadence in states ruled by Islam, the intellectual nullity of races which behold exclusively their culture and education to this religion.(Quoted in Taras 2012: 146)

Dutch Freedom Party leader, Geert Wilders, used crasser words: "I hate Islam . . . the ideology of a retarded culture" (*Guardian* 17 February 2008).

These harsh critics of Islam hurl even sharper barbs at liberal apprehension and vacillation. Indeed, their indignation over alleged liberal spinelessness points to the very kind of fragilization that we have been pursuing throughout this book. Paul Scheffer (2011: 325), for instance, denounces the "cosmopolitan disillusion" of the Dutch elite preaching multiculturalism. Pascal Bruckner (2007) inveighs against the communitarian influence that prompts European governments to tolerate "parallel societies" of "small, self-isolated social groups, each of which adheres to a different norm" and "enclaves in which individual autonomy is squashed." Thierry Chervel takes aim at postmodernism:

In the confrontation with Islamism, the Left has *abandoned its principles*. In the past it stood for cutting the ties to convention and tradition, but in the case of Islam it reinstates them in the name of multiculturalism. It is proud to have fought for women's rights, but in Islam it tolerates head scarves, arranged marriages, and wife-beating. It once stood for equal rights, now it preaches a right to difference—and thus different rights. It proclaims freedom of speech, but when it comes to Islam it coughs in embarrassment. It once supported gay rights, but now keeps silent about Islam's taboo on homosexuality. The West's long-due process of self-relativisation at the end of the colonial era, which was promoted by postmodernist and structuralist ideas, has led to cultural relativism and the loss of criteria.(*Der Tagesspiegel* 9 February 2009; emphasis in original)

"What has come of us," complains Ralph Giordano, "when we have to be concerned whether or not our actions and negotiations please radical Muslims?" (*Die Welt* 25 October 2008). The intended message is plain: European governments should side with liberalism and defend and spread its core values even if doing so offends Muslims (or communitarians and postmodernists for that matter). In the words of *Stern* editor Hans Ulrich Jörges, "We must defend and foment what the Islamic nations are lacking, democracy, minority rights, women's rights, the Enlightenment, and separation between Church and State" (*Stern* 14 February 2006). Likewise, Peter Michalzek argued in the left-leaning *Frankfurter Rundschau* (23 March 2007) that "one cannot consider Islam a religion among others, a religion that might have a right to exist under the big roof of European tolerance."

Some of the most vociferous and compelling proponents of liberal perfectionism are Muslims, typically ex-Muslims. These often highly prominent critics of Islam enjoy an exalted standing among European publics as "experts by real-life experience," insiders, so to speak, who purportedly "know" the true nature of Islam because they have suffered firsthand as victims of its smothering oppression. They appear frequently on talk shows, at public fora, and in governmental hearings. Many are the same women whose voices we heard in the previous chapter excoriating veiling as the outermost manifestation of pervasive misogyny in Islamic doctrine and practice. Whether male or female, they all tend to urge European governments to protect liberalism from Muslims who seek its demise. Germany's Seyran Ateş (2008: 199) denounces "kowtowing [*Kniefall*] to Islam" (quoted in Rommelspacher 2010: 449). Afshin Ellian (2006) of the Netherlands warns:

> Free speech is in danger of being increasingly restricted by invoking "Islamophobia" and "racism." . . . Intellectuals themselves are increasingly calling for self-censorship and politically correct reporting of intolerant tendencies. Has this country lost its appetite for freedom? Has the country where Pierre Bayle and John Locke published their books become a land of veiled opinions?

Following the Danish cartoon controversy, several prominent public intellectuals with Muslim backgrounds, including Salman Rushdie, Ayaan Hirsi Ali, Chahla Chafiq, Irshad Manji, Mehdi Mozaffari, Maryam Namazie, Taslima Nasreen, and Ibn Warraq published (with five non-Muslims as well) a manifesto against Islamist "totalitarianism":

> We reject "cultural relativism," which consists in accepting that men and women of Muslim culture should be deprived of the right to equality, freedom, and secular values in the name of respect for cultures and traditions. . . . We appeal to democrats and free spirits of all countries that our century should be one of Enlightenment, not of obscurantism.(*Jyllands-Posten* 28 February 2006)

Also prominently and often effectively warning against extremist Islam are the many migrant NGOs with a strong secularist leaning, such as the Mouvement des maghrébins laïques de France, the Türkische Gemeinde in Deutschland, the (Swiss) Forum for Progressive Islam, the Democratic

Muslims in Denmark, or the Central Committee for Ex-Muslims (Germany, U.K., Scandanavia and the Netherlands).

Politicians have responded by pledging to use the instruments of the state to prevent radical Islam and promote Euro-Islam. The next chapter focuses on governmental efforts to monitor and thwart suspected terrorists. Chapter 3 drew attention to mandatory civics courses and oaths of allegiance that seek to teach and test the internalization of liberal democratic values by Muslim citizens and residents. The previous chapter detailed policies in many European countries that proscribe veiling and thereby literally compel Muslim women and girls (depending on the context) to dress "secular" in the hope that by doing so they will learn to appreciate liberal democratic values. Such measures stem from a combined liberal perfectionist and Orientalist presupposition that Muslims require state assistance to "modernize" or "Westernize." They cannot be depended on to do it themselves.

This perfectionist logic is detectable in a spate of governmental initiatives designed to gain greater influence over the preaching and teaching of Islam in Europe. Britain, for example, introduced in 2004 mandatory English classes for imams before obtaining visas to enter the kingdom. Since 2002, the Dutch government requires a six-month training program in language, social and political institutions, and the "Dutch ways of life" for imams coming to serve in Islamic organizations in the Netherlands (Laurence 2012: 186). Belgium and France have similar programs in Morocco (Laurence 2012: 227). Following the *Charlie Hebdo* shootings, the French Interior Ministry announced that all imams who serve as chaplains in French prisons will be required to earn a diploma in civic responsibility to be offered by a dozen French universities. The University of Lyon has since 2012 offered a course in "Understanding Secularity" for imams (*France 24* 26 February 2015). Germany since 2006 has through the Goethe Institute and the Konrad Adenauer Foundation provided training in German language and values to imams in Turkey who plan to migrate to Germany. The municipal governments of Munich, Berlin, Stuttgart, and Frankfurt have offered parallel programs for imams already residing in Germany (Laurence 2012: 234). The same holds true in Spain, where the programs are administered by the publicly funded Foundation for Pluralism and Coexistence (Astor 2014: 1725–26). The French Interior Ministry established in 2007 a program at the Institut Catholique in Paris of "republican training" for imams and other Muslims who work with or for Islamic organizations (Laurence 2012: 227; Chebel d'Appollonia 2010: 132). Leiden University and the Free University of Amsterdam offer bachelor's and master's degrees in Islamic theology (Laurence 2012: 186). In its mandatory political education for the seventh through nineth grade the *Land* of Northrhine-Westphalia instructs teachers to make students aware of "Islamist extremism" and its "unconstitutionality" (Ministerium für Schule und Weiterbildung 2010: 3). Germany established in 2011 Islamic studies centers at the universities of Münster, Tübingen, Osnabrück, Giessen, and Frankfurt that train imams and teachers of Islamic religious education in public schools. Beginning in 2006, the University of Vienna has offered a master's degree in "Islamic Religious Pedagogy" (Drees and Konigsveld 2008).

The perfectionist logic also turns up in the various Islamic councils mentioned above. Though ostensibly motivated by a liberal multiculturalist desire to welcome Islam into the European secular order, the governmental sponsors of the councils tend to presume that interaction with properly secularized European officials will serve as a model for Muslims to emulate. Sarkozy, for example, contended when defending the establishment of the French Council:

> If you find Islam to be incompatible with the Republic, then what do you do with the five million people of Muslim origin living in France? Do you kick them out, or make them convert, or ask them not to practice their religion? . . . With the French Council for the Muslim Religion, we are organizing an Islam that is compatible with the values of the Republic. (*Le Figaro* 30 April 2003)

The dominant path-dependency approach to comparative migration studies would, of course, expect such a statement from France, where republican assimilationism is said to be ensconced. But listen to the justification of the new centers for Islamic studies in Germany from erstwhile education minister Annette Schavan:

> If it were the case that Islam and democracy or Islam and modern society could not be made compatible, then a Muslim must either depart from his belief or from Europe. But that cannot be the only option. The charge of theology is also to translate religion into the present. Theology can accomplish such an interpretation of Islam in keeping with our times. In addition to that these new professorships should educate imams for our mosques and teachers for Islamic education in the public schools. (*Die Zeit* 14 April 2011)

Both ministers start from the presumption that Islam is and will remain at odds with democracy if the state does not intervene to resocialize Muslims to liberal democratic norms and values. As mentioned in Chapter 3, Cameron had just such an intervention in mind in 2010 when he called for "a more active, more muscular liberalism" that does not "stand neutral between different values," but rather proudly and unflinchingly promotes "freedom of speech, freedom of worship, democracy, the rule of law, equal rights regardless of race, sex or sexuality" (quoted in Joppke and Torpey 2013: 153).

Nowhere is liberal perfectionism more pervasive than in public schools. No state that finances and superintends public education can fully avoid molding young minds (Bader 2007: 324; Gutmann 1994: 23; Macedo 2000: 3–5). Several European governments (Austria, the Netherlands, Belgium, Greece) already offer Islamic religious instruction in public schools. Many national, regional, or municipal governments are attempting or contemplating doing so (Fetzer and Soper 2005). Though the specifics of providing Islamic education (in public schools or state-funded and overseen private schools) as well as the complications (such as identifying a reliable representative of Islam with whom to collaborate) vary from place to place, all such efforts are motivated in part by the perfectionist desire not to leave the religious socialization of young Muslims to imams, parents, and peers fully independent of state oversight. Far more important, however, than a few hours per week of religious instruction is doubtless the fact that the overwhelming majority of European Muslim pupils and students attend public schools whose curricula for all subjects are either crafted or supervised by state officials. Muslim youth are, in other words, generally exposed to the same secularizing tendencies at school as their non-Muslim classmates. The fears and complaints of conservative Muslim parents who detest the secularist teachings, pressures, and temptations that their children encounter in public schools might be paranoid to a certain extent but they are hardly groundless. Of course, it would be foolish to suggest that schools impart purely unadulterated liberal secular values. Nevertheless, public schools, in both the formal setting of the classroom and the informal interactions that take place elsewhere on campus, surely represent powerful and pervasive loci of state-sponsored favoritism toward secularism in both public and private life (Roy 2007: 16–17).

Christian Favoritism

We can also hear voices calling for deliberate favoritism toward Christianity. Not surprisingly, the Vatican has led the charge. In Istanbul in 2006, Benedict XVI observed that Islamic civilization is on the rise "because of its people's conviction that [it] can provide a valid spiritual foundation to their lives. Such a foundation seems to have eluded old Europe, which, despite its enduring political and economic power, seems to be on the road to decline" (Ratzinger 2006: 65). The German pontiff implored all Christians to "renew Europe's awareness of its Christian roots, traditions and values" (quoted in Kaya 2012: 195). Two years later in a public spectacle adroitly orchestrated in St. Peter's Basilica, Benedict XVI baptized Magdi Allam. The prominent

Egypt-born and until then Muslim Italian journalist has since 2003 become a vehement and outspoken opponent of Islam. He, for example, rejects the ecumenical trend of including Islam among the three "Abrahamic" religions on grounds that it fosters "the de-legitimization of Christianity" (*Catholic World Report* 8 April 2013). Somewhat more surprisingly, given his afore-mentioned endorsement of integrating aspects of sharia into British law, Archbishop of Canterbury Williams warned that "moving toward a secular society in Christian Britain—where the Queen is the head of the Church of England and religion still features in public institutions—would be more radical than can be imagined" (*Jurist* 23 October 2006). The Church itself emphasized that "the contribution of the Church of England in particular and of Christianity in general to the underlying culture remains very sub-stantial. . . . It could certainly be argued that there is an agenda behind a claim that a five per cent adherence to 'other faiths' makes for a multifaith society" (*Telegraph* 8 October 2006). Even Baroness Warsi, a Muslim min-ister without portfolio in the Cameron Cabinet, claimed that Europe needs to be "more confident in its Christianity" (*BBC News* 14 February 2012). Matthias Koenig (2007: 928) discerns a wide-reaching "reinterpretation of Church-State relations as symbols of national identity."

More than a few politicians have jumped on the pro-Christianity band-wagon. Frau Merkel exclaimed at the annual party conference of her Chris-tian Democratic Union in 2010 that "the problem is not too much Islam, the problem is too little Christianity, too little discussion of the Christian view of man and of the Judeo-Christian ethical foundation" (*das islamische Portal* 19 November 2010). Several of her political allies, such as Interior Minister Hans-Peter Friedrich and former chancellor candidate Edmund Stoiber, have averred that "Islam does not belong to Germany" in a way that would merit treatment by the state as equal to Christianity (Friedrich quoted in *Die Welt* 3 March 2011; on Stoiber see *Süddeutsche Zeitung* 18 Feb-ruary 1999). And the chancellor herself opined that Germany is a country "in which we celebrate Christian, not Muslim holidays" (quoted in Cesari 2013: 8). Former vice-president of the European Parliament, Italian Mario Mauro (2004), averred that "Europe will be Christian or it will not be at all." Perhaps no one has articulated the Christian favoritism argument with greater pith or rhetorical force than Austria's Freedom Party, whose slogan for municipal elections in Vienna in 2005 read "*Pummerin statt Muezzin*" (Pummerin instead of Muezzin; "Pummerin" is the name of the bell at St. Stephen's Cathedral). Again, according to path-dependency theory, such particularist utterances are to be expected from leading politicians in coun-tries with a strong ethnonationalist heritage, such as Italy, Germany, and Austria. But then how do we explain Sarkozy, who at an audience with the pope in the Lateran Palace in 2007, proclaimed that a nation which ignores its ethnic, spiritual and religious heritage commits a crime against its culture . . . its patrimony, its arts and popular traditions, which deeply permeate our manner of living and thinking. Pulling out roots is to lose meaning, to weaken national identity, to further impoverish social relations which have such a need for symbols of memory. (Quoted in Taras 2012: 61)

Or what about David Cameron, who in his Easter message in 2014 said we need to be "more confident about our status as a Christian country" (*Church Times* 16 April 2014)? One might reply by saying that the French and British leaders, like the other politicians, were tailoring their words to fit their audience. That is precisely my point. Rather than consistently committing to a particular public philosophy, fragilized politicians employ and often combine fragments of liberalism, nationalism, or postmodernism whenever they seem likely to please a given audience.

A common conflation of universalist and particularist logic turns up in the oft-heard outcry to protect "our Judeo-Christian civilization" or "our Western way of life" from "creeping Islamization" (Sarrazin 2010; British National Party 2010: 17; Dippel and Prill 2007; Fortuyn 1997). The German movement European Patriots against the Islamization of the Occident (PEGIDA) is exemplary. The movement purports to protect modern universal liberal values, such as freedom and equality for all, that are presumed not only to have been championed and largely realized in Europe since the Enlightenment, but to have been foreshadowed in a longer Judeo-Christian heritage involving such important notions as the equality of all persons before God. The Germans are not alone. Prime Minister Berlusconi proclaimed in 2001:

> We are proud bearers of the supremacy of western civilisation, which has brought us democratic institutions, respect for the human, civil, religious and political rights of our citizens, openness to diversity and tolerance of everything. . . . Europe must revive on the basis of common Christian roots.(*Guardian* 27 September 2001)

In pure theory, of course, universal rights cannot belong to any specific person, people, or civilization in the sense of being "ours" and not "theirs." Their universality resides precisely in their belonging to all or to no one person or group particularly. However, logical consistency is rarely prized or efficacious in real politics. On the contrary, the inconsistent rhetoric packs greater political punch. The norms and values are worth protecting not only because they are universal and therefore ethically superior to all others; they are also "ours." The particularistic logic adds a powerful affective dimension akin to protecting one's (cultural) offspring. Moreover, if the superior morality is honored in "our way of life" and stems from "our Judeo-Christian heritage," so runs the particularistic (and culturist) thinking, then it cannot be part of "their (Muslims') way of life" or "their civilization" in anything like the profound way it is part of "ours." And this, in turn, represents (yet another) reason to distrust or fear "them." In this regard, it is interesting to note that in addition to very openly pro-Christian opinion leaders like Alain Besançon and Alexandre Del Valle, some prominent atheists such as Umberto Eco or Regis Debray have taken to calling themselves "cultural Christians" in an effort to underscore precisely this kind of purported cultural affinity among non-Muslim Europeans as well as the cultural "otherness" of those of Muslim heritage (Jenkins 2007: 263).

Both anti-Islamic and pro-Christian sentiment influence policy making. In 2009, for example, Switzerland banned (through a referendum) the erection of minarets. Movements to follow the Swiss example are being led by the Freedom Party in Austria, the Lega Nord in Italy, and the Danish People's Party in Denmark. Film star Brigitte Bardot has drawn much attention (and five fines for "inciting racial hatred") arguing that France has too many mosques and too few churches (Aidi 2014: 141). Though their success varies from neighborhood to neighborhood, campaigns to oppose the erection of individual mosques are nearly as common as the new mosques themselves. In addition to alleging that the mosques will harbor terrorists, the opponents also typically contend that the Islamic edifices besmirch the architectural integrity (its particular "European" charm or unity) of "our" cities (Astor 2014: 1725; Tyrer 2013: 77; Cesari 2013: 96–98; Alonso 2012: 479–80; Allievi 2010). Similarly, the Muslim call to prayer is forbidden by many but hardly all European municipalities. As reported in the previous chapter, France and Belgium in 2011 banned the full-face burqa from the public sphere, while prohibitions on other forms of Islamic covering in certain places are in force or under consideration in many European countries. The "tolerant" Netherlands passed a bill in 2011 making proper Islamic slaughtering (*halal*) illegal. Animal rights activists around Europe have lobbied with different degrees of success to outlaw the practice because it employs no anesthetic (*Financial Times* 3 August 2011).We should not overlook the anti-Islam undertones in widespread opposition to Turkey's membership in the EU. To be sure, the opposition goes far beyond Turkey's seventy-five million Muslims and involves economic, political, and military concerns that have little or nothing to do with Islam. Nonetheless, many sympathize with Pope Benedict XVI, who as cardinal in 2004 spoke out against Turkey's accession because Islam stands in "permanent contrast" to Europe's Christian tradition (quoted in Kaya 2012: 240). All this, of course, is to say nothing about the daily discrimination, institutional and personal, experienced by individual Muslims trying to find employment, education, housing, financing, and so on. The fact that most, not all, European governments have established anti-discrimination agencies only in the last ten or fifteen years (mainly in response to the 2000 EU Race Directive) testifies to the protracted de facto policy of tolerating discrimination against Muslims. After all, the Muslims began arriving in large numbers as early as the 1950s, meaning roughly five decades of the regularized sins of omission on the part of governments vis-à-vis the sins of commission of their non-Muslim citizens. Any suggestion that the recently formed agencies will swiftly eliminate anti-Muslim discrimination smacks of political naiveté of the highest order.

Far more pervasive, however, is blatant favoritism toward Christianity. In 2004, Pope John Paul II championed a nearly successful effort to have Europe's "Christian heritage" inserted in the preamble of the EU (draft) Constitution. Formally established Christian churches exist in Iceland, Lichtenstein, Greece, Denmark, and Britain. The latter's Parliament passed the UK Education Act of 1988, which stipulates that a majority of the acts of collective worship in state-run schools are to be "wholly or mainly of a broadly Christian character" and that in religious education the content "devoted to Christianity in the syllabus should predominate" (quoted in Fetzer and Soper 2005: 39). Similarly, Clause 140 of Bremen's Constitution obligates public schools to teach "Biblical history in a Christian context" (quoted in Fetzer and Soper 2005: 113). Until 2009, Catholic religious education was mandatory for all pupils in Spanish public schools (Zapata-Barrero and de Witte 2010: 185). Greek public schools mandate daily Orthodox prayers, except in Western Thrace with its large Turkish minority (Triandafyllidou 2010c: 208). Bavaria and Italy permit the display of crucifixes in all classrooms in public schools, a statute upheld by the European Court of Human Rights in *Lautsi v. Italy* in 2011 (Joppke and Torpey 2013: 154–58). The French province of Alsace-Moselle provides Catholic and Protestant (as well as Jewish) religious education in its public schools (Laborde 2008: 69). State aid for private religious schools overwhelmingly favors Christians. Germany has thousands of Christian schools compared to two Islamic schools (Monsma and Soper 2009: 196); the Netherlands 5,000 compared to 42 (Monsma and Soper 2009: 59; Sunier 2014: 60); Britain 7,000 compared to 140 (Cesari 2013: 100; Monsma and Soper 2009: 151), despite the fact that more Muslims weekly attend mosque than Anglicans weekly attend church (Berger 2007: 20). Even in *laïque* France, roughly a fifth of French pupils attend religious (mostly Christian) schools, 85 percent of whose costs are covered by the state (Adrian 2011: 422). By contrast, a mere twenty-nine private Islamic schools exist with only one (Lycée Averroes) subsidized by the French state (Cesari 2013: 100; see also Commission de réflexion 2006). Add to this the fact that European lands remain fully saturated in Christian lore, ritual, and symbolism, from hourly ringing of church bells to officially declared Christian holidays, all of which Muslims must suffer. The (Gregorian) calendar itself is of Christian origin! Laborde (2008: 17) labels such favoritism "soft rules," mostly unorchestrated, unofficial yet pervasive favoring of Christian norms, expectations, and presuppositions as "normal" and Muslim ones as "abnormal" (also see Bader 2007: 153–56). This represents the religious dimension of Billig's (1995) "banal nationalism" (mentioned in Chapter 3). As Davie (2007: 238) perspicaciously observes, "In European society, the religious playing field is not level, nor is it likely to become so in the foreseeable future." Even in the purportedly "multicultural" Netherlands, "in terms of institutional arrangements, there is no question of an Islamic pillar [state-funded religious organization] . . . or at least one that is in any way comparable to the Roman Catholic or Protestant pillars of the past" (Rath 1999: 59).

Islamophobic Hyperbole

Neither Christianity, then, nor liberal secular democracy, for that matter, lies gravely imperiled, at least not by Muslim Europeans, who comprise at most but 5 percent of Europe's population. And yet such exaggerated warnings are made with great frequency despite the existence of plentiful evidence (cited above) disproving them. Indeed, it is hard to imagine a political issue more saturated in humbug and hyperbole than the question of Islam in Europe. Here we can detect the considerable political sway of Hobbesian postmodernism. We encounter fragilization in particular toward the same two postmodern tenets or fragments that we encountered with regard to veiling: truth is what passes for truth, and what passes for truth does so as a result of shrewd manipulation of words, images, and symbols.

Deliberate distortions of Islam and Muslims have become nearly ubiquitous in Europe (Bowen 2012a; Lean 2012; Hafez 2011; Schneiders 2010b; Gardell 2010; Allen 2007; van Dijk 2007; Rigoni 2007; Deltombe 2005; Geissler and Pöttker 2005; Poole 2002). The previous chapter noted the frequent and risible comparison between allowing girls to don the hijab in public schools and Chamberlain's appeasement of Hitler in Munich in 1938. Wilders likened the Qur'an to *Mein Kampf*. Prominent French intellectual Bernhard Henri Lévy uses the catachresis "fascislamist," while *Le Figaro* columnist Yvan Rioufol prefers "nazislamist" (both quoted in Rigoni 2007: 109–10). British columnist Christopher Hitchens spoke of "fascism with an Islamic face" (*Slate* 22 October 2007) and best-selling Italian journalist Oriana Fallaci of "the new Nazi-Fascism" (quoted in *New Yorker* 5 June 2006). Necla Kelek (2005: 47) anathematized Islam for promoting a "slave mentality" among its adherents. Ayaan Hirsi Ali called Muhammad a "perverted tyrant whose teachings cannot be reconciled with democracy" (*Trouw* 25 January 2003) and compared him to "all those megalomaniac rulers in the Middle East: bin Laden, Khomeini, Saddam" (quoted in Jenkins 2007: 190).

Typically accompanying such distortions of Islamic doctrine are gross exaggerations of its impact in Europe. Populist politicians from Enoch Powell to Jörg Haider to Jean Marie Le Pen to Pim Fortuyn to Siv Jensen have shrewdly garnered votes spreading fear of the imminent Islamization of Europe. Mario Borghezio, an Italian member of the European Parliament, warns that soon Christmas songs will be banned at the behest of "a bunch of shit Islamic bastards" (quoted in Tyrer 2013: 118). Prominent German feminist Alice Schwarzer (2010: 17) lamented the "Shariazation of German law." Melanie Phillips (2007) entitled her bestseller *Londonistan*, while Bat Ye'or (2005) declared the entire continent "Eurabia." One Islamophobic YouTube video with over one million hits features a reconfigured map of "Europe 2015" on which France has been renamed "The Islamic Republic of New Algeria," the United Kingdom "North Pakistan," Germany "New Turkey," and so on (YouTube, youtube.com/watch?v=wiLdDe7Eha4). Indeed, dozens of Islamophobic websites such as Islam Watch, Politically Incorrect, Reposte Laique, Die Grüne Pest, Nürnberg 2.0, or Stop the Islamization of Europe regularly maintain a steady cyber-stream of unfiltered and hateful balderdash regarding Muslims.

Roy (2007: 88) aptly explains how the culturalizing and essentializing logic works:

> Islam is thus turned into an essence, as though it has become the invariant that determines attitudes in very different contexts. A murder with blows from a rock [as in the Ghofrane case in Marseille in 2004] is defined as a stoning. The macho attitudes of young men in the *banlieues*, regrettably similar in very different contexts (from Los Angeles to Moscow), is attributed to Islam. Adolescents' intentions to assert themselves by wearing provocative clothing is a banality in secondary schools, but the affair of the veil has been experienced as the penetration of the school system by Islamism.

Studies repeatedly find that the sobriquets most frequently associated with Muslims in reportage are "terrorist," "extremist," "militant," "fanatical," "radical," and the like. The overwhelming majority of media coverage depicts Muslims as "threats" or "problems" (Zick, Küpper, Hövermann 2011; Moore, Mason, and Lewis 2008; van Dijk 2007; Poole 2002). Bowen (2012a: 57) labels the approach "block thinking, whereby the diversity of perspectives within a social group are collapsed into a single caricature."

We need to recognize that these specious distortions are more often deliberate rather than merely ignorant. We need, that is, to comprehend them as being justified by a normative outlook, Hobbesian postmodernism, which justifies manipulating images if for no other reason than that it discerns no prudent alternative to doing so. First, there now exists so much credible evidence of the kind already mentioned above that refutes the stigmatizing stereotypes of Muslims that it no longer seems plausible that educated, intelligent Islam-bashers could be unaware of it. This means that the critics willfully choose to neglect evidence at odds with their own positions. For instance, precious few of the prominent Islam naysayers possess advanced degrees in any branch of Islamic studies and most exhibit little interest in learning from or contributing to that scholarly enterprise, though, as said, they have to be aware of its existence (Meijer 2013; Schneiders 2010b). Furthermore, we have to presume that the opponents of Islam are keenly aware of the equally large body of social scientific literature (also cited above) that demonstrates that the reductionist, essentializing stereotypes of Muslims shape mass public opinion far more extensively than more nuanced interpretations of specialists. Third, and perhaps most importantly, no political activist can be oblivious to the surge in fame and success of anti-Islamic parties and politicians in Europe that was discussed in Chapter 3 (European Commission against Racism and Intolerance 2011: 7; Art 2011; Howard 2010; Givens and Luedtke 2005). Indeed, "blaming Islam" (Bowen 2012a) has mushroomed into a full blown "industry" (Lean 2012). Scapegoating Islam and Muslims has become similar to an irresistible fad that power-hungry politicians, ambitious reporters, and greedy media moguls cannot afford to ignore. The prevaricators peddle it like a hot new product or brand. Robert Leiken (2012: 269) summarizes this mentality:

> Nuance, specificity, and complexity rank as outsiders in a political culture that rewards partisanship, a media that reduces complex stories to "sound bites," an academy that merchandizes what it calls "theory," agenda-driven foundations and a think-tank world where policy often precedes, or even precludes, research.

But the players in this game do more than capitalize on an existing discourse; they also help to produce and sustain it. They fashion "mediatized" Muslims who pass for actual Muslims amongst much of the general public (Sunier 2010: 133). As Hirsi Ali notoriously conceded once the lies of her autobiography were exposed, "Yes, I made it all up" (Quoted in *Qantara.de* 1 June 2015, http://en.qantara.de/content/ayaan-hirsi-alis-controversial-theories-on-islam-hailed-as-a-female-luther).

I do not wish to imply that anti-Islam political activists are postmodernists through and through, though surely some are. I do not doubt that many of them sincerely see themselves as striving to defend human rights or protect their national culture. However, they have fragilized enough toward postmodernism to deem it naïve to think that they can succeed politically without manipulating the truth. They find politically unsophisticated and reckless the notion that the mass public can or even cares to appreciate the objective facts in all their complexity. They accept that fear-mongering and scapegoating wins votes and that sensationalized reporting sells best. They recognize that politics is as much or more about symbols than about substance, that the polls are more important than the truth, and that we live in an age in which there is no business *but* show business (Postman 1985). They have internalized that fragment of Hobbesian postmodernism that interprets politics as a struggle to establish one's preferred discourse as the "prestige" discourse over and above rivals. They do not trust their opponents to play "fairly" and conclude, reluctantly and sadly perhaps, that they must demonize and dominate or be demonized and dominated. They agree, whether they have read Stanley Fish (1999: 240) or not, that since there is no escaping the political game, one should play it "and play it to win."

Europhobic Hyperbole

Hobbesian postmodernism manifests itself markedly in what some authors have called "the clash of perceptions" (Nyiri 2010). The notion denotes the widely documented phenomenon whereby non-Muslims perceive Muslims differently than the latter perceive themselves (see also Chebel d'Appollonia 2015: 28 and 88–89; Pew Global Attitudes Project 2006). The prevailing misperceptions of Muslims in Europe have reached the level of what Stanley Cohen (1980: 9) identifies as "moral panic" (also see Morgan and Poynting 2012a; Bahners 2011). Moral panic occurs when opportunistic political agents manage to stigmatize a targeted group in such a way that the group's purported moral deviance becomes convincingly portrayed as an existential threat to the society as a whole. Moral panics tend to take place largely in the realm of symbolic politics, having little or no basis in fact. However, the otherwise very important literature that documents the stigmatization of Muslims in Europe tends to overlook reverse stigmatization or what we might call "reciprocal moral panic." Islamists, for example, often invert the stigma of themselves to portray the West and Westerners as an existential threat to the *umma*. Non-Muslim Europeans (as well as lapsed Muslims) are represented as superficial and hedonistic, power-hungry and oppressive, promiscuous and lascivious, greedy and sly, even rapacious and sadistic. The Iranian intellectual Jalal al-e Ahmad's notion of "Westoxification" (*Gharbzadegi*) receives popular and simplified expression in dozens of vituperating pamphlets, websites, and films that warn pious Muslims to avoid exposure to, let alone emulation of Western ways, lest they steer the righteous into iniquity and eternal damnation. For example, the website www.einladungzumparadies (invitation to paradise) shows multiple images of supposed Western materialism and decadence and then claims that Muhammad "would say no, never [to these things] and spurn them (www.youtube.com/watch?v=8-YDZAPycnM). A piece translated and widely circulated by the Saudi-sponsored London publishing house Al-Firdous enjoins readers: "Do not take the Jews and Christians for friends." It is "forbidden for a Muslim to go to live amongst the infidels and acknowledge their authority over him" (Qahtani 1999: 3:2). A Belgian website goes so far as to assert that "he who does not consider to be an infidel one who follows a religion other than Islam, such as the Christians, or who doubts their vileness or approves of their ways, he himself is a infidel" (http://assabyle.com/index.php?id=510.). Hizb ut-Tahrir similarly contends: "If Muslims surrendered to these calls to assimilate into the system we would inevitably lose our distinct Islamic values" (quoted in Akbarzahdeh and Roose 2011: 314). One Milli Görüş imam posited that "if Turkey were allowed into the EU, the Turkish people would have to give up Islam, give up their culture and their history" (quoted in LeVine 2003: 122; also see Jonker 2006: 138). Such warnings are often accompanied by admonitions to the audience to dedicate their lives to the inevitably triumphant struggle against the perfidious West that will usher in a new golden age of genuine peace, prosperity, and justice for the global umma (Dinç 2014: 42–43; Ramadan 2001; Parvez 2000). The noble-sounding, international message seems to resonate particularly strongly among younger European Muslims who find it easier to identify with this heroic global movement than with the distant homeland of their immigrant parents or with the receiving country from which they feel rejected and marginalized (Cheleb d'Appollonia 2015: 89–90; Cesari 2013: 130–37; Ceylan and Kiefer 2013: 71–99; Leiken 2012: 47; Gest 2010; Jenkins 2007: 127; Roy 2004; Lepoutre 1997; Withol de Wenden 1996; Gardner and Shuker 1994: 164). A number of prominent European intellectuals of Muslim heritage, including Tariq Ramadan (1999a: 55–56), have warned that large segments of Muslim youth in Europe are being indoctrinated into dualistic and reductionist interpretations of the West as the Great Satan (also see Lewis 2006: 172–73).

It is important, especially in conjunction with Hobbesian postmodernism, to underscore this reciprocating stigmatization because the warring sides not only prey on, but also rely on one another. The preposterous deeds or sayings of the Islam-haters are spotlighted to corroborate the outlandish deeds and sayings of the Europe-haters and vice versa. To cite just one example, some Muslims became indignant when they learned that the Danish newspaper *Jyllands Posten* not only published an insulting cartoon of Muhammad in 2005 but refused to print an unflattering caricature of Jesus in 2003. Some of the protesters in a demonstration in Britain organized by al-Ghurabaa carried placards reading "Europe you will pay—Your 9/11 is on the way." Such belligerent threats then become the focus of editorials and statements claiming "Islam is intolerant" (Jenkins 2007: 238). We could cite additional examples ad infinitum and ad nauseam. The important point is that this vicious circle of mutual recriminations is auto-generating. The dueling sides at once berate but also create their rivals. They become locked in a hermetically sealed discourse of hyperbole and invective that neither pays nor draws attention to more nuanced discussion and analysis (O'Brien 2015; Tyrer 2013: 121; LeVine 2003: 102). Furthermore, much of this "hyperdiscourse" (Amir-Moazami and Salvatore 2003: 68) or "phantom controversy" (Foroutan 2011: 8) takes place exclusively in cyberspace where the ease and stakes of manipulating images increase exponentially. There the Hobbesian postmodern logic that one must "market" the "truth" in order to win the inevitable power struggle becomes all the more compelling.

Hospitable Postmodernism and the Third Space

Though largely drowned out by the obstreperous voices informed by Hobbesian postmodernism, the more accommodating sounds of hospitable postmodernism are audible. Briefly recalling from Chapter 2, hospitable postmodernism retains the nihilism of its scrappier ken and like it rejects the feasibility of an overlapping normative consensus, whether based on universal reason or cultural homogeneity. However, hospitable postmodernism refuses to jettison the possibility that rival parties adhering to fundamentally different worldviews can learn to interact with one another via mutually respectful and beneficial practices. Such cooperation, it is argued, becomes possible when combating parties relax or relinquish their insistence on possessing the moral high ground. When they forego the finger-pointing that goes with condemning the adversary as evil, they produce and enter a figurative or actual "third space" (Bhabha 1994: 38) that neither party presumes to own or to determine as "our territory." In such inchoate and anomic realms and relations unexpected hybrid combinations and cross-fertilizations can be encountered and explored that can yield previously unimagined solutions to seemingly intractable antagonisms. Such solutions, as noted in the previous chapter, will always have to be context-specific, pragmatic, and provisionary and must remain open to renegotiation. The ideas of hospitable postmodernism, even when not specifically labeled as such, are well established, widely circulated, and even directly applied to religious pluralism in Europe (see O'Brien 2015; Norton 2013; Göle 2011; Modood 2009; Schiffauer 2008a; Davie 2007; Volf 2007; Asad 1997).

Post-Islamism

Fragments of this friendlier reading of the postmodern condition are detectable in the words and deeds of political activists whom some observers dub "post-Islamists" (Mandaville 2014: 369–99; Bayat 2013b; Schiffauer 2010; Roy 1998). I adopt this admittedly less-than-perfect label to refer to a new generation of Muslim intellectuals and activists in search of a "fusion of religiosity and rights, faith and freedom, Islam and liberty [that] transcend[s] Islamism by building a pious society with a civil nonreligious state" (Bayat 2013a: x). While their critique of many aspects of modern Western societies is unmistakably informed by the thought of earlier Islamists such as Qutb or Maududi, post-Islamists eschew the wholesale rejection of Western society associated with both the Islamist pioneers as well as their contemporary orthodox adherents. "I don't deny my Muslim roots," claims Tariq Ramadan, "but I don't vilify Europe either" (*Time* 11 December 2000). Likewise, the London-based Quilliam Foundation aims to show "the public that it is possible to express legitimate grievances with social and political issues without having to adopt simplistic narratives of there being a 'war on Islam'" (Quilliam Foundation; http://www.quilliamfoundation.org/about/). The same holds true for the Muslim members of the popular Danish musical trio Outlandish (Aidi 2014: xxiv). The proponents of this "neo-Islam" (Foroutan and Schäfer 2009) in Europe tend to stem from the middle class and to be highly and mostly Western educated (Khosrokhavar 2010: 143–44; Ewing 2008: 79; Werbner 1996: 115). That said, they operate within a fully "transnational religious discourse" (Mandaville 2003: 129) that is profoundly in touch with and deeply colored by prominent reformist thinkers in the Middle East such as Abdolkarim Soroush, Muhammad Shahrur, Rachid al-Ghannouchi, Fatima Mernissi, and Jusuf al-Qaradawi. These mavericks in Europe are contesting for leadership, often with success, with an older, more strictly anti-Western guard in Islamist associations such as the UOIE, IGMG, or the U.K. Islamic Mission. They have also founded their own independent associations such as Young Muslims (U.K.), the Federation of Student Islamic Societies, the Union des Jeunes Musulmans (France), or the Association of Young Italian Muslims. They support or produce research in think tanks such as the Institut Européen des Sciences Humaines (Paris), the ECFR (Dublin), Ta-Ha (London), and the Islamic Foundation (Leicester). They publish their ideas in journals and magazines such as *Q-News*, *The Muslim News*, *La Medina*, and *Die Islamische Zeitung* or on websites such as islamonline.com, Islam21.net, oumma.com, Islam.de, and huda. de, as well as sponsoring conferences like those at Le Bourget or Chateau Chinon or Islam Expo (London), which attract thousands of mainly young Muslims (Jonker 2000; Mandaville 2000; Boubekeur 2007: 20–28). Their ideas reach a very wide audience. For example, Ramadan, arguably their most celebrated spokesman, made the list of 100 most influential persons at *Time* in 2004, *Prospect Magazine* in 2008, and *Foreign Policy* in 2010.

Post-Islamists adamantly reject the conventional binary opposition between Islam and liberalism that paints them as mutually exclusive normative outlooks. Ramadan (2010: 257), for instance, chides European Muslims for falling prey to "simplistic versions of 'us versus them'" that teach that "you are more Muslim when you are against the West." Post-Islamists genuinely laud European democracies for their protection of individual liberty, especially religious freedom. Ramadan (1999b: 18) reminds readers that it is precisely the separation of church and state that can "protect the total independence of Muslims in France." Similarly, the erstwhile leader of IGMG, Mehmet Erbakan, contends that European Muslims live in far superior conditions for freely exercising their religion than 90 percent of their Muslim brethren in the so-called "Islamic world," where authoritarian regimes have traditionally quashed religious freedom. Such authoritarian rule, even when done in the name of Islamic law, he maintains, "is not a fulfillment of God's will rather its perversion" (quoted in Schiffauer 2010: 258). So impressed by the conditions of religious freedom was the Tunisian exile (until 2011) al-Ghannouchi that he famously changed Europe's designation from the conventional *dar-al-harb* (abode of war) to *dar-al-Islam* (abode of Islam) (Kepel 1999: 152). Ramadan (1999a: 150) endorsed the Tunisian's recategorization but augmented it to *dar al-shahada* (abode of testimony). By taking full advantage of the extensive freedoms available to them in Europe, argued Ramadan (1999a: 142–50), European Muslims could realize a new kind of "Islamic citizenship" that could stand as a model (testimony) for the rest of the Islamic world to emulate. But this they will only achieve when they abandon their "Pakistani, Turkish or Arab" "ghettos" (both "social and intellectual") and "integrate themselves into European cultures, which become a new dimension of their own identity" (Ramadan 2010: 259–60). Similarly, Muhammad Abdul Bari, former general secretary of the MCB, stated: "In my view the moral and ethical principles of our faith urge us to become conscientious, responsible citizens and active participants in the life of our nation" (quoted in Akbarzahdeh and Roose 2011: 315). Indeed, on their websites the UOIF (uoif-online.com), the IGMG (igmg.de), and the MCB (mcb.org), despite their Islamist connections, each publicly proclaims in no uncertain terms its fidelity to the constitution of France, Germany, and Britain, respectively.

Post-Islamists, however, do not offer unconditional praise of European society. They retain significant dimensions of the critique of modern liberalism and secularism bequeathed by their Islamist forefathers. They are especially troubled by the vapid spirituality and triumphant materialism that they discern in modern Western lifestyles. Al-Ghannouchi, for example, argues that modernization eroded older values stemming from religious belief. "But no new morality could develop to fill the gap. It is in this moral vacuum that personal aggrandizement and socio-economic exploitation have become rampant. . . . Islamic resurgence represents a rebellion against this state of affairs" (Ghannouchi 2000: 117). The spiritual, and thereby the ethical, dimension of life is said to be neglected by Europeans who have become mesmerized by their admittedly impressive physical accomplishments and the comforts of modernization. "We do not want modernization without soul or values," asserts Ramadan. "We want ethical reform. We want to transform the world in the name of the justice and human dignity that, sadly, are often forgotten in the current inhumane global (dis)order" (*New-Statesman* 6 April 2006). For Ramadan, modern nationalism provides a jejune substitute for genuinely religious identity. The former teaches humans "how" to exist but not, like Islam, "why" they exist. It leaves them lacking a deeper meaning and purpose with which to assess rather than merely accept the latest trends and fashions of modern life. It no less than robs humankind of its proper and proportionate relationship to the rest of the universe by anthropomorphically and mistakenly placing man at the center of that universe (Ramadan 1999a: 172).

In the eyes of post-Islamists, Europe urgently needs an infusion of ethics of just the kind that a great religion like Islam can provide. They see Islam as a wellspring of transcendental values such as the fundamental equality of all humans before God, humility and respect for God's creation (environment), individual responsibility and industry, but also sympathy, aid, and justice for the downtrodden and unfortunate that if adapted and applied to modern life could greatly improve it (see Vidino 2010a; Hellyer 2009: 118; Ewing 2008: 79; Cesari 2007: 117–18; Modood and Ahmed 2007: 192; Fadil 2006). Jamal Badawi of the ECFR writes:

> Islam is a faith that resonates with pure human nature. . . . It also teaches universal morality, justice and compassion. We believe as Muslims that these positive and constructive qualities are not a monopoly of Muslims but are embedded in upright human nature. (Quoted in Pargeter 2008: 177)

Similarly, the IGMG maintains that "by orienting itself around the Islamic sources," it can constructively contribute to "protecting the poor and the needy, opposing injustice, disseminating what is good and rejecting what is bad, and establishing justice in social relations" (das islamische Portal, igmg. de/gemeinschaft/wir-ueber-uns). In contrast to conventional Islamists, who have traditionally been more oriented toward affecting change in the countries from which they emigrated, post-Islamists are keen to engage and improve politics in Europe. However, they want to do so *qua* Muslims. Thus did the founding members of the Union des Jeunes Musulmans enunciate in 1987 their goal to "live our spirituality in the open and not in a reclusive way in the private sphere" (quoted in Bowen 2010: 22). IGMG maintains that "Islam is a social and individual way of living, the influence of which certainly does not end at a mosque's doorstep" (das islamische Portal, igmg. de/gemeinschaft/wir-ueber-uns). Likewise, the Muslim Council of Britain (2007) strives for "a multi-faith, pluralist society with a conscious policy of recognizing that people's cultural and faith identities are not merely a private matter but have public implications." Each organization echoes the words of the influential leader of the ECFR, Jusuf al-Qaradawi, who asserts: "No Muslim who believes that Islam is the word of God can conceive that this great religion will ever accept being a mere appendix to socialism or any other ideology" (quoted in Soage 2010: 29).

Post-Islamists do not merely want to join European societies (integrate); they want to change them. The only way that Muslims can contribute to Europe *qua* Muslims is if the understanding of what it means to be European expands to include Muslims. This necessitates, according to post-Islamists, a rethinking of European identity and the norms and values that define it not as something fixed and preordained, but rather as an ongoing and evolving project in which Muslims become key players. This is Europe reimagined as a work in progress, indeed as one demanding still much work and much progress. Amir-Moazami and Armando Salvatore (2003: 73) call this outlook "the both/and logic" whereby post-Islamists demand to join the game of modern life but also to change the rules by which it is played (also see Cesari 2007: 116–18; Boubekeur 2007).

Post-Islamists are calling for just the type of open-endedness prescribed by hospitable postmodernism. Need I repeat the caveat that I do not mean to equate post-Islamists and hospitable postmodernists? Rather, pragmatic and ambitious Muslim activists who understandably seek to inject themselves and their ideas into the mainstream of the societies that they now consider home deploy fragments of postmodern (and other) logic in an effort to legitimize their political aspirations (Bayat 2013b: 8; Bowen 2010: 14; Rich 2010: 123; Jonker 2006: 136). Given that the mainstream generally paints and treats them as outsiders to Europe, these "autodidactic" "tinkerers" (Roy 1994: 95, 97) would be foolish not to echo a postmodern observation like that of Tal Asad (1997: 194), who contends that discussion has pivoted around the question of "whether Muslim communities can really adjust to Europe" rather than "whether the institutions and ideologies of Europe can adjust to a modern world of which culturally diverse immigrants are an integral part." The same holds true for arguments of, say, Derrida (1992: 29): "It is necessary to make ourselves the guardians of an idea of Europe . . . *but* of a Europe that consists precisely in not closing itself off in its identity and in advancing itself in an exemplary way towards what it is not, toward the other heading or the heading of the other."

Ramadan (2010: 262) captures and capitalizes on this postmodern spirit of open-endedness and indeterminacy with his call for a "new 'We.'" This is a new understanding of what it means to be European that includes rather than excludes Islam and that views "Muslims—with their spirituality, ethics and creativity"—as a "contribution" rather than a threat. This will demand recognition that

> European societies have been changing, and the presence of Muslims has forced them to experience an even greater diversity of cultures. As a result, a European identity has evolved that is open, plural and constantly in motion, thanks to the cross-fertilisation between reclaimed cultures of origin and the European cultures that now include new (Muslim) citizens. (Ramadan 2010: 258–59)

As Ramadan's remark makes clear, post-Islamists do not pretend to have all the answers. They seek dialogue but, in hospitable postmodern spirit, dialogue that remains open, even if uncomfortably so, to all participants willing to enter discussion. Dilwar Hussain (2011) of the European Muslim Network, for instance, insists that "we . . . need to reach a point where (sensible and rationally argued) religious voices can be given consideration and not automatically disregarded as 'superstitious.'" Likewise, foregone conclusions of where dialogue will lead have to be resisted. The UOIF's commitment to open dialogue is typical of other organizations with post-Islamist leanings:

> Diversity is inherent in human nature. The UOIF believes that dialogue is the best way to achieve mutual recognition among members of a common society. The UOIF opposes a rupturing discourse based on the hatred and rejection of others. . . . The only acceptable approach to dealing with the emergence of problems of misunderstanding is dialogue, explanation and education. (Union des Organisations Islamiques de France; www.uoif-online.com/v3/spip. php?article19)

Official and Unofficial Hospitable Postmodernism

Fragilization toward hospitable postmodernism admittedly remains slight among state officials but hardly nonexistent. We can discern, for instance, resistance to demonization in the decision of Britain's Home and Foreign Offices to fund the Radical Middle Way, a project that sponsors speeches and discussion groups, often led by prominent Islamist personalities such as Ramadan, Kemal Helbawi, or Shaykh Abdullah bin Bayyah. "Radical Middle Way," explains its webpage, "is a safe place for people to ask difficult questions and explore challenging issues" (Radical Middle Way; radicalmiddleway.org). We hear a similar openness toward indispensable but unsettling dialogue in Otto Schilly's remark as interior minister in 2002: "The state cannot afford to ignore the . . . dynamics and potentially explosive nature of religious questions. . . . Integration will only succeed when we take into account the new religious needs of Muslims" (quoted in Laurence 2012: 107). Something similar would seem to be the guiding spirit of Dusseldorf's "Ibrahim trifft [meets] Abraham" project, which brings disaffected youths of various faiths together to air their grievances in a non-judgmental atmosphere designed to foster exchange of perspectives (Ceylan and Kiefer 2013: 132–40). A similar program since 2005 under the label "Dialog macht Schule" in Essen, Stuttgart and Berlin challenges its teen participants to "suspend assumptions and value judgments" in the interest of fostering open exchange (quoted in Ceylan and Kiefer 2013: 142). Most European governments have experimented with supporting Muslim hip-hop artists due to their appeal among youth and despite their often vehement critique of European societies and regimes (Aidi 2014: 205–11). Likewise, we hear some of the postmodern spirit of reimagining Europe in the European Commission's call to "rewrite European history" so as to include the major transference of knowledge that came to Europe from the Islamic world during the Middle Ages in places like al-Andalus (Aidi 2014: 327). Austrian chancellor Wolfgang Schüssel claimed in 2006 that "Islam is a real component of the European identity through the accomplishments of its grand scientific and cultural heritage" (Quoted in Godard 2007: 200). In like spirit, Tony Blair (2001) has said: "It is time the west confronted its ignorance of Islam. Jews, Muslims and Christians are all children of Abraham. This is the moment to bring the faiths closer together in understanding of our common values and heritage, a source of unity and strength." His British Foreign Office sponsored in 2006 a conference of European Islamist organizations whose final resolution read: "Following the teachings of the Holy Qur'an and the high standard which it sets, Muslims can enrich Europe as exemplary members of society and role models of decency and goodness" (Topkapi Declaration 2006). Sarkozy has spoken approvingly of "the cross-fertilization of ideas, thinking and cultures . . . [which] means recognizing, understanding and respecting the Other," although in the same (highly fragmented and fragilized) editorial he also endorsed "assimilation" as well as the Swiss ban on minarets (*Le Monde* 9 December 2009). President Hollande stated in 2013 that "France knows that Islam and democracy are compatible" (quoted in Fredette 2014: 17). And the European Council has proclaimed that "integration is a dynamic, two-way process of mutual accommodation by all immigrants and residents of Member States" (Council of the EU, Justice and Home Affairs 2004: 19–24).

At this point in time, though, fragments of hospitable postmodernism are likelier to be found in far smaller and less grand contexts of private initiatives and lives. Not surprisingly, churches, synagogues, and mosques frequently organize ecumenical encounters open to the notion that "our social identities are not constituted by one exclusive set of relations or mode of belonging" (former archbishop Rowan Williams quoted in Bowen 2012a: 77; also see Laurence 2012: 217; Zapata-Barrero and de Witte 2010: 189; Otterbeck 2010: 114–16). Many churches allow mosque-less Muslim communities to use their Christian sanctuaries for worship, thereby temporarily turning them into sacred Islamic spaces. Not all these experiences are planned, but rather emerge serendipitously. In some cities where Muslims make up a large percentage of a neighborhood, non-Muslims have come to appreciate and partake in the fast-breaking feasts during the month of Ramadan (Roy 2007: 85). Or on a more intimate level, a Muslim falls in love with a Christian or an atheist—or Christian grandparents find themselves with a Muslim granddaughter. Such prosaic examples are, of course, far removed from the august halls where lawmakers make formal policy. However, a burgeoning body of research reveals that a rapidly increasing number of such small-scale experiences with unexpected but, in the end, managed hybridity is gradually but profoundly altering the way that people who reside in Europe understand themselves and their home (Berg and Sigona 2013; Norton 2013; Meyer and Brysac 2012; Yildiz 2012; Bowen 2010; Foroutan and Schäfer 2009; Wise and Velayutham 2009; Schmitt 2003).

Conclusion: Islam Councils

I conclude this chapter with a brief discussion of the Islam councils that have been established in many European countries to facilitate better relations between state and mosque. The unfurling dynamics of the councils nicely exemplify the central themes of this chapter: policies toward Islam are polymorphous and often contradictory and self-defeating; this messiness results in significant measure from the vying public philosophies of liberalism, nationalism, and postmodernism; fragilization among and fragmentation of the public philosophies lead policy makers to become increasingly comfortable with ambivalence and inconsistency; the normative pluralism and bricolage and their impact on policy are generally similar from one European polity to the next.

Initially, state officials justify the establishment of the councils by invoking the inclusiveness of liberal multiculturalism. Islam is to be welcomed into the political order so long as its representatives respect the values enshrined in the constitution. The following official mission of the Consulta per l'Islam Italiano is typical. It is

> a consultative body of the Interior Ministry that conducts research which formulates positions and proposals for the purpose of encouraging institutional dialogue with the Islamic communities in order to identify the most adequate solutions for a harmonious inclusion of Islam within the national community with respect to the laws of the Italian Republic.(Quoted in Spena 2010: 171)

The invitees initially endorse the official goals. The leader of L'Unione delle Comunità e Organizzazioni Islamiche in Italia (UCOII), for example, stated: "I want to make clear that we are for the respect of the Italian constitution" (quoted in Laurence 2012: 213).

However, it does not take long for fragilization in the direction of liberal perfectionism to emerge, especially in response to critics who charge that the councils consort with enemies of democracy. One French politician argued that "when one recognizes 'moderate Islamist' organizations as official interlocutors . . . are we aware that these are allies of Islamist totalitarianism who betray democracy?" (quoted in Laurence 2012: 202). This claim that Islamist organizations, despite their publicly stated allegiance to the constitution, cannot be trusted due to their duplicity can commonly be heard by Islam naysayers around Europe (Baran 2011: 173; Steinberg 2010: 153; Dippel and Prill 2007; Vidino 2006; Fourest 2004; also see Laurence 2012: 202, 243; Bahners 2011: 220–21).

Officials feel compelled to address the anti-Islamic allegations with guarantees of unflinching promotion and defense of democratic values. Sarkozy, who as interior minister formed the Conseil Français du Culte Musulman in 2003 and wrote that "secularism does not mean the refusal of all religions, but the respect of all beliefs" (*Le Monde* 9 December 2009), also maintained: "It is precisely because we recognize the right of Islam to sit at the table of the republic that we will not accept any deviation. Any prayer leader whose views run contrary to the values of the republic will be expelled" (quoted in Ross 2007: 212). Similarly, Interior Minister Manuel Valls in 2013 contended that it was "necessary to show" that Islam can be compatible with democracy. Valls's German counterpart, Wolfgang Schäuble (2009), who founded the Deutsche Islam Konferenz and who averred that "there is no alternative to integrating Islam in Europe," urged that "we must insist that Muslims identify with the constitution" (quoted in Laurence 2012: 101). The Christian Democratic interior minister went so far as to require the imams on the council to cross out passages in their Qur'ans at odds with gender equality (Amir-Moazami 2011). This demeaning gesture came in the wake of sensationalized coverage of and hysterical national focus on the honor killing of Hatan Sürücü in 2005. Despite the fact that none of the imams had anything to do with the crime, the hyperbole surrounding it influenced the conference's proceedings. Similarly, in the wake of the murder of Theo van Gogh, the anti-Islamic fervor reached such intensity in the Netherlands that the Contactorgaan Moslims en Overheid (Contact Body for Muslims and Government) began rolling back its cooperation with Islamic organizations (which too had nothing to do with the murder) until eventually it was defunded in 2009 (Laurence 2012: 187). Officials in Germany, Italy, and the United Kingdom expelled representatives from the IGMG, UCOII, and the MCB, respectively, due to allegations of close ties with the Muslim Brotherhood (Joppke and Torpey 2013: 82; Laurence 2012: 184, 213; Hellyer 2009: 158). Governments such as France, Italy, and Germany have also sought to stack the councils with "independent experts" (often non-Muslims or ex-Muslims) to dilute the presence of Islamic organizations (Laurence 2012: 173; Bader 2007: 337–38). This tactic tends to anger many Muslim participants, since the councils' ostensible mission is to facilitate dialogue and cooperation between the state and Muslims. As some imams from the German Islam Conference who were perturbed by the inclusion of prominent feminists sarcastically quipped, "This is as if we tried to enter into dialogue with Catholics, and for this purpose we invite the Pope and pop star Madonna" (*Tageszeitung* 29 September 2006). More importantly, such patronizing acts backfire. By expelling or alienating the Islamic organizations with the largest number of members, the councils are rendered dubious in the eyes of large segments of the Muslim population whom the councils were initially established to attract (Laurence 2012: 194).

For their part, Islamist organizations have been very wary about cooperating with the councils. In the first place, many of their actual and potential members are wont to believe Europhobic hyperbole that paints European governments as oppressive. As Roy (2007: 49) perspicaciously observes, so long as "Muslim identity is tinged with a strongly anti-imperialist hue," enthusiastic support from a European government can often "amount to giving them [the state-supported Muslim organizations] the kiss of death" (also see Laurence 2012: 194; Akbarzadeh and Roose 2011: 319; Pargeter 2008: 201; Patel 2007: 51–52; Scientific Council 2006: 202). When Islamist organizations do explore cooperation with the councils, they typically do so with communitarian expectations. They welcome the prospect of government assistance for the provision of religious services to Muslims but they fully expect that they themselves will determine the doctrinal content. They understandably resist when officials or other non-Muslims insist on reinterpreting and rewriting Islamic doctrine. The Islamic Council, for instance, refused to endorse the Islam Konferenz's statement on "German Societal Order and Value Consensus" because it allegedly falsely interpreted Islamic doctrine as a hindrance to integration (Joppke and Torpey 2013: 82). After stymied negotiations with the Dutch government over the content of imam training at public universities, the Contactorgaan Moslims en Overheid announced in 2005 that it intended to establish its own independent training institutions (Boender 2006: 11). Islamic organizations have often refused to accept any interpretation of the Qur'an other than their own. It deserves mention that many of the current councils have predecessors from the 1990s, most of which stalled or unraveled due in large part to refused or withdrawn cooperation from Islamic organizations (for details, see Laurence 2012: 159–62, 204–8; Amir-Moazami 2011; Silvestri 2010; Gest 2010: 140–41; Rigoni 2009: 483; Schiffauer 2008b; Godard 2007; Warner and Wenner 2006: 458). A French advisor to three interior ministers from those years vented his frustration: "One cannot negotiate with the Islamists—it's 'my way or the highway' with them, because what's in the Qur'an is law and superior to any administrative or historic arguments you can make [as an administrator]" (quoted in Laurence 2012: 205).

Nor have the embassies proven to be wholly supportive. Most welcome the public assistance from receiving country governments. However, for their own communitarian reasons, the embassy representatives have voiced robust opposition to the inclusion onto the councils of other Islamic associations independent of their governments. They have charged Islamists with radicalism and have played an important role in cajoling state officials to reduce or eliminate the representatives of Islamist organizations from the councils (Laurence 2012: 220–25). DITIB's position is typical: "We suggest that the German state try . . . making DITIB the monopoly, the official interlocutor of the government. If every federation is going to be treated equally, what is the motivation to refuse radicalism?" (quoted in Laurence 2012: 222). Needless to say, the Islamist NGOs have strongly criticized the undue influence of the embassies on the councils, further impeding orchestrated cooperation (Laurence 2012: 225–26).

Nativism too has hampered the councils. They are woefully underfunded, convene rarely, and accomplish nothing even remotely similar to the kind of cooperation that exists between church and state (Laurence 2012: 179, 194–95). One official in the French council observed: "We support it politically but we don't give any money" (quoted in Laurence 2012: 179). When a Lega Nord politico assumed the helm at the Interior Ministry in 2008, the meetings of the Consulta were suspended for two years (Laurence 2012: 179). In fact, the Charter of Values drawn up by the Consulta underscores Italy's Judeo-Christian character: "Italy . . . developed under Christianity, which permeated all aspects of its history and, together with Judaism, prepared the way to modernity and the principles of freedom and justice" (Quoted in Spena 2010: 174). No mention is made of the resplendent Arab Islamic cultural legacy from medieval Sicily. Likewise, at the 2006 German Islam Conference, Interior Minister Schäuble underscored that Germany was a country with "Christian roots and traditions" (*Frankfurter Allgemeine Zeitung* 27 September 2006) and demanded that the Muslim attendees identify with the "German value community" (*deutsche Wertgemeinschaft*), to which many Muslims objected on grounds that Muslims, as Schäuble made plain, were not traditionally considered part of this community (Amir-Moazami 2009: 203).

And yet the councils have a way of surviving or reviving despite their frustrations and failures (Laurence 2012: 196). The participants, as dissatisfied as they might be with the councils, fear the alternative: mounting antipathy and recrimination. They perceive the increasing ugliness of a Hobbesian war of all against all without limits. Whether by philosophical conviction or mere pragmatism, many who persevere do so with a new appreciation of the nonaccusatory and open-ended spirit of hospitable postmodernism. A British official for the Department for Community and Local Government, which deals extensively with the Mosques and Imams National Advisory Board, commented in 2010:

> Today we must have a relationship of semi-autonomy and arms-length distance, including criticizing where due, to keep the credibility within the Muslim communities themselves—many of whom are not happy with internal policies or foreign policies of the UK government. That space is crucial to the credibility of the new council."(Quoted in Laurence 2012: 194)

A Muslim participant in the German Islam Conference reflected:

> I was long of the opinion that we were working without achieving any results. That was frustrating. Today I must correct that assessment. We have achieved results at all levels. Islamic organizations and representatives who were not able to speak to one another have now found dialogue and discussion. We have also managed to dismantle some prejudices in Germany. The black box of Islam has become more transparent.(Quoted in Laurence 2012: 197)

Dilwar Hussain (2011) of the European Muslim Network, for example, argues that fruitful exchange comes "by fostering education and critical thinking, by encouraging open, pluralistic and free spaces of debate and by encouraging people to dialogue in safe spaces so they can build meaningful relationships that cut through the polarised impasse of today." In 2007, in reference to the rules governing the French council, Islamist leader Lhaj Thami Brèze invoked Churchill's well-known aphorism considering democracy: "We need to find the least worst system." This statement becomes even more significant when readers remember Brèze's previous quotation (from 2003), in which he obstinately insisted: "The Qur'an is our constitution" (quoted in Laurence 2012: 242). These expressions of moderation represent hopeful signs of an emerging third space in many corners of Europe.

6

Terrorism

All told, there were 65 jihadist terrorist incidents in Europe from
2001 to 2009, involving 336 people; this represents less than 1% of
all terrorist incidents on the continent during those years.
—Doug Saunders, *The Myth of the Muslim Tide*

If Europe cannot be articulated in terms of complex space and
complex time that allow for multiple ways of life (and not merely
multiple identities) to flourish, it may be fated to be no more than
the common market of an imperial civilization, always anxious
about (Muslim) exiles within its gates and (Muslim) barbarians
beyond.
—Tal Asad, *Formations of the Secular*

Terrorism is not new to Europe. In the 1970s, 1980s, and 1990s, for example, revolutionary political organizations such as the Red Army Faction (RAF) or the Red Brigades and irredentist groups like the Irish Republican Army (IRA) or the Euskadi Ta Askatasuna (ETA) committed acts of violence in efforts to advance their political agendas. Earlier, during the tumultuous interwar years, political violence in the form of paramilitary clashes regularly transpired in many European countries. Of course, the assassination of Archduke Franz Ferdinand of Austria and his wife in 1914 triggered World War I. However, Islamist terrorism carried out against targets in Europe is quite novel. There was, of course, the hostage-taking episode at the Munich Olympic Games of 1972, but it was directed at Israel by Palestinian gunmen who did not directly invoke Islam. European officials have over the last two decades had to show heightening attention to Islamist terrorism as a result of a succession of alarming events: a series of lethal bomb attacks in Paris carried out by the Groupe Islamique Armé (GIA) in 1995, the Hamburg Al Qaeda cell that led the attacks of 9/11, the involvement of residents of France and Spain in the Casablanca bombings of 2003, the Madrid rail bombings of 2004, the murder of Theo van Gogh in Amsterdam in 2004, the London Tube bombings on 7 July 2005 (7/7), the slaying of two U.S. airmen and the serious injury of two others by Arid Uka at the Frankfurt airport in 2011, Mohammad Merah's lethal shooting spree in Toulouse and Montauban in 2012, the bus bombing that killed six people in Burgas in 2012, the bloody slaying of Jeremy Rigby in 2013 in Woolwich, the murder of four persons at the Brussels Jewish Museum in 2014, the murderous gunning of over 200 persons in Paris during the year 2015 (*Charlie Hebdo* and the coordinated attacks of 13 November), and the lethal attack on a cultural center and synagogue in Copenhagen in 2015, not to mention abundant reports of young militants recruited from Europe to fight for jihadists in Afghanistan, Iraq, Syria, and elsewhere. Analysts regularly speak of "securitization"—the process by which issues such as immigration or cultural diversity come to be increasingly viewed and treated through the lens of their alleged impact on domestic security (Waever et al. 1993).

Several oversimplifications are common in the analysis of counterterrorism in Europe. One draws a firm distinction between U.S. and European strategies. The U.S. government allegedly treats terrorism primarily as an external threat and therefore prefers military action such as the invasions and occupations of Afghanistan and Iraq to thwart terrorists before they can reach U.S. shores; European governments purportedly consider terrorism largely "homegrown," such as in the case of the 7/7 bombers, and therefore prefer a combined strategy of domestic police action to arrest terrorists and integration to discourage radicalization (Andreas and Nadelmann 2006; Rees and Aldrich 2005; Leiken 2005; Kagan 2004). The theory downplays or altogether ignores the fact that several European governments have allied with the United States in international military operations, such as the International Security Assistance Force (ISAF) in Afghanistan or the "Coalition of the Willing" in Iraq (Keohane 2008). I hasten to add, however, that the present chapter focuses on terrorism and counter-terrorism *within* Europe while recognizing, of course, that both inevitably have extra-European dimensions (Vidino 2013; Kegley 2003).

The aforementioned claim that European governments employ the combined strategies of policing and integrating measures (Chebel d'Appollonia and Reich 2008: 1), while vaguely correct, nevertheless lacks nuance. As will become clear below, significant differences stemming from the differing normative logics of liberalism, nationalism, and postmodernism abound on how best to pursue either strategy. Relatedly, the common assertion that the issue of terrorism in the end normatively distills down to a preference for security generally favored by the Right versus a preference for liberty defended by the Left (Banks, De Nevers, and Wallerstein 2008: 4; Chebel d'Appollonia and Reich 2008: 2; Balzacq and Carrera 2006) proves to be too simplistic. Instead, mutual fragilization among liberal, nationalist, and postmodern moralities has led activists to propose and governments to adopt a varied, ever-changing, and jumbled conglomeration of counter-terrorism measures. The policies "pursue wide-ranging and cross-cutting objectives" stemming from an "incoherent and fragmented counter-terrorism agenda" (Bossong 2013: 13, 11). The result is "paradoxical effects and unintended consequences" (Friedrichs 2008: 3), producing "messy, localized, complicated realities" (Ireland 2010: 34). Such policy messiness turns up in most European governments and therefore casts doubt on the theory of distinct national styles of counter-terrorism such as French assimilation and deportation versus British multiculturalism and conciliation (Klausen 2010; Kirschner and Sperling 2010; Leiken 2005).

Finally, the analysis of this chapter belies the clash-of-civilizations thesis. The latter postulates a greater tolerance of and propensity for politically motivated violence among Muslims than among (Western) non-Muslims (Huntington 1996; see also Phillips 2007; Fallaci 2006; Besson 2005; Ye'or 2005; Schwarzer 2002a). Like the three preceding chapters, this one too will demonstrate that Muslim Europeans vehemently disagree among themselves and generally along the same liberal, nationalist, and postmodern contours that inform the differing views expressed by non-Muslim Europeans. However, as will become abundantly clear, the clash thesis, in spite of and very likely because of its distortions, enjoys considerable normative sway in the politics of terrorism and counter-terrorism in Europe.

Combatting Terrorism with Equal Rights

Guaranteeing equal rights to Muslims is ultimately the surest weapon against terrorism; inversely, denying equal rights is the surest way to foment terrorism. Some version or other of this fragment of cosmopolitan reasoning figures prominently in the political discourse regarding terrorism in Europe. The widely circulated British columnist Timothy Garton Ash provides a typical formulation:

> The profound alienation of many Muslims—especially the second and third generations of immigrant families, young men and women themselves born in Europe—is one of the most vexing problems facing the continent today. If things continue to go as badly as they are at the moment, this alienation, and the way it both feeds and is fed by the resentments of mainly white, Christian or post-Christian Europeans, could tear apart the civic fabric of Europe's most established democracies. It has already catalyzed the rise of populist anti-immigrant parties, and contributed very directly to the terrorist attacks on the United States [and Europe]. . . . If we, the—for want of a

better word—traditional Europeans, manage to reverse the current trend, and enable . . . [Muslims] to feel at home as new Muslim Europeans, they could be a source of cultural enrichment and economic dynamism, helping to compensate for the downward drag of Europe's rapidly aging population. If we fail, we shall face many more explosions.(*New York Review of Books* 5 October 2006)

According to this line of reasoning, often dubbed "winning hearts and minds" or "soft power," persons treated with respect and dignity will have no reason to commit acts of terror. Persons welcomed and enabled to participate fully and equally in society will do just that lawfully and peacefully (Chebel d'Appollonia and Reich 2010; Limbach 2007; Bader 2007: 258; Frey 2004; Ignatieff 2004: x; Williams 2003).

European Muslims, on the whole, would appear to represent no exception. Thus, survey evidence indicates that they have as much or more confidence in European democratic institutions as non-Muslims (Foroutan et al. 2015; Cesari 2013: 20–81; Saunders 2012: 62–66; Haug, Müssig, and Stichs 2010; Inglehart and Norris 2009; Gallop 2009; Diehl and Schnell 2006; Metroscopia 2006; Pew Global Attitudes Project 2006; Tribalat 1996). They equally abhor violence and terrorism as a means to political ends (Gallop 2009; 2007). As Kymlicka (2010: 44) succinctly states, relations between European states and Muslim residents should be "taken out of the 'security' box, and put in the 'democratic politics' box."

From the cosmopolitan perspective, the European Muslims most likely to entertain, abet, or commit terrorism are persons who feel alienated from and mistreated by the very European societies in which they make their homes. Most of the "Muslim" terrorists in Europe have not come straight from the battlefields of Iraq, mountains of Afghanistan, or deserts of Arabia but rather were long-term resident aliens or even citizens of the European societies that they sought to terrorize. Take the example of 7/7 suicide bomber Mohammad Sidique ("Sid") Khan, who came of age in Beeston, spoke English with a perfect Yorkshire accent, took a degree from Leeds Metropolitan University, and became a "learning mentor" at Hillside Primary School. Only after his exposure to and indignation over the deprived immigrant children and youth whom he served did Khan become enthralled with the ideas of jihadist mullahs such as Abdullah el-Faisal and Abu Hamza al-Masri. Indeed, a majority of jihadists active in Europe—Mohammad Atta (9/11 hijacker), Jamal Zougam (Madrid bomber), Khaled Kelkal (Paris Metro bomber), Mohammad Bouyeri (van Gogh assassin), Essid Sami Ben Khemais (Strasbourg and Rome cyanide plots), Mehdi Nemmouche (Brussels Jewish Museum suspect), Chérif and Said Kouachi (Paris *Charlie Hebdo* massacre), to name a few—appear to have radicalized after residing there for longer durations (Leiken 2012: 71; Chebel d'Appollonia and Reich 2010: 3–5; Tirman 2010: 67; Roy 2009; Pargeter 2008: 113–24; Banks, De Nevers, and Wallerstein 2008: 56–70; Bakker 2006). Social deprivation and alienation also help explain why Europe's prisons, disproportionately filled with inmates of Muslim heritage, make fertile recruiting ground for Islamist militants, as was the case with Chérif Kouachi (Beckford, Joly, and Khosrokhavar 2006).

The same explanation seems plausible for other forms of violence. The rioters of mainly Pakistani origin in Oldham, Leeds, Bradford, and Burnley in 2001 were responding to a brutalizing rampage by white thugs through the Glodwick neighborhood of Oldham on the night of 26 May. Thus did Tony Blair blame the riots on the "bad and regressive motive of white extremists" (*Spiked Online* 29 May 2001). Riots engaged in by youth of mostly North African descent in Paris in 2005, like those in Stockholm in 2013 involving disaffected immigrants from Africa and the Middle East, were sparked by allegations of police brutality. These instances of social unrest, like the riots in London in 2011 that did not involve large numbers of Muslims, appear to have been classic eruptions by underprivileged youth venting stored-up anger that had little or nothing to do with Islam per se.

The cosmopolitan logic makes good sense to many policy makers. For instance, the *EU Annual Report on Human Rights* asserts that "effective counter-terrorism measures and the protection of human rights are not conflicting but complementary and mutually reinforcing goals" (European Union 2007: 39; see also Organisation for Security and Cooperation in Europe 2007). The European Security Strategy maintains that terrorism "arises from complex causes [that] include . . . the alienation of young people living in foreign societies" (European Council 2003: 5). Prominent lawmakers endorse the idea of genuine equal rights as a potent antidote to homegrown terrorism. In 2003, for example, Interior Minister Sarkozy claimed that it is "catastrophic [to deny] the cultural and religious identity of Muslims. An identity denied is an identity that radicalizes" (quoted in Laurence 2012: 121). In 2008, President Sarkozy announced: "I want the state to be exemplary. Exemplary in the implementation of policies in favor of equal opportunity, exemplary in fighting against discrimination, exemplary in promoting diversity" (quoted in Geisser and Soum 2012: 55). At her "integration summit" of 2013, Chancellor Merkel averred that peace and harmony could prevail among traditional Germans and the immigrant community only if prejudices "vanish from our thoughts" (*raus aus den Köpfen*) (*Deutsche Welle* 28 May 2013). In 2011, in regard to young Muslims who entertain the idea of embracing radical Islamism, Prime Minister David Cameron conceded that "we have failed to provide a vision of society to which they feel they want to belong" (quoted in Goodman 2014: 142–43).

Cosmopolitanism has shaped a significant amount of soft-power policy. As for eliminating discrimination against Muslims, Chapter 3 treated the considerable anti-discrimination laws and measures, such as the Racial Equality Directive adopted by the EU in 2000 which was either antedated or emulated in most EU member states. Regarding Muslims and the fight against terrorism per se, the EU has pledged to observe human rights. For example, the EU's counter-terrorism coordinator, Gijs de Vries, maintained in 2006 that

> the struggle against terrorism is first and foremost a conflict over values. To win the battle for hearts and minds our policies to combat terrorism must respect the rights and values we have pledged to defend, including the rights of prisoners. Abu Grahib, Guantanamo and CIA renditions have damaged America's standing in the world and have compromised our common struggle against terrorism. Credibility matters. The European Union continues to believe that in this battle we should be guided by established international legal standards, including international human rights law. (Quoted in Keohane 2008: 137)

Indeed, the European Union Counter-Terrorism Strategy aims "to combat terrorism worldwide while honoring human rights to make possible for its citizens an area of freedom, security and justice (Council of the EU 2005: 2). In 2002, at the urging of the European Parliament (EP), the European Commission formed the EU Network of Independent Experts on Fundamental Rights. The group of legal specialists compiles annual reports that are designed to identify in counter-terrorism measures real or potential violations of the EU's Charter of Fundamental Rights (2000), such as invasion of privacy, refoulement, extraordinary rendition, and torture (Commentary of the Charter of Fundamental Rights of the European Union 2006, http://cridho/uclouvain.be/en/eu_experts_network/; see also Dalgaard-Nielsen: 2009: 254). For its part, the EP has proven itself to be a staunch defender of individual rights when it comes to counter-terrorism. To cite but two examples, the EP investigated and condemned the extraordinary rendition program of the Central Intelligence Agency (CIA), including the complicity of the European Council and several EU member states (Fava 2007). The EP also refused to ratify the 2009 SWIFT Agreement (on finance tracking of suspected terrorist organizations) until the U.S. government agreed to tighter controls on and monitoring of the acquired information (Bossong 2013: 114; Dalgaard-Nielsen 2009: 254).

All EU member states recognize the European Convention on Human Rights (1950). Article Three protects against torture ("inhuman or degrading treatment or punishment"), Article Five guarantees liberty and security (unless convicted of a crime), and Article Six guarantees a fair and public trial. Of course, sovereign states do not have to abide by the convention, but when they do not, they can and often do find themselves hauled before the European Court of Human Rights. It, for instance, ruled in *Othman v. United Kingdom* (2012) that alleged Al Qaeda conspirator Abu Qatada could not be deported to Jordan "given the real risk of the admission of evidence obtained by torture" (quoted in *Telegraph* 17 January 2012). Abu Qatada was finally deported in 2013. In 2010, the court postponed the extradition from the United Kingdom to the United States of five terrorist suspects, including the firebrand preacher Abu Hamza, until in 2012 the U.S. government agreed not to pursue the death penalty or to try them before military tribunals. It furthermore deserves mention that by virtue of the EU Treaties of Maastricht (1993), Amsterdam (1999), and Nice (2003), all of which commit signatories to the European Convention on Human Rights, the latter has become EU law. This means plaintiffs can also turn to the European Court of Justice (ECJ), whose decisions are not only binding on member states but also trump national laws whenever they conflict with EU law. For instance, in *M and Others v Her Majesty's Treasury* (2010), the ECJ ruled that social security benefits may not be denied to family members of suspected terrorists.

National courts have also assiduously defended human rights. In 2004, for instance, Britain's High Court ruled that the section of the Anti-Terrorism, Crime and Security Act of 2001 that allowed for indefinite detention of foreigners breached the European Convention on Human Rights, which had been incorporated into British law in the Human Rights Act of 1998. As Lord Hoffmann opined: "The real threat to the life of the nation, in the sense of a people living in accordance with its traditional laws and political values, comes not from terrorism but from laws such as these" (quoted in Tsoukala 2008: 81). Led by Interior Minister Jacqui Smith, the Brown government introduced and the House of Commons passed a bill in 2007 allowing forty-two days of detention without charges; the Law Lords again squashed it in 2008 (Klausen 2010: 52). In 2006, the German Constitutional Court ruled unconstitutional the police's practice of electronic dragnetting (*Rasterfahndung*), whereby data were collected on persons through a profiling scheme (for instance, young and of Arab origin), regardless of whether the persons were actually suspected of involvement with terrorism (Tyrer 2013: 56). Four years later, a Munich court found insufficient evidence to convict eight

Islamists, including prominent imams Reda Seyam and Hassan Dabbagh, of organizing to incite violence (*ARD-Terrorismus Blog* 30 March 2010). In 2012, the Norwegian Court of Appeal nullified an incitement-to-terrorism conviction against Mullah Krekar, who had purportedly threatened to kill Minister of Local Government and Regional Development Erna Solberg. In 2003, Norway had ordered the deportation of Krekar but did not implement the order because he could face the death penalty in Iraq (*Aftenposten* 6 December 2012). In 2008, the appeals court of The Hague acquitted or severely reduced the sentences of eight alleged members of the so-called "Hofstad Network" who had been found guilty in 2006 by the court of Rotterdam for plotting to bomb, among other targets, the Dutch parliament. Though the Brussels criminal court sentenced Abdelkader Hakimi to eight years in prison for his involvement with the Madrid bombings, the Belgium government refused to extradite him to Morocco, where he had been sentenced to death in absentia. In 2011, he was released after the European Court of Human Rights ruled that he had not received a fair trial. In 2013, the Court of Appeal in Milan sentenced the former director and deputy director of the Italian Military and Intelligence Security Service (SISMI) to ten years in prison for their cooperation with the CIA's abduction and extraordinary rendition of Hassan Mustafa Osama Nasr (commonly referred to as "Abu Omar") to Egypt in 2003 (although the Supreme Court of Cassation acquitted the directors in 2014).

Because freedom of religion represents one of the rights that Muslims should be guaranteed, the cosmopolitan approach to counter-terrorism necessarily entails a liberal multicultural facet. In this line of thinking, feeling unencumbered and, like many Christians, even being state-subsidized in the exercise of their faith should help prevent radicalization among European Muslims. Furthermore, the experience of freely determining their religious beliefs and practices is thought to foster among Muslims respect for the right of non-Muslims to do the same. This radicalization-prevention strategy loomed large in the motives and justifications of the many outreach programs (for instance, the Islamic councils) initiated by European governments in the wake of the 9/11 attacks and the Madrid and London bombings (and discussed in detail in the previous chapter; see also Laurence 2012: 7–11). Indeed, virtually all of the Muslim participants in the councils, including Islamists, publicly declared their loyalty to democracy and renounced terrorism in general and specific terrorist acts in particular. For instance, the general secretary of the Islamische Gemeinde Milli Görüş (IGMG), Oguz Ücüncü, stated in 2004: "We condemned the terrorist attacks of March 11 [in Madrid] as we did on September 11, and we condemn any other act of terror" (quoted in Laurence 2012: 211). In the same year, L'Unione delle Comunità e Organizzazioni Islamiche in Italia (UCOII) made public a "manifesto against terrorism and for life" and organized peace marches in several Italian cities on 11 September to demand the release of Italian hostages in Iraq (quoted in Laurence 2012: 212). Similarly, on 7/7, the Muslim Council of Britain (2005) released a statement "utterly" condemning the bombings. General Secretary Farooq Murad stated that the MCB "recognise that our community must remain vigilant and steadfast against those who commit such acts in the name of Islam and thus pervert our faith for their own ends."

These organizations were marching in lockstep with Jusuf al-Qaradawi, spiritual leader of the international Muslim Brotherhood movement, who two days following the 9/11 attacks issued a *fatwa* that condemned Al Qaeda's "illegal jihad"; "Our hearts bleed because of the attacks that have targeted the World Trade Center, as well as other institutions in the United States." The murders in the United States, he continued, could not be justified on any ground, including "the American biased policy toward Israel on the military, political and economic fronts" (Islam Online, www.islamonline. net, 13 September 2001). After riots broke out in the Paris suburbs in 2005, the UOIF issued a strong renunciation of violence: "It is strictly forbidden for any Muslim . . . to take part in any action that strikes blindly at private or public property or that could threaten the lives of others" (quoted in Khosrokhavar 2010: 139). A decade later in response to the attacks on the Paris offices of *Charlie Hebdo* in 2015, "The UOIF condemns in the strongest terms this criminal attack, and these horrible murders" (*Huffington Post* 7 January 2015). As the president of the British Muslim Council, Iqbal Sacranie, put the matter, "There is no such thing as an Islamic terrorist—that is offensive" (*Sunday Express* 10 July 2005). Similarly, the Islamic University of Rotterdam published on its website (www.islamicuniversity.nl) on 13 September 2001 a statement entitled "A Terrorist Cannot Be a Muslim, Nor Can a True Muslim Be a Terrorist."

Not surprisingly, detractors (treated below) cast doubt on the sincerity of the pronouncements, especially those emanating from Islamists (Baran 2011: 126–34; Khosrokhavar 2010: 143; Rich 2010: 132–33; Tibi 2008: 12). However, many, in keeping with the tradition of liberal voluntarism, retort that it suffices for Muslims to observe the rule of law in democracies and abstain from committing or facilitating terrorist acts. For peaceful and democratic order to prevail it is necessary neither that European Muslims demonstrate nor possess a deep and thorough commitment to democracy or even nonviolence. For instance, France's highly influential Islam expert, Olivier Roy (2007: 93), argues regarding the prevention of Islamist extremism:

It is, in fact, participation in the political process that leads believers with little inclination toward democracy as a social ideal to accept the rules of the game and often to become strong defenders of those rules. If we had to wait for everyone to become a democrat before creating democracy, France would still be a monarchy.

Community-Based Counter-Terrorism

At this juncture it becomes critical to draw attention to a fine but important distinction between liberal and communitarian interpretations. As Roy's remark manifests, liberal multiculturalism remains optimistic but not insistent that European Muslims internalize the democratic values that allegedly predominate in Europe. By contrast, communitarianism, with its emphasis on particularism, deems it neither likely, necessary, nor desirable that Muslims adopt "European" values. In the first place, Muslims by definition identify with Islam. The mores and customs that shape their daily lives stem from a long-standing Islamic tradition. Though they may not uncritically accept all of these traditions, it is very improbable that they sense a burning need significantly to alter or reform, let alone jettison, them. Furthermore, according to the communitarian outlook, Islam and Islamic civilization have unfolded more often than not in contradistinction to and even confrontation with Christianity and Western civilization, whether it be as a vying monotheistic creed, rival geopolitical region, or, more recently within Europe, as a minority immigrant community clearly distinguished from the majority culture. From the communitarian viewpoint, it is naively optimistic to think cosmopolitanism can overcome these profound differences between Muslim and non-Muslim Europeans. Even if integrative words and deeds could manage to heal the wounds incurred through decades of discrimination and under-privilege within Europe (doubtless an unlikely eventuality itself), there would still be foreign policy. Muslims belong not just to a local Islamic community but also identify with the international Islamic community (*umma*): "Hold firmly to the rope of Allah all together and do not become divided" (Qur'an 3:103). Needless to say, few Muslims have forgotten the Crusades or European colonialism. Moreover, recent European foreign policies have bitterly disappointed and angered untold European Muslims, whether much delayed intervention to protect persecuted Bosnian Muslims (1992–1995), the Iraq War (2003–2011), the EU's decision to cut aid to the Hamas-controlled Gaza Strip (2006), or enduring support of both Israel and dictatorial Arab regimes (Bilgrami 2014: 263–65; Bonino 2012: 22). Well-sounding pledges to "promote good governance, democracy, education and economic prosperity outside the EU" like that found in the European Council's *Strategy and Action Plan to Combat Terrorism* will unlikely succeed in placating European Muslims outraged by repeated injustices purportedly inflicted on the umma by Western governments (Council of the EU 2007).

The unappeasable nature of Muslim indignation and alienation does not, however, have to mean that European governments have no soft-power option at their disposal in the fight against terrorism. But it does mean, in the communitarian worldview, that an effective strategy of verbal persuasion needs to emanate from and be largely implemented by the Islamic community itself. Muslim organizations and personalities can use Islamic doctrine and reasoning, such as "there shall be no compulsion in religion" (Qur'an 2:256), to convince potential extremists to eschew terrorism. Particularly European Islamist organizations such as the MCB, UIOF, UCOII, and IGMG have assiduously and opportunistically sought since 9/11 to convince European officials of the merits of this strategy (Vidino 2012: 66; Baran 2011: 126; Rosen 2008; Kepel 2004: 266). Thus, IGMG's Oguz Ücüncü added to the condemnation of violence cited above:

> But what we did as an Islamic organization is more than just demonstrating. We have been using our infrastructure in order to condemn the terrorist attacks and violence in general, but also to inform our people to not give any kind of support or sympathy to terrorists. (Quoted in Laurence 2012: 211)

The Islamists urge European governments financially to back their organizations and simultaneously give them considerable discretion as to how they go about identifying, reaching, discouraging, and thwarting would-be terrorists.

Many governments at various levels have experimented with "community-based" approaches emphasizing "self-policing" (Briggs, Fieschi, and Lownsbrough 2006). Perhaps the most dramatic example unfolded in London in the wake of the 9/11 attacks. In the 1980s and 1990s the British government had gained a widespread reputation for granting asylum to Islamist militants fleeing authoritarian regimes in the Middle East and South Asia. A tacit understanding or "covenant of security" was said to exist between the radicals and officialdom: asylum, including the freedom to pursue their political agendas regarding their homelands, in exchange for not carrying out acts of political violence in the U.K. (Leiken 2012: 184–85; Pargeter 2008: 156–58). Omar Bakri Muhammad, who headed the British group Al-Muhajiroun, quipped to a television reporter in 1997: "If I lived in Saudi Arabia, I could never get away with what I do here, ha ha" (quoted in Pargeter 2008: 32). The covenant, if it ever existed, dissolved arguably with 9/11 but surely on 11 September 2002, on which day Abu Hamza al-Masri sponsored at the Finsbury Park Mosque in North London a conference entitled "September the 11th 2001: A Towering

Day in History." Speeches and leaflets lionized the hijackers as the "Magnifi-
cent 19." Subsequently, the Muslim Contact Unit of the Metropolitan Police
partnered with Salafists to identify the militants and their illegal activities.
Although "hard power" was ultimately used in the form of a raid in 2003 to
arrest the jihadists, including al-Masri, Scotland Yard acknowledged that the
operation could not have succeeded had the Salafists not convinced the con-
gregation that the obstreperous militants were misrepresenting Islam to the
world and transgressing its sacred dictates (Saunders 2012: 104–5). Eventually
in 2005, the Muslim Association of Britain, an organization with ties to the
Muslim Brotherhood movement, was "invited" to assume leadership of the
mosque (Baran 2011: 134).

At the national level, the Blair government made the Muslim Council of
Britain into a quasi-official interlocutor after 9/11. The prime minister made
numerous high-profile appearances with leaders of the organization. Following the Tube bombings in 2005, the Home Office turned primarily to the
MCB (despite allegations of its close ties to the Jama'at-i Islami, reportedly
the South Asian counterpart to the Muslim Brotherhood) to provide the
personnel for seven working groups tasked with investigating radicalism
in Muslim communities (Frampton and Maher 2013: 37; Mandaville 2010:
150–1; Awan 2007b: 208). Later that year, the groups submitted to Blair their
findings and recommendations in *Preventing Extremism Together* (Home
Office 2005). From the report emerged the Preventing Violent Extremism
Programme (commonly referred to simply as "Prevent"), which was placed
under the supervision of the Department for Communities and Local Government. Through its subsequently devised programs, like the Preventing
Violent Extremism Pathfinder Fund, hundreds of millions of pounds were
channeled to local Islamic associations to enable them to devise initiatives
designed to offer a rejection of terrorism targeting Muslims that was rooted
in Islamic doctrine (Frampton and Maher 2013: 40–47; Tyrer 2013: 108;
Klausen 2010: 53–54). The supervising minister justified the policy in unmistakably communitarian terms:

> Strong mosques positioned at the centre of the community and ef-
> fectively governed will be better able to withstand attempts to hijack
> them by certain groups supporting violent extremist interpretations
> of Islam. Thus, the goal of state outreach to Muslim communities
> was twofold: vaccination against radicalism, on the one hand, and
> the routinization of religious observance for Muslims, on the other.
> (Quoted in Laurence 2012: 149)

The approach seemed to bear fruit in 2011 when, according to Scotland
Yard, Salafist mosques in South London were principally responsible for

keeping Muslim youths from joining in the riots that ignited during August (Aidi 2014: 213).

The U.K. holds no monopoly on community-based counter-terrorism. In response to 9/11, Sarkozy insisted that the UIOF be included in the newly formed Conseil Français du Culte Musulman. The then interior minister and his advisors maintained that the UIOF eschewed political violence, had an impressive organizational infrastructure with long tentacles throughout the Muslim community that gave it clout on the streets, and therefore represented the most effective agent for persuading young Muslims to abstain from terrorism (Daguzan 2013: 105; Kepel 2004: 274). "What we should be afraid of," Sarkozy explained to his detractors who stressed no involvement with the UIOF, "is Islam gone astray, garage Islam, basement Islam, underground Islam" (quoted in Taras 2012: 152). Yves Bertrand, director of the Direction Centrale des Renseignements Généraux (Central Directorate of General Intelligence) from 1999 to 2004, commented that "many of [our] observers were expecting problems . . . [but] the mosque leaders and associations have controlled their troops very well" (quoted in Bonelli 2008: 107). Indeed, it was leaders of the Dhaou Meskine and Larbi Kechat mosques who had more success than the gendarmerie in quieting the 2005 riots in the banlieues of Paris (Bowen 2010: 43). A similar story holds for the riots that broke out in Antwerp after a Muslim schoolteacher was shot dead by a neighbor in 2002 (Fadil 2006: 57).

Communitarian reasoning also moved German interior minister Schäuble to insist that the IGMG be invited to join the Deutsche Islam Konferenz in 2006. The advisor to the chancellor on religious affairs said the government, if it were to have a good chance of reaching alienated young Muslims, had to be willing to explore "interacting with political Islamists in the grey zone" (quoted in Laurence 2012: 171). By the latter she meant an ideological orientation that does not perfectly accord with the German Constitution but that nonetheless rejects terrorism. Defending his decision to include the UCOII in the Consulta per l'Islam Italiano, Italian interior minister Giuseppe Pisanu similarly claimed: "I took into account what the UCOII is today—not its past—and the efforts it has made for a positive role of the Muslim Brotherhood in the whole world." After the council's first meeting in 2005, he observed that "anyone participating in this meeting would have understood that there is a moderate Islam in Italy" (quoted in Laurence 2012: 171, 216). In 2004, Spanish prime minister Zapatero, building off Iranian president Khatami's idea of a "Dialogue of Civilizations," proposed before the United Nations an Alliance of Civilizations, "a grand alliance with moderate Islam to isolate violent members" (quoted in Planet and de Larramendi 2013: 123). The domestic dimension of the eventually adopted program involved subsidizing initiatives of groups tied to the al-Adl wa al-Ihssane (Moroccan Muslim Brotherhood) to reach out to alienated Moroccan immigrants (Planet and de Larramendi 2013: 123). Zapatero's opponents, the People's Party, had already in its 1996 platform recommended "that simplistic formulas of a generalized rejection of these [Islamist] movements be eschewed and imaginative channels for relationships and dialogue be found with its moderate manifestations" (quoted in Planet and de Larramendi 2013: 121).

Not surprisingly, the communitarian strategy draws criticism. Particularly non-Islamist Muslim organizations and secular immigrant associations (often bypassed due to the strategy) contend that the policy is perilously imprudent. Even if Islamists manage to dissuade some potential terrorists from committing violence, the critique argues, they will do so not by spreading respect for democracy but rather theocracy. The Muslim Brotherhood movement, for example, has eschewed violence since the 1990s but only, according to critics, because its leaders concluded that terrorism is not the most efficient way to establish an Islamic state. The ultimate goal remains Islamization, not democratization. Moreover, given the continued popularity among Islamists in Europe of pioneering ideologues like Sayyid Qutb, whose famous book *Milestones* does espouse militancy, European states have no guarantee that Islamist organizations will not either turn a blind eye to terrorists within their ranks or, worse, surreptitiously aid and abet them, all the while using European taxpayers' money to do so (Meijer 2013: 72; Alonso 2012: 479; Bakker 2012: 186–87; Baran 2011: 13–14, 179; Khosrokhavar 2010; Rich 2010: 132–33; Mandaville 2010: 150–51; Patel 2007: 51–52; Jenkins 2007: 274; Jonker 2006: 131; Hirsi Ali 2006; Fourest 2004). "A choice must be made," avers Bassam Tibi (2008: 31), "between Qutb and Kant, or, in the case of Europe, between a Muslim Europe or Euro-Islam—that is, the Islamization of Europe or the Europeanization of Islam."

Liberal Perfectionist Soft Power

Such suspicion of unreliable commitment to counter-terrorism among some Islamic organizations predictably prompts fragilization toward liberal perfectionism. European officials feel moved to prescribe to Islamic organizations in no uncertain terms what constitutes proper counter-terrorism preaching and practice. In 2005, Dutch prime minister Balkenende presided over the publication of the *Behavioral Code against Extremism/Contract with Society* (*Gedragscode tegen extremism/Contract met de Samenleving*), which the leaders of several Amsterdam mosques publicly signed (Laurence 2012: 175). France and Spain each have produced guidebooks for how imams are to be trained to foster democracy and discourage extremism. France,

Germany, and Austria coordinated to draft a handbook for how Muslim clerics should preach counter-terrorism in prisons (Bossong 2013: 114). In 2006, Interior Minister Schäuble said that "the number of Islamists is not the same thing as the number of potential terrorists [but] Islamists have a vision of state order that we do not share. . . . We must insist that Muslims in Germany identify with [not merely observe] the constitution" (quoted in Laurence 2012: 101). Similarly, Sarkozy promised before the National Assembly in 2003 not to tolerate any "communities of immigrant origin [that] organize themselves to resist Republican integration" (quoted in Freedman 2006: 179). Denmark goes so far as to compel naturalizing immigrants (not, however, Nordics) to swear an oath to teach their children to reject terrorism (Sainsbury 2012: 111).

Even the reputedly permissive British government has set limits. In 2008 in a critique of the Labour government's support of allegedly extremist Islamic organizations, David Cameron asserted: "The message should be clear: to those who reject democracy; to those who preach hate; to those who encourage violence; you are not part of the mainstream. You will not get public funding. You are not a welcome part of our society" (quoted in Frampton and Maher 2013: 50). Actually, in that same year, however, the Brown regime, through the Department of Communities and Local Government as part of its Prevent strategy, had announced the formation of a board of hand-picked Islamic theologians who were to draft standards of good practice to which all members of the Mosques and Imams National Advisory Board would be held. The predictable indignation at such patronizing treatment came from several corners of the Muslim community. For instance, Muhammad Abdul Bari, general secretary of the Muslim Council of Britain, responded:

> In a country where the State is largely neutral on theological matters, and where no other similar arrangement exists for other minority faiths, such an initiative will inevitably be met with skepticism and mistrust. For too long now, British Muslims have been viewed by this government through the narrow prism of security. British Muslims—like all citizens—have every right to peacefully disagree with government policies if they wish and they do not need to be 're-programmed' by a government-approved list of theologians. (Muslim Council of Britain, 18 July 2008, www.mcb.org/uk/media/presstext.php?ann_id=303)

Indeed, it is not difficult to imagine the furor that would erupt if Christian organizations were compelled under strict governmental supervision to evince that they do not support terrorism.

Most European governments authorize surveillance by their police and intelligence services of Islamist organizations, including even those with which the government formally cooperates (Bundesministerium des Innern 2014: 19–25; Frampton and Maher 2013: 38; Bossong 2013: 115; Meijer 2013: 72; Bleich 2010b: 10; Bonelli 2008: 110; Algemene Inlichtingen- en Veiligheidsdienst 2007; 2002). As reported in the previous chapter, officials in Germany, Italy, and the United Kingdom have broken off relations (usually temporarily) with the IGMG, UCOII, and the MCB, respectively, as a result of intelligence reports alleging that the organizations did not unambiguously reject political extremism (Joppke and Torpey 2013: 82; Laurence 2012: 184, 213; Hellyer 2009: 158). In the British case, it became known (through an *Observer* article) that MCB general secretary Daoud Abdullah had joined ninety other Islamist leaders in signing a pro-Hamas declaration at the January 2009 Shura Council conference in Istanbul. The declaration implored the "Islamic Nation" to use any and all means to oppose Israel and its allies. In March, relations with the MCB were halted. The Home Office announced, in strong liberal perfectionist language, that it would no longer countenance views that "fall short of supporting violence and are within the law, but which reject and undermine our shared values and jeopardize community cohesion" (quoted in Baran 2011: 179). However, relations were restored in 2010 after the MCB publicly declared its reproof of violence (Baran 2011: 167).

Concern over Islamists' allegedly unreliable commitment to counter-terrorism is more likely to elicit calls for hard power. The sense of anxiety regarding partnering with Islamist associations comes forth clearly in the continuation of the above-cited quotation from Yves Bertrand, erstwhile director of French General Intelligence, that "the mosque leaders and associations have controlled their troops very well which, I would add, doesn't necessarily reassure us. It means that the very dense social fabric is in perfect working order . . . that the community is very well controlled by these associations" (quoted in Bonelli 2008: 107). Or as Lorenzo Vidino (2010b: 199) questions, are European governments aiding "firefighters or arsonists" (see also Alonso 2012: 486)?

Hard Power

No European state confines its counter-terrorism strategy to soft power, whether liberal or communitarian (more likely both at once, as we have seen). Hard power (on the domestic front) can entail surveillance, intelligence-gathering, search and seizure, arrest, prosecution, conviction, and imprisonment or deportation. Hard-power strategies presuppose the existence of militants actively plotting to commit acts of terrorism on European soil. They presuppose, in other words, that soft power alone does not suffice and perhaps even enables terrorists. Normative justifications for preferring hard to soft power vis-à-vis the Muslim community typically invoke fragments of liberal perfectionism or nativist nationalism. The former hypothesize such extensive animosity toward democracy in Islamic doctrine and practice that use of political violence on the part of Muslims to subvert democratic governments and principles should not be ruled out but, on the contrary, expected. Nativism tends to be somewhat more oriented toward defending native territory rather than democracy per se, perceiving Islam as an inherently expansivist civilization that will stop at nothing to extend the borders of the *dar al-Islam* (abode of Islam). These represent fine theoretical distinctions that become wholly blurred and blended in the arguments of harsh Islam critics who endorse hard power. Moreover, it is difficult to point to another political stance in Europe that has benefited more from essentializing distortion and exaggeration than the claim that Islam and Muslims pose a serious terrorist threat in Europe. Put differently, we cannot fully explain the frequency and extent to which European governments deploy hard power without attending to the role played by what we in previous chapters have been calling postmodernist hyperbole.

Fear of Aggressive Islam

The previous three chapters covered, respectively, the common allegations that Islam, and by extension its believers, are anti-democratic, misogynist, and theocratic. Here we focus on the charge that they are violent, or at least more prone to violence than non-Muslim Europeans. Hirsi Ali alleged in an interview with the *Evening Standard* (2 February 2007) that "violence is inherent in Islam. It's a destructive, nihilistic cult of death. It legitimizes murder." On the website islamwatch.org, she further explained:

> Muhammad built the House of Islam using military tactics that included mass killing, torture, targeted assassination, lying and the indiscriminate destruction of productive goods. . . . A close look at the propaganda produced by the terrorists [of today] reveals constant quotation of Muhammad's deeds and edicts to justify their actions and to call on other Muslims to support their cause. (Hirsi Ali 2006)

Such charges often point to verses in the Qur'an that purportedly command believers to exercise violence. Favorites (often taken out of context) read "when you encounter the unbelievers strike off their heads" (47:4) or "slay them wherever ye find them and drive them out of the places whence they drove you out" (2:191–93). Indeed, Hirsi Ali's former political partner in the

Dutch parliament, Geert Wilders, produced in 2008 a YouTube film, *Fitna*, which plucks numerous quotations from the Qur'an while surrounding them with images of the most heinous acts of terrorism—a tactic used by numerous Islamophobic websites such as Islam Watch, Politically Incorrect, Die Grüne Pest, Nürnberg 2.0, or Stop the Islamization of Europe, which reach millions of viewers. The same year also saw publication of Hans Jansen's *Islam for Pigs, Monkeys, Donkeys and Other Animals,* epithets allegedly used in the Qur'an to refer to non-Muslims. Jansen too blamed the world religion with an estimated 1.6 billion adherents for promoting and legitimizing terrorism of the kind practiced by Al Qaeda against non-Muslims.

Dutch Islam-bashers are not alone. The prolific and frequently interviewed Spanish professor of political science Antonio Elorza (2004: 156) calls Islam "a religion of combat." The German orientalist Hans-Peter Raddatz (2006), who frequently appears on TV as an "Islam expert," answers his own provocative question of whether there is a direct link "from Allah to terror" with the answer: "Put simply, the Christian misuses his religion when he uses violence, the Muslim misuses his religion when he does not use violence" (quoted in Bahners 2011: 77). The prominent French essayist Pascal Bruckner (2007) warns that soft power appeasement will not sway Muslims to forgo terrorism, noting that "the more we give in to the radicalism of the bearded, the more they will harden their tone. Appeasement politics only increase their appetite. The hope that benevolence alone will disarm the brutes remains for the moment unfounded." As we have seen in previous chapters, the hyperbolic allusion to Hitler usually proves irresistible. Thus in her bestseller *The Force of Reason*, Oriana Fallaci (2006: 306) accuses:

> The Qur'an is the *Mein Kampf* of this [Islamist] movement. The Qur'an demands the annihilation or subjugation of the other, and wants to substitute totalitarianism for democracy. . . . All the evil that the sons of Allah commit against themselves and against others is in it.

Fallaci's accusation voices the common anxiety over Islam's alleged expansionism. Muhammad is said to have cast the mold by establishing an army of holy warriors in Medina that went on to wage *jihad* (or struggle) against the infidels controlling Mecca. Of course, such expansionist militancy was attributed to the prophet not only in the controversial cartoon published by *Jylland-Postens* in 2005 but also in the notorious Regensburg speech of 2006, in which Pope Benedict XVI (2006), quoting a Byzantine emperor, referred to Muhammad's "command to spread by sword the faith he preached." Many maintain that the covetous Muslims have their eyes trained on Europe. "A youthful Muslim society to the south and east of the Mediterranean is poised to colonize—the term is not too strong—a senescent Europe," warns Niall Ferguson (quoted in Saunders 2012: 55). "Wake up, people," thundered Fallaci following 9/11, "what is under way here is a reverse crusade. . . . They will feel authorized to kill you and your children because you drink wine or beer, because you don't wear a long beard or chador, because you go to the theatre and cinemas, because you listen to music and sing songs" (quoted in Kaya 2012: 6–7). Søren Krarup warns of "the slow extermination of the Danish people" (quoted in Hedetoft 2003), while Melanie Phillips (2007: 66) contends that "the job of subjugating the West is half done" and is being carried out by a "lethal and many-headed hydra" (11) of Al Qaeda affiliates in Europe. Alice Schwarzer (2002b), whose 2002 bestseller was titled *The Holy Warriors and the Misguided Tolerance*, drew the predictable comparison to the Nazis: "The parallels to 1933 are emerging. . . . The holy warriors have already made Italy their logistical basis, England their propoganda center and Germany their European hub." Elsewhere she warned that the Islamists "have already won an unsettling amount of terrain and unfortunately can no longer be stopped with democratic measures alone" (quoted in Bahners 2011: 246). Sorbonne history professor Guy Millière (2004) went so far as to claim that the Muslim question "will determine whether France survives or perishes" in the twenty-first century. There would appear to be no limit to the number of journalists and other authors who catapult themselves onto bestseller lists with books purporting to expose the designs of radical Muslim cells to transform Europe into "Eurabia" (Ye'or 2005; see also Marchand 2013; Ulfkotte 2013; Broder 2006; Besson 2005). As mentioned above, Islamophobic websites abound, often deploying captivating graphs and images that depict the impending Islamization of Europe.

The menacing quality of these alarmist warnings relies for its effect on explicit or implicit essentialization. Islam is presented as a static, monolithic collective religion, civilization, and psyche that envelope all Muslims. No differentiation, diversity, or change is acknowledged. The reductionist logic concludes that if some Muslims invoke Islam to legitimize terror, then all Muslims must have a propensity to do so: within every Muslim there lies a real or potential Osama Bin Laden. "A direct line leads from Al Qaeda in Iraq and the Intifada in Palestine to the youth with 'migration background' in Neukölln and Moabit [boroughs of Berlin]," claims German columnist Henryk Broder (2006: 115). Similarly, while writing in the weekly *L'Express*, André Glucksmann linked French Muslims to hijab-wearing women in Algeria who allegedly engaged in terrorism: "*Hijab* is a terrorist operation. . . . In France, the zealous pupils know that their *hijab* is covered with blood" (quoted in Rigoni 2009: 478). Even Zinedine Zidane's infamous head butt

during the soccer World Cup final in 2006 was widely discussed as a manifestation of a greater propensity toward violence and against the rule of law
among persons of Islamic heritage (Amiraux 2010: 146). Two years earlier,
French opinion leaders had erupted with indignation over Islam's supposed
violent culture in response to the alleged assault by Muslim youths against
the so-called "Marie L.," who, it turned out, had faked the story (Fredette
2014: 136). Given the nigh ubiquity of anti-Islam hyperbole, it should come
as no surprise that more than two-thirds of those polled in France, Britain,
the United States, and Germany "are worried about Islamic extremists in
their country" (Pew Research 2012).

Studies abound that demonstrate the frequency, the potency, as well as
the utter falsity of such essentializing tropes that necessarily associate Islam
and being Muslim with terrorism (Lynch 2013; Tyrer 2013; Bonino 2012;
Morgan and Poynting 2012a; Mudde 2012; Triadafilopolous 2011; Hickman
et al. 2011; Jacoby 2010; Schneiders 2010b; Terrio 2009; Zapata-Barrero and
Qasem 2008; Green-Pedersen and Krogstrup 2008: 616–18; Franz 2007). All
three qualities point to the influential sway of Hobbesian postmodernism,
at least of its fragment teaching that a commitment to objectivity makes for
naïve and therefore unsuccessful politicking. After all, it is hard to imagine successfully spurring liberals to defend democracy or natives to defend
the homeland with the argument that they are 33 times likelier to die from
meningitis, 822 times likelier to be murdered for nonpolitical reasons, and
1,833 times likelier to perish in a car accident than to fall victim to terrorist
attacks, of which only 1 percent are committed by persons invoking Islam
(Katzenstein 2003: 734; Saunders 2012: 107). Instead media and political actors find it nearly irresistible to engage in what Michael Murphy (2012: 3)
calls "the gross exaggeration of the Islamic threat." We see here nicely how
mutual fragilization, normative fragmentation, and political bricolage function together, for Hobbesian postmodern hyperbole is pressed into service
for a liberal perfectionist (save democracy!) or nativist nationalist (save our
land!) end, or very often for a combination of both (save "our" democratic
homeland from the "Islamic" terrorists!).

The "New Terrorism"

The hyperbole has clearly influenced policy makers who want to be seen
to be protecting their country from the perceived menace. A particularly
consequential aspect of this reaction issues forth through the declaration
of a new kind of terrorism that demands extraordinary measures. In the aftermath of 7/7, Tony Blair exclaimed: "Let no one be in any doubt, the rules
of the game are changing" (quoted in Dalgaard-Nielsen 2009: 245). The war
metaphor is also very common. Although most frequently associated with

George Bush's proclamation of a "war on terrorism," it was Chancellor Gerhard Schröder who on 11 September 2001 itself labeled the attacks "a declaration of war against the entire civilized world" (*Agence France Presse* 11 September 2001). European Parliament president Pat Cox denounced the Madrid attacks as "a declaration of war on democracy" (quoted in Bossong 2013: 39), while German interior minister Otto Schilly discerned in them "a new quality of threat for all of Europe" (*United Press International* 14 March 2004). A few months later, Dutch prime minister Jan Peter Balkenende would call the slaying of van Gogh a "declaration of war" against the Netherlands: "These people do not want to change our society, they want to destroy it" (*Associated Press* 6 November 2004, http://www.boston.com/news/world/europe/articles/2004/11/06/dutch_political_leader_cites_arrival_of_jihad/). President Hollande likewise following the *Charlie Hebdo* attacks in 2015 maintained that France found itself at "war" against terrorism (*National Public Radio Morning Edition*, 16 January 2015, http://www.npr.org/programs/morning-edition/2015/01/16/377634660?showDate=2015-01-16).

Security experts have heralded the dawn of a novel breed of terrorism. Its unique features are said to lie in its more sweeping, messianic motivation in contrast to the very specific aims of conventional terrorism, such as unseating a government, gaining independence for a territory, or prompting the release of jailed comrades. The goal would appear to be the humiliation of the West by inflicting maximum damage on its interests and people. The new terrorism purportedly exhibits an indiscriminate disrespect for human life, even for its own agents in the form of suicide bombers. Despite the media concentration on Al Qaeda, Islamist terrorist attacks do not seem to be centrally organized or commanded. Decentralization combined with the independence of the operatives purportedly lends Islamist terrorism both a global reach and an unprecedentedly high degree of unpredictability (Sageman 2008). Small cells or even a "lone wolf" can strike anywhere at any time. As Eliza Manningham-Buller, chief of the U.K. Security Service from 2002 to 2007, observed, the new breed of terrorist has the ability to "hide in plain sight, to be seen but not noticed" (quoted in Bonelli 2008: 112). Finally, the new terrorism is said to operate with a high degree of technological sophistication in terms of both weaponry (for example, smart bombs, jet airliners) and, perhaps more importantly, logistic support (for example, dissemination of information or transfer of funds via the internet) (Kegley 2003: 1–14; see also Weimann 2015; Younas 2014; Lynch and Ryder 2012; Awan 2007a; Duyvesteyn 2004).

European governments have enhanced hard-power measures to deal with the "new" threat. The national models paradigm highlights France in this regard (Leiken 2005: 130). Indeed, in the wake of the 1995 Paris Metro bombings, France did expand its *Vigipirate* emergency plan to allow French troops to be deployed to assist police, suspects to be arrested and held for four days without access to a lawyer, and non-Frenchmen to be summarily deported if suspected of involvement with terrorism (Leiken 2012: 16; Guittet 2008: 137–38). Over the course of the next two years, French police arrested 173 persons on charges of involvement with the Groupe Islamique Armé (GIA), 138 of whom were subjected to a highly controversial mass trial held in the gym of the Fleury-Mèrogis prison. In the end, police and prosecutors had collected enough evidence to convict and jail only twenty-one suspects (Pargeter 2008: 57–58). The heightened stages of alert stipulated in Vigipirate also empowered police and private security firms to carry out unimpeded search and seizure so that the stopping and questioning of young men who "look" North African by police has become routine on the streets (Human Rights Watch 2012; Hillebrand 2012: 102; Schneider 2008). A 2009 study of the Open Society Justice Initiative found that Arabs and blacks in France were eight times more likely than whites to be stopped by police (*New York Times* 3 October 2013). Small wonder that half of the incarcerated in France are Muslim despite the fact that Muslims comprise less than 10 percent of the total population (Taras 2012: 145). In 2003, the National Assembly passed legislation making it easier to arrest and deport religious leaders who preach violence or values incompatible with the French Constitution. As of 2012, 125 deportation orders had been issued to "radical" Islamists (*France24* 30 January 2013). "We will expel all these imams . . . who hold views that run counter to our values and say there is a need to combat France," said Interior Minister Manuel Valls (*Huffington Post* 30 January 2013). In 2014, in the wake of the alleged murder of four persons at the Jewish Museum in Brussels by purported Islamic State (ISIS) sympathizer and French national Mehdi Nemmouche, Interior Minister Bernard Cazeneuve announced that suspected ISIS supporters would be stripped of their passports and restricted from leaving France (*International Business Times* 10 July 2014).

The United Kingdom, conventionally dubbed soft on terrorism due to a penchant for protecting civil liberties (Klausen 2010; Leiken 2005), has in fact passed legislation similar to that of France. Even before 9/11, Parliament had enacted the Terrorism Act of 2000, Section 44 of which authorized police in designated areas to "stop and search" any persons regardless of whether they are suspected of terrorist activity. In addition, the home secretary subsequently clarified that officers may "take account of a person's ethnic origin in selecting persons to be stopped in response to a specific terrorist threat" (House of Commons 2005: 16). Minister of State for Community Safety, Crime Reduction, Policing and Counter-Terrorism Hazel Blears conceded that "some of our counter-terrorism powers will be disproportionately experienced by people in the Muslim community" (House of

Commons 2005: 46). In fact, stop and search procedures rose 302 percent for Asians compared to 230 percent for black people and 118 percent for white people between 2001 and 2003 (Tsoukala 2008: 71–72). Since the Tube bombings in 2005, Asians are five times likelier than whites to be stopped and searched by police (Bonino 2012: 18). According to the Home Office, of the 1,228 terror-related arrests made between 2001 and 2007 only 132 resulted in formal prosecution (Pargeter 2008: 163–64). In 2010, the European Court of Human Rights ruled Section 44 unlawful. The Protection of Freedoms Act of 2012 repealed Section 44 but still allowed for search and seizure without suspicion—however, under significantly narrower conditions of "extreme emergency."

The 2001 Anti-Terrorism, Crime and Security Act enhanced the government's powers to freeze and seize assets, confiscate information, detain suspects indefinitely without trial, and, most controversially, derogate from the European Convention on Human Rights due to a "state of emergency threatening the life of the nation" (Section 30). The Nationality, Immigration and Asylum Act of 2002 sought to ease deportation by making it legal for the home secretary to strip terrorist suspects with dual nationality of their British citizenship. In 2006, Parliament expanded the power by changing the language describing the triggering conditions for the act from "seriously prejudicial to the UK" to the vaguer "conducive to the public good." Finally in 2014, the Immigration Bill made it legal to strip citizenship even when it renders the party in question stateless. Home Secretary Theresa May asserted that citizenship "is a privilege, not a right" (*New York Times* 9 April 2014). Forty-six persons were stripped of British citizenship between 2006 and 2014 (*New York Times* 14 May 2014). To deal with those who could not be (easily) deported, the Prevention of Terrorism Act of 2005 empowered the home secretary to issue "control orders" against terrorist suspects, including no right for the suspects to examine the evidence against them. Amounting to a de facto house arrest, control orders allowed for electronic tagging as well as restriction of suspects' communication and movement. In 2014, May recommended banning jihadists (and neo-Nazis) from the airwaves, as the Thatcher regime had done to Sinn Féin and the IRA in the 1980s (*Guardian* 29 September 2014), as well as confiscating the passports of both British citizens and resident aliens suspected of traveling to fight with Islamists abroad, such as ISIS (*New York Times* 24 November 2014). Hurried through Parliament after 7/7 in order to "close the gaps" according to Home Secretary Charles Clark, the Terrorism Act of 2006 extended from fourteen to twenty-eight days the duration that suspects can be held without trial. The law also made into punishable offenses the "glorification" of terrorism as well as the participation in or facilitation of terrorism training. Tony Blair defended the measures: "We need to make our country safe. You can't do it by the rules of the game we have at the moment: it's too complicated, too laborious; the police are hidebound by restrictions" (*Telegraph* 12 October 2012). Not to be outdone, David Cameron advocated refusing reentry to British citizens who leave Britain to help ISIS abroad, though the Liberal Democrats stymied the proposal (*Guardian* 1 September 2014).

The Netherlands, also conventionally considered soft on extremism, passed several laws enhancing hard power in the wake of the murder of Theo van Gogh. Most notably, the Crimes of Terrorism Act of 2004 criminalized joining a terrorist organization or recruiting for jihad, in addition to stiffening sentences for crimes committed with the intent of carrying out or aiding terrorist attacks. The Witness Identity Protection Act (2006) allowed reports of the General Intelligence and Security Service to be entered into court proceedings as documentary evidence, and the Investigation and Prosecution of Terrorist Offences (2007) expanded search-and-seizure powers (including third parties not suspected of terrorism) and legalized the denial to suspects of full access to evidence (Buijs 2010).

The German Bundestag legislated in 2002 and renewed in 2007 the Law to Combat Terrorism. Among other things, it vastly expanded the power of police and intelligence agencies to monitor and archive private information from financial transactions to telephone correspondence to internet surfing. The law empowered the Agency for the Protection of the Constitution to ban any organization with a large number of aliens in its leadership or membership that in deed or word supports political violence as well the disruption of the public peace or the democratic process. By 2004, authorities had initiated 194 cases against alleged terrorists (Handcock et al. 2015: 719). The Taiba Mosque in Hamburg, where the 9/11 plotters had met, was closed in 2010. In 2014, the "Islamic State" (ISIS) was banned, including even its banner in physical or cyber space (*Deutsche Welle* 12 September 2014). Resident aliens and refugees may be brought in for questioning regarding their identity or activities at any time and they may be deported for crimes committed not only inside but also outside of Germany so long as the latter transgress the fundamental conventions of the United Nations. For example, Abdelghani Mzoudi was deported in 2005 despite having been found innocent in 2004 of plotting the 9/11 attacks. In the same year, Yakup Taşçı, imam at the Mevlana Mosque in Berlin, was deported for having praised suicide bombers in a sermon. In 2014, Germany instituted a ban on exiting the country for German Islamists suspected of aiding ISIS.

With passage in 2005 of the so-called "Package Pisanu," Italy gave the interior minister the power to declare "quick expulsions" or expedited deportations of persons suspected of involvement with terrorism. Recruiting for and engaging in terrorist training were made illegal, the duration that police may hold suspects without formally charging them was lengthened from twelve to twenty-four hours, and powers to track private information were broadened (Bleich 2010b: 17). In 2012, for example, Italy deported Mohamed Mannai to Tunisia in defiance of the European Court of Human Rights, which fined Rome 21,500 euros. Spain, due to its long battle with ETA, already before the Madrid attacks had had tough anti-terror measures in place in its Code of Criminal Procedure. These included holding suspects up to thirteen days incommunicado and up to four years in pretrial detention. In 2004, dormant statutes from the Law on Foreigners were reactivated to facilitate rapid deportation of suspected Islamist terrorists such as Mohamed Berzizoui, who had been arrested in connection with the Casablanca bombings of 2003 but later released (Human Rights Watch 2005). Prime Minister Mariano Rajoy has maintained "not everyone fits here" (*El Pais* 11 November 2010). Police interrogation of young Arab men has become commonplace in neighborhoods with a large concentration of immigrants (Gest 2010: 133). Even the Swedes increased hard power with the Act on Criminal Responsibility for Terrorist Offences of 2003. Although member states are wont to obstinately protect their unilateral sovereignty when it comes to counter-terrorism, the EU has endeavored to encourage hard-power cooperation. Through statutes such as the Action Plan on Combating Terrorism of 2001, the European Union Counter-Terrorism Strategy of 2005, and the Prüm Convention of 2005 (not ratified by all EU member states), the EU facilitates international sharing of police and intelligence information as well as cross-border pursuit of suspects (Bossong 2013). In 2007, the European Commission also took steps to criminalize terrorist training and recruitment as well as "the public provocation to commit terrorist offenses" (quoted in Handcock et al. 2015: 719).

While pledging to respect the civil liberties of Muslims and often doing so, most European governments have simultaneously curtailed them through enhanced hard power. Across Europe, in the name of fighting terrorism, millions of Muslims have been electronically monitored, thousands physically searched or arrested, and hundreds convicted, jailed, or deported. In addition, dozens of Islamic organizations have been banned or defunded (Bleich 2010b; Neal 2010). Stefano Bonino (2012: 19) speaks of the "criminalization of a whole population [European Muslims]" and Werner Schiffauer (2008b: 225) of the "Muslimization" of the terror threat. Human rights NGOs such as the German Institute for Human Rights, the Islamic Human Rights Commission, Human Rights Watch, and Mouvement contre le racisme et pour l'amitié entre les peoples (Movement against Racism and for Friendship between Peoples) regularly record and condemn the widespread violation of Muslims' human rights through counter-terrorism measures. The following assessment regarding Italy in Amnesty International's *Annual Report 2013* is typical: "The authorities regularly failed to protect the rights of refugees, asylum-seekers and migrants. . . . No systemic measures were taken to prevent human rights violations by police and ensure accountability" (www.amnesty.org/en/region/italy/report-2013). French political scientist Laurent Bonelli (2008) coined the clever term "liberticide" to describe the phenomenon whereby a majority of the citizens of liberal democracies out of fear of terrorism support (or at least do not resist) grave curtailments of civil rights (*Le Monde* 11 September 2008). Ariane Chebel d'Appollonia (2010: 130) maintains that human rights abuses have become so rampant that "the victims of counterterrorism . . . today outnumber the victims of terrorism." To cite one example that sparked public outrage and mass demonstrations, London police raided two homes at the Forest Gate apartment complex on 2 June 2006, arrested two Muslims, one of whom was shot, and yet failed to find any evidence of their complicity in a terrorist plot involving chemical explosives. Other critics contend that the resources devoted to hard-power counter-terrorism measures are not only vastly disproportionate to a deliberately exaggerated threat, but also inefficiently and ineffectively deployed by overzealous and poorly informed security agents (Chowdhury and Fitzsimmons 2013; Bossong 2013: 5–6; Bonino 2012: 9; Croft and Moore 2010: 834; Bigo and Tsoukala 2008). In 2012, for example, 3 percent of failed, foiled, or completed terrorist attacks in Europe were religiously motivated compared to 76 percent planned by separatists (Europol 2013). Of the 2,139 failed, foiled, or completed terrorist attacks in Europe between 2006 and 2010, ten involved Muslims (Europol 2011). In 2008 and 2009, two-thirds of those arrested on suspicion of Islamist terrorism could not be linked to a known terrorist act or organization (Europol 2010). Similarly, the EU's three "terrorists lists" have been harshly criticized for including persons for whom there is no credible evidence to suspect involvement with terrorism (Hillebrand 2012: 164–69).

Yet security officials retort that the resources and measures are justified because "Islamist terrorism is still perceived as the biggest threat to most Member States" (Europol 2010). They claim to have saved thousands of lives by foiling attacks like the 2005 plot to blow up the Eiffel Tower, the 2006 plan to board seven jets in London bound for North America and set off liquid explosives concealed in soda bottles, the 2007 conspiracy of the so-called "Sauerland Cell" to murder U.S. soldiers stationed in Germany, the 2008 planned simultaneous attacks on Barcelona's mass transit system by fourteen conspirators, the 2009 design to explode bombs in several popular retail stores in Amsterdam, the 2014 attack on the European Commission building in Brussels allegedly planned by ISIS sympathizers, the 2015 conspiracy to target Belgian police, and the 2015 plot to bomb the Frankfurt financial district cycling race. Security officials also tend to claim that laypersons cannot understand the severity or magnitude of the threat because they are not privy to sensitive intelligence. The British home secretary, for example, stated that "all those who tell me we are not [under threat] are the ones who do not have the security and intelligence information which for my sins I carry" (quoted in Tsoukala 2008: 80). Security officials remind critics that liberty is meaningless if one is dead. Security has to come before civil rights. With terrorism, we are dealing no longer with merely a threat to our way of life but to our life itself.

State of Exception

It makes sense at this juncture to revisit the notion of "Schmittian liberalism" introduced in Chapter 3 (Triadafilopolous 2011: 863). Schmittian liberalism marries liberal perfectionism with nativist nationalism in a revealing example of what we have been calling "mutual fragilization." Schmittian liberalism borrows from Schmitt's nationalism (discussed in Chapter 2) the idea of a specific mortal enemy (Muslims) against whom the nation must ready itself to fight. The enemy's most menacing quality, however, is alleged to be its unswerving hatred of liberal democratic values and societies. Put differently, the most serious terrorist threat to liberal democracies is said to emanate from Muslims because they adhere to an illiberal creed that legitimizes terrorism. Inversely, non-Muslim Europeans are presumed to be friendly toward liberal democracy and toward one another precisely because they are not Muslims.

I do not mean to suggest the total eclipsing of either liberal perfectionism or nativist nationalism by Schmittian liberalism. One would be hard pressed, for example, to find a European government that does not officially condemn *all* forms of terrorism. Several European states are engaged in extensive campaigns to thwart separatist violence, such as from ETA in Spain, or anarchist violence, such as from Conspiracy of Fire Cells in Greece. Furthermore, especially since Anders Behring Breivik's murder of seventy-seven people in Norway in 2011 and the uncovering in the same year of the National Socialist Underground cell that killed nine immigrants and a police officer in Germany between 2001 and 2007, several European governments have stepped up hard-power measures against Radical Right organizations. The murders themselves seem to have been motivated primarily by the kind of nativism keen to protect racial purity. These developments notwithstanding, the rhetoric and resources expended to combat political violence exercised in the name of Islam are hugely disproportionate to the number of actual acts, whether planned or carried out. For example, according to Europol, whereas failed, foiled, or completed terrorist attacks invoking Islam comprised under 3 percent of all terrorist attacks reported in the EU in 2012, Muslim suspects comprised 30 percent of terrorist-related arrests; in 2013 the numbers were 0 percent and 40 percent, respectively (Europol 2013: 42–43; Europol 2014: 46–47).

The reference to Schmitt becomes even more apposite due to the German thinker's influential theory of the state of exception. The theory conceptualizes and justifies the moment when states allow themselves to derogate from their own laws. Schmitt (1985: 5) famously wrote: "Sovereign is he who decides on the exception." For Schmitt, politics, in its profoundest moments, necessarily boils down to the friend-enemy (*Freund-Feind*) confrontation: "The high points of politics are simultaneously the moments in which the enemy is, in concrete clarity, recognized as the enemy" (Schmitt 1996: 67). No sovereign can perfectly predict how, when, and where the enemy will attack. Therefore, no state can write into its formal laws exactly what measures will be necessary to prevent annihilation.

> The exception, which is not codified in the existing legal order, can at best be characterized as a case of extreme peril, a danger to the existence of the state, or the like. But it cannot be circumscribed factually and made to conform to a preformed law. . . . The precise details of an emergency cannot be anticipated, nor can one spell out what may take place in such a case, especially when it is truly a matter of an extreme emergency and of how it is to be eliminated. (Schmitt 1985: 6)

Thus, any state that restricts its actions to the constitutional order invites its own demise. Ironically, according to Schmitt, the rule of law can ultimately only be secured through its suspension.

As mentioned in Chapter 2, the last quarter century has seen a revival of interest in Schmitt's political thought, especially among postmodern theorists. They take interest not in the racist dimensions of the ex-Nazi's theories, but rather in his insistence on the insurmountably antagonistic nature of politics (Tralau 2010; Agamben 2005; Mouffe 2000). Some of his ideas jibe well with the postmodern tenet regarding the will to power and the resulting irreconcilable clash of opposing worldviews. For postmodernists, the clashing parties do not necessarily have to be nation-states, as in Schmitt's rendering. They can be any parties advancing incompatible and incommensurable stances. Moreover, Schmitt's concept of the "enemy" can be married with postmodernism's focus on the "Other," though postmodernists see no need to postulate an ultimately mortal clash (Mouffe 2000).

Particularly those scholars working in Foucault's shadow interpret counter-terrorism from the perspective of governmentality. On this reading, a multifaceted array of interlocking institutions—police, military, academia, media, and more—form a power nexus that without being orchestrated from a single locus nevertheless effectively constructs and represents what passes for terrorism and terrorists, including how they should be thwarted (Agamben 1998; 2005). For example, Ole Waever (1995: 54–55) and his colleagues from the Copenhagen School of Security Studies, following John Searle's theory of language, resist the temptation to analyze terrorism as an objective phenomenon or "real thing" and urge reading it as a "speech act":

> In naming a certain development a security problem, the "state" can claim a special right, one that will, in the final instance, always be defined by the state and its elites. . . . By definition, something is a security problem when the elites declare it to be so.

Similarly, Tal Asad (2007: 26) explains that "my argument . . . is directed against thinking of terrorism simply as an illegal and immoral form of violence and advocates an examination of what the discourse of terror—and the preparation of terror—does in the world of power." Since 9/11, discourse theory has drawn much attention to the constructed images of "Islamic terrorism" and the "Muslim terrorist," which in turn are invoked to justify enhanced soft but especially hard power to combat the threat (Fredette 2014: 126–40; Kaya 2012: 201–18; Schiffauer 2008b: 206–7; Peter 2008; Asad 2007: 28–38; Inda 2006: 53). Tim Jacoby's (2010: 167) analysis is standard:

> While this culturalist discourse continues to operate as a means of explaining such violence outside the West, its primary function has been (particularly since the attacks in New York, Washington and Pennsylvania in 2001) to construct and maintain a connection between Muslims, Islam and violence, and then to present this as the primary threat—both internal and external—to the West "itself."

From the postcolonial perspective, the manufactured threat of Islamic terrorism has been exploited to extend even further the reach and grip of the West's neocolonial empire. In the name of security, Muslim lands have been newly occupied and their resources, such as Iraq's oil reserves, secured for Western exploitation (Douzinas 2007; Jabri 2007). These "new Crusades" have replaced the Cold War dichotomy by "constructing the Muslim enemy" (Qureshi and Sells 2003a) to stand in for the Soviet bogeyman (Ruf 2010; Said 2003: 69).

> The proclamation by individual writers of a clash between civilizations does not have the formal performative effect of a declaration of war. Yet it is more than a description. To warn that an entire civilization and religion is, by definition, "our" enemy is to raise a call to arms. (Qureshi and Sells 2003b: 2)

The colonial distinction between the "rational" Occident and "irrational" Orient is said to have been revived in the clash-of-civilizations thesis to predict a greater threat of terrorism emanating from the Muslim world and to justify differential treatment of Muslims, whether in the form of drone killings, the reapplication of torture, or the erection of specialized prisons like Guantanamo Bay or Abu Ghraib for suspected terrorists. David Tyrer (2013: 140) writes that

> this postcolonial condition appears to be embodied in the figure of the Muslim, at once racially recognizable and yet somehow excessively different, and yet this problem is radicalized within the war on terror because of the threat of terrorism that knows no boundaries, as the official discourse reminded us.

Likewise, the West allegedly tolerates or supports Israel's apartheid-like treatment of Palestinians and imperious relations with neighboring Arab countries on grounds that the Jewish state faces terrorist foes who are not capable or deserving of the kind of rational negotiation among disputing parties common in, say, the EU (Yaqoob 2007). Within Europe itself, Muslims are treated as delinquent interlopers who bring their violent ways into an otherwise peaceful Europe (Amin 2011; Terrio 2009).

Postcolonial Violent Resistance

I mention postmodern and postcolonial readings of counter-terrorism not to test their validity, but rather to shed light on their role as normative forces in politics. Islamists who advocate or exercise nonstate political violence directed at European targets often invoke fragments of postcolonial and postmodern thought. Two caveats deserve immediate mention. First, only a tiny proportion of Islamist, let alone Muslim, Europeans engage in terrorism. However, they represent more than a mere phantom construction of Islamophobic media and politics; they do exist (though in small numbers) and they do strike (though very infrequently, as the Europol numbers cited above attest). They are organized in groups such as Al Qaeda, Al-Muhajiroun, Hizb ut-Tahrir, Supporters of Shariah, Al-Jama'a Al-Islamiya, Groupe Islamique Armé, the Salafist Group for Preaching and Combat, and the International Mujahadeen Uzbekistan; they are also known to frequent mosques such as Finsbury Park in London, Al-Quds in Hamburg, Al-Tawhid in Amsterdam, Grimhøjvej in Aarhus, and the Islamic Cultural Institute of Milan (Wiktorowicz 2005: 2–3).

Second, I do not wish to imply that violent Islamists are committed postmodernists or that they do not draw on arguments from within the Islamic tradition in an effort to legitimize their actions. Omar Bakri, for instance, exclaimed shortly after 9/11:

The Islamic Movements have not used the real weapon yet. . . . Oh Osama . . . you and your brothers are now breathing life and dignity into the body of the *umma*. Our main mission as Muslims is to carry the Islamic message to the entire world. . . . We are an *umma* of jihad and beyond doubt, we have been chosen by Allah to lead the whole world if we hold to his command. (Quoted in Strindberg and Wärn 2011: 179)

Qutb's *Milestones* is known to be very influential among militant jihadists. In it, the Egyptian Islamist advocated perpetual violent and nonviolent jihad to "abolish injustice from the earth, to bring people to the worship of God alone, and to bring them out of servitude to others into the servants of the Lord" (Qutb 1981: 56). However, as previously stated, the theory of fragilization does not necessitate the total conversion to postmodernism and rejection of Islam. The theory posits only a softening or opening toward some fragmentary aspects of a public philosophy with which one does not explicitly identify. Presumably, violent Islamists consider the Qur'an Absolute Truth and therefore do not share postmodernism's thoroughgoing moral relativism. However, they borrow from Hobbesian postmodernism the contention that the Western state lacks a solid moral foundation and as a result exercises arbitrary and biased power. The claim that Western states have no superior moral foundation to legitimize their treatment of Muslims is critical in justifying the violent Islamists' decision to contravene the conventional monopoly on political violence declared by European governments. Similarly, fragments of Frantz Fanon's influential theory of postcolonial liberation echo through militant Islamist discourse. The Martinique-born psychiatrist and revolutionary for Algerian independence theorized that the colonized could only exorcise the inferior self-image imposed on them through violence by exercising like violence ("absolute violence") against the colonizer (Fanon 1965a: 37). It is just this notion that Omar Bakri invokes in the aforementioned quotation when he lauds Bin Laden for "breathing life and dignity into the body of the *umma*."

Several studies of militant international jihadism underscore the adoption and adaptation of anti-Western rhetoric in the wake of Marxism's waning appeal. Thus, Roy (2005: 324) contends that "Osama Bin Laden is far more within the legacy of a tradition of Western radicalism than merely an expression of traditional political violence in Islam."

Al Qaeda is heir to the ultra-leftist and Third Worldist movements of the 1970s. The left aspect fizzled and has been replaced by Islamic radicalism: the only networks of radical protest are Islamic, but they recruit from among the same categories (outcasts from the educated middle class and dropouts from the working class), carry the same hatred for "bourgeois" values and attitudes, have the same targets (imperialists) and often the same pet guerrillas (Palestine), claim to be internationalist (*ummah* instead of the international working class), and are built on the same generation gap. (Roy 2005: 324)

Robert Leiken (2005: 127) refers to the same phenomenon as "anti-West westernization" (see also Pargeter 2008).

Of particular interest in this regard is Al Qaeda's emphasis on the "Far Enemy." In 1996, Bin Laden began encouraging his sympathizers to strike the "Far Enemy," a strategy subsequently endorsed by Ayman Al-Zawahiri. The two Al Qaeda leaders urged militants to strike the Western "occupiers" not only in the traditional and sacred lands of Islam from which they were to be expelled but also at home (Gerges 2005). Needless to say, ISIS carried out this strategy in Paris on 13 November 2015. In audiotapes, Al-Zawraa TV, online magazines such as *Inspire* and *Dabiq,* or webchat fora like Bab-ul-Islam and Ansarullah, not to mention YouTube, Twitter and Facebook, international jihadists of various stripes, using many languages beyond Arabic and English, increasingly reach out to militant zealots living in the West with the message that they should "strike at the heart of the unbeliev-ers" (Quoted in Weimann 2015: 71; see also Younas 2014; Davies, et al. 2011). In a 2002 letter to Mullah Omar in Afghanistan, Bin Laden is said to have written: "It is obvious that the media war in this century is one of the stron-gest methods; in fact, its ratio may reach 90% of the total preparation for the [our] battles" (quoted in Younas 2014: 11). The Global Islamic Media Front tells its internet visitors:

> This is the Internet that Allah has enlisted in the service of jihad and of the Mujahedeen, which has come to serve your interests—given that half the battle of the Mujahedeen is being waged on the pages of the Internet—the sole outlet for Mujahedeen media. (Quoted in Awan 2007b: 222)

If militant Islamists want to inspire Westerners to embrace their cause, it makes sense to speak to them using normative fragments that likely reso-nate with them. The trope of the imperialist West bent on subjugating Mus-lims worldwide offers itself as an irresistible ideological tool.

It should come as no surprise, then, that the trope turns up in ratio-nalizations of acts of terror committed by violent Islamists. Mohammed Bouyeri, murderer of Theo van Gogh and alleged member of the Hofstad Network, claimed:

There are dark Satanic forces that have sown their seed of evil everywhere in the world. This seed has been sown in the Islamic world in the times of colonialism . . . Since the fall of the Ottoman Empire . . . the enemies of Islam have been active in gradually carrying out their plans aiming at the total destruction of Islam. (Quoted in Peters 2011: 153)

The 7/7 bomber Shehzad Tanweer explained in a YouTube video released one year after the bombing: "Your government continues to oppress our women and children, our brothers and sisters in Palestine, Afghanistan, Iraq and Chechnya." He pledged that his deeds represented "only the beginning of a string of attacks that will continue and become stronger until you pull your forces out of Afghanistan and Iraq and until you stop your financial and military support to America and Israel" ("7/7 Bomber's Will;" youtube.com/watch?v=FG6a26uXleA). Likewise, Michael Adebolajo, who cut down British soldier Lee Rigby with a machete in 2013, claimed: "Muslims are dying daily by British soldiers. . . . We swear by Allah . . . we will never stop fighting you until you leave us alone" (youtube.com/watch?v=WxrtaHkyw5w, though YouTube subsequently took down the video). Amedy Coulibaly, who killed four hostages in Paris in 2015, complained: "They need to stop bombing ISIS. . . . They need to stop forcing our women to remove *hijab*. . . . They need to stop holding our men in jail" (*CNN* 11 January 2015). The Madrid bombers justified their actions as "a response to the crimes you have committed in the world, particularly in Iraq and Afghanistan" (quoted in Forest 2015: 284). The alleged German ISIS sympathizer Silvio K pledged attacks on German soil as revenge for German arms delivery to Kurdish fighters in Syria combating ISIS encroachment (*Hamburger Morgenpost* 10 September 2014). Similarly, the Moroccan-German Chouka brothers, who grew up in Bonn but now reside in the borderlands between Afghanistan and Pakistan, regularly send internet videos from the camp of the International Mujahadeen Uzbekistan exhorting Germans, in German, to commit acts of terrorism against trains, shopping centers, restaurants, and discotheques in Germany. In one video from 2011 entitled *Evil Fatherland* (*Böses Vaterland*), Mounir promises that "there must and will be, God willing, a series of attacks against the German people" in retaliation for the injustices its government has perpetrated against Muslims in Afghanistan. In subsequent videos, such as *Yes, We Are Terrorists*, the brothers praise Arid Uka and Mohammad Merah ("the knight of Toulouse") as exemplary Muslims whose murderous deeds merit emulation (quoted in Steinberg 2013: 198). For his part, Merah claimed to be motivated by French involvement in Afghanistan, the burqa ban, and Israel's persecution of Palestinians: "The Jews kill our brothers and sisters in Palestine" (*Telegraph* 10 April 2012). ISIS contends: "Oh Americans, and oh Europeans, the Islamic State did not initiate a war against you as your governments and media try to make you believe. It is you who started the transgression against us, and thus you deserve blame and you will pay a great price" (*CNN* 22 September 2014). Following the attacks on *Charlie Hebdo* in 2015, ISIS exclaimed: "These are the first drops of terror that will be rained down on the West" (*Arutz Sheva* 8 January 2015).

Islamist organizations that do not necessarily commit but nevertheless seem to condone acts of terrorism in Europe also deploy the postcolonial fragment. On 21 May 2013, Hizb ut-Tahrir published on its website (hizb. org.uk) the following statement:

> Ultimately such demonization of Islam and Muslims by the British political establishment has one main purpose for the UK and other Western Governments and that is to justify their foreign policy of interference or wars in the Muslim world as in Iraq, Afghanistan, Mali or Somalia which is aimed at securing their economic interests. We must fight back.

Similarly, Abou Jahjah, leader of the Antwerp-based Arab-European League, complains: "We're Belgian citizens but they treat us like foreigners. The whole system is rigged to exclude us from jobs, houses and everything. So we must force them to give us our rights" (*Telegraph* 29 November 2002). Before being deported from Germany to Turkey in 2004, Metin Kaplan had implored his followers: "Yes, it is time to strike; both in Turkey and in Europe. . . . The enemies of Islam assume they can attack our religion, beliefs, and worship and we Muslims keep silent like sheep" (quoted in Yükleyen 2012: 239). At times, the popular rap and hip-hop scene would seem to condone violence against the West. In 2006, for instance, the British group Fun-da-Mental released *All Is War (The Benefits of G-had)*. Lead vocalist Aki Nawaz, who likened bin Laden to Che Guevara, sings: "I'm strapped up cross my chest bomb belt attached/Deeply satisfied with the plan I hatched" (*Guardian* 28 June 2006).

Europhobic Hyperbole

Islamists who condone or commit violence against European targets often employ deliberate hyperbole to justify their cause. Much of their anti-Western rhetoric overlaps with the Europhobic hyperbole that we detailed in the previous two chapters and, therefore, does not need to be rehashed here. The jihadist spin comes in contending that the West is so irrevocably impious, decadent, and sadistic that violent attacks against its people are necessary and justified to counter its dangerous and lethal impact on Muslims (Parekh 2008: 168). The most blatantly hyperbolic distortion in this act of recriminating stigmatization comes forth in the outlandish claim that Western governments themselves have committed the terrorist attacks spuriously attributed to Muslims. The most common accusation in this regard is that the 9/11 attacks were either orchestrated or faked by the Central Intelligence Agency (or in some accounts by or with the Israeli Mossad), but similar claims have been made about, for example, Britain's MI5 (Secret Intelligence Service) and the 7/7 bombings (Leiken 2012: 57; Buijs 2010: 78; Jenkins 2007: 166). It testifies to the power of persuasion that the jihadist websites and other publications possess that a Pew Global Attitudes Project (2006: 49) survey found that, among polled Muslims, 56 percent in Britain, 46 percent in France, and 44 percent in Germany refused to believe that Arabs were involved in the 9/11 attacks. Likewise, half of the 500 British Muslims surveyed for *Channel Four News* (4 June 2007) believed that the government trumped up charges against the convicted 7/7 bombers, with a quarter convinced that the government itself masterminded the attacks.

The rapidly proliferating jihadist websites typically style themselves as alternative sources of news and information to the "lies or misconceptions that are present in Kuffar (infidel) sources such as the BBC or CNN," to quote almuhajiroun.com (quoted in Wiktorowicz 2005: 158–59). The Global Islamic Media Front, for example, stages its hooded spokesman in the same kind of setting as a news anchor, behind a desk with projected news feeds (Awan 2007b: 221). Such sites portray Western foreign policy as nothing short of a thinly veiled crusade ("Crusader West") bent on destroying Islam (quoted in Weimann 2015: 70). Typically, physical injuries to innocent women and children allegedly inflicted by Western government action are highlighted and depicted not as unintended and regretted, but rather deliberate and wanton (Leiken 2012: 232; Pargeter 2008: 198; Wiktorowicz 2005: 68; Kepel 2004: 289). By contrast, in publications such as the ISIS magazine *Dabiq* or the film *Flames of War,* jihadists are one-dimensionally lionized as heroic defenders of Islam, miraculously overcoming tremendous odds to triumph over Western persecutors (Awan 2007b: 221–22; Sageman 2008: 113–15). The numbers supporting the jihadist movements are also typically inflated several-fold (Wiktorowicz 2005: 193). Whether true or false, such fulminations can and do influence European Muslims. For instance, Arid Uka, who shot dead two U.S. airmen in the Frankfurt airport in 2011, claimed that he was motivated by a YouTube video depicting U.S. soldiers raping Muslim women in Iraq. In fact, the clip originated from the Hollywood film *Redacted* directed by Brian De Palma (*Der Spiegel* 10 February 2012). My intention is neither to bore nor to astound readers with jihadist apocrypha; rather, my point is to shed light on the widespread normative sway of the postmodernist tenet that "truth" is what passes for the truth.

Non-Muslim Terror

Lest the reader receive the false impression that terrorism in Europe mainly involves Muslims, some mention of non-Muslim terrorism is in order. As reported by Europol's annual *European Union Terrorism Situation and Trend Report,* acts of political violence invoking Islam typically range from 0 to 3 percent of all terrorist attacks in the EU in any given year. They are annually far outnumbered by "separatist" and "leftwing" acts, which fall outside the scope of this project. What falls within the purview of this study, however, are terrorizing acts of violence directed at Muslims and their places of residence, business, or worship in Europe. Such attacks antedate 9/11 but have increased since 2001, often spiking after high-profile incidents such as the slayings of Theo van Gogh and Jeremy Rigby, 7/7, the Madrid bombings, or the lethal attack on *Charlie Hebdo* (Tyrer 2013: 62–63; also see the "Right-Wing Terrorism" chapters of the annual Europol reports). As with Islamist violence, anti-Muslim violence is often implicitly incited or condoned, if not directly organized, by Radical Right organizations such as the various national Defense Leagues and Stop Islamisation of Europe associations, Golden Dawn (Greece), Nordisk (Norway), PEGIDA (Germany), or Europe-wide neo-Nazi networks such as the National Socialist Underground. Like jihadists, their efforts are increasingly backed by extensive internet and social media sites such as Nuke all Mosques, Islam versus Europe, Pro-Reconquista-Europa, Riposte Laique, Die gruene Pest, The Brussels Journal, Jihad Watch, Gates of Vienna, or Politically Incorrect, all of which make extensive use of anti-Islamic hyperbole in their odious propaganda. A Pro-Reconquista-Europa headline from 22 July 2014, for example, read: "Madrid to Fall [to jihadists] in 2020" (forum.pro-reconquista-europa.com/viewtopic.php?f=93&t=2267); the headline at Islam versus Europe from 16 June 2014 was "Black flag of Jihad Will Fly over London" (http://islamversuseurope.blogspot.com).

Though undeniably informed by radically xenophobic nativism, the anti-Muslim militants often manifest considerable fragilization toward postmodernism's notion of the systematically biased state. However, in their worldview, the state is systematically biased in favor of multiculturalism in a way that would seem to call for radical action to counter the threat that multiculturalism allegedly poses to the homogenous nation (Fekete 2012). Mass murderer Anders Behring Breivik, for example, asked in his manifesto "how many thousands of Europeans must die, how many hundreds of European women must be raped, millions robbed and bullied" before

Europe wakes up to the threat posed by Islam (quoted in Fekete 2012: 34). He hoped his killings would inspire a modern-day crusade to stave off what he discerned as the galloping Islamization of Europe. But Breivik also despised democratic socialism for allegedly enabling Islamization—ostensibly the reason why he bombed a government building in Oslo and conducted his shooting spree at a Workers' Youth League camp thought to be grooming future social democratic leaders.

European states are not above lawlessness. For instance, several European governments, including Austria, Belgium, Cyprus, Denmark, Germany, Greece, Ireland, Italy, Poland, Portugal, Romania, Spain, Sweden, and the United Kingdom, have, in unequivocal violation of the European Convention on Human Rights, tolerated or facilitated over one thousand extraordinary renditions of suspected Muslim terrorists by the CIA to "black sites" where the apprehended have been tortured (Fava 2007; also see Hillebrand 2012: 96–99 and 126–30). In a related high-profile case, Abu Omar, an imam in Milan, was abducted in a joint operation by the CIA and SISMI on 17 February 2003, transferred to Egypt, and there interrogated and tortured until his release in 2007 (*BBC News* 4 November 2009). Swedish police had in 2001 handed over Egyptian asylum-seekers Ahmed Agiza and Muhammad al-Zery to the CIA at Stockholm's Bromma airport, where the prisoners were stripped, drugged, and chained before being transferred to Egypt for interrogation that included torture (*Washington Post* 21 May 2005). Likewise, the German citizen Khaled el-Masri was apprehended in Skopje by Macedonian police in 2003 and delivered to the CIA, whose agents tortured him for four months before releasing him in a forest in Albania. In 2004, U.S. ambassador to Germany Daniel Coats convinced German interior minister Otto Schilly not to make the case public (*Washington Post* 4 December 2005). A similarly grizzly fate befell Abd al-Rahim al-Nashiri and Abu Zubaydah, who were tortured by the CIA at a military base in Poland. In 2014, the European Court of Human Rights found "coherent, clear, and categorical" evidence that the Polish government "facilitated the whole process, created the conditions for it to happen and made no attempt to prevent it from occurring" (*Los Angeles Times* 26 July 2014). Similar cases are pending before the court against Lithuania and Romania. Many European governments are known to have made bilateral agreements with the United States to allow CIA flights to refuel or to land under false pretenses. Given the profound lack of transparency of cross-national counter-terrorism working groups like the G6 (Germany, France, U.K., Italy, Spain, and Poland) or the EU's Policy Working Group on Terrorism and the Counter-Terrorism Group (made up of intelligence heads of each EU member state), it is nearly impossible to know what, if any, laws they are breaking behind closed doors (Hillebrand 2012; Den Boer, Hillebrand, and Nölke 2008). It is public knowledge that the governments of Germany and France agreed to provide the United States with information on the alleged 9/11 conspirator Zacarias Moussouai, even though they knew that the prosecution was seeking the death penalty (Keohane 2008: 129).

Finally, readers should not overlook the fact that government officials are known at times to turn a blind eye to acts of violence against Muslims planned by private citizens. George Morgan and Scott Poynting (2012b: 8) refer to this phenomenon as an unofficial "permission to hate." Perhaps the most famous case involved the exposure of several employees of Germany's Agency for the Protection of the Constitution as alleged sympathizers with the National Socialist Underground, whose Zwickau cell murdered nine immigrants and a police officer (Aust and Laabs 2014).

These various forms of governmental lawlessness manifest consequential fragilization in the direction of Hobbesian postmodernism. They reflect, in particular, the expanding sway of the nihilistic tenet that moral rectitude represents an unsophisticated, Pollyannaish approach to politics that all but ensures the ultimate victory of one's adversaries. Such lawlessness in the name of fighting terrorism reflects the growing attitude that politics is about winning—and winning only—at whatever price.

Conviviality without Consensus

The extensive mark of postmodern thought does not necessarily have to motivate violent antagonism in which opposing parties seek to terrorize their adversaries. Hospitable postmodernism theorizes conviviality without consensus (Norton 2013: 226; Hall 2012: 11; Gilroy 2006: 40). To be sure, swaying persons inclined to terrorize one another to live peacefully together represents a daunting challenge, and hospitable postmodernism does not pretend to assure that the attempt to do so will succeed. However, the attempt can seem prudent in light of the apparent difficulty, if not impossibility, of forging an overlapping consensus around liberalism's insistence on the autonomy of the individual or around nationalism's loyalty to the nation.

Hospitable postmodern encounters aim not at consensus, but simply the regularized act or experience of interacting with adversaries without recourse to violence. The goal is to habituate nonviolent interaction so that it is given a chance to become the norm rather than the exception. To succeed among parties with vehemently opposing positions, hospitable postmodernism teaches that participants should be permitted to air their views and grievances in an atmosphere free of moral condemnation. Interlocutors suspend their claims to moral superiority in a wager, not a guarantee, that doing so can open modes and means of nonviolent communication not yet tried or even imagined by participants. Tariq Modood (2009: 180), for example, argues that participants must disavow "an ideological 'drawing a line in the sand' mentality." Resolutions, whether sought after or achieved, should be considered pragmatic, local, and provisionary rather than principled, universal, or permanent (Schiffauer 2008a: 129).

How do hospitable postmodern tenets apply to counter-terrorism per se? In the first place, European officialdom (the state) would have to relax its proclaimed monopoly on defining terrorism long enough to enable dialogue with (some of) those it otherwise considers Islamist terrorists and their allies. Like liberal cosmopolitanism, the hospitable postmodern approach does not discriminate against Muslims as a category of persons deserving greater suspicion of terrorism. However, the postmodern tactic goes beyond the liberal strategy in not refusing to cooperate with persons who do not necessarily put first, like liberalism, the sanctity of the individual human being. Similarly, like the community-based approach, hospitable postmodernism does open the door to cooperation with non-liberal Muslims but, unlike communitarianism, does not retain the state's monopoly on defining what constitutes terrorism. Indeed, the postmodern strategy does not exclude from dialogue those perspectives that contend the European state itself sponsors terrorist deeds. For their part, militant Islamists would need to suspend their conclusion that the Western state is incapable of treating Muslims as anything other than objects of derision and subjugation and that not all of its intentions vis-à-vis Muslims are mean-spirited.

Admittedly, hospitable postmodernism shapes the politics of counter-terrorism less than any of the other six normative stances analyzed above, but its mark is nonetheless discernible. Those whom we dubbed "Post-Islamists" in the previous chapter have taken the critical step of declassifying Europe as the *dar-al-harb* (abode of war). Due to its extensive religious freedoms, Europe deserves to be thought of by Muslims as the *dar-al-aman* (abode of truce); Tariq Ramadan (1999a: 150) prefers *dar al-shahada* (abode of testimony), Jusuf Qaradawi *dar-al-dawa* (abode of proselytization), Rachid al-Ghannouchi *dar-al-Islam* (LeVine 2003: 105). The reclassification means that the violent methods of warfare are no longer justified in Europe. Qaradawi, for example, has predicted that "Islam would return to Europe as a victorious conqueror, after having been twice expelled. I maintain that this time the conquest will not come of the sword, but of preaching and ideology" (quoted in Bruckner 2007). As already mentioned, Qaradawi has condemned the terrorist attacks carried out in the name of Islam in the West. Ramadan too has condemned terrorist attacks in the West and denounced "the adolescent stupidity" of the rioters in the Paris suburbs in 2005 (quoted in Leiken 2012: 19). Indeed, virtually all of the major Islamist organizations in Europe have rejected Al Qaeda's "Far Enemy" strategy as both unnecessary and un-Islamic (Gerges 2005: 233). For example, after the

U.S.-led invasion of Iraq in 2003, many fatwas issued forth from the Middle East calling on Muslims to strike back against Western targets. However, the president of the Federation of Islamic Organizations in Europe, Ahmed al Rawi, stated: "Muslims living in Europe should not follow fatwas given on this subject in Muslim countries, because Muslims in Europe have a specific character, which means that those fatwas are not incumbent upon them" (quoted in Bowen 2010: 145).

Here we can detect fragilization toward hospitable postmodernism's contextualism and its related rejection of moral universalism. Al Rawi did not categorically condemn the fatwas as immoral; rather, he maintained that they were not morally applicable to Muslims residing in Europe. Like-wise, most post-Islamists refuse to condemn violent defense of Muslims in Muslim lands occupied by non-Muslims (Bowen 2012: 121; Bakker 2012: 184; Jenkins 2007: 252; Gerges 2005: 210–28). While both Ramadan and Qa-radawi, for example, reject violent resistance in Europe, both condoned it in (occupied) Afghanistan, Iraq, and Palestine. Furthermore, Qaradawi drew much criticism in Europe for endorsing suicide bombings against Israel: "It's not suicide, it is martyrdom in the name of God. . . . The Israelis might have nuclear bombs but we have the children bomb and these human bombs must continue until liberation" (quoted in Jenkins 2007: 252).

In 2005, the British Foreign and Commonwealth Office (FCO) recom-mended granting an entry visa to Qaradawi to address the Muslim Unity Conference in Manchester. Although Qaradawi did not ultimately attend, the visa sparked controversy because of the cleric's endorsement of suicide bombings. Qaradawi had been fêted in 2004 by London mayor Ken Livings-ton. The latter invited the cleric to address a conference sponsored by the Muslim Contact Unit of the Metropolitan Police, whose mission since its founding in 2002 has been to combat terrorism emanating from the Muslim community. Although plainly informed by the communitarian notion of discouraging radicalization through Islam-based arguments, the sponsored visits also revealed significant fragilization toward hospitable postmodern-ism. The FCO, the mayor's office, and the Metropolitan Police were perfectly aware of the cleric's endorsement of suicide bombings in Palestine (not to mention violent resistance to occupying troops in Afghanistan and Iraq that included British soldiers). Moreover, Prime Minister Blair had reacted to the invitation by stating that all those who advocate suicide bombing, "whether it's in London, whether it's in Afghanistan or Iraq, or it's in Palestine or it's in Turkey or Kashmir, or anywhere . . . have got no place in our coun-try" (*Telegraph* 20 July 2005). Nevertheless, the officials in favor of the visit were willing to suspend the judgment on Qaradawi as a supporter of terror-ist tactics in Palestine to enable his renunciation of terrorism in the U.K., including his unequivocal condemnation of the 7/7 bombings. Thus Chief

Constable Ian Blair of the Metropolitan Police publicly confirmed that Qaradawi held "views on the Palestinian intifada that probably would not be
very acceptable" but defended the visit because the beloved sheikh could
"command an audience of 50,000 young people at the drop of a hat." The
constable also expressed the hospitable postmodern emphasis on unavoidable risk taking: "We are going to talk to him [Qaradawi] however difficult
that becomes" (quoted in Frampton and Maher 2013: 43–44). Postmodern
contextualism and pragmatism also influenced the advocates of the visits.
They focused their energies on discouraging radicalization within the context of the U.K. rather than in general or in Palestine. Indeed, the Muslim
Contact Unit not only foresaw in Qaradawi's visit

> a positive Muslim community impact in the fight against Al Qaida
> propaganda in the UK. His support for Palestinian suicide bombers
> adds credibility to his condemnation of Al Qaida in those sections of
> the community most susceptible to the blandishments of Al Qaida
> terrorist propaganda. (Quoted in Frampton and Maher 2013: 44)

Thus, in the specific context of thwarting Islamist terrorism in the U.K.,
Qaradawi's endorsement of suicide bombings was viewed as a pragmatic
asset rather than grounds for a categorical rejection of cooperation with the
cleric based on the kind of moral absolutism expressed by the prime minister. I should add that similar pragmatic, context-specific reasoning moved
the Italian and French foreign ministries to work with Qaradawi in 2004, in
both cases in conjunction with attempts to free hostages abducted in Iraq.

Conclusion

The case of Qaradawi exemplifies the main theme of this chapter (and book)
regarding messy policy making. The same Qaradawi who was granted a visa
in 2004 and 2005 by the British government because, in the words of the
FCO, "having individuals like Qaradawi on our side should be our aim," was
denied entry in 2008. The Home Office maintained that it would "not tolerate the presence of those who seek to justify any acts of terrorist violence or
express views that could foster inter-community violence" (quotations from
Vidino 2010a: 114). Likewise, despite having worked with Qaradawi in 2004
to secure the release of two French hostages in Iraq, the French government
in 2012 denied him an entry visa to France, where he was scheduled to address a conference sponsored by the UOIF, a participating organization in
the Conseil Français du Culte Musulman. Although Qaradawi had publicly
condemned Merah's lethal attack on a Jewish school in that same year, President Sarkozy defended the decision by saying that people "who maintain or

would like to take positions that are incompatible with the republican ideal would not be welcome" (*Al Jazeera*, 27 March 2012, http://www.aljazeera. com/news/europe/2012/03/201232745312479784.html). A year earlier, Ireland had denied a visa to Qaradawi, even though he heads the European Council for Fatwa and Research, which is legally headquartered in Dublin.

The inconsistencies in Qaradawi's case are hardly unique. As this chapter has demonstrated, the same governments that pledge to and often do respect the equal rights of Muslims in an effort to discourage their radicalization also simultaneously order and oversee unreasonable and even unlawful arrests, detentions, and renditions of Muslim suspects on a regular basis. With equally blatant inconsistency, European governments that work with Islamist organizations in community-based efforts to counter terrorism authorize the surveillance of the same organizations by the police and intelligence services. On some occasions, the surveillance so angers the targeted organizations that they break off ties with officials. On other occasions, (typically sensationalized) media coverage of the intelligence reports leads officials temporarily to cease cooperation with Islamists. Small wonder, then, that analysts find "a multiple set of strategies and tactics" (Banks, De Nevers, and Wallerstein 2008: 4) "beset with contradictions" (Asad 2007: 2) that "often produce paradoxical and unforeseen consequences" (Chebel d'Appollonia and Reich 2008: 5; see also Argomaniz 2011; Bleich 2010b; Croft and Moore 2010).

Granted, much of this policy messiness stems from the fact that counter-terrorism policies are devised and implemented in many different and often disparate offices, ministries, and branches of government (Heath-Kelly, Jarvis, and Baker-Beall 2014). The argument advanced here, however, is that profound normative dissonance plays a significant role as well. Moreover, the abiding *Kulturkampf* among liberalism, nationalism, and postmodernism has occasioned in politics considerable mutual fragilization among the public philosophies. Despite their purely theoretical incompatibility, normative fragments from each—torture is wrong, don't trust Islamists, do whatever it takes to stop terrorism—nevertheless come forth as persuasive in various contexts. In their effort to sway diverse and highly fragilized publics, policy makers grow accustomed to moral ambivalence and paradox. The result is counter-terrorism measures that regularly contradict and even undercut one another.

7

Conclusion: Messy Politics

> The image of the world daily generated by present-day life concerns is now devoid of the genuine or assumed solidity and continuity which used to be the trademark of modern "structures." The dominant sentiment is the feeling of uncertainty—about the future shape of the world, about the right way of living in it, and about the criteria by which to judge the rights and wrongs of one's way of living. Uncertainty is not exactly a newcomer in the modern world, with its past. What is new, however, is that it is no longer seen as a mere temporary nuisance which, with due effort, may be either mitigated or completely overcome. The postmodern world is bracing itself for life under a condition of uncertainty which is permanent and irreducible.
>
> —ZYGMUNT BAUMAN, "The Making and Unmaking of Strangers"

This book has argued against viewing European Muslims as a distinct group of political actors. Instead it has urged readers to see Muslims and non-Muslims alike as inhabiting a normative landscape in Europe dominated by the vying public philosophies of liberalism, nationalism, and postmodernism. This is not to contend that Islam does not shape the political agendas of (some) Muslims. Rather, it makes good sense to couch one's political goals, however informed, in the language of liberalism, nationalism, and/or postmodernism, because those three public philosophies carry substantial political clout in Europe.

I have employed the notion of *Kulturkampf* to underscore that none of the public philosophies enjoys decisively more political clout than its rivals. Furthermore, the persistence of an inconclusive *Kulturkampf* has occasioned mutual fragilization—that is, widespread ambivalence and diffidence regarding the moral superiority of any one public philosophy. Rather than try to fit Muslim and non-Muslim actors into ideological straitjackets, in particular the Left versus Right paradigms so common in political analysis (Goodman 2014; Koopmans, Michalowski, and Waibel 2012; Bornschier 2010; Joppke 2010; Janoski 2010; Howard 2009; Lahav 2004), this study has found it more illuminating to analyze them as pragmatic bricoleurs who

opportunistically exploit liberal, nationalist, and/or postmodern public philosophies to suit a particular political goal, space, moment, and audience.
Thus, we saw, for instance, that IGMG deployed liberal rhetoric to argue
that female Muslims should have the same right to don the hijab as others have to wear a miniskirt, communitarian logic to contend that Muslims
alone should determine what is proper Islamic practice in the diaspora, and
postmodern logic to complain that European governments and mainstream
media stigmatize and marginalize Muslims as potential terrorists—that is,
as the proverbial negative other. Such bricolage is further facilitated through
ideological fragmentation. Rhetorical fragments are used as performative
utterances detached from the more systematic argumentation of a given
public philosophy as pure theory. Fragmentation helps inconsistencies to
go less noticed, which in turn fosters greater normative ambivalence. No
wonder that recent studies uncovered "increased ideological uncertainty"
(Odmalm 2014: 112) and "deep ambivalence about immigration" across
migrant-importing countries (Hollifield, Martin, and Orrenius 2014b: 26).

This book has maintained that ideological bricolage contributes significantly to policy messiness. If the analysis presented here convinces readers
of anything, it ought to be of the messy—that is, polymorphous, multilayered, incoherent, and contradictory—policies concerning Muslims across
issues and across Europe. This finding sheds revealing light on the prominent debate in comparative immigration studies about policy convergence
versus national distinctiveness (Goodman 2014: 65). In none of the four case
studies were we able to identify the kind of distinct, coherent, persistent
national approaches posited by the defenders of unique national paradigms
(Goodman 2014; Korteweg and Yurdakul 2014; Joppke and Torpey 2013;
Koopmans, Michalowski, and Waibel 2012; Klausen 2010; Kirschner and
Sperling 2010; Joppke 2009; Howard 2009; Saharso 2007; Amir-Moazami
2007; Bader 2007; Koopmans et al. 2005; Fetzer and Soper 2005; Leiken
2005; Brochmann and Hammar 1999; Favell 1998; Joppke 1996; Brubaker
1992). Instead, in concurrence with other critics of methodological nationalism, the present study has also found "complexity" (Banting and Kymlicka 2013: 591), "contradictions and inefficiencies in policy" (Boswell 2007:
93), and "conflicting policy outputs" (Hampshire 2013: 12). To be sure, for
instance, the French do demand that Muslims assimilate to liberal "republican" values. However, we have also unearthed intermingled with assimilative policies not only toleration of but considerable deliberate support for
communitarian separatism practiced by Muslim associations. Likewise,
"multicultural" Britain surely implements "community-based" approaches
to counter-terrorism. But the British government no more shrinks from applying extensive hard power than the French government does from exploring self-policing programs within Muslim communities. Similar messiness

turned up in "ethnonational" Germany, where only half of the *Länder* proscribed the hijab (but not the habit or yarmulke) for public school teachers. Furthermore, we encountered in the previous chapters governments across Europe that turn a blind eye to the relentless and ruthless exploitation of undocumented migrants as well as illegal and intimidating discrimination against "legal" Muslims in myriad walks of life. These "policies" appear nowhere "on the books," but, as we have stressed, this makes them no less real for the victims. Analysis that limits itself to official policies occludes a large dimension of what is actually transpiring.

This study does not, however, corroborate the convergence thesis, at least not as it is putatively formulated. The typical formulation hypothesizes that Europe-wide consensus is congealing around a single normative outlook, such as endorsement of "postnational" (Soysal 1994: 3) values and "diversity" (Joppke 2009: 120) or, by contrast, around "the return of assimilation" (Brubaker 2001: 531). The most conspicuous similarity throughout Europe that has emerged in this study is normative *Kulturkampf* and policy messiness. Everywhere we found vehement and enduring political controversy surrounding citizenship, veiling, secularism, and terrorism. Even regarding the use of torture we found no unequivocal consensus, at least not once we considered the unofficial or downplayed assistance that many European governments have lent to the extraordinary renditions of Muslim suspects. Consensus appears to be elusive rather than imminent. As Jock Young (1999: 15) perspicaciously notes, "the deviant other is everywhere" but "everyone is a potential deviant."

Perhaps the time has come to relax or relinquish altogether the search for overarching consensus. Europe has a long and complicated tradition of normative diversity and discord. Needless to say, it would be wrong and indeed unconscionable to deny or dismiss the immense human suffering that has erupted and too often recrudesced in Europe in conjunction with ideological conflict. But has not much of this suffering resulted from perpetrators insisting on consensus, insisting that my view be everyone's view? Isaiah Berlin concluded his famous essay "Two Concepts of Liberty" by quoting Joseph Schumpeter: "To realize the relative validity of one's convictions and yet stand for them unflinchingly, is what distinguishes a civilized man from a barbarian." Berlin added: "To demand more than this is perhaps a deep and incurable metaphysical need; but to allow it to determine one's practice is a symptom of an equally deep, and more dangerous, moral and political immaturity" (Berlin 1969: 172).

Afterword: Paris, November 13, 2015

The page proof for this book were finalized only a few hours before the deplorable attacks transpired in Paris on November 13, 2015. Therefore, no systematic analysis of the tragic events appears in the body of the text. However, at this time, only a few days after the events, they do not appear to undermine or alter the lessons and conclusions of this study. Rather, the latter can enable a more nuanced comprehension of the events as well as a more sophisticated anticipation of their political fallout than is common, for example, in the flood of media reports.

The most important lesson, and one happily receiving at least lip service from many prominent political actors, is that the attacks signal no war of all Muslims (Islam) against all non-Muslims (France/Europe/the West). Muslim Europeans are not a monolithic community. Their views are as differentiated as those of non-Muslim Europeans. For all those who have applauded the attacks, for instance via Twitter, there are many more who have condemned them. L'union des Organisations Islamique de France (UOIF), for example, immediately announced that it was "horrified and shocked by . . . this barbaric terrorism" (*Anadolu* Post 15 November 2015). We should keep in mind the observation from chapter six of the president of the British Muslim Council, Iqbal Sacranie: "There is no such thing as an Islamic terrorist—that is offensive." The same sentiment has been expressed by millions in the wake of the attacks via the Twitter hashtag "#NotInMyName."

Readers should resist reductionist arguments that try to attribute a greater propensity for violence to "Muslims" in general. Claims such that France was struck because it has the largest Muslim minority in Europe conveniently ignore the fact that European countries with much smaller Muslim populations (most notably Spain and the U.K.) have also been targeted. The same criticism holds for assertions or insinuations that, say, refugees from predominantly Muslim countries such as Iraq or Syria present a greater security risk. Most of these refugees are themselves fleeing constant terrorizing circumstances and thus presumably are even more sensitized and opposed to terrorism. Nor should we lose sight of the fact that Muslims were among the victims on November 13.

Even more importantly, this book has shown that especially Muslims number among the victims of overzealous counter-terrorism. President Hollande immediately declared a state of emergency, requested its extension for three months, and proposed changes to the constitution to enhance police powers. He ordered over 100,000 security officials to stabilize the country, including searching and arresting hundreds of suspects. Neighboring lands such as Belgium and Germany joined the hunt. Readers know from previous chapters that it would be naïve not to presume that security agents will employ racial profiling that is often profoundly informed by the essentializing stereotypes generated by both Islamophobic and Europhobic hyperbole. Furthermore, these mutually reinforcing discourses that already significantly influence the politics of diversity are likely to intensify as political opportunists seek to exploit the attacks for political gain. Though November 13 dramatically demonstrated that political violence is real, this does not change the important insight that what counts as "terrorists" and "terrorism" remains ultimately a social construct formed through ongoing political contestation typically among unevenly powerful parties.

Ironically, we can expect the surest protection of and compensation for those Muslims wrongly accused of involvement with terrorism to come from the same French and European governments, especially from their courts of law. Such irony and paradox are what this book has sought to stress with its central theme of normative and policy messiness. Especially in Europe's courts, but also among its citizens, both Muslim and non-Muslim, the normative sway of liberalism's insistence on the sanctity of equal rights for each individual human being remains robust. And yet the prevalence of messiness also means that France, despite initially deploying mainly hard power inside and outside of its borders, will likely explore soft-power options, including community-based counter-terrorism. Such programs, we saw, tend to function best in terms of preventing violent radicalization when they relax or suspend the ethical hegemony of liberalism, including the closely associated presumption of Europe's moral superiority. Much (understandable and surely consoling) self-adulation about the resilience and greatness of French and European civilization ensued in the immediate aftermath of the attacks. Looking to the longer term, however, Europe, if it truly wishes to incorporate Muslims into the very essence of its identity, will have to enable an open and likely unsettling and uncertain dialog about why so much of its foreign policy seems to place lesser value on Muslim lives, whether through border controls, economic sanctions, military interventions, or support for authoritarian regimes in the Middle East.

The attacks of November 13, 2015 were abominable and tragic. However, we should not let them obscure the reality of "everyday multiculturalism," namely, that millions of Muslim and non-Muslim Europeans daily manage to live peacefully together side by side, and they have been doing so for decades. The potential for and power of mutually agreeable cooperation far outweigh the forces of violence.

Berlin, November 18, 2015

References

Abadan-Unat, Nermin. 2011. *Turks in Europe: From Guest Worker to Transnational Citizen*. New York: Berghahn.

Abbas, Tahir, ed. 2007. *Islamic Political Radicalism: A European Perspective*. Edinburgh: Edinburgh University Press.

Abizadeh, Arash. 2012. "On the Demos and Its Kin: Nationalism, Democracy, and the Boundary Problem." *American Political Science Review* 106 (4): 867–82.

Abu-Lughod, Lila. 2013. *Do Muslim Women Need Saving?* Cambridge, MA: Harvard University Press.

Abu Zayd, Nasr Hamid. 1996. *Vernieuwing in het islamitisch denken: De roots van een vrijheidsstrijd*. Amsterdam: Bulaaq.

———. 2006. *Reformation of Islamic Thought. A Critical Historical Analysis*. Amsterdam: Amsterdam University Press.

Adrian, Melanie. 2011. "A Common Life amidst Fragmentation: A Consideration of German and French Approaches to the Integration of Muslims." *Journal of Muslim Minority Affairs* 31 (3): 411–22.

Afonso, Alexandre. 2013. "Whose Interests Do Radical Right Parties Really Represent? The Migration Policy Agenda of the Swiss People's Party between Nativism and Neoliberalism." In Umut Korkut et al. 2013, pp. 17–36.

Agamben, Giorgio. 1998. *Homo Sacer: Sovereign Power and Bare Life*. Trans. Daniel Heller-Roazen. Stanford, CA: Stanford University Press.

———. 1993. *The Coming Community*. Trans. Michael Hardt. Minneapolis: University of Minnesota Press.

———. 2005. *State of Exception*. Trans. Kevin Attell. Chicago: University of Chicago Press.

Ahmed, Faisal Z. 2012. "The Perils of Unearned Foreign Income: Aid, Remittances, and Government Survival." *American Political Science Review* 106 (1): 146–65.

Ahmed, Leyla. 1992. *Women and Gender in Islam.* New Haven, CT: Yale University Press.

Aidi, Hisham D. 2014. *Rebel Music: Race, Empire, and the New Muslim Youth Culture.* New York: Vintage Books.Akbarzadeh, Shahram, and Joshua M. Roose. 2011. "Muslims, Multiculturalism and the Question of the Silent Majority." *Journal of Muslim Minority Affairs* 31 (3): 309–25.

Alba, Richard, and Jennifer Holdaway, eds. 2013. *The Children of Immigrants at School: A Comparative Look at Integration in the United States and Western Europe.* New York: New York University Press.

Aleinikoff, Thomas, and Douglas Klusmeyer. 2002. *Citizenship Policies for an Age of Migration.* Washington, DC: Carnegie Endowment for International Peace and Migration Policy Institute.

Alesina, Alberto, and Edward Glaeser. 2006. *Fighting Poverty in the US and Europe: A World of Difference.* New York: Oxford University Press.

Algan, Yann, and Mariya Aleksynska. 2012. "Conclusion: Cultural Integration of Immigrants in Europe." In *Cultural Integration of Immigrants in Europe,* ed. Yann Algan et al., pp. 301–32. Oxford: Oxford University Press.

Algemene Inlichtingen- en Veiligheidsdienst (AIVD). 2002. *Rekrutering in Nederland voor de jihad, van incident tot trend.* The Hague: Algemene Inlichtingen- en Veiligheidsdienst.

———. 2007. *The Radical Dawa in Transition: The Rise of Islamic Neo-radicalism in the Netherlands.* The Hague: Algemene Inlichtingen- en Veiligheidsdienst.

Ali, Monica. 2004. *Brick Lane.* New York: Scribner.

Allen, Chris. 2007. "Islamophobia and Its Consequences." In Amghar, Boubekeur, and Emerson 2007, pp. 144–68.

Allievi, Stefano. 2003. "Islam in the Public Space: Social Networks, Media and Neo-communities." In Allievi and Nielsen 2003, pp. 1–27.

———, ed. 2010. *Mosques in Europe: Why a Solution Has Become a Problem.* London: Alliance Publishing Trust.

———, and Jørgen Nielsen, eds. 2003. *Muslim Networks and Transnational Communities in and across Europe.* Leiden, Netherlands: Brill.

Alonso, Rogelio. 2012. "The Spread of Radical Islam in Spain: Challenges Ahead." *Studies in Conflict and Terrorism* 35 (6): 471–91.

Alter, Peter. 1994. *Nationalism.* New York: Edward Arnold.

Altinbaş, Nihan. 2013. "Honor-Related Violence in the Context of Patriarchy, Multicultural Politics, and Islamophobia after 9/11." *American Journal of Islamic Social Sciences* 30 (3): 1–19.

Amara, Fadela. 2003. *Ni putes, ni soumises.* Paris: La Découverte.

———. 2006. *Breaking the Silence: French Women's Voices from the Ghetto.* Trans. Helen Harden Chenut. Berkeley: University of California Press.

Amghar, Samir, Amel Boubekeur, and Michael Emerson, eds. 2007. *European Islam: Challenges for Public Policy and Society.* Brussels: Centre for European Policy Studies.

Amin, Ash. 2002. "Ethnicity and the Multicultural City: Living with Diversity." *Environment and Planning A* 34: 958–80.

———. 2011. "Xenophobic Europe." openDemocracy, 9 May. Available at http://www.opendemocracy.net/ash-amin/xenophobic-europe.

Amiraux, Valérie. 2006. "Speaking as a Muslim: Avoiding Religion in French Public Space." In Jonker and Amiraux 2006, pp. 21–52.

———. 2007. "The Headscarf Question: What Is Really the Issue?" In Amghar, Boubekeur, and Emerson 2007, pp. 124–43.

———. 2010. "From Empire to Republic: The French Muslim Dilemma." In Triandafyllidou 2010a, pp. 137–59.

Amir-Moazami, Schirin. 2007. *Politisierte Religion. Der Kopftuchstreit in Deutschland und Frankreich*. Bielefeld, Germany: Transcript.

———. 2009. "Islam und Geschlecht unter liberal-säkularer Regierungsführung: die Deutsche Islam Konferenz." *Telaviver Jahrbuch für deutsche Geschichte* 37: 187–203.

———. 2011. "Pitfalls of Consensus-oriented Dialogue: The German Islam Conference (Deutsche Islam Konferenz)." *Approaching Religion* 1 (May): 1–14.

———, and Armando Salvatore. 2003. "Gender, Generation, and the Reform of Tradition: From Muslim Majority Societies to Western Europe." In Allievi and Nielsen 2003, pp. 52–77.

Amnesty International. 2012. *Choice and Prejudice: Discrimination against Muslims in Europe*. London: Amnesty International.

Andall, Jacqueline. 2003. "Hierarchy and Independence: The Emergence of a Service Caste in Europe." In *Gender and Ethnicity in Contemporary Europe*, ed. Jacqueline Andall, pp. 39–60. Oxford: Berg.

Anderson, Benedict. 1991. *Imagined Communities: Reflections on the Origins and Spread of Nationalism*. London: Verso.

Anderson, Bridget. 2000. *Doing the Dirty Work: The Global Politics of Domestic Labour*. London: Zed Books.

———. 2013. *Us and Them: The Dangerous Politics of Immigration Control*. Oxford: Oxford University Press.

Anderson, Christopher J. 1996. "Economics, Politics, and Foreigners: Populist Party Support in Denmark and Norway." *Electoral Studies* 15 (4): 497–511.

Andreas, Peter, and Ethan Nadelmann. 2006. *Policing the Globe and Crime Control in International Relations*. Oxford: Oxford University Press.

Andreassen, Rikke, and Doutje Lettinga. 2012. "Veiled Debates: Gender and Gender Equality in European Narratives." In Rosenberger and Sauer 2012b, pp. 17–36.

Ang, Ien. 2001. *On Not Speaking Chinese: Living between Asia and the West*. London: Routledge.

Ansari, Humayun. 2004. *"The Infidel Within": Muslims in Britain since 1800*. London: Hurst.

———, and Farid Hafez, eds. 2012. *From the Far Right to the Mainstream: Islamophobia in Party Politics and the Media*. Frankfurt: Campus Verlag.

Anthias, Floya, and Gabriella Lazaridis, eds. 1999. *Into the Margins: Migration and Exclusion in Southern Europe*. Aldershot, U.K.: Ashgate.

Antidiskriminierungsstelle des Bundes. 2013. *Diskriminierung im Bildungsbereich und im Arbeitsleben*. Berlin: Antidiskriminierungsstelle des Bundes.

Arendt, Hannah. 1958. *The Human Condition*. Chicago: University of Chicago Press.

———. 1966. *The Origins of Totalitarianism*. New York: Harcourt, Brace and World.

Argomaniz, Javier. 2011. *The EU and Counter-Terrorism: Politics, Polity and Policies after 9/11*. Milton Park, U.K.: Routledge.

Arkoun, Mohammed. 1994. *Rethinking Islam: Common Questions, Uncommon Answers*. Trans. Robert D. Lee. Boulder, CO: Westview.

Armstrong, John. 1982. *Nations before Nationalism*. Chapel Hill: University of North Carolina Press.

Art, David. 2011. *Inside the Radical Right: The Development of Anti-immigration Parties in Western Europe*. New York: Cambridge University Press.

Asad, Tal. 1997. "Europe against Islam: Islam in Europe." *The Muslim World* 37 (2): 183–95.

———. 2003. *Formations of the Secular: Christianity, Islam, Modernity*. Stanford, CA: Stanford University Press.

———. 2006. "Trying to Understand French Secularism." In *Political Theologies: Public Religions in a Post-secular World*, ed. Hent de Vries and Lawrence E. Sullivan, pp. 494–526. New York: Fordham University Press.

———. 2007. *On Suicide Bombing*. New York: Columbia University Press.

Ashfar, Haleh. 1994. "Muslim Women in West Yorkshire: Growing Up with Real and Imaginary Values amidst Conflicting Views of Self and Society." In *The Dynamics of "Race" and Gender: Some Feminist Interventions*, ed. Haleh Ashfar and Mary Maynard, pp. 127–47. London: Taylor and Francis.

Astor, Avi. 2014. "Religious Governance and the Accommodation of Islam in Contemporary Spain." *Journal of Ethnic and Migration Studies* 40 (1): 1716–35.

Ataç, Ilker, and Sieglinde Rosenberger, eds. 2013. *Politik der Inklusion und Exklusion*. Vienna: University of Vienna Press.

Ateş, Seyran. 2008. *Der Multikulti-irrtum. Wie wir in Deutschland besser zusammen leben können*. Berlin: Ullstein.

Aust, Stefan, and Dirk Laabs. 2014. *Heimatschutz: Der Staat und die Mordserie des NSU*. Munich: Pantheon.

Avramopoulou, Eirini, Gül Çorbacioğlu, and Maria Eleonora Sanna. 2012. "Thinking through Secularism: Debates on the Muslim Veil in Europe." In Rosenberger and Sauer 2012b, pp. 37–54.

Awan, Akil N. 2007a. "Virtual Jihadist Media: Function, Legitimacy, and Radicalizing Efficacy." *European Journal of Cultural Studies* 110 (3): 389–408.

———. 2007b. "Transitional Religiosity Experiences: Contextual Disjuncture and Islamic Political Radicalism." In Abbas 2007, pp. 207–30.

Bader, Veit. 2007. *Democracy or Secularism? Associational Governance of Religious Diversity*. Amsterdam: Amsterdam University Press.

Bahners, Patrick. 2011. *Die Panikmacher: Die deutsche Angst vor dem Islam—Eine Streitschrift*. Munich: Beck.

Bakker, Edwin. 2006. *Jihadi Terrorists in Europe: Their Characteristics and the Circumstances in Which They Joined the Jihad—An Explanatory Study*. The Hague: Netherlands Institute of International Relations.

———. 2012. "The Public Image of the Muslim Brotherhood in the Netherlands." In Meijer and Bakker 2012, pp. 169–88.

Baldwin-Edwards, Martin, and Joaquin Arango, eds. 1999. *Immigrants and the Informal Economy in Southern Europe*. London: Frank Cass.

Balibar, Etienne. 2004. *We, the People of Europe? Reflections on Transnational Citizenship*. Princeton, NJ: Princeton University Press.

———. 2007. "Postface." In *European Anti-Discrimination and the Politics of Citizenship: Britain and France*, ed. Christophe Bertossi, pp. 237–44. Basingstoke, U.K.: Palgrave.

————, and Immanuel Wallerstein. 1991. *Race, Nation, Class: Ambiguous Identities.* London: Verso.

Balzacq, Thierry, and Sergio Carrera, eds. 2006. *Security versus Freedom? A Challenge for Europe's Future.* Aldershot, U.K.: Ashgate.

Banchoff, Thomas, ed. 2007a. *Democracy and the New Religious Pluralism.* Oxford: Oxford University Press.

————. 2007b. Introduction to Banchoff 2007a, pp. 3–18.

Banks, William, Renée De Nevers, and Mitchel Wallerstein. 2008. *Combating Terrorism: Strategies and Approaches.* Washington, DC: CQ Press.

Banting, Keith, and Will Kymlicka. 2013. "Is There Really a Retreat from Multiculturalism Policies? New Evidence from the Multiculturalism Policy Index." *Comparative European Politics* 11 (5): 577–98.

Baran, Zeyno. 2011. *Citizen Islam: The Future of Muslim Integration in the West.* London: Continuum.

Barber, Benjamin. 1984. *Strong Democracy: Participatory Politics for a New Age.* Berkeley: University of California Press.

Barker, Martin. 1981. *The New Racism: Conservatives and the Ideology of the Tribe.* London: Junction Books.

Barlas, Asma. 2002. *"Believing Women" in Islam: Unreading Patriarchal Interpretations of the Quran.* Austin: University of Texas Press.

Barry, Brian. 1996. "Political Theory, Old and New." In *A New Handbook of Political Science,* ed. Robert Goodin and Hans-Dieter Klingemann, pp. 531–48. Oxford: Oxford University Press.

Barzun, Jacques. 2001. *From Dawn to Decadence: 500 Years of Western Cultural Life.* New York: Harper.

Bauböck, Rainer. 1994. *Transnational Citizenship: Membership and Rights in International Migration.* Aldershot, U.K.: Edward Elgar.

————. 2002. "Cultural Minority Rights in Public Education: Religious and Language Instruction for Immigrant Communities in Western Europe." In *West European Immigration and Immigrant Policy in the New Century,* ed. Anthony Messina, pp. 161–89. Westport, CT: Praeger.

————. 2007. "Stakeholder Citizenship and Transnational Political Participation: A Normative Evaluation of External Voting." *Fordham Law Review* 75 (5): 2393–447.

————, Bernhard Perching, and Wiebke Sievers, eds. 2007. *Citizenship Policies in the New Europe.* Amsterdam: Amsterdam University Press.

————, Eva Ersbøll, Kees Groenendijk, and Harald Waldrauch, eds. 2006. *Acquisition and Loss of Nationality: Policies and Trends in 15 European States.* 2 vols. Amsterdam: Amsterdam University Press.

Bauder, Harald. 2006. *Labour Movement: How Migration Regulates Labour Markets.* Oxford: Oxford University Press.

Bauman, Zygmunt. 1993. *Modernity and Ambivalence.* Oxford: Polity.

————. 1997. "The Making and Unmaking of Strangers." In *Debating Cultural Hybridity,* ed. Pnina Werbner and Tariq Modood, pp. 50–88. London: Zed.

————. 2003. *City of Fears, City of Hopes.* London: Goldsmiths College, University of London, Centre for Urban and Community Research.

————. 2011. *Collateral Damage: Social Inequalities in a Global Age.* Cambridge: Polity.

Bayat, Asef. 2013a. Preface to *Post-Islamism: The Changing Faces of Political Islam,* ed. Asef Bayat, pp. ix–xi. New York: Oxford University Press.

———. 2013b. "Post-Islamism at Large." In *Post-Islamism: The Changing Faces of Political Islam,* ed. Asef Bayat, pp. 3–34. New York: Oxford University Press.

Beck, Ulrich. 1998. *Politik der Globalisierung.* Frankfurt: Suhrkamp.

———. 2000. "The Cosmopolitan Perspective: Sociology of the Second Age of Modernity." *British Journal of Sociology* 51 (1): 79–105.

———, and Edgar Grande. 2007. *Cosmopolitan Europe.* Cambridge: Polity.

Beckford, James A., Daniele Joly, and Farhad Khosrokhavar. 2006. *Muslims in Prison: Challenge and Change in Britain and France.* London: Palgrave.

Béland, Daniel, and Robert Henry Cox, eds. 2011. *Ideas and Politics in Social Science Research.* Oxford: Oxford University Press.

Bell, Daniel.1960. *The End of Ideology: On the Exhaustion of Political Ideas in the Fifties.* Glencoe, IL: Free Press.

Bellil, Samira. 2002. *Dans l'enfer des tournantes.* Paris: Denoël.

Bencheikh, Soheib. 1998. *Marianne et le Prophète: L'Islam dans la France laïque.* Paris: Bernard Grasset.

Benhabib, Seyla. 1996. *Democracy and Difference: Contesting the Boundaries of the Political.* Princeton, NJ: Princeton University Press.

———. 2004. *The Rights of Others: Aliens, Residents, and Citizens.* Cambridge: Cambridge University Press.

———. 2005. "Border, Boundaries, and Citizenship." *Political Science and Politics* 38 (4): 673–78.

———. 2007. "Twilight of Sovereignty or the Emergence of Cosmopolitan Norms? Rethinking Citizenship in Volatile Times." *Citizenship Studies* 11 (1): 19–36.

Benoist, Alain de. 1977. *Dix ans de combat culturel pour une Renaissance.* Paris: GRECE.

———. 1979. *Vu de droite. Anthologie critique des idées contemporaines.* Paris: Copernic.

———, and Charles Champetier. 2012. *Manifesto for a European Renaissance.* London: ARKTOS.

Berezin, Mabel. 2009. *Illiberal Politics in Neoliberal Times: Culture, Security and Populism in the New Europe.* New York: Cambridge University Press.

Berg, Mette Louise, and Nando Sigona. 2013. "Ethnography, Diversity and Urban Space." *Identities: Global Studies in Culture and Power* 20 (4): 347–60.

Berger, Peter. 2007. "Pluralism, Protestantization, and the Voluntary Principle." In Banchoff 2007a, pp. 19–30.

Berger, Peter, and Thomas Luckmann. 1967. *The Social Construction of Reality: A Treatise in the Sociology of Knowledge.* Garden City, NY: Anchor Books.

Berghahn, Sabine. 2009. "Deutschlands konfrontiver Umgang mit dem Kopftuch der Lehrerin." In *Der Stoff, aus dem Konflikte sind: Debatten um das Kopftuch in Deutschland, Österreich und der Schweiz,* ed. Sabine Berghahn, pp. 33–72. Bielefeld, Germany: Transcript.

———. 2012. "Legal Regulations: Responses to the Muslim Headscarf in Europe." In Rosenberger and Sauer 2012b, pp. 97–115.

Berlin, Isaiah. 1969. *Four Essays on Liberty.* London: Oxford University Press.

———. 1991. *The Crooked Timber of Humanity.* Princeton, NJ: Princeton University Press.

———. 2002. "Two Concepts of Liberty." In *Liberty,* ed. Henry Hardy, pp. 166–217. Oxford: Oxford University Press.

Berman, Sheri. 2011. "Ideology, History, and Politics." In Béland and Cox 2011, pp. 105–26.

Bertossi, Christophe. 2012. "French Republicanism and the Problem of Normative Density." *Comparative European Politics* 10 (3): 248–65.

———. 2014. "French 'Muslim' Soldiers? Social Change and Pragmatism in a Military Institution." In Bowen et al. 2014a, pp. 73–103.

———, and John R. Bowen. 2014. "Practical Schemas, Conjunctures, and Social Locations: *Laïcité* in French Schools and Hospitals." In Bowen et al. 2014a, pp. 104–34.

———, and Willem Jan Duyvendak. 2012. "National Models of Immigrant Integration: The Costs for Comparative Research." *Comparative European Politics* 10 (3): 237–47.

Besson, Samantha, and André Etzinger. 2007. "Introduction: Future Challenges of European Citizenship—Facing a Wide-open Pandora's Box." *European Law Journal* 13 (5): 573–90.

Besson, Sylvain. 2005. *La conquête de l'Ocident: Le project secret des islamistes*. Paris: Le Seuil.

Betts, Andrew, ed. 2011. *Global Migration Governance*. Oxford: Oxford University Press.

Bhabha, Homi. 1994. *The Location of Culture*. London: Routledge.

Bielefeldt, Heiner. 2007. *Menschenrechte in der Einwanderungsgesellschaft: Plädoyer für einen aufgeklärten Multikulturalismus*. Bielefeld, Germany: Transcript.

———, and M. Bahmanpour. 2002. "The Politics of Social Justice: Religion versus Human Rights?" openDemocracy, 7 November. Available at www.openDemocracy.net.

Bigo, Didier, and Anastassia Tsoukala, eds. 2008. *Terror, Insecurity and Liberty: Illiberal Practices of Liberal Regimes after 9/11*. New York: Routledge.

Bilgrami, Akeel. 2014. *Secularism, Identity, and Enchantment*. Cambridge, MA: Harvard University Press.

Billig, Michael. 1995. *Banal Nationalism*. London: Sage.

Bin Bayyah, Abdullah. 2002. "Muslims Living in Non-Muslim Lands." Zaytuna College. Available at www.zaytuna.org/specials/muslims_living_in_non_muslim_lands.html (accessed 6 February 2013).

Blair, Tony. 2001. "Speech to Labour Party." Brighton, 2 October. Available at http://www.britishpoliticalspeech.org/speech-archive.htm?speech=186 (accessed 6 June 2014).

———. 2006. *Our Nation's Future: Multiculturalism and Integration*. Available at www.number10.gov.uk/, p. 11923.

Bleich, Erik. 2003. *Race Politics in Britain and France: Ideas and Policymaking since the 1960s*. Cambridge: Cambridge University Press.

———, ed. 2010a. *Muslims and the State in the Post 9/11 West*. New York: Routledge.

———. 2010b. "State Responses to 'Muslim' Violence: A Comparison of Six West European Countries." In Bleich 2010a, pp. 9–27.

———. 2011. *The Freedom to Be Racist? How the United States and Europe Struggle to Preserve Freedom and Combat Racism*. Oxford: Oxford University Press.

Bloemraad, Irene, Anna Korteweg, and Gökçe Yurdakul. 2008. "Citizenship and Integration: Multiculturalism, Assimilation, and Challenges to the Nation-state." *Annual Review of Sociology* 34: 153–79.

Blyth, Mark. 2011. "Ideas, Uncertainty, and Evolution." In Béland and Cox 2011, pp. 83–101.

Boender, Welmoet. 2006. "From Migrant to Citizen: The Role of the Islamic University of Rotterdam in the Formulation of Dutch Citizenship." In Jonker and Amiraux 2006, pp. 103–22.

Bohman, James. 2007. *Democracy across Borders: From* Dêmos *to* Dêmoi. Cambridge, MA: MIT Press.

Bolkenstein, Frits. 1991. "Integratie van minderheden moet met lef worden aangepakt." *De Volkskrant,* 12 September.

Bommes, Michael, and Andrew Geddes, eds. 2000. *Immigration and Welfare: Challenging the Borders of the Welfare State.* London: Routledge.

Bonelli, Laurent. 2008. "Hidden in Plain Sight: Intelligence, Exception and Suspicion after 11 September 2001." In Bigo and Tsoukala 2008, pp. 101–20.

Bonino, Stefano. 2012. "Policing Strategies against Islamic Terrorism in the UK after 9/11: The Socio-political Realities for British Muslims." *Journal of Muslim Minority Affairs* 32 (1): 5–31.

Börkenförde, Ernst-Wolfgang. 1995. "Die Nation." *Frankfurter Allgemeine Zeitung,* 30 September.

Bornschier, Simon. 2010. *Cleavage Politics and the Populist Right: The New Cultural Conflict in Western Europe.* Philadelphia: Temple University Press.

Bos, Wouter. 2005. "Europe's Social Democrats, Solidarity and Muslim Immigration." *The Globalist,* 9 December. Available at www.theglobalist.com/DBWeb/printStoryId.aspx?StoryId=4976.

Bosniak, Linda. 2006. *The Citizen and the Alien: Dilemmas of Contemporary Membership.* Princeton, NJ: Princeton University Press.

Bossong, Raphael. 2013. *The Evolution of EU Counter-terrorism: European Security Policy after 9/11.* New York: Routledge.

Boswell, Christina. 2003. *European Migration Policies in Flux: Changing Patterns of Inclusion and Exclusion.* Oxford: Blackwell.

———. 2005. *The Ethics of Refugee Policy.* Aldershot, U.K.: Ashgate.

———. 2007. "Theorizing Immigration Policy: Is There a Third Way?" *International Migration Review* 41 (1): 75–100.

———. 2009. *The Practical Uses of Expert Knowledge: Immigration Policy and Social Research.* Cambridge: Cambridge University Press.

———, and Andrew Geddes. 2011. *Migration and Mobility in the European Union.* Basingstoke, U.K.: Palgrave.

Boubekeur, Amel. 2005. "Cool and Competitive: Muslim Culture in the West." *ISIM Review* 16 (Autumn): 12–13.

———. 2007. "Political Islam in Europe." In Amghar, Boubekeur, and Emerson 2007, pp. 14–37.

———, and Samir Amghar. 2006. "Islamist Parties in the Maghreb and Their Links with EU: Mutual Influences and the Dynamics of Democratization." EuroMeSCo Exchange Facility. Available at www.euromesco.net/images/55_eng.pdf (accessed 7 January 2012).

Bouteldja, Houria. 2004. "De la cérémonie du dévoilement à Alger (1958) à Ni Putes Ni Soumises: l'instrumentalisation colonial et néo-coloniale de las cause des femmes." *TouTes égaux,* 1 December.

———Bouteldja, Naima. 2011. "Behind the 'Burqa Ban.'" European Muslim Network, 11 November. Available at http://www.euro-muslims.eu/#/articles/all/all_articles_15 (accessed 28 June 2012).

Bouzar, Dounia. 2004. *"Monsieur Islam" n'existe pas: Pour une déislamisation des débats*. Paris: Hachette.

Bowen, John R. 2010. *Can Islam Be French? Pluralism and Pragmatism in a Secularist State*. Princeton, NJ: Princeton University Press.

———. 2012a. *Blaming Islam*. Cambridge, MA: MIT Press.

——— 2012b. *A New Anthropology of Islam*. Cambridge: Cambridge University Press.

———, Christophe Bertossi, Jan Willem Duyvendak, and Mona Lena Krook, eds. 2014a. *European States and Their Muslim Citizens: The Impact of Institutions on Perceptions and Boundaries*. New York: Cambridge University Press.

———, Christophe Bertossi, Jan Willem Duyvendak, and Mona Lena Krook. 2014b. "An Institutional Approach to Framing Muslims in Europe." In Bowen et al. 2014a, pp. 1–26.

———, and Mathias Rohe. 2014. "Juridical Framings of Muslims and Islam in France and Germany." In Bowen et al. 2014a, pp. 135–63.

Brand, Laurie. 2006. *Citizens Abroad: Emigration and the State in the Middle East and North Africa*. Cambridge: Cambridge University Press.

Brenner, Emmanuel, ed. 2002. *Les territoires perdus de la république*. Paris: Mille et Une Nuits.

Brettfeld, Katrin, and Peter Wetzels. 2007. *Muslime in Deutschland: Integration, Integrationsbarrieren, Religion sowie Einstellungen zu Demokratie, Rechtsstaatund politisch-religiös motivierter Gewalt—Ergebnisse von Befragungen im Rahmen einer multizentrischen Studie in städtischen Lebensräume*. Bonn: Bundesministerium des Inneren.

Briggs, Rachel, Catherine Fieschi, and Hannah Lownsbrough. 2006. *Bringing It Home: Community-based Approaches to Counter-terrorism*. London: Demos.

British National Party. 2010. "Democracy, Freedom, Culture and Identity." British Nation Party General Elections Manifesto 2010. Available at http//:bnptv.org.uk (accessed 11 August 2013).

Brochmann, Grete, and Tomas Hammar, eds. 1999. *Mechanisms of Immigration Control: A Comparative Analysis of European Regulation Policies*. Oxford: Berg.

Broder, Henryk. 2006. *Hurra, wir kapitulieren: Von der Lust am Einknicken*. Berlin: WJS.

Brohi, A. K. 1980. "Problems of Minorities." In *Muslim Communities in Non-Muslim States*, ed. Islamic Council of Europe, pp. 31–42. London: Islamic Council of Europe.

Bronner, Stephen E. 2004. *Reclaiming the Enlightenment: Toward a Politics of Radical Engagement*. New York: Columbia University Press.

Brouwer, Lenie. 2004. "Dutch-Muslims on the Internet: A New Discussion Platform." *Journal of Muslim Minority Affairs* 24 (1): 47–55.

Brubaker, William Rogers. 1992. *Citizenship and Nationhood in France and Germany*. Cambridge, MA: Harvard University Press.

———. 2001. "The Return of Assimilation? Changing Perspectives on Immigration and Its Sequels in France, Germany, and the United States." *Ethnic and Racial Studies* 24 (4): 531–47.

Bruckner, Pascal. 2007. "Enlightenment Fundamentalism or Racism of the Anti-racists?" signandsight.com, 24 January. Available at http://www.signandsight.com/features/1146.html.

Buchstein, Hubertus. 1995. "Die Zumutungen der Demokratie. Von der normativen Theorie des Bürgers zur institutionell vermittelten Präferenzkompetenz." *Politische Vierteljahresschrift* 26 (*Politische Theorien in der Ära der Transformation*): 295–324.

Buijs, Frank. 2010. "Muslims in the Netherlands: Social and Political Developments after 9/11." In Bleich 2010a, pp. 68–85.

Bukow, Wolf-Dietrich, Claudia Nikodem, Erika Schulze, and Erol Yildiz. 2007. "Was heisst hier Parallelgesellschaft? Zum Umgang mit Differenzen." In *Was heisst hier Parallelgesellschaft? Zum Umgang mit Differenzen,* ed. Wolf-Dietrich Bukow, Claudia Nikodem, Erika Schulze, and Erol Yildiz, pp. 11–28. Wiesbaden: VS Verlag für Sozialwissenschaften.

Bundesamt für Verfassungsschutz. 2005. *Annual Report of the Office for the Protection of the Constitution.* Cologne: Bundesamt für Verfassungsschutz. Available at http://www.verfassungsschutz.de/en/en_publications/annual_reports/vsbericht2005_engl.

Bundesministerium des Innern. 2008. *Verfassungsschutzbericht 2008.* Berlin: Bundesministerium des Innern. Available at www.verfassungsschutz.de (accessed 28 January 2013).

———. 2014. *2013 Annual Report of the Office for the Protection of the Constitution.* Berlin: Bundesministerium des Innern.

Bunt, Gary. 2009. *iMuslims: Rewriting the House of Islam.* Chapel Hill: University of North Carolina Press.

Burke, Edmund. 1803–1827. *Works.* 16 vols. London: F.C.J. Rivington.

———. 1973. *Reflections on the Revolution in France.* New York: Doubleday.

———. 2006. *The Works of the Right Honourable Edmund Burke.* 12 vols. Salt Lake City, UT: Project Gutenberg.

Buruma, Ian. 2006. *Murder in Amsterdam.* New York: Penguin.

———. 2010. *Taming the Gods, Religion and Democracy on Three Continents.* Princeton, NJ: Princeton University Press.

Calavita, Kitty. 2005. *Immigrants at the Margins: Law, Race, and Exclusion in Southern Europe.* New York: Cambridge University Press.

Canovan, Margaret. 1996. *Nationhood and Political Theory.* Cheltenham, U.K.: Edward Elgar.

Cantle Report. 2001. *Community Cohesion.* London: Government Printing Office.

Carens, Joseph. 2013. *The Ethics of Immigration.* Oxford: Oxford University Press.

Carstensen, Martin B. 2011. "Paradigm Man vs. the Bricoleur: Bricolage as an Alternative Vision of Agency in Ideational Change." *European Political Science Review* 3 (1): 147–67.

Casanova, José. 1994. *Public Religions in the Modern World.* Chicago: University of Chicago Press.

———. 2006. "Religion, European Secular Identities, and European Integration." In *Religion in an Expanding Europe,* ed. Peter Katzenstein and Timothy Byrnes, pp. 65–92. Cambridge: Cambridge University Press.

———. 2007. "Immigration and the New Religious Pluralism: A European/United States Comparison." In Banchoff 2007a, pp. 59–84.

Castells, Manuel. 1975. "Immigrant Workers and Class Struggles in Advanced Capitalism: The West European Experience." *Politics and Society* 5 (1): 33–66.

Castles, Stephen. 2012. "Migration, Crisis and the Global Labour Market." In *Migration, Work and Citizenship in the New Global Order,* ed. Ronaldo Munck, Carl Ulrik Schierup, and Raúl Delgado Wise, pp. 63–76. London: Routledge.

———, and Alastair Davidson. 2000. *Citizenship and Migration: Globalization and the Politics of Belonging.* London: Routledge.

———, and Godula Kosack. 1973. *Immigrant Workers and Class Structure in Western Europe.* Oxford: Oxford University Press.

———, and Mark J. Miller. 2009. *The Age of Migration: International Population Movements in the Modern World.* New York: Guilford Press.

Cesari, Jocelyn. 1994. *Etre musulman in France.* Paris: Kathala-Iremam.

———. 2007. "The Hybrid and Globalized Islam of Western Europe." In Samad and Sen 2007, pp. 108–22.

———. 2013. *Why the West Fears Islam: An Exploration of Muslims in Liberal Democracies.* New York: Palgrave.

Ceylan, Rauf. 2006. *Ethnische Kolonien: Entstehung, Funktion und Wandel am Beispiel türkischer Moscheen und Cafés.* Wiesbaden, Germany: VS Verlag Sozialwissenschaften.

———, and Michael Kiefer. 2013. *Salafismus: Fundamentalische Strömungen und Radikalisierungsprävention.* Wiesbaden, Germany: Springer VS.

Champetier, Charles, and Alain de Benoist. 1999. "La Nouvelle Droite de l'an 2000." *Elements* 94 (February): 10–23.

Chebel d'Appollonia, Ariane. 2010. "How to Make Enemies: A Transatlantic Perspective on the Radicalization Process and Integration Issues." In Chebel d'Appollonia and Reich 2010, pp. 114–36.

———. 2015. *Migrant Mobilization and Securitization in the US and Europe: How Does It Feel to Be a Threat?* New York: Palgrave.

———, and Simon Reich. 2008. "The Securitization of Immigration: Multiple Countries, Multiple Dimensions." In *Immigration, Integration, and Security,* ed. Ariane Chebel d'Appollonia and Simon Reich, pp. 1–22. Pittsburgh, PA: Pittsburgh University Press.

———, and Simon Reich, eds. 2010. *Managing Ethnic Diversity after 9/11: Integration, Security, and Civil Liberties in Transatlantic Perspective.* New Brunswick, NJ: Rutgers University Press.

Cheleb, Malek. 2004. *Manifeste pour un Islam des lumières: 27 propositions pour faire bouger l'Islam.* Paris: Hachette Littératures.

Chesler, Phyllis. 2010. "Ban the Burqa? The Argument in Favor." *Middle East Quarterly* 17 (4): 33–45.

Chimienti, Milena, and John Solomos. 2012. "Social Movements of Irregular Migrants, Recognition and Citizenship." In *Migration, Work and Citizenship in the New Global Order,* ed. Ronaldo Munck, Carl Ulrik Schierup, and Raúl Delgado Wise, pp. 95–112. London: Routledge.

Chin, Rita. 2007. *The Guest Worker Question in Postwar Germany.* Cambridge: Cambridge University Press.

———. 2010. "Turkish Women, West German Feminists, and the Gendered Discourse on Muslim Cultural Difference." *Public Culture* 22 (3): 557–81.

Chowdhury, Arjun, and Scott Fitzsimmons. 2013. "Effective but Inefficient: Understanding the Costs of Counterterrorism." *Critical Studies on Terrorism* 6 (3): 447–56.

Çileli, Serap. 2002. *Wir sind eure Töchter, nicht eure Ehre.* Michelstadt, Germany: Neuthor.

Cohen, Elizabeth. 2009. *Semi-citizenship in Democratic Politics.* Cambridge: Cambridge University Press.

Cohen, Robin. 2006. *Migration and Its Enemies.* Aldershot, U.K.: Ashgate.

Cohen, Stanley. 1980. *Folk Devils and Moral Panics: The Creation of the Mods and Rockers.* New York: St. Martin's.

Collet, Beate. 2004. "Muslim Headscarves in Four Nation-states and Schools." In *Civil Enculturation: Nation-state, Schools and Ethnic Difference in Four European Countries,* ed. Werner Schiffauer, Gerd Baumann, Riva Kastoryano, and Steven Vertovec, pp. 119–44. New York: Berghahn.

Commission de réflexion juridique sur les relations des cultes avec les pouvoirs publics. 2006. 20 September. Paris: Interior Ministry. Available at http://lesraports.ladocumentationfrancaise.fr/BRP/064000727/0000.pdf (accessed 5 January 2008).

Commission Nationale Consultative des Droits de l'Homme. 2008. *Rapport de la Commission Nationale Consultative des Droits de l'Homme.* Paris: La Documentation Française.

Commission of the European Communities. 2000. *On a Community Immigration Policy.* Brussels: Commission of the European Communities.

Commission on British Muslims and Islamophobia. 2004. *Islamophobia: Issues, Challenges and Action.* Stoke-on-Trent, U.K.: Trentham Books.

Condorcet, Marquis de Jean Antoine Nicolas Caritat. 1804. *Oeuvres Complètes.* Vol. 8. Paris: Chez Viewig.

Connolly, William. 1993. *The Terms of Political Discourse.* Princeton, NJ: Princeton University Press.

———. 2005. *Pluralism.* Durham, NC: Duke University Press.

Conseil d'Etat. 2010. *Study of Possible Legal Grounds for Banning the Full Veil: Report Adopted by the Plenary General Assembly of the Conseil d'Etat.* 25 March. Paris: Conseil d'Etat.

Cornelius, Wayne, Takeyuki Tsuda, Philip Martin, and James Hollifield, eds. 2002. *Controlling Migration: A Global Perspective.* Stanford, CA: Stanford University Press.

Corvalho, João. 2013. "British and French Policies towards High-skilled Immigration during the 2000s: Policy Outplays Politics or Politics Trumps Policy?" *Ethnic and Racial Studies* (24 September). Available at http://www.tandfonline.com/doi/abs/10.1080/01419870.2013.833645#.UqIts9JDu18 (accessed 4 December 2013).

Council of the EU. 2000a. "Council Directive 2000/43/EC of 29 June 2000 Implementing the Principle of Equal Treatment between Persons Irrespective of Racial or Ethnic Origin." *Official Journal of the European Communities,* L 180, 19.7.

———. 2000b. "Council Decision of 27 November 2000 Establishing a Community Action Programme to Combat Discrimination (2001 to 2006)." *Official Journal of the European Communities,* L 303, 21.12.

_____. 2005. *The European Union Counter-Terrorism Strategy.* 30 November. Brussels: Council of the EU. Available at http://register.consilium.europa.eu/doc/srv?l=EN&f=ST+14469+2005+REV+4.

———. 2007. *Implementation of the Strategy and Action Plan to Combat Terrorism.* 20 May. Brussels: Council of the EU. Available at http://register.consilium.eu.int/pdf/en/05/st14/st14469-re04.en05.pdf.

Council of the EU, Justice and Home Affairs. 2004. "Press Release." 2618th Council Meeting (19 November), pp. 19–24.

Cousin, Bruno, and Tommaso Vitale. 2012. "Italian Intellectuals and the Promotion of Islamophobia after 9/11." In *Global Islamophobia: Muslims and Moral Panic in the West,* ed. George Morgan and Scott Poynting, pp. 47–65. Burlington, VT: Ashgate.

Craig, Sarah. 2013. "Struggling with EU Safe Country Practices in Asylum." In Korkut et al. 2013, pp. 53–72.

Croft, Stuart, and Cerwyn Moore. 2010. "The Evolution of Threat Narrative in the Age of Terror: Understanding Terrorist Threats in Britain." *International Affairs* 86 (4): 821–35.

Cross, Hannah. 2012. *Migrants, Borders and Global Capitalism.* New York: Routledge.

Cyrus, Norbert, and Vesela Kovacheva. 2010. "Undocumented Migration in Germany: Many Figures, Little Comprehension." In Triandafyllidou 2010e, pp. 125–44.

Daguzan, Jean-François. 2013. "France and Islamist Movements: A Long Non-dialogue." In Vidino 2013, pp. 101–13.

Dalgaard-Nielsen, Anja. 2009. "Counterterrorism and the Civil Rights of Muslim Minorities in the European Union." In *Muslims in Western Politics,* ed. Abdulkader H. Sinno, pp. 245–63. Bloomington: Indiana University Press.

Dalton, Russell. 2006. *Citizen Politics: Public Opinion and Political Parties in Advanced Industrial Democracies.* Washington, DC: CQ Press.

Dancygier, Rafaela M. 2010. *Immigration and Conflict in Europe.* Cambridge: Cambridge University Press.

Dassetto, Felice, ed. 2000. *Paroles d'islam: Individus, societies et discours dans l'islam européen contemporain.* Paris: European Science Foundation.

Davie, Grace. 1994. *Religion in Britain since 1945: Believing without Belonging.* Oxford: Blackwell.

———. 2007. "Pluralism, Tolerance, and Democracy: Theory and Practice in Europe." In Banchoff 2007a, pp. 223–42.

Davies, Garth, Martin Bouchard, Edith Wu, Kila Joffres, and Richard Frank. 2011. "Terrorist and Extremist Organizations' Use of the Internet for Recruitment." In *Jihadi Terrorism and the Radicalisation Challenge,* ed. Rik Coolsaet, pp. 105–27. Farnham: Ashgate.

Debray, Régis. 2003. *Ce que nous voile le voile: la République et le sacré.* Paris: Gallimard.

Delanty, Gerard. 2009. *Cosmopolitan Imagination: The Renewal of Social Critical Theory.* Cambridge: Cambridge University Press.

Deleuze, Gilles, and Felix Guattari. 1994. *What Is Philosophy?* Trans. Hugh Tomlinson and Graham Burchell. New York: Columbia University Press.

Deltombe, Thomas. 2005. *L'islam imaginaire. La construction médiatique de l'islamophobie en France, 1975–2005.* Paris: La Découverte.

Den Boer, Monica, Claudia Hillebrand, and Andreas Nölke. 2008. "Legitimacy under Pressure: The European Web of Counter-terrorism Networks." *Journal of Common Market Studies* 46 (1): 101–24.

Dere, Ali. 2008. "The PRA of Turkey: The Emergence, Evolution and Perception of Its Religious Services outside of Turkey." *The Muslim World* 98 (2): 292–93.

Derrida, Jacques. 1976. *Of Grammatology.* Trans. G. C. Spivak. Chicago: University of Chicago Press.

————. 1991. "Différance." In *A Derrida Reader: Between the Blinds,* ed. Peggy Kamuf, pp. 59–79. New York: Columbia University Press.

————. 1992. *The Other Heading: Reflections on Today's Europe.* Bloomington: University of Indiana Press.

————. 2001. *On Cosmopolitanism and Forgiveness.* Trans. Mark Dooley and Michael Hughes. London: Routledge.

Descartes, René. 1971. *Philosophical Writings.* Trans. Elizabeth Anscombe and Peter Thomas Geach. New York: Macmillan.

Deutsche Islam Konferenz. 2009. "Deutsche Islam Konferenz." 14 April. Available at http://www.deutsche-islam-konferenz.de/nn_1864594/SubSites/DIK/DE/Kopf-tuchGender/Kelek/kelek-node.html?__nnn=true) (accessed 15 April 2014).

Dewinter, Filip. 2000. *Baas in eigen land.* Brussels: Egmont.

Diehl, Claudia, and Rainer Schnell. 2006. "'Reactive Ethnicity' or 'Assimilation'? Statements, Arguments, and First Empirical Evidence for Labor Migrants in Germany." *International Migration Review* 40 (4): 786–816.Dinç, Cüneyd. 2014. "New and Old Identity Patterns of Religious Young Muslims in Germany." In *New Multicultural Identities in Europe: Religion and Ethnicity in Secular Societies*, eds. Erkan Toğuşlu, Johan Leman & İsmail Mesut Sezgin (eds.), pp. 37–53. Leuven: Leuven University Press.

Dippel, Andreas, and Egmond Prill, eds. 2007. *Die schleichende Islamisierung? Beiträge, Fakten und Hintergründe.* Leipzig: Hännsler Verlag.

Dirie, Waris. 1999. *Desert Flower: The Extraordinary Journey of a Desert Nomad.* New York: Harper Perennial.

Djavann, Chahadortt (2004). *Que pense Allah de l'Europe.* Paris: Gallimard.

Douzinas, Costas. 2007. *Human Rights and Empire: The Political Philosophy of Cosmopolitanism.* London: Routledge.

Drees Willem B., and Pieter Sjoerd van Konigsveld, eds. 2008. *The Study of Religion and the Training of Muslim Clergy in Europe.* Leiden, Netherlands: Leiden University Press.

Drysek, John. 2000. *Deliberative Democracy and Beyond: Liberals, Critics, Contestations.* Oxford: Oxford University Press.

Dumbrava, Costica. 2014. *Nationality, Citizenship and Ethno-cultural Belonging: Preferential Membership Policies in Europe.* London: Palgrave.

Düvell, Franck, ed. 2006. *Illegal Immigration in Europe: Beyond Control?* New York: Palgrave.

————. 2011. "Paths into Irregularity: The Legal and Social Construction of Irregular Migration." *European Journal for Migration and Law* 13 (3): 275–95.

Duyvendak, Jan Willem. 2011. *The Politics of Home: Belonging and Nostalgia in Western Europe and the United States.* New York: Palgrave.

————, and Peter Scholten. 2012. "Deconstructing the Dutch Multicultural Model: A Frame Perspective on Dutch Immigrant Integration Policymaking." *Comparative European Politics* 10: 262–82.

Duyvesteyn, Isabelle. 2004. "How New Is New Terrorism?" *Studies in Conflict and Terrorism* 27 (5): 439–54.

Dwyer, Claire. 1999. "Veiled Meanings: Young British Muslim Women and the Negotiation of Difference." *Gender, Place and Culture* 6 (1): 5–26.

Dzankic, Jelena. 2012. "The Pros and Cons of Ius Peceniae: Investor Citizenship in Comparative Perspective." RSCAS Working Paper 2012/14. Florence: European University Institute.

El Guindi, Fadwa. 1999. *Veil: Modesty, Privacy and Resistance.* London: Berg.

Ellermann, Antje. 2008. "The Limits of Unilateral Migration Control: Deportation and Inter-state Cooperation." *Government and Opposition* 43 (2): 168–89.

———. 2009. *States against Migrants: Deportation in Germany and the United States.* New York: Cambridge University Press.

———. 2014. "The Rule of Law and the Right to Stay: The Moral Claims of Undocumented Migrants." *Politics and Society* 42 (3): 293–308.

Ellian, Afshin. 2006. "Stop Capitulating to Threats." The Power of Culture, February. Available at http://www.krachtvancultuur.nl/en/current/2006/february/afshin_ellian (accessed 19 June 2013).

Elorza, Antonio. 2004. "Terrorismo islámico: Las raíces doctrinales." In *El neuvo terrorismo islamista,* ed. Fernando Reinares and Antonio Elorza, pp. 156–57. Madrid: Temas de Hoy.

Engbersen, Gottfried. 2001. "The Unanticipated Consequences of Panopticon Europe: Residence Strategies for Illegal Immigrants." In *Controlling a New Migration World,* ed. Virginie Guiraudon and Christian Joppke, pp. 222–46. London: Routledge.

Ersbøll, Eva, Dora Kostakopoulou, and Ricky Van Oers. 2011. *A Re-definition of Belonging? Language and Integration Tests in Europe.* Leiden, Netherlands: Brill.

Esping-Andersen, Gøsta, Duncan Gallie, Anton Hemerijck, and John Myles. 2002. *Why We Need a New Welfare State.* Oxford: Oxford University Press.

European Commission against Racism and Intolerance. 2011. *Annual Report on ECRI's Activities.* Strasbourg: Council of Europe.

European Council. 2003. *A Secure Europe in a Better World? European Security Strategy.* Brussels: European Council.

European Union. 2007. *EU Annual Report on Human Rights.* Brussels: European External Action Service.

European Union Agency for Fundamental Rights. 2009. *EU-MIDIS at a Glance: Introduction to FRA's EU-wide Discrimination Survey.* Vienna: European Union Agency for Fundamental Rights. Available at http://fra.europa.eu/fraWebsite/attachments/EU-MIDIS_GLANCE_EN.pdf (accessed 12 February 2012).

European Union Monitoring Centre on Racism and Xenophobia. 2006. *Muslims in the European Union: Discrimination and Islamophobia.* Vienna: EUMC.

Europol. 2010. *European Union Terrorism Situation and Trend Report 2010 (TE-SAT 2010).* Brussels: European Police Office.

———. 2011. *European Union Terrorism Situation and Trend Report 2011 (TE-SAT 2011).* Brussels: European Police Office.

———. 2013. *European Union Terrorism Situation and Trend Report 2013 (TE-SAT 2013).* Brussels: European Police Office

———. 2014. *European Union Terrorism Situation and Trend Report 2014 (TE-SAT 2014).* Brussels: European Police Office.

Eurostat. 2008. *Population Projections 2008–2060.* Available at http://europa.eu/rapid/press-release_STAT-08-119_en.htm (accessed 17 February 2013).

Ewing, Katherine Pratt. 2008. *Stolen Honor: Stigmatizing Muslim Men in Berlin.* Stanford, CA: Stanford University Press.

Fadil, Nadia. 2006. "'We Should Be Walking Qurans': The Making of an Islamic Political Subject." In Jonker and Amiraux 2006, pp. 53–78.

Faist, Thomas. 2000. *The Volume and Dynamics of International Migration and Transnational Social Spaces.* Oxford: Oxford University Press.

———. 2009. "Diversity—A New Mode of Incorporation?" *Ethnic and Racial Studies* 32 (1): 171–90.

———, and Andreas Ette, eds. 2007. *The Europeanization of National Policies and Politics of Immigration: Between Autonomy and the European Union.* New York: Palgrave.

Fallaci, Oriana. 2006. *The Force of Reason.* New York: Rizzoli International.

Fanon, Frantz. 1965a. *The Wretched of the Earth.* Trans. Constance Farrington. New York: Grove Press.

———. 1965b. *A Dying Colonialism.* Trans. Haakon Chevalier. New York: Grove Press.

Fasani, Francesco. 2010. "The Quest for La Dolce Vita? Undocumented Migration in Italy." In Triandafyllidou 2010e, pp. 167–86.

Fava, Giovanni Claudio. 2007. "Report on the Alleged Use of European Countries by the CIA for the Transportation and Illegal Detention of Prisoners." Document A6-0020/2007, 30 January. Brussels: European Parliament.

Favell, Adrian. 1998. *Philosophies of Integration.* London: Macmillan.

Fekete, Liz. 2012. "The Muslim Conspiracy Theory and the Oslo Massacre." *Race and Class* 53 (3): 30–47.

Ferrera, Maurizio. 2005. *The Boundaries of Welfare: European Integration and the New Spacial Politics of Social Protection.* Oxford: Oxford University Press.

Fetzer, Joel, and Christopher Soper. 2005. *Muslims and the State in Britain, France and Germany.* Cambridge: Cambridge University Press.

Fichte, Johann Gottlieb. 1968. *Addresses to the German Nation.* New York: Harper Torchbooks.

Fillitz, Thomas. 2006. "'Being the Native's Friend Does Not Make You the Foreigner's Enemy!' Neo-Nationalism, the Freedom Party and Jörg Haider in Austria." In *Neonationalism in Europe and Beyond,* ed. Andre Gingrich and Marcus Banks, pp. 138–62. New York: Berghahn Books.

Fish, Stanley. 1999. *The Trouble with Principle.* Cambridge, MA: Harvard University Press.

Foblets, Marie-Claire, and Sander Loones. 2006. "Belgium." In Bauböck et al. 2006, pp. 2:63–104.

Forest, James J.F. 2015. *The Terrorism Lectures: A Comprehensive Collection for Students of Terrorism, Counterterrorism, and National Security.* Santa Ana, CA: Nortia Press.

Foroutan, Naika, ed. 2011. *Sarrazins Thesen auf dem Prüfstand: Ein empirischer Gegenentwurf zu Thilo Sarrazins Thesen zu Muslimen in Deutschland.* VW Forschungsprojekt "Hybride europäische-muslimische Identitätsmodelle (HEYMAT)." Berlin: Humboldt University.

——— et al. 2015. *Deutschland postmigrantisch I. Gesellschaft, Religion, Identität.* Berlin: Berliner Institut für empirische Integrations- und Migrationsforschung (BIM).

———, and Isabel Schäfer. 2009. "Hybride Identitäten—muslimische Migrantinnen und Migranten in Deutschland und Europa." *Aus Politik und Zeitgeschichte* 5 (23 January).

Fortuyn, Pim. 1997. *Tegen de islamisering van onze cultuur*. Utrecht, Netherlands: A. W. Bruno.

Forum against Islamophobia and Racism. 2002. *Towards Equality and Diversity—Implementing the Employment and Race Directives*. London: Forum against Islamophobia and Racism.

Foucault, Michel. 1978. *The History of Sexuality*. Trans. Robert Hurley. New York: Pantheon.

———. 1979. *Discipline and Punish: The Birth of the Prison*. Trans. Alan Sheridan. New York: Vintage.

———. 1980. *Power/Knowledge: Selected Interviews and Writings, 1972–1977*. Ed. C. Gordon. New York: Pantheon.

———. 1984. *The Foucault Reader*. Ed. Paul Rabinow. New York: Pantheon.

———. 1988. *Madness and Civilization: A History of Insanity in the Age of Reason*. Trans. Richard Howard. New York: Vintage.

Fourest, Caroline. 2004. *Frère Tariq. Discours, stratégie et méthode de Tariq Ramadan*. Paris: Grasset and Fasquelle.

Frampton, Martyn, and Shiraz Maher. 2013. "Between 'Engagement' and a 'Values-led' Approach: Britain and the Muslim Brotherhood from 9/11 to the Arab Spring." In Vidino 2013, pp. 32–55.

Franz, Barbara. 2007. "Europe's Muslim Youth: An Inquiry into the Politics of Discrimination, Relative Deprivation, and Identity Formation." *Mediterranean Quarterly* 18 (1): 89–112.

Fredette, Jennifer. 2014. *Constructing Muslims in France: Discourse, Public Identity, and the Politics of Citizenship*. Philadelphia: Temple University Press.

Freeden, Michael. 1996. *Ideologies and Political Theory: A Conceptual Approach*. Oxford: Clarendon Press.

Freedman, Jane. 2006. "The Headscarf Debate: Muslim Women in Europe and the 'War on Terror.'" In *(En)Gendering the War on Terror: War Stories and Camouflaged Politics,* ed. Krista Hunt and Kim Rygiel, pp. 169–90. Aldershot, U.K.: Ashgate.

———. 2011. "The Réseau Education sans Frontières: Reframing the Campaign against the Deportation of Migrants." *Citizenship Studies* 7 (3/4): 613–26.

Freeman, Gary. 1995. "Modes of Immigration Politics in Liberal Democratic States." *International Migration Review* 29 (4): 881–92.

———. 2004. "Immigrant Incorporation in Western Democracies." *International Migration Review* 38 (146): 945–69.

———, and Nedem Ögelman. 1998. "Homeland Citizenship Policies and the Status of Third Country Nationals in the European Union." *Journal of Ethnic and Migration Studies* 24 (4): 769–88.

Frey, Bruno (2004). *Dealing With Terrorism – Stick or Carrot?* Cheltenham and Northampton: Edward Elgar.

Friedrichs, Jörg. 2008. *Fighting Terrorism and Drugs: Europe and International Police Cooperation*. London: Routledge.

Frisch, Max. 1983. *Die Tagebücher, 1964–1966 und 1966–1971*. Frankfurt: Suhrkamp.

Fung, Archon, and Erik Olin Wright. 2001. "Deepening Democracy: Innovations in Empowered Participatory Governance." *Politics and Society* 29 (1): 5–41.

Gadamer, Hans-Georg. 1975. *Wahrheit und Methode*. Tübingen: Mohr.

———. 2007. *The Gadamer Reader: A Bouquet of the Later Writings*. Ed. Richard Palmer. Evanston, IL: Northwestern University Press.

Gallop. 2007. *Gallop World Poll: Muslims*. Princeton, NJ: The Gallup Organization.

———. 2009. *The Gallop Coexist Index 2009: A Global Study of Interfaith Relations*. Abu Dhabi: Gallup, Inc.

Garbaye, Romain. 2010. "Toward a European Policy of Integration? Divergence and Convergence of Immigrant Integration Policy in Britain and France." In Chebel d'Appollonia and Reich 2010, pp. 165–77.

Gardell, Mattias. 2010. *Islamofobi*. Stockholm: Leopard.

Gardner, Katy. 1995. *Global Migrants, Local Lives: Travel and Transformation in Rural Bangladesh*. Oxford: Clarendon.

———, and Abdus Shuker. 1994. "'I'm a Bengali, I'm Asian and I'm Living Here': The Changing Identity of British Bengalis." In *Desh Pardesh: The South Asian Presence in Britain*, ed. Roger Ballard, pp. 142–64. London: C. Hurst.

Garton Ash, Timothy. 2006. "Islam in Europe." *New York Review of Books*, 5 October.

Gaspard, Françoise, and Farhad Khosrokhavar. 1995. *Le Foulard et la république*. Paris: Découverte.

Gauci, Jean-Pierre. 2012. *Racism in Europe: ENAR Shadow Report 2010–11*. Brussels: European Network against Racism.

Gay, Peter. 2002. *Schnitzler's Century*. New York: Norton.

Geddes, Andrew. 2000. "Thin Europeanisation: The Social Rights of Migrants in an Integrating Europe." In Bommes and Geddes 2000, pp. 209–26.

Geisser, Vincent, and El Yamine Soum. 2012. "The Legacies of Colonialism: Migrant-origin Minorities in French Politics." In Givens and Maxwell 2012, pp. 53–66.

Geissler, Rainer, and Horst Pöttker, eds. 2005. *Massenmedien und die Integration ethnischer Minderheiten in Deutschland*. Bielefeld, Germany: Transcript.

Gellner, Ernest. 1983. *Nations and Nationalism*. Ithaca, NY: Cornell University Press.

Gerges, Fawaz A. 2005. *The Far Enemy: Why Jihad Went Global*. Cambridge: Cambridge University Press.

Gerlach, Julia. 2006. *Zwischen Pop und Dschihad: Muslimische Jugend in Deutschland*. Berlin: Christoph Links Verlag.

Gest, Justin. 2010. *Apart: Alienated and Engaged Muslims in the West*. New York: Columbia University Press.

Geuss, Raymond. 2008. *Philosophy and Real Politics*. Princeton, NJ: Princeton University Press.

al-Ghannouchi, Rashid. 2000. "Arab Secularism in the Maghreb." In *Islam and Secularism in the Middle East*, ed. Azzam Tamimi and John L. Esposito, pp. 97–123. New York: New York University Press.

Ghodsee, Kristen. 2012. "Regulating Religious Symbols in Public Schools: The Legal Status of the Islamic Headscarf in Bulgaria." In Rosenberger and Sauer 2012b, pp. 116–31.

Gibney, Matthew. 2004. *The Ethics and Politics of Asylum: Liberal Democracy and the Response to Refugees*. Cambridge: Cambridge University Press.

Gillies, Alexander. 1945. *Herder*. Oxford: Blackwell.

Gilroy, Paul. 2006. "Multiculture in Times of War." *Critical Quarterly* 48 (4): 27–43.

Givens, Terri, and Adam Luedtke. 2005. "European Immigration Policies in Comparative Perspective: Issue Salience, Partisanship and Immigrant Rights." *Comparative European Politics* 3 (1): 1–22.

———, Gary Freeman, and David Leal, eds. 2008. *Immigration Policy and Security: U.S., European, and Commonwealth Perspectives*. London: Routledge.

————, and Rahsaan Maxwell, eds. 2012. *Immigrant Politics: Race and Representation in Western Europe.* Boulder, CO: Lynne Rienner.

Glover, Jonathan. 1997. "Nations, Identity and Conflict." In *The Morality of Nationalism,* ed. Robert McKim and Jeff McMahan, pp. 11–30. Oxford: Oxford University Press.

Godard, Bernard. 2007. "Official Recognition of Islam." In Amghar, Boubekeur, and Emerson 2007, pp. 183–203.

Göle, Nilüfer. 2003. "The Voluntary Adoption of Islamic Stigma Symbols." *Social Research* 70 (3): 809–28.

————. 2004. "Die sichtbare Präzens des Islam und die Grenzen der Öffentlichkeit." In *Islam in Sicht: Der Auftritt von Muslimen im öffentlichen Raum,* ed. Nilüfer Göle and Ludwig Ammann, pp. 11–44. Bielefeld, Germany: Transcript.

————. 2011. *Islam in Europe: The Lure of Fundamentalism and the Allure of Cosmopolitanism.* Trans. Steven Rendall. Princeton, NJ: Marcus Wiener.

Gonzalez-Enriquez, Carmen. 2010. "Spain: Irregularity as a Rule." In Triandafyllidou 2010e, pp. 227–46.

Goodman, Sara Wallace. 2010. "Integration Requirements for Integration's Sake? Identifying, Categorising and Comparing Civic Integration Policies." *Journal of Ethnic and Migration Studies* 36 (5): 753–73.

————. 2014. *Immigration and Membership: Politics in Western Europe.* Cambridge: Cambridge University Press.

Gould, Andrew C. 2009. "Muslim Elites and Ideologies in Portugal and Spain." *West European Politics* 32 (1): 55–76.

Gray, John. 1995. *Liberalism.* Minneapolis: University of Minnesota Press.

————. 1996. *Isaiah Berlin.* Princeton, NJ: Princeton University Press.

————. 2003. *Al Qaeda and What It Means to Be Modern.* London: Faber and Faber.

Green, Simon. 2005. "Between Ideology and Pragmatism: The Politics of Dual Nationality in Germany." *International Migration Review* 39 (4): 921–52.

Green-Pedersen, Christoffer, and Jesper Krogstrup. 2008. "Immigration as a Political Issue in Denmark and Sweden." *European Journal of Political Research* 47 (5): 610–34.

Gresch, Nora, Petra Rostock, and Sevgi Kiliç (2012. "Negotiating Belonging: Or How a Differentiated Citizenship Is Legitimized in European Headscarf Debates." In Rosenberger and Sauer 2012b, pp. 55–73.

Griffith-Jones, Robin, ed. 2013. *Islam and English Law.* Cambridge: Cambridge University Press.

Grillo, Ralph D. 1998. *Pluralism and the Politics of Difference.* Oxford: Clarendon.

————. 2005. *Backlash against Diversity.* Working Paper 14. Oxford: Centre on Migration, Policy and Society, University of Oxford.

Groot, Gerard-René de, Jan-Jaap Kuipers, and Franziska Weber. 2009. "Passing Citizenship Tests as a Requirement for Naturalization: A Comparative Perspective." In Guild, Groenendijk, and Carrera 2009, pp. 51–78.Guénif-Souilamas, Nacira. 2006. *Des beurettes.* Paris: Grasset and Frasquelle.

Guild, Elspeth, Kees Groenendijk, and Sergio Carrera, eds. 2009. *Illiberal Liberal States: Immigration, Citizenship and Integration in the EU.* Burlington, VT: Ashgate.

Guiraudon, Virginie. 1998. "Citizenship Rights for Non-citizens: France, Germany and the Netherlands." In *Challenge to the Nation-state: Immigration in Western Europe and the United States,* ed. Christian Joppke, pp. 272–304. Oxford: Oxford University Press.

———. 2000. "The Marshallian Triptych Reordered: The Role of Courts and Bureaucracies in Furthering Migrants' Social Rights." In Bommes and Geddes 2000, pp. 72–89.

———. 2003. "The Constitution of a European Immigration Policy Domain: A Political Sociology Approach." *Journal of European Public Policy* 10 (2): 263–82.

———. 2006. "Different Nation, Same Nationhood: The Challenges of Immigration Policy." In *Changing France: The Politics That Markets Make,* ed. Pepper D. Culpepper, Peter Hall, and Bruno Palier, pp. 137–40. Basingstoke, U.K.: Palgrave.

Guittet, Emmanuel-Pierre. 2008. "Military Activities within National Boundaries: The French Case." In Bigo and Tsoukala 2008, pp. 121–45.

Gutmann, Amy. 1994. Introduction to *Multiculturalism,* ed. Amy Gutmann, pp. 1–25. Princeton, NJ: Princeton University Press.

———, and Dennis Thompson. 2004. *Why Deliberative Democracy?* Princeton, NJ: Princeton University Press.

Habermas, Jürgen. 1962. *Strukturwandel der Öffentlichkeit: Untersuchungen zu einer Kategorie der bürgerlichen Gesellschaft.* Berlin: Luchterhand.

———. 1984. *The Theory of Communicative Action.* Vol. 1: *Reason and Rationalization of Society.* Cambridge: Polity.

———. 1987a. *The Theory of Communicative Action.* Vol. 2: *The Critique of Functionalist Reason.* Cambridge: Polity.

———. 1987b. *The Philosophical Discourse of Modernity.* Trans. Frederick Lawrence. Cambridge, MA: MIT Press.

———. 1998. *The Inclusion of the Other.* Ed. Ciaran Cronin and Pablo De Greiff. Cambridge, MA: MIT Press.

———. 2003. *The Future of Human Nature.* London: Polity.

———. 2006. "Religion in the Public Sphere." *European Journal of Philosophy* 14 (1): 1–25.

———. 2008a. "Notes on Post-secular Society." *New Perspectives Quarterly* 25 (4): 17–29.

———. 2008b. "A 'Post-secular Society'—What Does That Mean?" Reset Dialogue on Civilizations, 16 September. Available at http://www.resetdoc.org/story/00000000926 (accessed 28 May 2013).

Hadj-Abdou, Leila, and Linda Woodhead. 2012. "Muslim Women's Participation in the Veil Controversy: Austria and the UK Compared." In Rosenberger and Sauer 2012b, pp. 186–204.

Hafez, Farid, ed. 2011. *Jahrbuch für Islamophobieforschung.* Innsbruck, Austria: Studienverlag.

———, ed. 2014. *Jahrbuch für Islamophobieforschung 2014.* Vienna: New Academic Press.

Hagedorn, Heike. 2007. "Föderalismus und die duetsche Staatsangehörigkeit: Die Einbürgerungspolitik der Bundesländer." In *Integrationspolitik in föderalistischen Systemen (Jarhbuch Migration),* ed. Lale Akgün and Dietrich Thränhardt, pp. 91–117. Munster, Germany: LIT.

Hainmueller, Jens, and Dominik Hangartner. 2013. "Who Gets a Swiss Passport? A Natural Experiment in Immigrant Discrimination." *American Political Science Review* 107 (1): 159–87.

Hall, Peter. 1993. "Policy Paradigms, Social Learning, and the State: the Case of Economic Policymaking in Britain." *Comparative Politics* 25 (3): 275–96.

Hall, Stuart. 1992. "The Question of Cultural Identity." In *Modernity and its Futures,* ed. Stuart Hall, David Held, and T. McGrew, pp. 274–325. Cambridge: Polity.

———. 2000. "Conclusion: The Multi-cultural Question." In *Un/settled Multiculturalisms: Diasporas, Entanglements, Transruptions,* ed. Barnor Hesser, pp. 209–41. London: Zed.

Hall, Suzanne. 2012. *City, Street and Citizen: The Measure of the Ordinary.* London: Routledge.

Hamidi, Malika. 2009. *From the Construction of a European Muslim Feminine Identity to the Emergence of a Feminist Consciousness.* 18 February. Brussels: European Muslim Network. Available at http://www.euro-muslims.eu/#/articles/gender-issue/gender_issue_3 (accessed 21 June 2012).

Hammar, Thomas. 1990. *Democracy and the Nation State.* London: Gower.

———. 2013. *The Politics of Immigration: The Contradictions of the Liberal State.* Oxford: Polity.

Handcock, M. Donald Christopher Carman, Marjorie Castle, David P. Conradt Raffoila Y. Nanetti, Y. B. Guy Peters, William Saffran, and Stephen White 2015. *Politics in Europe.* Los Angeles: Sage.

Hansen, Peo, and Sandy Brian Hager. 2010. *The Politics of European Citizenship: Deepening Contradictions in Social Rights and Migration Policy.* Oxford: Berghahn.

Hansen, Randall. 2000. *Citizenship and Immigration in Post-war Britain.* Oxford: Oxford University Press.

———. 2003. "Citizenship and Integration in Europe." In *Toward Assimilation and Citizenship: Immigrants in Liberal Nation-states,* ed. Christian Joppke and Ewa Morawska, pp. 87–109. New York: Palgrave.

———, and Patrick Weil, eds. 2001. *Toward a European Nationality: Citizenship, Immigration and Nationality Law in the EU.* London: Palgrave.

Hargreaves, Alec. 2007. *Multi-ethnic France: Immigration, Politics, Culture and Society.* New York: Routledge.

Harvey, David. 1989. *The Condition of Postmodernity: An Enquiry into the Conditions of Social Change.* Oxford: Oxford University Press.

Hatton, Timothy. 2009. "The Rise and Fall of Asylum: What Happened and Why?" *Economic Journal* 119 (535): F183–F213.

Haug, Habil Sonja, Stephanie Müssig, and Anya Stichs. 2010. *Muslim Life in Germany.* Berlin: Federal Office of Migration and Refugees.

Haut Conseil à l'Intégration. 1995. *Liens culturels et integration.* Paris: Documentation Française.

———. 1997. *Affaiblissement du lien social, enfermement dans les particularisms et intégration dans la cite.* Paris: Documentation Française.

———. 2000. *L'Islam dans la république.* Paris: Documentation Française.

Hayes, Carlton. 1931. *The Historical Evolution of Modern Nationalism.* New York: Richard R. Smith.

Hazán, Miryam. 2014. "Spain." In Hollifield, Martin, and Orrenius 2014a, pp. 371–94.

Heath, Anthony F., Catherine Rothon, and Elina Kilpi. 2007. "The Second Generation in Western Europe: Education, Unemployment, and Occupational Attainment." *Annual Review of Sociology* 34 (1): 211–35.

Heath-Kelly, Charlotte, Lee Jarvis, and Christopher Baker-Beall. 2014. "Editors' Introduction: Critical Terrorism Studies: Practice, Limits and Experience." *Critical Studies on Terrorism* 7 (1): 1–10.

Hebling, Marc. 2013. "Local Citizenship Politics in Switzerland: Between National Justice and Municipal Particularities." In Maas 2013b, pp. 149–67.

Hedetoft, Ulf. 2003. "Cultural Transformation: How Denmark Faces Immigration." openDemocracy, 30 October. Available at http://www.opendemocracy.net/people-migrationeurope/article_1563.jsp (accessed 12 July 2014).

Hegel, Georg Wilhelm Friedrich. 1953. *Reason in History: A General Introduction to the Philosophy of History.* Trans. Robert Hartman. New York: Bobbs-Merrill.

Heidegger, Martin. 1977. *The Question Concerning Technology and Other Essays.* Trans. William Lovitt. New York: Harper and Row.

Heisler, Martin. 1998. "Contextualizing Global Migration: Sketching the Socio-political Landscape in Europe." *Journal of International Law and Foreign Affairs* 3 (2): 557–93.

Held, David. 1995. *Democracy and the Global Order.* Stanford, CA: Stanford University Press.

Hellyer, H. A. 2006. "Muslims and Multiculturalism in the European Union." *Journal of Muslim Minority Affairs* 26 (3): 329–51.

———. 2009. *Muslims of Europe: The 'Other' Europeans.* Edinburgh: Edinburgh University Press.

Hemerijck, Anton. 2013. *Changing Welfare States.* Oxford: Oxford University Press.

Herder, Johann Gottfried. 1877–1913. *Sämtliche Werke.* Ed. B. Suphan. Berlin: Hildesheim Olms.

———. 1984. *Werke.* 3 vols. Ed. Wolfgang Pross. Munich: Carl Hansen.

Hervieu-Léger, Danièle. 2001. *La religion en miettes ou la question des sects.* Paris: Calmann Lévy.

———. 2004. "Religion und Sozialer Zusammenhalt." *Transit: Europäische Revue* 26 (Summer): 101–19.

———. 2007. "Islam and the Republic: The French Case." In Banchoff 2007a, pp. 203–22.

Heywood, Andrew. 2012. *Political Ideologies: An Introduction.* New York: Palgrave.

Hickman, Mary, Lyn Thomas, Sara Silvestri, and Henri Nickels. 2011. *Suspect Communities? Counter Terrorism Policy, the Press, and the Impact on Irish and Muslim Communities in Britain.* London: London Metropolitan University.

Hillebrand, Claudia. 2012. *Counter-Terrorism Networks in the European Union: Maintaining Democratic Legitimacy after 9/11.* Oxford: Oxford University Press.

Hirsi Ali, Ayaan. 2006. "There Is an Alternative to Islam's Example." Islam Watch, 1 July. Available at www.islamwatch.org/ExMuslims/AHirsi/Alternative2Islam.htm (accessed 15 June 2013).

Holbach, Paul-Henri Baron d'. 1970. *The System of Nature.* Trans. H. D. Robinson. New York: Burt Franklin.

Hollifield, James. 1992. *Immigrants, Markets, and States: The Political Economy of Postwar Europe.* Cambridge, MA: Harvard University Press.

———. 1997. "Immigration and Integration in Western Europe: A Comparative Analysis." In *Immigration into Western Societies,* ed. Emek Ucarer and Donald Puchala, pp. 28–70. London: Pinter.

———. 2014. "France: Immigration and the Republican Tradition in France." In Hollifield, Martin, and Orrenius 2014a, pp. 156–87.

———, Philip Martin, and Pia Orrenius, eds. 2014a. *Controlling Immigration: A Global Perspective*. Stanford, CA: Stanford University Press.

———, Philip Martin, and Pia Orrenius. 2014b. "Introduction: The Dilemmas of Immigration Control." In Hollifield, Martin, and Orrenius 2014a, pp. 3–34.

Holmes, Douglas R. 2000. *Integral Europe: Fast-capitalism, Multiculturalism, Neo-fascism*. Princeton, NJ: Princeton University Press.

Home Office. 2001. *Community Cohesion Report*. London: HMSO.

———. 2002. *Secure Borders, Safe Haven: Integration with Diversity in Modern Britain*. London: HMSO.

———. 2005. *Preventing Extremism Together Working Groups August–October 2005*. London: HMSO.

———. 2008. *The Path to Citizenship*. Available at www.ukba.homeoffice.gov.uk/sitecontents/documents/aboutus/consultations/closedconsultations/pathtocitizenship/pathtocitizenship? (accessed 20 June 2012).

———. 2011. *Family Migration: A Consultation*. London: HMSO.

———. 2013. *Life in the United Kingdom: A Guide for New Residents*. London: HMSO.

Honig, Bonnie. 2001. *Democracy and the Foreigner*. Princeton, NJ: Princeton University Press.

———. 2009. *Emergency Politics: Paradox, Law, Democracy*. Princeton, NJ: Princeton University Press.

Honohan, Iseult. 2010. *The Theory and Practice of Jus Soli*. Florence: EUDO Citizenship Observatory, European University Institute.

Horowitz, Donald L. 1985. *Ethnic Groups in Conflict*. Berkeley: University of California Press.

House of Commons. 2005. *Terrorism and Community Relations—Sixth Report of Session 2004–2005*. Vol. 1, 6 April. London: House of Commons.

Howard, Marc Morjé. 2006. "Comparative Citizenship: An Agenda for Cross-national Research." *Perspectives on Politics* 4 (3): 443–55.

———. 2009. *The Politics of Citizenship in Europe*. Cambridge: Cambridge University Press.

———. 2010. "The Impact of the Far Right on Citizenship Policy in Europe: Explaining Continuity and Change." *Journal of Ethnic and Migration Studies* 36 (5): 735–51.

Human Rights Watch. 2005. "Setting an Example? Counter-terrorism Measures in Spain." *Human Rights Watch* 17 (1): 1–65. Available at http://www.hrw.org/sites/default/files/reports/spain0105.pdf (accessed 3 July 2014).

———. 2008. *Stuck in a Revolving Door: Iraqis and Other Asylum Seekers and Migrants at the Greece/Turkey Entrance to the European Union*. Available at www.hrw.org/en/node/76211/section/1.

———. 2012. "The Root of Humiliation: Abusive Identity Checks in France." Available at https://www.hrw.org/sites/default/files/reports/france0112ForUpload.pdf (accessed 18 September 2014).

Hume, David. 1754. *Treatises on Several Subjects*. Vol. 4. London: A. Millar.

Huntington, Samuel. 1996. *The Clash of Civilizations*. New York: Simon and Schuster.

———. 2004. *Who Are We?* New York: Simon & Schuster.

Hussain, Dilwar. 2011. "Secularism and Islam." European Muslim Network, 25 May. Available at http://www.euro-muslims.eu/#/articles/religious-public-sphere/religious_and_public_sphere_1 (accessed 21 June 2012).

Ignatieff, Michael. 2004. *The Lesser Evil: Political Ethics in an Age of Terror.* Princeton, NJ: Princeton University Press.

Inda, Jonathan. 2006. *Targeting Immigrants: Government, Technology and Ethics.* Oxford: Blackwell.

Inglehart, Ronald, and Christian Welzel. 2005. *Modernization, Cultural Change, and Democracy: The Human Development Sequence.* Cambridge: Cambridge University Press.

————, and Pippa Norris. 2009. "Muslim Integration into Western Cultures: Between Origins and Destinations." Faculty Research Working Paper Series RWP09-007, March. Cambridge, MA: Kennedy School of Government, Harvard University.

Ireland, Patrick. 2004. *Becoming Europe: Immigration, Integration and the Welfare State.* Pittsburgh, PA: University of Pittsburgh Press.

————. 2010. "Security and/or Participation: On the Need to Reconcile Differing Conceptions of Migrant Integration." In Chebel d'Appollonia and Reich 2010, pp. 20–39.

Isin, Engin F., and Peter Nyers. 2014. "Introduction: Globalizing Citizenship Studies." In *Routledge Handbook of Global Citizenship Studies,* ed. Engin F. Isin and Peter Nyers, pp. 1–11. New York: Routledge.

Israel, Jonathan. 2006. *Enlightenment Contested: Philosophy, Modernity, and the Emancipation of Man 1670–1752.* Oxford: Oxford University Press.

Jabri, Vivienne. 2007. *War and the Transformation of Global Politics.* Basingstoke, U.K.: Palgrave.

Jacobson, David. 1996. *Rights across Borders: Immigration and the Decline of Citizenship.* Baltimore: Johns Hopkins University Press.

Jacoby, Tim. 2010. "The 'Muslim Menace,' Violence and the De-politising Elements of the New Culturalism." *Journal of Muslim Minority Affairs* 30 (2): 167–81.

Janoski, Thomas. 2010. *The Ironies of Citizenship: Naturalization and Integration in Industrialized Countries.* New York: Cambridge University Press.

Jenkins, Philip. 2007. *God's Continent: Christianity, Islam, and Europe's Religious Crisis.* Oxford: Oxford University Press.

Jessen, Frank, and Ulrich von Wilamowitz-Moellendorff. 2006. *Das Kopftuch. Die Entschleierung eines Symbols?* Sankt Augustin, Germany: Konrad Adenauer Stiftung.

Jonker, Gerdien. 2000. "Islamic Television 'Made in Berlin.'" In Dassetto 2000, pp. 265–80.

————. 2006. "Islamist or Pietist? Muslim Responses to the German Security Framework." In Jonker and Amiraux 2006, pp. 123–50.

————, and Valérie Amiraux, eds. 2006. *Politics of Visibility: Young Muslims in European Public Spaces.* Bielefeld, Germany: Transcript.

Joppke, Christian. 1996. "Multiculturalism and Immigration: A Comparison of the United States, Germany, and Great Britain." *Theory and Society* 25 (4): 449–500.

————. 1998. "Why Liberal States Accept Unwanted Immigration." *World Politics* 50 (2): 266–93.

————. 2001. "The Legal-domestic Sources of Immigrant Rights: The United States, Germany, and the European Union." *Comparative Political Studies* 34 (4): 339–66.

————. 2004. "The Retreat of Multiculturalism in the Liberal State: Theory and Policy." *British Journal of Sociology* 55 (2): 237–57.

————. 2009. *Veil: Mirror of Identity.* Cambridge: Polity.

————. 2010. *Citizenship and Immigration.* Cambridge: Polity.

————. 2011. "European Immigration Policies: Between Stemming and Soliciting Still." In *Developments in European Politics,* ed. Erik Jones et al., pp. 220–40. New York: Palgrave.

————, and Ewa Morawska. 2003. "Integrating Immigrants in Liberal Nation-states: Policies and Practices." In *Toward Assimilation and Citizenship: Immigrants in Liberal Nation-states,* ed. C. Joppke and Ewa Moawska, pp. 1–36. New York: Palgrave.

————, and John Torpey. 2013. *Legal Integration of Islam: A Transatlantic Perspective.* Cambridge, MA: Harvard University Press.

Kaddor, Lamya. 2010. "Warum das islamische Kopftuch obsolet geworden ist: Eine theologische Untersuchung anhand einschlägiger Quellen." In *Islamverherrlichung. Wenn die Kritik zum Tabu wird,* ed. Thorsten Schneiders, pp. 131–58. Wiesbaden, Germany: VS Verlag für Sozialwissenschaften.

Kagan, Robert. 2004. *Of Paradise and Power: America and Europe in the New World Order.* New York: Vintage.

Kant, Immanuel. 1838. *Sämtliche Werke. Religion innerhalb der Grenzen der blossen Vernunft und Streit der Facultäten.* Vol. 10. Ed. Karl Rosenkranz. Leipzig, Germany: Leopold Voss.

————. 1949. *The Philosophy of Kant: Immanuel Kant's Moral and Political Writings.* Trans. Carl J. Friedrich. New York: Modern Library.

————. 1991. *Kant: Political Writings.* Ed. Hans Reiss. Cambridge: Cambridge University Press.

————. 1996. *Practical Philosophy.* Trans. M. J. Gregor. Cambridge: Cambridge University Press.

————. 1998. *Religion within the Boundaries of Mere Reason.* Trans. Allen Wood and George Di Giovanni. Cambridge: Cambridge University Press.

Karakaşoğlu-Aydin, Yasemin. 2000. *Muslimische Religiosität und Erziehungsvorstellungen: eine Untersuchung bei türkischen Pädagogikstudentinnen in Deutschland.* Frankfurt: IKO Verlag für Interkulturelle Kommunikation.

Karakayali, Serhat. 2008. *Gespenster der Migration. Zur Genealogie der illegaler Einwanderung in der Bundesrepublik Deutschland.* Bielefeld, Germany: Transcript.

Karich, Imane. 2007. "Economic Development of Muslim Communities." In Amghar, Boubekeur, and Emerson 2007, pp. 62–76.

Kastoryano, Riva. 2006. "French Secularism and Islam: France's Headscarf Affair." In Modood, Triandafyllidou, and Zapata-Barrero 2006, pp. 57–69.

Katzenstein, Peter. 2003. "Same War—Different Views: Germany, Japan and Counterterrorism." *International Organization* 57 (4): 731–60.

Kawar, Leila. 2015. *Contesting Immigration Policy in Court: Legal Activism and Its Radiating Effects in the United States and France.* Cambridge: Cambridge University Press.

Kaya, Ayhan. 2012. *Islam, Migration and Integration: The Age of Securitisation.* Basingstoke, UK: Palgrave.

Keenan, Alan. 2003. *Democracy in Question: Democratic Openness in a Time of Political Closure.* Stanford, CA: Stanford University Press.

Kegley, Charles W. 2003. *The New Global Terrorism: Characteristics, Causes, Controls*. Upper Saddle River, NJ: Prentice Hall.

Kelek, Necla. 2005. *Die fremde Braut: Ein Bericht aus dem Innern des türkischen Lebens in Deutschland*. Cologne: Kiepenheuer and Witsch.

———. 2007. "Die Stereotype des Mr. Buruma." In *Islam in Europa: Eine Internationale Debatte*, ed. Thierry Chervel and Anja Seeliger, pp. 110–16. Frankfurt: Suhrkamp.

Keohane, Daniel. 2008. "The Absent Friend: EU Foreign Policy and Counter-terrorism." *Journal of Common Market Studies* 46 (1): 125–46.

Kepel, Giles. 1997. *Allah in the West: Islamic Movements in America and Europe*. Stanford, CA: Stanford University Press.

———. 1999. *Allah in the West: Islamic Movements in America and Europe (Mestizo Spaces)*. Paris: Broché.

———. 2004. *The War for Muslim Minds: Islam and the West*. Cambridge, MA: Harvard University Press.

Kersten, Carool. 2011. *Cosmopolitans and Heretics: New Muslim Intellectuals and the Study of Islam*. New York: Columbia University Press.

Kezjar, Barbara. 2009. "Dual Citizenship as an Element of the Integration Process in Receiving Countries: The Case of Slovenia." In Guild, Groenendijk, and Carrera 2009, pp. 131–47.

Khosravi, Shahram. 2012. "An Ethnography of Migrant 'Illegality' in Sweden: Included yet Excepted?" In van den Anke and van Liempt 2012, pp. 46–66.

Khosrokhavar, Farhad. 2010. "The Muslim Brotherhood in France." In Rubin 2010, pp. 137–48.

Kiliç, Sevgi, Sawitri Saharso, and Birgit Sauer. 2008. "Introduction—The VEIL: Debating Citizenship, Gender and Religious Diversity." *Social Politics: International Studies in Gender, State and Society* 15 (4): 397–410.

Kiliçarslan, Ayten. 2014. "Zum Kopftuch als Thema in der deutschen Öffentlichkeit." *Deutsche Islam Konferenz Magazin Muslime in Deutschland*. Available at http://www.deutsche-islam-konferenz.de/DIK/DE/Magazin/MedienPolitik/Diskussion/Kopftuch/Kommentare/kommentar-ayten-kilicarslan-inhalt.html (accessed 29 October 2014).

King, Russell. 2000. "Southern Europe in the Changing Global Map of Migration." In *Eldorado or Fortress? Migration in Southern Europe*, ed. Russell King, Gabriella Lazaridis, and Charalambos Tsardanidis, pp. 3–26. London: Macmillan.

Kintzler, Catherine. 1996. *La république en questions*. Paris: Minerve.

Kirschner, Emil, and James Sperling. 2010. *National Security Cultures: Patterns of Global Governance*. London: Routledge.

Klausen, Jytte. 2005. *The Islamic Challenge*. Oxford: Oxford University Press.

———. 2010. "British Counter-terrorism after 7/7: Adapting Community Policing to the Fight against Domestic Terrorism." In Bleich 2010a, pp. 50–67.

Klekowski von Koppenfels, Amanda. 2013. "Testing for Integration and Belonging or a New Barrier to Entry? Citizenship Tests in the United States and Germany." In Ataç and Rosenberger 2013, pp. 135–54.

Klinkhammer, Gritt. 2000. *Moderne Formen islamischer Lebensführung. Eine qualitative empirische Untersuchung zur Religiosität sunnitisch geprägter Türkinnen in Deutschland*. Marburg, Germany: Diagonal Verlag.

Kneip, Sascha. 2008. "Verfeassungsgerichtbarkeit im Vergleich." In *Die EU-Staaten im Vergleich: Strukturen, Prozesse, Politikinhalte,* ed. Oscar Gabriel and Sabine Krop, pp. 631–55. Wiesbaden, Germany: VS Verlag für Sozialwissenschaften.

Koenig, Matthias. 2007. "Europeanising the Governance of Religious Diversity." *Journal of Ethnic and Migration Studies* 33 (6): 911–32.

Kohn, Hans. 1946. *The Idea of Nationalism.* New York: Macmillan.

———. 1955. *Nationalism: Its Meaning and History.* Princeton, NJ: Princeton University Press.

Konsta, Anna-Maria, and Gabriella Lazaridis. 2010. "Civic Stratification, 'Plastic' Citizenship and 'Plastic Subjectivities' in Greek Immigration Policy." *Journal of International Migration and Integration* 11 (4): 365–82.

Koopmans, Ruud. 1999. "Germany and Its Immigrants: An Ambivalent Relationship." *Journal of Ethnic and Migration Studies* 25 (4): 627–47.

———, Ines Michalowski, and Stine Waibel. 2012. "Citizenship Rights for Immigrants: National Political Processes and Cross-national Convergence in Western Europe, 1980–2008." *American Journal of Sociology* 117 (4): 1202–45.

———, Paul Statham, Marco Guigni, and Florence Passy. 2005. *Contested Citizenship: Immigration and Cultural Diversity in Europe.* Minneapolis: University of Minnesota Press.

Korteweg, Anna C., and Gökçe Yurdakul. 2014. *The Headscarf Debates: Conflicts of National Belonging.* Stanford, CA: Stanford University Press.

Korkut, Umut et al., eds. 2013. *The Discourses and Politics of Immigration in Europe.* New York: Palgrave.

Koser, K. 2008. "Why Migrant Smuggling Pays." *International Migration* 46 (2): 3–26.

Kosic Ankica, and Karen Phalet. 2006. "Ethnic Categorization of Immigrants: The Role of Prejudice, Perceived Acculturation Strategies and Group Size." *International Journal of Intercultural Relations* 30: 769–82.

Kraler, Albert. 2010. *Civic Stratification, Gender and Family Migration Policies in Europe.* Vienna: ICMPD.

Krämer, Gudrun. 2011. "Fighting Islamophobia with Rational Arguments." *Qantara.de* (4 February). Available at http://www.qantara.de/webcom/show_article.php?wc_c=478&wc_id=1155 (accessed 14 June 2012).

Kriese, Hanspeter, Ruud Koopmans, Jan Willem Duyvendak, and Marco Giugni. 1995. *New Social Movements in Western Europe: A Comparative Analysis.* Minneapolis: University of Minnesota Press.

Kristeva, Julia. 1991. *Strangers to Ourselves.* Trans. Leon Roudiez. New York: Columbia University Press.

Kuisma, Mikko. 2013. "'Good' and 'Bad' Immigrants: The Economic Nationalism of the True Finns' Immigration Discourse." In Korkut et al. 2013, pp. 93–108.

Kymlicka, Will. 1995. *Multicultural Citizenship: A Liberal Theory of Minority Rights.* Oxford: Oxford University Press.

———. 2010. "The Rise and Fall of Multiculturalism? New Debates on Inclusion and Accommodation in Diverse Societies." In Vertovec and Wessendorf 2010, pp. 32–49.

———, and Wayne Norman. 2000. "Citizenship in Culturally Diverse Societies: Issues, Contexts, Concepts." In *Citizenship in Diverse Societies,* ed. Will Kymlicka and Wayne Norman, pp. 1–44. Oxford: Oxford University Press.

Laborde, Cécile. 2002. "From Constitutional to Civic Patriotism." *British Journal of Political Science* 32 (4): 591–612.

———. 2008. *Critical Republicanism: The Hijab Controversy and Political Philosophy.* Oxford: Oxford University Press.

Lahav, Gallya. 2004. *Immigration and Politics in the New Europe: Reinventing Borders.* Cambridge: Cambridge University Press.

Lalani, Mumtaz. 2011. *Stop the Abuse.* London: Kalayaan.

Lamont, Michele. 2000. *The Dignity of Working Men: Morality and the Boundaries of Race, Class, and Immigration.* Cambridge, MA: Harvard University Press.

Landau, Jacob. 1990. *The Politics of Pan-Islam.* Oxford: Oxford University Press.

Laurence, Jonathan. 2012. *The Emancipation of Europe's Muslims: The State's Role in Minority Integration.* Princeton, NJ: Princeton University Press.

Lean, Nathan. 2012. *The Islamophobia Industry: How the Right Manufactures Fear of Muslims.* London: Pluto Press.

Lefort, Claude. 1988. *Democracy and Political Theory.* Minneapolis: University of Minnesota Press.

Leiken, Robert S. 2005. "Europe's Angry Muslims." *Foreign Affairs* 84 (4): 120–35.

———. 2012. *Europe's Angry Muslims: The Revolt of the Second Generation.* Oxford: Oxford University Press.

Lepoutre, David. 1997. *Coeur de Banlieue.* Paris: Odile Jacob.

Levi, Margaret. 2013. "Can Nations Succeed?" *Perspectives on Politics* 11 (1): 187–92.

LeVine, Mark. 2003. "'Human Nationalisms' versus 'Inhuman Globalisms': Cultural Economies of Globalisation and the Re-Imagining of Muslim Identities in Europe and the Middle East." In Allievi and Nielsen 2003, pp. 78–126.

Lévi-Straus, Claude. 1985. *The View from Afar.* Trans. Joachim Neugroschel and Phoebe Hoss. New York: Basic Books.

Lewis, Bernard. 2002. *What Went Wrong? Western Impact and Middle Eastern Response.* New York: Oxford University Press.

Lewis, Philip. 1994. *Islamic Britain: Religion, Politics and Identity. Bradford in the 1990s.* London: Tauris.

———. 2006. "From Seclusion to Inclusion: British *'Ulama* and the Politics of Social Visibility." In Jonker and Amiraux 2006, pp. 169–90.

Limbach, Jutta. 2007. "Making Multiculturalism Work." signandsight.com, 17 August. Available at http://www.signandsight.com/features/313.html.

Linklater, Andrew. 1998. *The Transformation of Political Community: Ethical Foundations of a Post-Westphalian Era.* Cambridge: Polity.

Locke, John. 1980. *Second Treatise of Government.* Indianapolis, IN: Hackett.

Lord Bingham of Cornhill. 2006. *Opinions of the Lords of Appeal.* UKHL 15.

Löwenheim, Oded, and Orit Gazit. 2009. "Power and Examination: A Critique of Citizenship Tests." *Security Dialogue* 40 (2): 145–67.

Lowi, Theodore. 1969. *The End of Liberalism.* New York: W. W. Norton.

Lucasson, Leo. 2005. *The Immigrant Threat: the Integration of Old and New Migrants in Western Europe since 1890.* Urbana: University of Illinois Press.

Lynch, Orla. 2013. "British Muslim Youth: Radicalisation, Terrorism and the Construction of the 'Other.'" *Critical Studies on Terrorism* 6 (2): 641–61.

————, and Christopher Ryder. 2012. "Deadliness, Organisational Change and Suicide Attacks: Understanding the Assumptions Inherent in the Use of the Term 'New Terrorism.'" *Critical Studies on Terrorism* 5 (2): 257–75.

Lyotard, Jean-François. 1984. *The Postmodern Condition: A Report on Knowledge.* Trans. G. Bennington and B. Massumi. Minneapolis: University of Minnesota Press.

Maas, Willem. 2007. *Creating European Citizens.* Lanham, MD: Rowman and Littlefield.

————. 2013a. "Varieties of Multilevel Citizenship." In Maas 2013b, pp. 1–24.

————, ed. 2013b. *Multilevel Citizenship.* Philadelphia: University of Pennsylvania Press.

————. 2013c. "Equality and the Free Movement of People: Citizenship and Internal Migration." In *Democratic Citizenship and the Free Movement of People,* ed. Willem Maas, pp. 9–30. Leiden, Netherlands: Martinus Nijhoff.

Macedo, Stephen. 2000. *Diversity and Distrust: Civic Education in a Multicultural Democracy.* Cambridge, MA: Harvard University Press.

Macey, Marie. 1999. "Class, Gender and Religious Influences on Changing Patterns of Pakistani Muslim Male Violence in Bradford." *Ethnic and Racial Studies* 22 (5): 845–66.

MacIntyre, Alasdair. 1984. *After Virtue.* Notre Dame, IN: University of Notre Dame Press.

Maistre, Joseph de. 1884–1887. *Euvres completes de J. de Maistre.* 14 vols. Lyon: Vitte et Perrussel.

————. 1989. "Considérations sur la France." In *Écrits sur la Révolution.* Paris: Presses universitaires de France.

Majid, Anouar. 2000. *Unveiling Traditions: Postcolonial Islam in a Polycentric World.* Durham, NC: Duke University Press.

Mandaville, Peter. 2000. "Information Technology and the Changing Boundaries of European Islam." In Dassetto 2000, pp. 281–94.

————. 2003. "Towards a Critical Islam: European Muslims and the Changing Boundaries of Transnational Religious Discourse." In Allievi and Nielsen 2003, pp. 127–45.

————. 2010. "Muslim Transnationality and State Responses in Europe and the UK after 9/11: Political Community, Ideology and Authority." In Bleich 2010a, pp. 138–53.

————. 2014. *Islam and Politics.* New York: Routledge.

Mandel, Ruth. 2008. *Cosmopolitan Anxieties: Turkish Challenges to Citizenship and Belonging in Germany.* Durham, NC: Duke University Press.

Mann, Michael. 1987. "Ruling Class Strategies and Citizenship." *Sociology* 21 (3): 339–54.

Mantouvalou, Virginia. 2014. "Workers without Rights as Citizens at the Margins." In *The Margins of Citizenship,* ed. Philip Cook and Jonathan Seglow, pp. 48–64. New York: Routledge.

March, James, and Johan Olsen. 1989. *Rediscovering Institutions: The Organizational Basis of Politics.* New York: Free Press.

Marchand, René. 2013. *Reconquista ou mort de l'Europe: L'enjou de la guerre islamique.* Paris: Editions Riposte Laique.

Marcouch, Ahmend. 2008. *Mijn vader kwam te voet.* Amsterdam: Waterlandstichting.

Maréchal, Brigitte (2008). *The Muslim Brothers in Europe: Roots and Discourse.* Leiden: Brill.

Maroukis, Thanos. 2010. "Irregular Migration in Greece: Size and Features, Causes and Discourses." In Triandafyllidou 2010e, pp. 93–114.

Marshall, T. H. 1950. *Citizenship and Social Class*. Cambridge: Cambridge University Press.

Marty, Martin. 2005. *When Faiths Collide*. Malden: Blackwell.

Marx, Anthony. 2003. *Faith in Nation: Exclusionary Origins of Nationalism*. Princeton, NJ: Princeton University Press.

Mas, Ruth. 2006. "Compelling the Muslim Subject. Memory as Post-colonial Violence and the Public Performativity of 'Secular and Cultural Islam.'" *The Muslim World* 96 (4): 585–616.

Mauro, Mario. 2004. *L'Europa sarà cristiana o non sarà*. Milan: Spirali.

Maussen, Marcel. 2009. *Constructing Mosques: The Governance of Islam in France and the Netherlands*. Amsterdam: Amsterdam School for Social Science Research.

Mavelli, Luca. 2012. *Europe's Encounter with Islam: The Secular and Postsecular*. London: Routledge.

Mehta, Jal. 2011. "The Varied Roles of Ideas in Politics." In *Ideas and Politics in Social Science Research*, ed. Daniel Béland and Robert Henry Cox, pp. 23–46. Oxford: Oxford University Press.

Meijer, Roel. 2013. "Political Islam According to the Dutch." In Vidino 2013, pp. 68–85.

———, and Edwin Bakker, eds. 2012. *The Muslim Brotherhood in Europe*. New York: Columbia University Press.

Meining, Stefan. 2012. "The Islamic Community in Germany: An Organization under Observation." In Meijer and Bakker 2012a, pp. 209–33.

Menz, George. 2009. *The Political Economy of Managed Migration: Nonstate Actors, Europeanization, and the Politics of Designing Migration Policies*. Oxford: Oxford University Press.

Merleau-Ponty, Maurice. 1962. *Phenomenology of Perception*. Trans. Colin Smith. London: Routledge and Kegan Paul.

Messina, Anthony. 2007. *The Logics and Politics of Post-WWII Migration to Western Europe*. Cambridge: Cambridge University Press.

Metcalf, Barbara, ed. 1996. *Making Muslim Space in North America and Europe*. Berkeley: University of California Press.

Metroscopia. 2006, November. *La Comunidad Musulman en España*. Madrid: Ministerio del Interior.

Meyer, Karl E., and Shareen Blair Brysac. 2012. *Pax Ethnica: Where and How Diversity Succeeds*. New York: Public Affairs.

Michalowski, Ines. 2009. "Citizenship Tests in Five Countries—An Expression of Political Liberalism?" Discussion Paper SP IV 2009-702. Berlin: Wissenschaftszentrum Berlin für Sozialforsching.

———. 2014. "Legitimizing Host Country Institutions: A Comparative Analysis of the Content of Civic Education Courses in France and Germany." In Bowen et al. 2014a, pp. 164–88.

Midtbøen, Arnfinn. 2014. "The Invisible Second Generation? Statistical Discrimination and Immigrant Stereotypes in Employment Processes in Norway." *Journal of Ethnic and Migration Studies* 40 (10): 1657–75.

Mill, John Stuart. 1975. *Three Essays: On Liberty, Representative Government, The Subjection of Women*. Oxford: Oxford University Press.

Miller, David. 1989. "In What Sense Must Socialism Be Communitarian?" *Social Philosophy and Policy* 6(2): 51–73.

————. 1992. "Community and Citizenship." In *Communitarianism and Individualism,* ed. Shlomo Avineri and Avner de Shalit, pp. 85–100. Oxford: Oxford University Press.

————. 1995. *On Nationality.* Oxford: Clarendon.

————. 2000. *Citizenship and National Identity.* Cambridge: Polity.

Millière, Guy. 2004. *Qui a peur de l'islam! La dèmocratie est-elle soluble dans l'islam?* Paris: Editions Michalon.

Ministerium für Schule und Weiterbildung NRW (2010). "Demokratie – Islam – Islamismus. Andi2: Handreichung füden Politikunterricht." Dusseldorf: Ministerium für Schule und Weiterbildung.

Modood, Tariq. 1990. "British Asian Muslims and the Rushdie Affair." *Political Quarterly* 61 (2): 143–60.

————. 1994. "Establishment, Multiculturalism and British Citizenship." *Political Quarterly* 65 (1): 53–73.

————. 2003. *Multiculturalism, Muslims and the British State.* London: British Association for the Study of Religion.

————. 2007. *Multiculturalism.* Oxford: Polity.

————. 2009. "Muslims, Religious Equality and Secularism." In *Secularism, Religion and Multicultural Citizenship,* ed. Geoffrey Brahm Levey and Tariq Modood, pp. 164–185. Cambridge: Cambridge University Press.

————, Anna Triandafyllidou, and Ricard Zapata-Barrero, eds. 2006. *Multiculturalism, Muslims and Citizenship: A European Approach.* London: Routledge.

————, and Fauzia Ahmad. 2007. "British Muslim Perspectives on Multiculturalism." *Theory, Culture and Society* 24 (2): 186–99.

Mohr, Irka-Christin. 2006. *Islamischer Religionsunterricht in Europe: Lehrtexte als Instrumente muslimischer Selbstverortung im Vergleich.* Bielefeld, Germany: Transcript.

Money, Jeannette. 1999. *Fences and Neighbors: The Political Geography of Immigration Control.* Ithaca, NY: Cornell University Press.

Monsma, Stephen, and Christopher Soper. 2009. *The Challenge of Pluralism: Church and State in Five Democracies.* Lanham, MD: Rowman and Littlefield.

Montesquieu, Charles-Louis. 1950–1955. *De l'esprit des lois.* Reprinted in *Oeuvres completes de Montesquieu,* ed. André Masson. 3 vols. Paris: Nagel.

————. 1989. *The Spirit of the Laws.* Ed. Anne Cohler, Basia Miller, and Harold Stone. Cambridge: Cambridge University Press.

Moore, Kerry, Paul Mason, and Justin Lewis. 2008. "Images of Islam in the UK: The Representation of British Muslims in the National Print News Media 2000–2008." *Cardiff School of Journalism, Media and Cultural Studies Report* (7 July).

Moors, Anneliese. 2009. "The Dutch and the Face-Veil: The Politics of Discomfort." *Social Anthropology* 17 (4): 393–408.

Morgan, George, and Scott Poynting, eds. 2012a. *Global Islamophobia: Muslims and Moral Panic in the West.* Burlington, VT: Ashgate.

————, and Scott Poynting. 2012b. "Introduction: The Transnational Folk Devil." In Morgan and Poynting 2012a, pp. 1–14.

Mouffe, Chantal. 2000. *The Democratic Paradox.* London: Verso.

Mourão Permoser, Julia. 2013. "The *Integrationsvereinbarung* in Austria: Exclusion in the Name of Integration?" In Ataç and Rosenberger 2013, pp. 155–76.

Mouritsen, Per. 2006. "The Particular Universalism of a Nordic Civic Nation: Common Values, State Religion and Islam in Danish Political Culture." In Modood, Triandafyllidou, and Zapata-Barrero 2006, pp. 70–93.

———. 2009. "The Culture of Citizenship. A Reflection on Civic Integration in Europe." In *Citizenship Policies in an Age of Diversity: Europe at the Crossroads,* ed. Ricard Zapata-Barrero, pp. 23–35. Barcelona: CIDOB.

Muchielli, Laurent. 2005. *Scandale des "tournantes."* Paris: La Découverte.

Mudde, Cas. 2012. *The Relationship between Immigration and Nativism in Europe and North America.* Washington, DC: Migration Policy Institute.

Müller, Jan Werner. 2007. *Constitutional Patriotism.* Princeton, NJ: Princeton University Press.

"Multiculturalism Policy Index at Queens University: Findings." 2012. Multiculturalism Policies in Contemporary Democracies. Available at www.queensu.ca/mcp/Findings.html (accessed 12 June 2012).

Munck, Ronaldo, Carl Ulrik Schierup, and Raúl Delgado Wise. 2012. "Migration, Work, and Citizenship in the New World Order." In *Migration, Work and Citizenship in the New Global Order,* ed. Ronaldo Munck, Carl Ulrik Schierup, and Raúl Delgado Wise, pp. 1–12. London: Routledge.

Muñoz, Gema Martín. 1994. "El Islam en España Hoy." In *Hablar y Dejar Hablar (Sobre racism y xenophobia),* ed. Luisa Martín Rojo et al., pp. 212–27. Madrid: Universidad Autónomoma de Madrid.

———, Francisco Javier Garcia Castaño, Ana López Sala, and Rafael Crespo. 2003. *Marroquies en España, Estudio sobre su integración.* Madrid: Fundación Repsol.

Murphy, Michael. 2012. *Multiculturalism: A Critical Introduction.* New York: Routledge.

Muslim Council of Britain. 2005. "British Muslims Utterly Condemn Acts of Terrorism." 7 July. Available at www.mcb.org.uk/media/presstext.php?ann_id=30 (accessed 12 June 2014).

———. 2007. "Our Stand on Multiculturalism, Citizenship, Extremism and Expectations from the Commission of Integration and Cohesion." January. Available at www.mcb.org.uk/downloads/MCB%20ReDoc%20Briefing%20Paper%20.

Nancy, Jean-Luc. 1991. *The Inoperative Community.* Trans. P. Connor et al. Minneapolis: University of Minnesota Press.

———. 2000. *Being Singular Plural.* Trans. R. Richardson and A. O'Byrne. Stanford, CA: Stanford University Press.

Nandy, Ashis. 1988. *The Intimate Enemy: Loss and Recovery of Self under Colonialism.* Delhi: Oxford University Press.

Navarro, Laura. 2008. *Contra el Islam. La visión deformada del mundo árabe en Occidente.* Cordoba: Almuzara.

Neal, Andrew. 2010. *Exceptionalism and the Politics of Counter-terrorism: Liberty, Security and the War on Terror.* London: Routledge.

Netherlands Ministry of the Interior and Kingdom Relations. 2007. *Polarisation and Radicalisation: Action Plan 2002–2011.* The Hague: Ministry of the Interior and Kingdom Relations.

Neveu, Catherine. 2013. "Sites of Citizenship, Politics of Scales." In Maas 2013b, pp. 203–12.

Nielsen, Jørgen. 1999. *Toward a European Islam.* New York: St. Martin's.

———. 2003. "Transnational Islam and the Integration of Islam in Europe." In Allievi and Nielsen 2003, pp. 28–51.

————, ed. 2009. *Yearbook of Muslims in Europe.* Vol. 1. Leiden, Netherlands: Brill.

Nietzsche, Friedrich. 1954. "On Truth and Lies in a Non-moral Sense." In *The Portable Nietzsche,* ed. Walter Kaufmann. New York: Viking.

————. 1966. *Beyond Good and Evil.* New York: Vintage.

————. 1967–1977. *Sämtliche Werke. Kritische Gesamtausgabe.* Ed. Giorgio Colli and Mazzino Montinari. Berlin: de Gruyter.

————. 1968. *The Will to Power.* Trans. Walter Kaufmann and R. J. Hollingdale. New York: Vintage Books.

————. 1974. *The Gay Science.* Trans. Walter Kaufmann. New York: Vintage.

Nordmann, Charlotte, and Jérôme Vidal. 2004. "La République à l'épreuve des discriminations." In *Le foulard islamique en questions,* ed. C. Nordmann, pp. 1–11. Paris: Editions Amsterdam.

Norris, Pippa. 2005. *Radical Right: Voters and Parties in the Electoral Market.* Cambridge: Cambridge University Press.

Norton, Anne. 2013. *On the Muslim Question.* Princeton, NJ: Princeton University Press.

Nozick, Robert. 1974. *Anarchy, State, and Utopia.* New York: Basic Books.

Nyiri, Zsolt. 2010. "The Clash of Perceptions: Comparison of Views among Muslims in Paris, London, and Berlin with Those among the General Public." In Chebel d'Appollonia and Reich 2010, pp. 98–113.

Obin, Jean Pierre. 2004. *Les signes et manifestations d'appartenance religieuse dans les établissements scolaires.* Paris: Ministère de l'education nationale.

O'Brien, Peter. 1996. *Beyond the Swastika.* London: Routledge.

————. 2009. "Making (Normative) Sense of the Headscarf Debate in Europe." *German Politics and Society* 27 (3): 50–76.

————. 2013a. "Islamophobia, Euro-Islam, Islamism and Post-Islamism: Changing Patterns of Secularism in Europe." *American Journal of the Islamic Social Sciences* 30 (3): 59–93.

————. 2013b. "Clashes within Western Civilization: Debating Citizenship for European Muslims." *Migration Studies* 1 (2): 131–55.

————. 2015. "Postmodern Politics: Manipulating Images of Islam in Contemporary Europe." In *Muhammad in the Digital Age,* ed. Ruqayya J. Khan, pp. 83–105. Austin: University of Texas Press.

Odmalm, Pontus. 2014. *The Party Politics of the EU and Immigration.* Houndmills: Palgrave.

Oestreich, Heide. 2004. *Der Kopftuch-Streit.* Frankfurt: Brandes und Apsel.

O'Malley, Pat. 1996. "Risk and Responsibility." In *Foucault and Political Reason: Liberalism, Neo-liberalism and Rationalities of Government,* ed. Andrew Barry, Thomas Osborne, and Nikolas Rose, pp. 189–208. Chicago: University of Chicago Press.

Ong, Aihwa. 1999. *Flexible Citizenship: The Cultural Logics of Transnationality.* Durham, NC: Duke University Press.

openDemocracy. 2004. "The War for Muslim Minds: An Interview with Gilles Kepel." 11 November. Available at http://www.opendemocracy.net/debates/article-5-57-2216.jsp (accessed 13 March 2014).

Open Society Institute. 2002. *Monitoring the EU Accession Process: Minority Protection Volume II—Case Studies in Selected Member States.* Budapest: Open Society Institute.

————. 2010. *Muslims in Europe: A Report on 11 EU Cities*. Budapest: Open Society Institute.

Orgad, Liav. 2010. "Illiberal Liberalism." *American Journal of Comparative Law* 58 (1): 53–106.

Organisation for Economic Cooperation and Development. 2011. *International Migration Outlook 2011*. Paris: OECD.

————. 2013. *International Migration Outlook 2013*. Paris: OECD.

Organisation for Security and Cooperation in Europe. 2007. *Countering Terrorism, Protecting Human Rights*. Warsaw: OSCE Office for Democratic Institutions and Human Rights.

Otterbeck, Jonas. 2000. "Local Islamic Universalism: Analyses of an Islamic Journal in Sweden." In Dassetto 2000, pp. 247–66.

————. 2010. "Sweden: Cooperation and Conflict." In Triandafyllidou 2010a, pp. 103–20.

Parekh, Bhikhu. 1999. "A Varied Moral World." In *Is Multiculturalism Bad for Women?* ed. Susan Moller-Okin, pp. 69–75. Princeton, NJ: Princeton University Press.

————. 2000. *Rethinking Multiculturalism: Cultural Diversity and Political Theory*. Cambridge, MA: Harvard University Press.

————. 2008. *A New Politics of Identity: Political Principles for an Interdependent World*. New York: Palgrave.

Pargeter, Alison. 2008. *The New Frontier of Jihad: Radical Islam in Europe*. Philadelphia: University of Pennsylvania Press.

Parray, Tauseef Ahmad. 2012. "The Legal Methodology of '*Fiqh al-Aqalliyyat*' and Its Critics: An Analytical Study." *Journal of Muslim Minority Affairs* 32 (1): 88–107.

Parvez, Zahid. 2000. *Building a New Society: An Islamic Approach to Social Change*. London: Revival Publications.

Patel, Ismail Adam. 2007. "The Scales for Defining Islamic Political Radicalism." In Abbas 2007, pp. 42–56.

Pędziwiatr, Konrad. 2007. "Muslims in Europe: Demography and Organizations." In Samad and Sen 2007, pp. 26–59.

Pera, Marcello, and Joseph Ratzinger. 2004. *Senza radici. Europa, relativismo, Cristeanesimo, Islam*. Milan: Mondadori.

Peter, Frank. 2006. "Individualization and Religious Authority in Western European Islam." *Islam and Christian-Muslim Relations* 17 (1): 105–18.

————. 2008. "Political Rationalities: Counter-terrorism and Policies on Islam in the United Kingdom and France." In *The Social Life of Anti-terrorism Laws*, ed. Julia M. Eckert, pp. 79–108. Bielefeld, Germany: Transcript.

Peters, Rudolph. 2011. "Dutch Extremist Islamism: Van Gogh's Murderer and his Ideas." In *Jihadi Terrorism and the Radicalisation Challenge*, ed. Rik Coolsaet, pp. 145–60. Farnham: Ashgate.

Peucker, Mario. 2010. "Islamfeindlichkeit—die empirischen Grundlagen." In Schneiders 2010b, pp. 155–66.

Pew Global Attitudes Project. 2006. *The Great Divide: How Westerners and Muslims View Each Other*. Washington, DC: Pew Research Center. Available at Pewglobal. org/reports/display.phpeportID=253.

Pew Research. 2012. "Muslim-Western Tensions Persist." July 21. Available at http://pewresearch.org/pubs/2066/muslims-westerners-christians-jews-islamic-extremism-september-11 (accessed 22 July 2012).

Phillips, Melanie. 2007. *Londonistan*. New York: Encounter Books.

Pickles, Margaret. 1995. "Muslim Immigration Stress in Australia." In *Muslim Minorities in the West*, ed. Ziauddin Sardar, pp. 105–17. London: Grey Seal.

Piela, Anna. 2010. "Muslim Women's Online Discussions of Gender Relations in Islam." *Journal of Muslim Minority Affairs* 30 (3): 425–35.

———. 2012. *Muslim Women Online: Faith and Identity in Virtual Space*. London: Routledge.

Planet, Ana I., and Miguel Hernando de Larramendi. 2013. "Spain and Islamist Movements: From the Victory of the FIS to the Arab Spring." In Vidino 2013, pp. 114–29.

Pocock, John G. A. 1975. *The Machiavellian Moment: Florentine Political Thought and the Atlantic Republican Tradition*. Princeton, NJ: Princeton University Press.

Pollack, Detlef, and Olaf Müller. 2013. *Religionsmonitor: Verstehen was verbindedt—Religiosität und Zusammenhalt in Deutschland*. Gütersloh: Bertelsmann-Stiftung.

Poole, Elizabeth. 2002. *Reporting Islam: Media Representations of British Muslims*. London: I. B. Taurus.

Pope Benedict XVI. 2006. "Faith, Reason and the University: Reflections and Memories." Speech, 12 September, Regensburg. Available at http://w2.vatican.va/content/benedict-xvi/en/speeches/2006/september/documents/hf_ben-xvi_spe_20060912_university-regensburg.html.

Postman, Neil. 1985. *Amusing Ourselves to Death: Public Discourse in the Age of Show Business*. New York: Penguin.

Putnam, Robert. 2007. "E Pluribus Unum: Diversity and Community in the Twenty-first Century." *Scandinavian Political Studies*. 30 (2): 137–74.

al-Qahtani, Shaykh Muhammad Saeed. 1999. *Loyalty and Repudiation*. London: Al-Firdous.

al-Qaradawi, Jusuf. 1999. *The Lawful and the Prohibited in Islam*. Oak Brook, IL: American Trust Publications.

Qureshi, Emran, and Michael A. Sells, eds. 2003a. *The New Crusades: Constructing the Muslim Enemy*. New York: Columbia University Press.

———, and Michael A. Sells. 2003b. "Introduction: Constructing the Muslim Identity." In Qureshi and Sells 2003a, pp. 2–47.

Qutb, Sayyid. 1981. *Milestones*. Cedar Rapids, IA: The Mother Mosque Foundation.

———. 2007. *Milestones*. Chicago: Kazi Publications.

Raday, Frances. 2003. "Culture, Religion and Gender." *International Journal of Constitutional Law* 1 (4): 663–715.

Radditz, Hans-Peter. 2006. *Von Allah zum Terror? Der Djihad und der Deformierung des Westens*. Munich: Herbig.

Radtke, Frank-Olaf. 1997. "Multiculturalism in Welfare States: The Case of Germany." In *The Ethnicity Reader: Nationalism, Multiculturalism and Migration*, ed. M. Guibernau and John Rex, pp. 248–56. Cambridge: Polity.

———. 2011. *Kulturen sprechen nicht. Die Politik grenzüberschreitender Diologe*. Hamburg: Hamburger Edition.

Ragazzi, Francesco. 2014. "Post-territorial Citizenship in Post-communist Europe." In *Routledge Handbook of Global Citizenship Studies,* ed. Engin F. Isin and Peter Nyers, pp. 489–97. New York: Routledge.

Ramadan, Hani. 2001. *L'islam et la derive de l'Occident.* Paris: Editions Maison d'Ennour.

Ramadan, Tariq. 1999a. *To Be a European Muslim: A Study of Islamic Sources in the European Context.* Leicester, U.K.: The Islamic Foundation.

———. 1999b. *Muslims in France: The Way towards Coexistence.* Leicester, U.K.: The Islamic Foundation.

———. 2009. "Globalisation Critics Are Naïve." *Qantara.de* (15 September). Available at http://en.quantara.de/Globalisation-Critics-Are-Na%C3%AFve/9571c9670i1p227/index.html (accessed 2 November 2011).

———. 2010. "Islam and Muslims in Europe: Change and Challenges." In *Political Islam: Context versus Ideology,* ed. Khaled Hroub, pp. 253–64. London: SAQI.

Ranstorp, Magnus, and Josefine Dos Santos. 2009. *Hot mot demokrati och värdegrund: en lägesbild från Malmö.* Stockholm: Centrum för Asymmetriska Hot och TerrorismStudier.

Rath, Jan. 1999. "The Netherlands: A Dutch Treat for Anti-social Families and Immigrant Minorities." In *The European Union and Migrant Labour,* ed. Mike Cole and Gareth Dale, pp. 48–60. Oxford: Berg.

Ratzinger, Joseph. 2006. "The Spiritual Roots of Europe: Yesterday, Today, and Tomorrow." In *Without Roots: The West, Relativism, Christianity, Islam,* by Marcello Pera and Joseph Ratzinger, pp. 51–80. New York: Basic Books.

Rawls, John. 2001. *Justice as Fairness: A Restatement.* Cambridge, MA: Harvard University Press.

Raz, Joseph. 1994a. *Ethics in the Public Domain.* Oxford: Clarendon.

———. 1994b. "Multiculturalism: A Liberal Perspective." *Dissent* 41 (1): 67–79.

Rees, Wyn, and Richard Aldrich. 2005. "Contending Cultures of Counter-terrorism: Transatlantic Divergence or Convergence?' *International Affairs* 81 (5): 905–23.

Rex, John. 1996. *Ethnic Minorities in the Modern Nation State.* Houndmills/Basingstoke, U.K.: Macmillan.

Reyneri, Emilio. 2003. "Immigration and the Underground Economy in New Receiving South European Countries: Manifold Negative Effects, Manifold Deep-rooted Causes." *International Journal of Sociology* 13 (1): 117–43.

Rich, David. 2010. "The Very Model of a British Muslim Brotherhood." In Rubin 2010, pp. 117–36.

Richardson, Henry S. 2002. *Democratic Autonomy: Public Reasoning about the Ends of Policy.* Oxford: Oxford University Press.

Rigoni, Isabelle. 2007. "Access to Media for European Muslims." In Amghar, Boubekeur, and Emerson 2007, pp. 107–23.

———. 2009. "Media and Muslims in Europe." In Nielsen 2009, pp. 475–506.

Rogstad, Jon. 2007. *Demokratisk fellesskap: Politisk inkludering og etnisk mobilisering.* Oslo: Universitetsforlaget.

Rohe, Mathias. 2004. "The Legal Treatment of Muslims in Germany." In *The Legal Treatment of Islamic Minorities in Europe,* ed. Roberta Aluffi Beck-Peccoz and Giovanna Zincone, pp. 83–107. Leuven, Belgium: Peeters.

Rommelspacher, Birgit. 2010. "Islamkritik und antimuslimische Positionen—am Beispiel von Necla Kelek und Seyran Ateş." In Schneiders 2010b, pp. 433–56.

Room, Graham, Roger Lawson, and Frank Laczko. 1989. "The 'New Poverty' in the European Community." *Policy and Politics* 17 (2): 165–76.

Rorty, Richard. 1989. *Contingency, Irony and Solidarity*. Cambridge: Cambridge University Press.

Rosanvallon, Pierre. 2013. *The Society of Equals*. Trans. Arthur Goldhammer. Cambridge, MA: Harvard University Press.

Rose, Nikolas. 1996. "Governing 'Advanced' Liberal Democracies." In *Foucault and Political Reason: Liberalism, Neo-liberalism and Rationalities of Government*, ed. Andrew Barry, Thomas Osborne, and Nikolas Rose, pp. 37–64. Chicago: University of Chicago Press.

Rosen, Ehud. 2008. "The Muslim Brotherhood's Concept of Education." *Current Trends in Islamist Ideology* 7 (85): 115–29.

Rosenberger, Sieglinde, and Birgit Sauer. 2012a. "Framing and Regulating the Veil: An Introduction." In Rosenberger and Sauer 2012b, pp. 1–14.

———, and Birgit Sauer, eds. 2012b. *Politics, Religion and Gender: Framing and Regulating the Veil*. London: Routledge.

——— and Winkler, Jacob. 2013. "Anti-Abschiebungsproteste: Mit Empathie gegen die Exklusion." In Ataç and Rosenberger 2013, pp. 111–34.

Ross, Marc H. 2007. *Cultural Contestation in Ethnic Conflict*. Cambridge: Cambridge University Press.

Rousseau, Jean Jacques. 1967. *The Social Contract and Discourse on the Origin of Inequality*. Ed. Lester G. Crocker. New York: Pocket Books.

Roy, Olivier. 1994. *The Failure of Political Islam*. London: I. B. Tauris.

———. 1998. "Le post-islamisme." *Revue des mondes musulmans et de la Méditerranée* 85–86: 11–30.

———. 2000. "L'individualisation dans l'islam européen contemporain." In Dassetto 2000, pp. 69–84.

———. 2004. *Globalised Islam*. London: Hurst.

———. 2005. *Globalized Islam*. New York: Columbia University Press.

———. 2007. *Secularism Confronts Islam*. Trans. George Holoch. New York: Columbia University Press.

———. 2009. "Al-Qaeda in the West as a Youth Movement: The Power of a Narrative." In *Ethno-religious Conflict in Europe: Typologies of Radicalisation in Europe's Muslim Communities*, ed. Michael Emerson, pp. 11–26. Brussels: Centre for European Policy Studies.

Rubery, Jill, Mark Smith, and Collete Fagan. 1999. *Women's Employment in Europe: Trends and Prospects*. London: Routledge.

Rubin, Barry, ed. 2010. *The Muslim Brotherhood: The Organization and Policies of a Global Islamist Movement*. New York: Palgrave.

Rubio-Marin, Ruth. 2000. *Immigration as a Democratic Challenge: Citizenship and Inclusion in Germany and the United States*. Cambridge: Cambridge University Press.

Rudolph, Christopher. 2010. "Security and the Immigration of Immigrants in Europe and the United States." In Chebel d'Appollonia and Reich 2010, pp. 40–58.

Ruf, Werner. 2010. "Muslime in den internationalen Beziehungen—das neue Feindbild." In Schneiders 2010b, pp. 121–30.

Ruffer, Galya Benarieh. 2011. "Pushed beyond Recognition? The *Liberality* of Family Reunification Policies in the EU." *Journal of Ethnic and Migration Studies* 37 (6): 935–51.

Ruggerio, Guido de. 1927. *The History of European Liberalism*. Trans. R. G. Colling-wood. Oxford: Oxford University Press.

Runnymede Trust Commission on British Muslims and Islamophobia. 1997. *Islamo-phobia—A Challenge for Us All*. London: Runnymede Trust.

Ryan, Alan. 2012. *The Making of Modern Liberalism*. Princeton, NJ: Princeton University Press.

Ryan, Bernard. 2009. "The Integration Agenda in British Migration Law." In Guild, Groenendijk, and Carrera 2009, pp. 277–98.

Safi, Omid, ed. 2003. *Progressive Muslims. On Justice, Gender, and Pluralism*. Oxford: Oneworld.

Sageman, Marc. 2008. *Leaderless Jihad: Terror Networks in the Twenty First Century*. Philadelphia: University of Pennsylvania Press.

Saharso, Sawitri. 2007. "Headscarves: A Comparison of Public Thought and Public Policy in Germany and the Netherlands." *Critical Review of International Social and Political Philosophy* 10 (4): 513–50.

Said, Edward. 1978. *Orientalism*. New York: Basic Books.

———. 1993. *Culture and Imperialism*. New York: Knopf.

———. 2003. "The Clash of Definitions." In Qureshi and Sells 2003a, pp. 68–87.

Sainsbury, Diane. 2012. *Welfare States and Immigrant Rights: The Politics of Inclusion and Exclusion*. Oxford: Oxford University Press.

Samad, Yunas. 2007. "Ethnicization of Religion." In Samad and Sen 2007, pp. 160–69.

———, and Katsuri Sen, eds. 2007. *Islam in the European Union: Transnationalism, Youth and the War on Terror*. Oxford: Oxford University Press.

Sarrazin, Thilo. 2010. *Deutschland schafft sich ab: Wie wir unser Land aufs Spiel setzen*. Munich: Deutsche Verlags-Anstalt.

Sassen, Saskia. 1996. *Losing Control: Sovereignty in the Age of Globalization*. New York: Columbia University Press.

———. 1998. *Globalization and Its Discontents: Essays on the New Mobility of People and Money*. New York: The New Press.

———. 2002. "The Repositioning of Citizenship: Emergent Subjects and Spaces for Politics." *Berkeley Journal of Sociology* 46: 4–26.

———. 2003. "A Universal Harm: Making Criminals of Migrants." openDemocracy, 20 August. Available at http://www.opendemocracy.net/people-migrationeurope/article_1444.jsp (accessed 4 June 2013).

Saunders, Doug. 2012. *The Myth of the Muslim Tide: Do Immigrants Threaten the West?* New York: Vintage.

Sayyid, Bobby S. 2009. "Contemporary Politics of Secularism." In *Secularism, Religion and Multicultural Citizenship*, ed. Geoffrey Brahm Levey and Tariq Modood, pp. 186–99. Cambridge: Cambridge University Press.

Schain, Martin A. 1999. "Minorities and Immigrant Incorporation in France: The State and the Dynamics of Multiculturalism." In *Multicultural Questions*, ed. Christian Joppke and Steven Lukes, pp. 199–223. Oxford: Oxford University Press.

———. 2008. *The Politics of Immigration in France, Britain, and the United States*. New York: Palgrave.

———. 2010. "Security and Immigrant Immigration Policy in France and the United States: Evaluating Convergence and Success." In Chebel d'Appollonia and Reich 2010, pp. 137–64.

———. 2012. "On Models and Politics." *Comparative European Politics* 10 (3): 369–76.

Schäuble, Wolfgang. 2009. *Braucht unsere Gesellschaft Religion?—Vom Wert des Glaubens*. Berlin: Berlin University Press.

Scheffer, Paul. 2011. *Immigrant Nations*. Cambridge: Polity.

Schierup, Carl-Ulrik, Peo Hansen, and Stephen Castles. 2006. *Migration, Citizenship, and the European Welfare State*. Oxford: Oxford University Press.

Schiffauer, Werner. 2000. *Die Gottesmänner: Türkische Islamisten in Deutschland*. Frankfurt: Suhrkamp.

———. 2002. *Migration und kulturelle Differenz*. Berlin: Büro der Aufländerbeautragten des Senats.

———. 2006. "Enemies within the Gates: The Debate about the Citizenship of Muslims in Germany." In Modood, Triandafyllidou, and Zapata-Barrero 2006, pp. 94–116.

———. 2007. "From Exile to Diaspora: The Development of Transnational Islam in Europe." In *Islam in Europe: Diversity, Identity and Influence*, ed. Aziz Al-Azmeh and Effie Fokas, pp. 68–97. Cambridge: Cambridge University Press.

———. 2008a. *Parallelgesellschaften. Wie viel Wertkonsens braucht unsere Gesellschaft? Für eine kluge Politik der Differenz*. Bielefeld, Germany: Transcript.

———. 2008b. "Zur Konstruktion von Sicherheitspartnerschaften." In *Migrationsreport 2008: Fakten-Analysen-Perspektiven*, ed. Michael Bommes and Marianne Krüger-Potratz, pp. 205–37. Frankfurt: Campus.

———. 2010. *Nach dem Islamismus: Eine Ethnographie der Islamischen Gemeinschaft Milli Görüş*. Frankfurt: Suhrkamp.

Schmidt, Helmut. 2011. *Religion in der Verantwortung: Gefährdungen des Friedens im Zeitalter der Globalisierung*. Berlin: Propyläen Verlag.

Schmidt, Vivien A. 2010. "Taking Ideas and Discourses Seriously: Explaining Change through Discursive Institutionalism as the Fourth 'New Institutionalism.'" *European Political Science Review* 2 (1): 1–25.

Schmidtke, Oliver, and Adrej Zaslove. 2014. "Why Regions Matter in Immigrant Integration Policies: North Rhine-Westphalia and Emilia-Romagna in Comparative Perspective." *Journal of Ethnic and Migration Studies* 40 (12): 1854–74.

Schmitt, Carl. 1976. *The Concept of the Political*. Trans. George Schwab. New Brunswick, NJ: Rutgers University Press.

———. 1983. *Verfassungslehre*. Berlin: Duncker.

———. 1985. *Political Theology*. Trans. George Schwab. Cambridge, MA: MIT Press.

———. 1996. *The Concept of the Political*. Trans. George Schwab. Chicago: University of Chicago Press.

Schmitt, Thomas. 2003. *Moscheen in Deutschland: Konflikte um ihre Errichtung und Nutzung*. Flensburg, Germany: Deutsche Akadamie für Landeskunde.

Schnabel, Paul. 1999. *De multiculturele illusive—Een pleidooi voor aanpassing en assimilatie* Utrecht, Netherlands: Forum.

Schnapper, Dominique. 1994. *La Communautédes citoyens: Sur l'idée moderne de nation*. Paris: Gallimard.

———. 1998. *Community of Citizens: On the Modern Idea of Nationality*. Trans. Severine Rosée. New Brunswick, NJ: Transaction.

Schneider, Cathy Lisa. 2008. "Police Power and Race Riots in Paris." *Politics and Society* 36 (1): 133–59.

Schneiders, Thorsten Gerald. 2010a. "Die Schattenseite der Islamkritik. Darlegung und Analyse der Argumentationsstrategien von Henryk M. Broder, Ralph Giordano, Necla Kelak, Alice Schwarzer und anderen." In Schneiders 2010b, pp. 417–46.

————, ed. 2010b. *Islamfeindlichkeit: Wenn die Grenzen der Kritik verschwimmen*. Wiesbaden, Germany: VS Verlag für Sozialwissenschaften.

Scholten, Peter. 2011. *Framing Immigrant Integration: Dutch Research-policy Dialogues in Comparative Perspective*. Amsterdam: University of Amsterdam Press.

Schwarzer, Alice, ed. 2002a. *Die Gotteskrieger und die falsche Toleranz*. Cologne: Kieperheuer and Witsch.

————. 2002b. "Vorwort." In *Die Gotteskrieger und die falsche Toleranz*, ed. Alice Schwarzer. Cologne: Kieperheuer and Witsch.

————. 2010. "Die Realität in Deutschland." In *Die grosse Verschleierung. Für Integration. Gegen Islamismus*, ed. Alice Schwarzer, pp. 10–17. Cologne: Kieperheuer and Witsch.

Scientific Council for Government Policy. 2006. *Dynamism in Islamic Activism: Reference Points for Democratization and Human Rights*. Amsterdam: University of Amsterdam Press.

Sciortino, Guiseppe. 2004. "Immigration in a Mediterranean Welfare State." *Journal of Comparative Policy Analysis* 6 (2): 111–29.

Scott, Joan Wallach. 2007. *The Politics of the Veil*. Princeton, NJ: Princeton University Press.

Shachar, Ayelet. 2009. *The Birthright Lottery: Citizenship and Global Inequality*. Cambridge, MA: Harvard University Press.

Shadid, W.A.R., and P. S. van Koningsveld. 2005. "Muslim Dress in Europe: Debates on the Headscarf." *Journal of Islamic Studies* 16 (1): 35–61.

Shavit, Uriya. 2007. "Should Muslims Integrate into the West?" *Middle East Quarterly* 14 (4): 13–21.

————, and Frederic Wiesenbach. 2009. "Muslim Strategies to Convert Western Christians." *Middle East Quarterly* 16 (2): 3–14.

————, and Frederic Wiesenbach. 2012. "An Integrative Enclave: The Case of Al-Hayat, Germany's First Islamic Fitness Center for Women in Cologne." *Journal of Muslim Minority Affairs* 32 (1): 47–61.

Shaw, Alison. 2000. *Kinship and Continuity: Pakistani Families in Britain*. Amsterdam: Harwood Academic.

Sigona, Nando. 2012. "'I've Too Much Baggage': The Impact of Legal Status on the Social Worlds of Irregular Migrants." *Social Anthropology/Anthropologie Sociale* 20: 50–65.

————, and Vanessa Hughes. 2012. *No Way Out, No Way In: Irregular Migrant Children and Families in the UK*. Oxford: ESRC Centre on Migration, Policy and Society, Oxford University.

Siim, Birte. 2014. "How Institutional Context Shapes Head Scarf Debates across Scandinavia." In Bowen et al. 2014a, pp. 216–34.

Silvestri, Sara. 2010. "Public Policies towards Muslims and the Institutionalization of 'Moderate Islam' in Europe: Some Critical Reflections." In Triandafyllidou 2010a, pp. 45–58.

Simonsen, Jørgen Baek. 2000. "From Defensive Silence to Creative Participation: Muslim Discourse in Denmark." In Dassetto 2000, pp. 145–55.

Skinner, Quentin. 1990. "The Republican Ideal of Political Liberty." In *Machiavelli and Republicanism*, ed. G. Bock, Q. Skinner, and M. Violi, pp. 293–309. Cambridge: Cambridge University Press.

Slaughter, Anne-Marie. 2004. *A New World Order*. Princeton, NJ: Princeton University Press.

Smith, Anthony D. 1986. *The Ethnic Origins of Nations*. Oxford: Blackwell.

———. 1991. *National Identity*. Reno: University of Nevada Press.

Smith, Rogers. 1999. *Civic Ideals: Conflicting Visions of Citizenship in U.S. History*. New Haven, CT: Yale University Press.

Sniderman, Paul M., and Louk Hagendoorn. 2007. *When Ways of Life Collide: Multiculturalism and Its Discontents in the Netherlands*. Princeton, NJ: Princeton University Press.

Sniderman, Paul, Louk Hagendoorn, and M. Prior. 2004. "Predisposing Factors and Situational Triggers: Exclusionary Reactions to Immigrant Minorities." *American Political Science Review* 98 (1): 35–49.

Soage, Ana Belén. 2010. "Yusuf al-Qaradawi: The Muslim Brothers' Favorite Ideological Guide." In Rubin 2010, pp. 19–38.

Soysal, Yasemin. 1994. *Limits of Citizenship: Migrants and Postnational Membership in Europe*. Chicago: University of Chicago Press.

Spena, Maurizia Russo. 2010. "Muslims in Italy: Models of Integration and New Citizenship." In Triandafyllidou 2010a, pp. 160–80.

Spinner-Halev, Jeff. 1999. "Cultural Pluralism and Partial Citizenship." In *Multicultural Questions*, ed. Christian Joppke and Steven Lukes, pp. 107–30. Oxford University Press.

Spinoza, Baruch. 1951. *Tractacus Theologico-Politicus*. Trans. R.H.M. Elwes. New York: Dover.

Spragens, Thomas. 1981. *The Irony of Liberal Reason*. Chicago: University of Chicago Press.

Stasi, Bernard. 2004. *Laïcité et République*. Paris: La Documentation française.

Stasi Commission. 2003. *Rapport au Président de la Republique*. Paris: Commission de réflexion sur l'application du principe de laïcité dans la république.

Stasiulis, Daiva. 2004. "Hybrid Citizenship and What's Left." *Citizenship Studies* 8 (3): 295–303.

Statens-offentliga-utredningar (SOU). 2003. *Unga utanför. Slutbetäkande av utreningen om unga utanför*. SOU 2003: 92. Stockholm: Näringsdepartementet.

Staver, Anne. 2013. "Free Movement of Workers or Citizens? Reverse Discrimination in European Family Reunification Policies." In *Democratic Citizenship and the Free Movement of People*, ed. Willem Maas, pp. 57–89. Leiden, Netherlands: Martinus Nijhoff.

Steinberg, Guido. 2010. "The Muslim Brotherhood in Germany." In Rubin 2010, pp. 149–60.

———. 2013. *German Jihad: On the Internationalization of Islamist Terrorism*. New York: Columbia University Press.

Sternhell, Zeev. 2010. *The Anti-Enlightenment Tradition*. Trans. David Maisel. New Haven, CT: Yale University Press.

Stolz, Jörg. 2000. *Soziologie der Fremdfeinlichkeit: Theoretische und empirische Analysen*. Frankfurt am Main: Campus Verlag.

Strassburger, Gaby. 2000. "Fundamentalism versus Human Rights: Headscarf Discourses in an Established-outsider-figuration in France." In Dassetto 2000, pp. 125–44.

Strindberg, Anders, and Mats Wärn. 2011. *Islamism.* Cambridge: Polity.

Sunier, Thijl. 2010. "Islam in the Netherlands, Dutch Islam." In Triandafyllidou 2010a, pp. 121–36.

———. 2014. "Schooling and New Religious Diversity across Four European Countries." In Bowen et al. 2014a, pp. 54–72.

Surkis, Judith. 2010. "Hymenal Politics: Marriage, Secularism and French Sovereignty." *Public Culture* 22 (3): 531–54.

Sutherland, Claire. 2012. *Nationalism in the Twenty-first Century: Challenges and Responses.* London: Palgrave.

Taguieff, Pierre-André. 1988. *La Force du préjugé. Essai sur le racisme et ses doubles.* Paris: La Découverte.

Taheri, Amir. 2005. "France's Ticking Time Bomb." *Arab News* 5 November. Available at www.benadorassociates.com/article/18823.

Tajfel, Henri. 1982. "Social Psychology of Intergroup Relations." *American Review of Psychology* 33: 1–39.

Tamir, Yael. 1993. *Liberal Nationalism.* Princeton, NJ: Princeton University Press.

Taras, Raymond. 2012. *Xenophobia and Islamophobia in Europe.* Edinburgh: Edinburgh University Press.

Taylor, Charles. 1985. *Philosophy and the Human Sciences: Philosophical Papers II.* Cambridge: Cambridge University Press.

———. 1994. "The Politics of Recognition." In *Multiculturalism: Examining the Politics of Recognition,* ed. Amy Guttman, pp. 25–74. Princeton, NJ: Princeton University Press.

———. 1995. *Philosophical Arguments.* Cambridge, MA: Harvard University Press.

———. 2007. *A Secular Age.* Cambridge, MA: The Belknap Press of Harvard University Press.

Terkessidis, Mark, and Yasemin Karakaşoğlu. 2006. "Gerechtigkeit für die Muslime!" *Die Zeit,* 6 February.

Terray, Emmanuel. 2004. *La question du voile: une hystérie politique.* Ghent, Belgium: Centrum voor Islam in Europa. Available at http://www.flw.ugent.be/cie/CIE/terray.htm.

Terrio, Susan J. 2009. *Judging Muhammad: Juvenile Delinquency, Immigration, and Exclusion at the Paris Palace of Justice.* Stanford, CA: Stanford University Press.

Thaa, Winfried. 2001. "'Lean Citizenship': The Fading Away of the Political in Transnational Democracy." *European Journal of International Relations* 7 (4): 503–23.

Tibi, Bassam. 2002. "Muslim Migrants in Europe: Between Euro-Islam and Ghettoization." In *Muslim Europe or Euro-Islam: Politics, Culture, and Citizenship in the Age of Globalization,* ed. Nezar AlSayyad and Manuel Castells, pp. 31–52. New York: Lexington Books.

———. 2008. *Political Islam, World Politics and Europe: Democratic Peace and Euro-Islam versus Global Jihad.* London: Routledge.

Tichenor, Daniel. 2002. *Dividing Lines: The Politics of Immigration Control in America.* Princeton, NJ: Princeton University Press.

Tirman, John. 2010. "Security and Antiterror Policies in America and Europe." In Chebel d'Appollonia and Reich 2010, pp. 59–78.

Tocqueville, Alexis de. 1952. *L'Ancien Régime et la Révolution*. Reprinted in *Oevres completes*, vol. 2, pt. 1, ed. J.-P. Mayer. Paris.

Tonkiss, Katherine. 2013. *Migration and Identity in a Post-national World*. London: Palgrave.

Topkapi Declaration. 2006, July 2. Available at www.muslimsofeurope.com/topkapi. php (accessed 7 May 2014).

Toulmin, Stephen. 1990. *Cosmopolis*. New York: Free Press.

Tralau, Johan, ed. 2010. *Thomas Hobbes and Carl Schmitt: The Politics of Order and Myth*. London: Routledge.

Triadafilopolous, Triadafilos. 2011. "Illiberal Means to Liberal Ends? Understanding Recent Immigrant Integration Policies in Europe." *Journal of Ethnic and Migration Studies* 37 (6): 861–80.

Triandafyllidou, Anna. 2006. "Religious Diversity and Multiculturalism in Southern Europe: The Italian Mosque Debate." In Modood, Triandafyllidou, and Zapata-Barrero 2006, pp. 116–42.

———, ed. 2010a. *Muslims in 21st Century Europe: Structural and Cultural Perspectives*. London: Routledge.

———. 2010b. "Muslims in 21st Century Europe: Structural and Cultural Perspectives." In Triandafyllidou 2010a, pp. 1–26.

———. 2010c. "Greece: The Challenge of Native and Immigrant Muslim Populations." In Triandafyllidou 2010a, pp. 199–217.

———. 2010d. "Irregular Migration in Europe in the Early 21st Century." In Triandafyllidou 2010e, pp. 1–22.

———, ed. 2010e. *Irregular Migration in Europe: Myths and Realities*. Farnham, U.K.: Ashgate.

———, and Dita Vogel. 2010. "Irregular Migration in the European Union: Evidence, Facts and Myths." In Triandafyllidou 2010e, pp. 291–99.

Tribalat, Michèle. 1996. *De l'immigration à l'assimilation. Enquéte sur les populations d'origine étrangère en France*. Paris: La Decouverte.

Tsoukala, Anastassia. 2008. "Defining the Terrorist Threat in the Post–September 11 Era." In Bigo and Tsoukala 2008, pp. 49–100.

Tyerman, Christopher. 2006. *God's War: A New History of the Crusades*. Cambridge, MA: Belknap.

Tyrer, David. 2013. *The Politics of Islamophobia: Race, Power and Fantasy*. London: PlutoPress.

Uitermark, Justus, Paul Mepschen, and Jan Willem Duyvendak. 2014. "Populism, Sexual Politics, and the Exclusion of Muslims in the Netherlands." In Bowen et al. 2014a, pp. 235–55.

Ulfkotte, Udo. 2013. *Vorsicht Bürgerkrieg! Was lange gärt, wird endlich Wut*. Rottenburg, Germany: Kopp.

United Nations. 2000. *Replacement Migration: Is It a Solution to Declining and Ageing Populations?* New York: United Nations Population Division.

———. 2005. "Special Rapporteur on Freedom of Religion Ends Visit to France." 30 September. Available at www.un.org (accessed 10 February 2014).

Vakulenko, Anastasia. 2012. *Islamic Veiling in Legal Discourse*. New York: Routledge.

van den Anke, Christien, and Ilse van Liempt, eds. 2012. *Human Rights and Migration: Trafficking for Forced Labour*. London: Palgrave.

van Dijk, Teun A. 2007. "El racismo y la prensa en España." In *Discurso periodístico y procesos migratorios*, ed. Hernández Antonio Bañón, pp. 27–80. Donostia-San Sebastián, Spain: Gakoa.

van Oers, Ricky. 2009. "Justifying Citizenship Tests in the Netherlands and the UK." In Guild, Groenendijk, and Carrera 2009, pp. 113–30.

Vattimo, Gianni. 2006. *Dialogue with Nietzsche*. Trans. William McCuaig. New York: Columbia University Press.

Vergès, François. 2011. "Xenophobia and the Civilizing Mission." openDemocracy, 13 May. Available at http:www.opendemocracy.net/fran%C3%A7oise-verg%C3%A8s/xenophobia-and-civilizing-mission?utm_source=feedblitz&utm_medium_FeedBlitzEmail&utm_content=201210&utm_campaign=Nightly_%272011-05-16%20 05%3a30%3a00%27.

Verkaaik, Oskar. 2010. "The Cachet Dilemma: Ritual and Agency in New Dutch Nationalism." *American Ethnologist* 37 (1): 69–82.

Verstraete, Ginette. 2003. "Technological Frontiers and the Politics of Mobility in the European Union." In *Uprootings/Regroundings: Questions of Home and Migration*, ed. Sara Ahmed et al. pp. 225–49. Oxford: Berg.

———, and Susanne Wessendorf, eds. 2010. *The Multiculturalism Backlash: European Discourses, Policies, and Practices*. New York: Routledge.

Vico, Giovanni Battista. 1948. *New Science*. Trans. T. G. Bergin and M. H. Fisch. Ithaca, NY: Cornell University Press.

Vidino, Lorenzo. 2006. "Aims and Methods of Europe's Muslim Brotherhood." Hudson Institute, 1 November. Available at www.investigativeproject.org/173/aims-and-methods-of-europes-muslim-brotherhood (accessed 9 June 2013).

———. 2010a. "The Muslim Brotherhood in Europe." In Rubin 2010, pp. 106–16.

———. 2010b. *The New Muslim Brotherhood in the West*. New York: Columbia University Press.

———. 2012. "The European Organisation of the Muslim Brotherhood: Myth or Reality?" In Meijer and Bakker 2012a, pp. 51–70.

———, ed. 2013. *The West and the Muslim Brotherhood after the Arab Spring*. Dubai: Al Mesbar Studies and Research Center.

Villiers, Philippe de. 2006. *Les mosqueés de Roissy: Nouvelles révélations sur l'islamisation en France*. Paris: Broché.

Vink, Maarten. 2007. "Dutch 'Multiculturalism' Beyond the Pillarisation Myth." *Political Studies Review* 5 (3): 337–50.

———, and Gerard René de Groot. 2010. "Citizenship Attribution in Western Europe: Framework and Domestic Trends." *Journal of Ethnic and Migration Studies* 36 (5): 713–34.

Viroli, Maurizio. 1997. *For Love of Country: An Essay on Patriotism and Nationalism*. Oxford: Oxford University Press.

Vivar, Maria Teresa Herrera. 2012. "'The Right to Always Wear a Smile': Migration Policies and the Exploitation of Domestic Workers in Germany." In van den Anke and van Liempt 2012, pp. 109–26.

Volf, Miroslav. 2007. "A Voice of One's Own: Public Faith in a Pluralistic World." In Banchoff 2007a, pp. 271–82.

Voltaire. 1969. *Essai sur les moeurs et l'espirit des nations*. Paris: Classiques Garnier.

von Blumenthal, Julia. 2009. *Das Kopftuch in der Landesgesetzgebung: Governance im Bundesstaat zwischen Unitarisierung und Föderalisierung*. Baden-Baden, Germany: Nomos.

Wacquant, Loïc. 1996. "The Rise of Advanced Marginality: Notes on Its Nature and Implications." *Acta Sociologica* 39 (2): 121–39.

Waever, Ole. 1995. "Securitization and Desecuritization." In *On Security*, ed. Ronnie D. Lipschutz, pp. 46–86. New York: Columbia University Press.

————, Barry Buzan, Morten Kelstrup, and Pierre Lemaitre, eds. 1993. *Identity, Migration and the New Security Agenda in Europe*. London: Palgrave.

Walten, Eric. 1689. *De Regtsinnige Policey*. The Hague: Meindert Uitwerf.

Walzer, Michael. 1983. *Spheres of Justice: A Defense of Pluralism and Equality*. New York: Basic Books.

————. 2004. *Politics and Passion: Toward a More Egalitarian Liberalism*. New Haven, CT: Yale University Press.

Warner, Carolyn M., and Manfred W. Wenner. 2006. "Religion and the Political Organization of Muslims in Europe." *Perspectives on Politics* 4 (3): 457–79.

Weber, Max. 1922. *Gesammelte Aufsätze zur Wissenschaftslehre*. Tübingen, Germany: Mohr.

————. 1949. "'Objectivity' in Social Science and Social Policy." In *The Methodology of the Social Sciences*, ed. E. Shils and H. Finch, pp. 72–111. Glencoe, IL: Free Press.

Weil, Patrick. 2004. *Qu-est-ce qu'un Français?* Paris: Gallimard.

Weimann, Gabriel. 2015. *Terrorism in Cyberspace: The Next Generation*. New York: Columbia University Press.

Werbner, Pnina. 1996. "The Making of Muslim Dissent: Hybridized Discourses, Lay Preachers and Radical Rhetoric among British Pakistanis." *American Ethnologist* 23 (1): 102–29.

————. 2002. *Imagined Diasporas among Manchester Muslims: The Public Performance of Pakistani Transnational Identity Politics*. Oxford: James Curry.

————. 2004. "The Predicament of Diaspora and Millennial Islam: Reflections on September 11, 2001." *Ethnicities* 4 (4): 451–76.

Wetenschappelijke Raad voor het Regeringsbeleid (WRR). 1989. *Allochtonenbeleid*. Rapporten aan de Regering, No. 36. The Hague: SDU Uitgeverij.

Wiener, Antje, and Vincent Della Sala. 1997. "Constitution-making and Citizenship Practice—Bridging the Democracy Gap in the EU." *Journal of Common Market Studies* 35 (4): 595–614.

Wieviorka, Michel. 2002. "Race, Culture and Society: The French Experience with Muslims." In *Muslim Europe or Euro-Islam: Politics, Culture, and Citizenship in the Age of Globalization*, ed. Nezar AlSayyad and Manuel Castells, pp. 131–46. New York: Lexington Books.

Wiktorowicz, Quintan. 2005. *Radical Islam Rising: Muslim Extremism in the West*. New York: Rowan and Littlefield.

Williams, Michael C. 2003. "Words, Images, Enemies: Securitization and International Politics." *International Studies Quarterly* 47 (4): 511–31.

Wilpert, Czarina, and Smailin Laacher. 1999. "New Forms of Migration and the Informal Labour Market in Old Receiving Countries." In *Migrant Insertion in the Informal Economy, Deviant Behaviour and the Impact on Receiving Societies,* ed. Emilio Reyneri, pp. 39–56. Brussels: European Commission.

Wise, Amanda, and Selvaraj Velayutham, eds. 2009. *Everyday Multiculturalism.* New York: Palgrave.

Withol de Wenden, Catherine. 1992. "Les associations 'beur' et immigrés, leurs leaders, leurs strategies." *Regards sur l'actualité,* no. 178.

———. 1996. "Muslims in France." In *Muslims in the Margin: Political Responses to the Presence of Islam in Western Europe,* ed. W.A.R. Shadid and P. S. van Koningsveld, pp. 218–42. Kampen, Netherlands: KOK Pharos.

———. 2010. "Irregular Migration in France." In Triandafyllidou 2010e, pp. 115–24.

Wittgenstein, Ludwig. 1922. *Tractatus Logico-Philosophicus.* Trans. C. K. Ogden. London: Routledge and Kegan Paul.

———. 1958. *Philosophical Investigations.* Trans. G.E.M. Anscombe. New York: Macmillan.

———. 1969. *On Certainty.* Ed. G.E.M. Anscombe and G. H. von Wright. New York: Harper.

———. 1993. *Philosophical Occasions, 1912–1951.* Ed. James C. Klagge and Alfred Nordmann. Indianapolis, IN: Hackett.

Wright, Matthew, and Irene Bloemraad. 2012. "Is There a Trade-off between Multiculturalism and Socio-political Integration? Policy Regimes and Immigrant Incorporation in Comparative Perspective." *Perspectives on Politics* 10 (1): 77–95.

Wuthnow, Robert. 2005. *America and the Challenges of Religious Diversity.* Princeton, NJ: Princeton University Press.

Yaqoob, Salma. 2007. "British Islamic Political Radicalism." In Abbas 2007, pp. 279–94.

Ye'or, Bat. 2005. *Eurabia: The Euro-Arab Axis.* Madison, NJ: Fairleigh Dickinson Press.

Yildiz, Erol. 2012. *Die weltoffene Stadt: Wie Migration Globalisierung zum urbanen Alltag macht.* Bielefeld, Germany: Transcript.

Yilner, Nadja. 2012. "Undercover Report: Muslim Leaders Urge Women to Total Submission." Uppdrag granskning, 16 May. Available at http://www.svt.se/ug/undercover-report-muslim-leaders-urges-women-to-total-submission (accessed 6 June 2014).

Younas , Muhammad Ahsan. 2014. "'Digital Jihad' and Its Significance to Counterterrorism." *Counter Terrorist Trends and Analysis.* 6 (2): 10–17.

Young, Jock. 1999. *The Exclusive Society: Social Exclusion, Crime and Difference in Late Modernity.* London: Sage.

Yükleyen, Ahment. 2012. *Localizing Islam in Europe: Turkish Islamic Communities in Germany and the Netherlands.* Syracuse, NY: Syracuse University Press.

Yurdakul, Gökçe. 2006. "Secular versus Islamist: The Headscarf Debate in Germany." In Jonker and Amiraux 2006, pp. 151–68.

———. 2009. *From Guest Workers into Muslims: The Transformation of Turkish Immigrant Associations in Germany.* Newcastle upon Tyne, U.K.: Cambridge Scholars Publishing.

Yuval-Davis, Nira. 1999. "Multi-layered Citizenship in the Era of 'Glocalization.'" *International Feminist Journal of Politics* 1 (1): 119–37.

Zapata-Barrero, Ricard. 2006. "The Muslim Community and Spanish Tradition: Maurophobia as a Fact, and Impartiality as a Desidiratum." In Modood, Triandafyllidou, and Zapata-Barrero 2006, pp. 142–61.

————, and I. Qasem. 2008. "The Politics of Discourse towards Islam and Muslim Communities in Europe." In *Constituting Communities: Political Solutions to Cultural Conflict,* ed. P. Mouritsen and K. E. Jørgensen, pp. 73–93. New York: Palgrave.

————, and Nynke de Witte. 2010. "Muslims in Spain: Blurring Past and Present Moors." In Triandafyllidou 2010a, pp. 181–98.

Zeeuw, Mohammad de. 1998. *Islamistisch godsdienstlesmateriaal in Nederland.* Nieuwegein, Netherlands: IPC.

Zick, Andreas, Beate Küpper, and Andreas Hövermann. 2011. *Intolerance, Prejudice and Discrimination: A European Report.* Berlin: Friedrich Ebert Stiftung.

Zivilcourage und Anti-Rassismus Arbeit (ZARA). 2011. *Jahrbuch*

Index

Peter O'Brien is Professor of Political Science at Trinity University in San Antonio, Texas. He is the author of *European Perceptions of Islam and America from Saladin to George W. Bush: Europe's Fragile Ego Uncovered*, and *Beyond the Swastika*. He has been a Social Science Research Council Fellow at the Free University in Berlin, and Fulbright Visiting Professor at Boğaziçi University in Istanbul and at the Humboldt University in Berlin.